KU-510-983

Joe Yogerst, born in San Diego, California in 1956, graduated in geography from the University of California at Los Angeles and in journalism from the University of Oregon.

He has worked as a freelance writer and photographer in Africa, Asia, Europe and North America and has contributed to such publications as *The Geographical Magazine, The Washington Post, The Los Angeles Times* and *The San Francisco Examiner and Chronicle.* For the last three years he has contributed a monthly column on Asia and Africa to *International Travel News* magazine.

Publication Data

Title	Paris Confidential
Typeface	Phototypeset in Compugraphic Times
Photographs	By the Author.
Printing	Kelso Graphics, Kelso, Scotland.
ISBN	0 903909 30 8
Edition	This first September, 1985
Publisher	Roger Lascelles
	47 York Road, Brentford, Middlesex, TW8 0QP.
Copyright	Joseph R. Yogerst

All rights reserved. Other than brief extracts for purposes of review no part of this publication may be produced in any form without the written consent of the publisher and copyright owner.

Distribution

Africa:	Enquiries invited	
Americas:	Canada —	International Travel Maps & Books, P.O. Box 2290, Vancouver B.C.
	U.S.A. —	Bradt Enterprises, 95 Harvey Street, Cambridge, MA. 02140
Asia:	Hong Kong —	The Book Society, G.P.O. Box 7804, Hong Kong Tel: 5-241901
	India —	English Book Store, New Delhi
Australasia	Australia —	Rex Map Centre, 413 Pacific Highway, Artarmon NSW 2064
	New Zealand —	International Travel Guides, P.O. Box 4397, Christchurch 1
Europe:	Belgium —	Brussels, Peuples et Continents
	GB/Ireland —	Available through all booksellers with a good foreign travel section.
	Italy —	Libreria dell'Automobile, Milano
	Netherlands —	Nilsson & Lamm BV, Weesp
	Denmark —	Copenhagen — Arnold Busck, G.E.C. Gad, Boghallen
	Finland —	Oslo - Arne Gimnes/J.G. Tanum
	Sweden —	Stockholm - Esselte/Akademi Bokhandel Fritzes/Hedengrens
		Gothenburg - Gumperts/Esselte
		Lund - Gleerupska
	Switzerland —	The Travel Bookshop, Seilergraben 11, 8001 Zurich
		Librairie Artou, 8 rue de Rive, 1204 Geneve.

PARIS

Joseph R. Yogerst

Roger Lascelles, Cartographic and Travel Publisher
47 York Road, Brentford, Middlesex TW8 0QP Telephone: 01-847 0935

Contents

1 Ici Paris!

2 Getting there and back

3 Getting around town

4 Where to stay

5 Where to eat

6 Where to drink

7 Performing arts

8 Nightlife

9 Sightseeing

10 Shopping

11 Sports and recreation

CHAPTER ONE

Ici Paris!

Paris is an easy city for the visitor to get to know, for it is relatively compact compared with other major capitals, it has a number of world-famous landmarks and the winding Seine from which to orient yourself, and there is an easy-to-understand network of boulevards and avenues. It is these immense streets — engineered by Baron Haussmann just over one hundred years ago — which set Paris apart from other medieval cities and give it such a feeling of spaciousness.

More importantly, Paris is divided into 20 districts or *arrondissements* around which the Parisian conscience is permanently fixed. Knowing these arrondissements is the key to quickly finding your way from A to B in Paris. The postal codes of every address include the arrondissement number (75001 refers to the first district, 75002 to the second district and so on), and we have included that number with almost every listing in this book (written thus: 1er, 2e, 3e — that is to say 1st, 2nd, 3rd — and so on).

The city is governed by the Mairie de Paris, situated in the Hotel de Ville which has an elected mayor and 100 municipal councillors. But each of the 20 districts also has a *mairie* or town hall responsible for public services and activities in each area.

But Paris is more than a city of numbers, for it is the historic names of each district which are firmly etched on the visitor's mind. The Rive Gauche is the Left Bank as you look downstream, the Rive Droit the Right Bank. Over the centuries the Rive Gauche has come to stand for student, arty, avant-garde Paris, home of the anti-establishment folks. The Rive Droit, on the other hand, has always stood for conservative and wealthy Paris. In the past, it was the home of royalty and the aristocracy, but today it embraces the smartest hotels and shops in Paris.

The fifth and sixth arrondissements comprise the famous Latin Quarter of the Left Bank, which derives its name from the Roman town which once stood upon the spot. But Parisians rarely use this touristy term, preferring to divide the quarter in two: St Michel 5e and St Germain 6e. Likewise, the historic Marais of the Right Bank, the oldest neighbourhood in Paris, is divided between the 3rd and 4th districts. And Montparnasse with its artists' quarter and urban renewal is split between the 14th and 15th districts.

There are many famous arrondissements: the old artists' district of Montmartre with its quaint streets and magnificent vistas, 18e; seedy Pigalle, 9e with its hookers and sex shows; the redeveloped Beaubourg, 4e with the Pompidou Centre as its heart and soul; and Les Halles, 1er, the old market quarter of Paris which is rapidly becoming its most popular shopping area.

All of these quarters await your eager exploration with a multitude of historic sights, lovely squares, delicious restaurants and romantic cafés. Just pick yourself up a good map and guide from the Tourist Office or a bookstore and off you go. There is no better city on earth in which to absorb yourself completely.

Information

Tourist Office
127, avenue des Champs-Elysées, 1er. (tel: 723.61.72 Metro: Etoile). Paris's immense central tourist office with all the information you could ever want on the city and the surrounding Ile de France. Free maps, brochures and current

listings of Paris theatre, cinema and arts. Hotel booking service for a 10-35F fee. Special book shop with travel books and maps on all of France. They also run a tourist information service in English on tel: 720.88.98. Open Monday to Saturday 9 am to 10 pm and Sunday 9 am to 8 pm.

The Office de Tourisme also has offices at four railway stations: Gare de l'Est (8 am to 1 pm and 5 to 7 pm); Gare des Invalides (noon to 7 pm); Gare de Lyon (8 am to 1 pm and 5 to 7 pm); and Gare du Nord (8 am to 8 pm). The railway station offices are closed on Sunday. In addition, there are tourists offices at the following air terminals: Le Bourget, Charles de Gaulle/Roissy, Orly South and Orly West.

Publications

The best publication for current happenings in Paris is the weekly *Pariscope,* available for 2.80F at almost every newsagent, Tabac shop and bookstore in town. It has extensive listings of cinema, theatre, cabaret, music, sex shows, dance, concerts, fine arts, sports, bars, cafés, discos, television and restaurants. Two other similar weekly publications are *'Allo Paris* (free) and *Official des Spectacles* (2F), but neither is as extensive as *Pariscope.*

Those who are seeking more in-depth reading on current trends and events in Paris should pick up a copy of *Passion* (9F), the monthly English-language magazine on Paris. It's published by a young, energetic staff of expatriate Americans from a tiny office near Les Halles, and offers regular features on Paris restaurants, bars, music, art, fashion, politics, transportation, theatre and sports. Lots of very interesting interviews with local personalities, and excellent black and white photo essays in each issue.

Probably the best street plan of the city is the Plan Guide Blay 1:14000 because in one compact pocket edition it offers a detailed plan of every street in Paris with a full index, metro and RER (Réseau Express Régional) map. Best of all, it's very easy to read and it shows all those nasty one-way streets with distinct green arrows. Plan Guide Blay also publish street maps on suburban Versailles, Boulogne-

Billancourt and some 120 other French towns.

The best street atlas of Paris is the comprehensive *Paris par Arrondissement* by Editions l'Indispensable, the book used by the national police to find their way around town! It has an alphabetical index, individual maps of each arrondissement, special maps of La Defense, the Bois de Boulogne and Bois de Vincennes, plus a giant fold-out map of the metropolitan area showing all the suburbs.

Michelin too offer an extensive collection of maps and books on Paris and the surrounding region. The Michelin green guide to Paris is legendary, the most detailed guide to be found on the city, listing the most intimate facts on every museum, church and monument. The guide offers 30 interesting walking tours in the city.

Students

The Centre for International Educational Exchange (CIEE) can issue you with an International Student ID Card from offices at 51, rue Dauphine, 6e (tel: 326.79.65; metro: Odéon) or 16, rue de Vaugirard, 6e (tel: 634.02.90; metro: Odéon).

Detailed information on education, language courses, youth groups, au pair work and other jobs, rooms in private homes and travel can be had from the Centre d'Information et de Documentation Jeunesse at 101, quai Branly, 7e (tel: 566.40.20; metro: Bir-Hakeim). It's open Monday to Saturday 9 am to 7 pm. Au pair listings can also be found at the Accueil Familial des Jeunes Etrangers at 23, rue de Cherche-Midi, 6e (tel: 222.50.34; metro: Sèvres-Babylone).

Information and bookings of student and youth accommodation can be found at the offices of the Accueil des Jeunes en France (AJF), Union des Centres de Rencontres Internationales de France (UCRIF), International Youth Hostel Federation (IYHF) and OTU-Accueil. See the Youth Hostel section on page 90 for addresses and telephone numbers, plus a detailed listing of all the Paris hostels.

One of the better student travel agencies in Paris is the popular Centre Touristique des Etudiants et de la Jeunesse (CTEJ) at 20, rue des Carmes, 5e (tel: 325.00.76; metro: Maubert-Mutualité). They have cheap air tickets to almost anywhere in the world, plus TransAlpino rail tickets. There's also a postal service similar in form and function to the American Express mail service. Open Monday to Friday 9.30 am to 6 pm, Saturday 9.30 am to 1 p.m.

Another good youth travel agency is Central Voyages at 29, rue Pont Neuf, 1er (tel: 233.85.34; metro: Les Halles). They also have cheap air tickets and TransAlpino service.

Those searching for a Youth Hostel card can obtain one at the Paris IYHF offices at 6, rue Mesnil, 16e (tel: 261.84.03; metro: Victor Hugo) or 38, boulevard Raspail, 7e (tel: 548.69.84; metro: Sevres-Babylone).

Money

Parisian banks are generally open from 9 am to 4.30 pm on Monday to Friday, but you will find major branches, change bureaux and travellers cheques offices which are open earlier, later or on weekends. Most bank branches are closed on weekends, and they normally close at noon on holiday eves (i.e. Christmas Eve).

Exchange rates have fluctuated much in recent years, but as of 1984 they were 12F to £1 and 7.80F to U.S. $1. French banks will accept all major traveller's cheques including American Express, Thomas Cook and Barclays. Any bank which displays a VISA sign in the window will give you cash on presentation of the VISA card and identification. Most banks and change bureaux will hit you with a 10-12F commission for cashing traveller's cheques or foreign currency. To avoid this, cash your cheques at the Paris office of the company which issued them back home (i.e. Barclays, Thomas Cook or American Express). And always remember that rates of exchange can vary slightly from bank to bank, so do a bit of shopping before you change money.

Those who want to avoid carrying around a lot of cash (Paris has a high crime rate just like any other big city) will be comforted with the knowledge that many hotels, restaurants and travel agencies, as well as many of the shops, accept VISA, Diners Club, American Express, Eurocard and

Classical French facade of the International Westminster Bank branch in the Place Vendome, which is directly opposite the Ritz Hotel in the most fashionable part of Paris.

13

Carte Bleue cards. Look for the appropriate card sign in the window or behind the desk.

Airport exchange
Charles de Gaulle/Roissy: Société Général; open daily 6 am to 11 pm on the departure level and 6 am to 1 am on the arrival level.

Orly South: Société Général; open daily 6.30 am to 11.30 pm.

Orly West: Société Général; open daily 7 am to 11 pm

Railway station exchange
Gare d'Austerlitz: Monday to Friday 9 am to 4.45 pm.

Gare de l'Est: Monday to Friday 7.30 am to 8 pm.

Gare de Lyon: daily 6.30 am to 11 pm.

Gare Montparnasse: daily 9 am to 7 pm.

Gare du Nord: daily 6.30 to 10 pm.

Gare Saint-Lazare: Monday to Friday 7.30 am to 8 pm.

Bus terminal exchange
Air France Gare des Invalides: Société Général; open daily 6.30 am to 10.30 pm. Air France Palais des Congres: Société Général on Level One; open Monday to Friday 9 am to 12.30 pm and 1.45 to 4.30 pm.

City exchange
American Express: 11, rue Scribe 9e; (tel: 073.42.90. metro: Opéra). Open Monday to Friday 9 am to 5.45 pm., Saturday 9 am to noon.

Bank of America: 43-47, avenue de la Grande-Armée, 16e; (tel: 501.54.12. metro: Argentine). Open Monday to Friday 9 am to 1 pm.

Barclays: 33, rue de 4 Septembre, 2e; (tel: 265.65.65. metro: 4 Septembre). 157, boulevard St Germain, 6e; (metro: St Germain). 6, Rond Point des Champs-Elysées, 8e; (metro: Roosevelt). 24, avenue Kleber, 16e; (metro: Kleber). All branches are open Monday to Friday 9 am to 4.30 pm.

Citibank: 60, avenue des Champs-Elysées, 8e; (tel: 266.33.60; metro: Roosevelt). Open Monday to Friday 9 am to 12.30 pm.

Thomas Cook : 2, place de la Madeleine, 8e; (tel: 260.33.20; metro: Madeleine). 32, rue 4 Septembre, 2e; (metro: 4 Septembre). 14, boulevard des Capucines, 9e; (metro: Opera). Open Monday to Friday 9 am to 6 pm. Exchange service only at the Madeleine branch (9 am to 5.45 pm). Also, Thomas Cook exchange bureaux at the Eiffel Tower (11 am to 7 pm) and the Gare St Lazare, Gare de l'Est and Gare du Nord (7 am to 9 pm).

Westminster (International) Bank: 18, place Vendome, 8e; (tel: 260.37.40; metro: Tuileries, Opera). Open 9 am to 4 pm Monday to Friday, bureau de change closed noon to 2 pm.

Communications

Post and telegraph

French post offices are open Monday to Friday from 8 am to 7 pm, and Saturday from 8 am to noon. There is a special 24-hour post office at 52, rue du Louvre, 1er (metro: Louvre) and a late-night and weekend post office at 71, avenue des Champs-Elysées, 8e (metro: George V) which is open Monday to Saturday from 8 am to 11 pm and Sunday from 10 am to noon and 2 to 8 pm.

Stamps can also be purchased at most Tabac shops. A special message service is available from all post offices within the Paris city limits, in which your note will be delivered to any address in the city within two hours.

Poste restante letters and packages will be directed to the huge postal facility at 52, rue du Louvre unless otherwise stated. The great thing about having your post sent there is that you can collect it 24 hours a day.

Post boxes are painted yellow and are found throughout the city. At post offices you may be presented with a choice of mail slots: *Paris unique* (Paris only), *avion* (overseas air-mail) and *départements étrangers* (France beyond Paris). Other important postal terms: *timbres* (stamps), *timbres de collection* (special commemorative stamps), *aerogram* (air letter), *récommander* (registered post), *paquet* (parcel post).

Telegrams can be sent from any post office, or by ringing 233.21.11. (English service). There is a seven word minimum including the address.

Post offices are also equipped with a bank of telephones from which you can make domestic and overseas calls.

Postal information: tel: 280.67.89.

Telephones

Public telephones are found in post offices, railway stations, airports, hotels, drugstores, shopping complexes, theatres and cafes. There are also multiple phone boxes spread around Paris, but at any given time it seems as if half of these don't work and the other half are situated next to busy streets where you can hardly hear yourself think, let alone talk. But the French telephone service has improved by leaps and bounds in the last decade and it's now equal to most other systems in Europe (although Americans will find it no match for Ma Bell).

Making a telephone call from a box is quite simple, made easier by multi-language instructions on the wall. If these instructions are ripped down or written over it's still easy. Depending on the phone, the slots should take 5F, 1F, 50 centimes and 10 centimes coins. There are not many around which will accept the newer 2F and 20 centimes coins. Put enough coins in to last you a minimum three minutes, say 3F in the case of Britain. Then dial the number: 19 to get you out of France, followed by the country code, the local or regional code, then the local number. To call London for example, you would dial 19-44-01 and then the house or office number. For local Paris calls just drop the money in the slot and dial the number. Your money will be returned to you if the party at the other end doesn't answer, or if the phone is engaged. If you connect, the money will slowly drop out of sight according to the length of the call. The phone will start beeping ten seconds before your time is up, so you should have more coins ready to deposit if you want to talk longer. All unused coins will be returned at the end of the call, in other words, any coins you can still see in the plastic slots.

You can also make telephone calls from cafés and Tabac shops by purchasing a *jeton* or token for 70 centimes from the proprietor. Deposit the jeton in the slot and then press the button to the right of the telephone when the party answers (if you don't they won't be able to hear you talking).

Most hotels will also let you make local and overseas calls from their phones, but you will get hit with a hefty service charge on top of the call charge.

Collect or reverse charge calls (P.C.V. in French) can be made from post offices or hotels, but you may wait several hours for the call to go through if it's overseas. Collect calls are not allowed on Sunday.

Telex
Paris's main telex office is at 7, rue Feydeau, 2e (tel: 233.20.12 or 233.20.13; metro: Bourse). It's open daily 8 am to 8 pm. Almost every hotel above two stars has its own telex machine for the use of hotel guests. These are particularly convenient for business travellers.

Television
Paris has three television stations, all government controlled and all broadcasting in original or dubbed French. The programme selection is a mixture of news, old movies, sit-coms, soap operas, documentaries, sports and cops and robber shows, as in America or Britain. Not too many British shows, but the Yanks might want to tune into *Dallas, Starsky and Hutch* or *Chips* dubbed into French. (What does J.R. sound like with a French accent? Check Channel One on Saturday at 8.35 pm.)

Radio
The only English-language radio station in Paris is ENS (European News Service) cable radio which broadcasts into 30 major hotels. It's a 24-hour a day station which features reports from the *International Herald Tribune, Time* magazine, AP Radio service, the *Financial Times* and *Passion* magazine.

There are at least 40 free airwave stations in the Paris

17

region (a deregulated situation which makes Britain look downright medieval) broadcasting news, music, sports, radio soap operas and features. There are even special stations for minority groups like the North Africans and Latin Americans. Stations which might be of interest to English-speaking visitors include:

ABC (100.6 MHz): Rock and news radio.

Radio Canal (89 MHz): Rock, jazz, funk and classics 24 hours a day.

Radio Cité (92.6 MHz): Top 40 rock'n'roll.

Radio-Classique (101.8 MHz): Music of the 18th and 19th centuries.

Radio Latina (101.8 MHz): South American sounds in alternation with Radio-Classique.

Radio Libre Paris (106 MHz): Rock, pop,, funk, new wave, classic and folk music 24 hours a day.

Radio Montmartre (90.7 MHz): French chanson and folk songs.

Radio Solidarnosc (89 MHz): Radio Free Poland in the West.

NRJ (89.4 MHz): 24-hour a day stereo radio with 99 per cent music and 1 per cent news. Includes rock, funk, country western, pop and French folk.

Finally, a selection of English-language services which can be picked up in Paris depending on the strength of your receiver:

BBC Radio Four (1,500 LW): British news, weather, sports and classical music.

BBC World Service (29.0 MHz): The famous 'Beeb' news station.

US Armed Forces Network (28.5 MHz): Top 40 music, news and live sports broadcasts from the DJs who keep the American army happy. Fast-paced, slick format.

Voice of America (24 MHz): US news and propaganda station meant primarily for Eastern European ears.

Health

Visiting Paris isn't quite as risky as travelling to the tropics, you won't have to worry about taking your malaria pills or getting a yellow fever injection! But you can have health problems anywhere on this globe, ranging from a mild headache to emergency surgery. France is one of the most advanced nations on earth in the area of modern medical treatment, and Paris has more than its share of clinic and hospital facilities if something goes wrong.

Pharmacies and drug stores are your most likely health destination, probably for something to cure a cold or headache. You can spot them quite easily, for they each have a large green cross posted outside which is illuminated at night.

If it's something more serious and you need a doctor in a hurry try the 24-hour **SOS Medicins** on 377.77.77 or 707.77.77. or the 24-hour **General Practitioner Service** on 542.37.00. If it's a throbbing tooth ache which ails you, try **SOS Dentist** on 337.51.00 Both the SOS and GP services make house calls on request.

Ambulances can be obtained by calling SAMU 75 on 567.50.50. or City of Paris on 887.27.50.

Finally, if it's a hospital you need, some place where everyone speaks your language (English) is probably desired. Try the American Hospital at 63, boulevard Victor Hugo in suburban Neuilly (tel: 747.53.00; metro: Sablons, Louise Michel), or the British Hospital of Paris at 48, rue de Villiers in suburban Levallois-Perret (tel: 757.24.10; metro: Anatole France). There are nearly 100 other hospitals and clinics in metropolitan Paris.

Pharmacies
Dhery - Pharmacie des Champs-Elysées: 84, avenue des Champs-Elysées, 8e; (tel: 562.02.41; metro: Roosevelt). Open 24 hours a day, 365 days a year.
Drugstore Champs-Elysées: 133, avenue des Champs-Elysées, 8e; (metro: Etoile). Open until 2 am nightly.
Drugstore Matignon: 1, avenue Matignon, 8e; (metro:

Roosevelt). Open until 2 am nightly.

Drugstore Opera: 6, boulevard des Capucines, 9e; (metro: Opera). Open until 2 am nightly.

Drugstore Saint-Germain: 149, boulevard St Germain, 6e; (tel: 222.80.00; metro: St Germain). Open until 2 am nightly.

Pharmacie Anglaise: English pharmacy at 62, avenue des Champs-Elysées, 8e; (tel: 359.22.52; metro: Roosevelt). Open Monday to Saturday 9 am to 10.30 pm.

Pharmacie Anglo-Americaine: 6, rue Castiglione, 1er; (tel: 260.72.96; metro: Tuileries). Combination American drugstore and English chemist, across the street from the Hotel Inter-Continental with all your favourite drugs, cosmetics, perfumes and toiletries.

Pharmacie des Arts: 106, boulevard Montparnasse, 14e; (tel: 326.56.20; metro: Montparnasse). Opposite the Maine-Montparnasse Centre. Open daily 8 am to midnight.

Emergency phone numbers

Alcoholics anonymous (AA): 634.59.65.

Ambulance: SAMU 75 on 567.50.50 or the City of Paris on 887.27.50.

Burn centre: 344.33.33. ext. (poste) 2360, or 329.32.32. ext. (poste) 73.

Dentist: SOS Dentist on 337.51.00. 24 hours a day.

Doctor: SOS Médicin on 377.77.77. or 707.77.77. 24 hours a day.

Drug crisis centre: 581.11.20. ext (poste) 4150.

Fire dept: 18.

Food poisoning: 260.33.22. ext. (poste) 4430.

Pacemakers: SOS Pacemaker on 828.76.99. 24 hours a day.

Poison centre: 205.63.29.

Police: 17

Pregnancy: Emergencies only on 887.27.50.

Rape crisis centre: 348.24.91.

Vets: SOS Veterinarian on 871.20.60. from 8 pm to 8 am only.

VD clinic: Dispensaire de la Croix-Rouge (Red Cross) on 261.30.04. or Institut Prophylactique on 544.38.94.

Houses of worship

Paris is a predominantly Roman Catholic city (the third largest Catholic population in the world after Mexico City and São Paulo) with numerous patron saints and their imposing medieval shrines. There are hundreds of Catholic churches in the metropolitan area, ranging from the Gothic masterpiece of Notre Dame to the tiny parish chapels of the suburbs. Notre Dame is the diocesan seat, and a wonderfully inspiring place to witness a Catholic Mass. Finding a non-Catholic religious service is not so easy, but the following list of houses of worship might help:

Armenian Catholic: Eglise Armenienne, 8, rue des Ternes, 17e; (tel: 375.11.25; metro: Porte Maillot).

Baptist: Eglise Evangelique Baptiste de Paris, 72, rue de Sèvres, 7e; (tel: 273.35.07; metro: Duroc).

Christian Science: Deuxième Eglise de Christ Scientiste, 58, boulevard Flandrin, 16e, (tel: 504.37.74; metro: Porte Dauphine).

Church of England: St Michael's (British Embassy Church), 5, rue d'Aguesseau, 8e; (tel: 073.09.00; metro: Madeleine).

Episcopal: American Cathedral of the Holy Trinity, 23, avenue George V, 8e; (tel: 359.17.90; metro: Alma).

Greek Orthodox: Notre-Dame des Affliges et Ste Genevieve, 36, rue de la Montagne Ste Genevieve, 5e; (metro: Maubert-Mutualité).

Islam: Institut Musulman et Mosquée de Paris, Place du Puits de l'Ermite, 5e; (tel: 535.97.33; metro: Monge).

Judaism: Consistoire Central (Great Synagogue of Paris), 44, rue de la Victoire, 9e; (tel: 285.71.09; metro: Le Peletier).

Lutheran. Eglise Allemande Lutherienne, 25, rue Blanche, 9e; (tel: 526.79.43; metro: Trinité).

Methodist: Wesleyan Methodist Church, 5, rue Rocquepine, 8e; (tel: 265.43.58; metro: St Augustin).

Non-Denominational Christian: American Church, 65, quai d'Orsay, 7e; (tel: 551.38.90; metro: Invalides).

Romanian Orthodox: Saints Archanges, 9 bis, rue Jean-de-Beauvais, 5e; (tel: 033.67.47; metro: Maubert-Mutualité).

A worshipper lights holy candles in one of the side chapels of Notre Dame Cathedral, the seat of Roman Catholic worship in Paris.

Russian Orthodox: St Alexandre-Newsky Cathedral, 12, rue
 Daru, 8e; (tel: 727.37.34; metro: Courcelles).
Scottish/Presbyterian: Skots Kirk, 17, rue Bayard, 8e;
 (metro: Roosevelt).
Serbian Orthodox: Saint-Save, 9 bis, rue Jean-de-Beauvais,
 (metro: Maubert-Mutualité).
Seventh Day Adventist: 63, rue du Faubourg Poissonnière, 9e;
 (tel: 824.95.26; Poissonnière).

Embassies

Australia: 4, rue Jean-Rey, 15e; (tel: 575.62.00; metro:
 Bir-Hakeim). Consulate: 28, rue de la Pepiniere, 8e; (tel:
 292.24.81; metro: Saint-Lazare).
Canada: 35, avenue Montaigne, 8e; (tel: 723.01.01; metro:
 Alma). Consulate: 4, rue Ventadour, 1er; (tel: 296.87.19;
 metro: Pyramides).
Ireland: 12, avenue Foch, 16e; (tel: 500.20.87; metro: Etoile).
New Zealand: 9, rue Leonard-de-Vinci, 16e; (tel: 500.24.11;
 metro Victor Hugo).
United Kingdom: 35, rue du Faubourg St Honore, 8e; (tel:
 266.91.42; metro: Madeleine). Consulate: 109, rue du
 Faubourg St Honore 8e; (tel. 260.33.06; metro:
 Miromesnil).
United States: 2, avenue Gabriel, 8e; (tel: 296.12.02; metro:
 Concorde). Consulate: 2, rue St Florentine, 1er;
 (tel: 260.14.88; metro: Concorde).

Holidays

The following public holidays are observed in France.
Expect most government offices and shops to be closed, plus
reduced service on all public transit.
New Year's Day (January 1)
Easter Sunday and Monday (March or April)
Labour Day (May 1)
Ascension Day (May, movable)

Whit Monday (May, movable)
Bastille Day (July 14)
Assumption Day (August 15)
All Saint's Day (November 1)
Armistice Day (November 11)
Christmas (December 25)

Miscellaneous services

Baby sitting: La Panthere Rose (The Pink Panther) at 1, rue Cherubini, 2e; (tel: 296.05.69; metro. Pyramides). Fees are 20F per hour plus transportation costs. Minimum age of one month. Centre Regional des Oeuvres Universitaires et Scolaires de Paris (University Work Centre) at 39, avenue Georges-Bernanos, 5e; (tel: 329.97.10 or 329.12.43. ext. poste 437 and 447; metro Porte Royal). Fees are 20F per hour plus 2F per infant supplement. Minimum stay of three hours.

Camera repair: Special camera repair desk at the FNAC department store in the Forum des Halles complex (Etage -1); (tel: 261.81.18; metro: Les Halles).

Interpreters: If you have a business deal or complex shopping to undertake in Paris and your French isn't up to the task, you may want to engage the services of an English-French interpreter. One of the best agencies is Interpreter Service (tel. 278.13.25.) which charges 500F minimum for up to two and a half hours and then 200F per hour thereafter. Weekend rates are 250F per hour and the day-rate for eight hours is 1,500F.

Legal aid: SOS Lawyer on 329.33.00 from 6 pm to 12 pm each evening.

Locksmith: 707.99.99. 24 hours a day or 722.02.64. for duplicates of car keys.

Lost and found: Bureau des Objets Trouvés at 36, rue des

Morillons, 15e; (metro: Convention).

Time: tel: 463.84.00.

Wake-up service: tel: 688.71.11. or 463.71.11. Paris uses the 24-hour clock which means 13.00 instead of 1 pm.

Weather: tel: 555.95.90.(local) or 555.95.02. (international).

Women's centre. tel: 348.24.91. on Wednesday from 6 pm to 10 pm.

CHAPTER 2

Getting there and back

Paris hasn't always been easy to reach. The ancient Romans had to march hundreds of miles through enemy territory and then cross to the Cité island in wooden boats. Attila the Hun was met with a somewhat violent reception and wound up skipping the city altogether. And Kaiser Wilhelm's troops couldn't get past the Marne.

Fortunately for us, this situation has been amended in this age of supersonic jet travel and high-speed trains. Paris is now easy to reach from almost every major city in the world via a wide range of transport modes. There are hundreds of daily flights between Paris and the urban centres of Europe and North America, the SNCF (Société Nationale des Chemins de Fer) provides rapid rail service to provincial towns and other Western European capitals, and there are coach companies which have slow but cheap connections with other cities.

Those who want to drive themselves will find excellent cross-Channel connections and then the impressive network of French national roads. The 'N' numbers are national highways, double-lane or dual carriageway roads which are kept in tip-top condition, while the 'A' roads are *autoroutes* or motorways which provide the quickest means of vehicle travel between major cities. By the end of the decade there should be an autoroute from Calais all the way to Paris, for only the last 20 kilometres from Nordausques to Calais have yet to be built. And once you get into Paris there is a speedy inner peripheral road (sadly lacking in London) and plenty of public car parks.

Flights

Almost every major national carrier which serves Heathrow and Gatwick airports flies the London-Paris route. British Airways, for instance, has six daily flights between Heathrow and Roissy/Charles de Gaulle. Flight time is about 90 minutes from take-off to touch-down.

The bad news for air passengers is that the national airlines have formed a monopolistic cartel which keeps inter-European fares sky-high. The standard cost on the London-Paris route is £68 single and £136 return on tourist economy class, and £84 single and £168 return on business/first class. This makes it one of the most expensive routes in the world in terms of cost per mile.

The good news is that British Airways and Air France have finally responded to passenger pressure and competition from bucket shops and charter companies by offering a special low fare to Paris of just £74 return. Sounds great, but there are two hitches: you must spend at least one Saturday night in Paris and you must travel on certain off-peak flights. For information and reservations telephone British Airways on (01) 370 5411.

Anyone possessing an International Student I.D. Card can buy a London-Paris return for only £47 through the numerous youth travel and bucket shops in London. For a list of reputable agents, contact the Air Travel Advisory Bureau on (01) 636 5000.

Airport information
The following numbers should be called for general information on arriving and departing flights:
Orly: 884.32.10.
Roissy/Charles de Gaulle: 862.22.80.

Le Bourget: 862.52.52
Information on the major airlines serving Paris can be gained
by calling the following numbers:
Air France: 535.61.61. or 535.66.00. from 8 am to 8 pm
  (passenger tickets and reservations).
British Airways: 778.14.14.
British Caledonian: 261.50.21.
Pan Am: 266.45.45.
TWA: 720.75.79.
UTA: 266.30.30.
Air Canada: 320.14.21.

Getting into town

From Roissy-Charles de Gaulle
1. Roissy-Rail: RER train service from airport to Gare du
Nord in the centre of Paris, where you can link up with the
regular metro, bus and taxi service. Trains every 15 minutes
in both directions from 5.30 am to 11.30 pm. Tickets: 20F
single second class and 30F single first class. This service
is also available from the Chatelet/Les Halles and Luxembourg RER stations.

2. Air France Bus: Speedy coach service from the airport
to the Aerogare Maillot under the Palais des Congres (metro:
Porte Maillot). Service in both directions every 15-20 minutes
from 6 am to 11 pm daily, plus special service during the
night on the arrival of scheduled flights. Tickets: 27F one
way, children under four free. Information: 758.20.17.

3. RATP Bus: Number 350 to/from Gare de l'Est (metro:
Gare de l'Est) and number 351 to/from Place de la Nation
(metro: Nation). Service every 5-10 minutes from 5.30 am
to 8.30 pm. Tickets: 15F.

4. Taxis: Available at the taxi stands *(tête de station)* in front
of the terminals 24 hours a day. Fares into the centre of Paris
are higher than normal taxi rates, so be prepared to pay about
100F from 6.30 am to 11 pm, and 150F during the night. Add
an extra 1.50F per piece for luggage which must be carried

SNCF high-speed trains whisk visitors from the Channel ports into the centre of Paris in just three hours.

in the boot or on the roof rack, and the driver will expect a 15 per cent tip at the end. Not your cheapest means of getting into town, but the fastest.

5. Driving: From the terminals take the easily-marked route to Autoroute A1 following the signs toward Paris. The A1 terminates at the Porte de la Chapelle, where you can pick up the Boulevard Périphérique around Paris, or follow the Rue de la Chapelle into the centre of town.

From Orly
1. Orly-Rail: RER train service from the airport to the Gare d'Austerlitz (metro: Austerlitz), Gare St Michel (metro: St Michel) and Gare d'Orsay (metro: Solferino). Service every 15 minutes from 5.44 am to 10.44 pm. Tickets: 17F single second class and 25F single first class. Information: 261.50.50.

2. Air France Bus: Coach service from the Orly Ouest and Sud every 12 minutes to the Aerogare des Invalides (metro: Invalides) in central Paris. Scheduled stop at Gare Montparnasse and request stops at Porte d'Orléans. Service every 12 minutes from 5.50 am to 11 pm, with special night service upon the arrival of scheduled flights. Tickets: 24F single, with children under four free. The journey takes 30 minutes. Information: 551.96.20.

3. RATP Bus: Number 215 to/from Denfert-Rochereau and number 183A to/from Porte de Choisy (metro: Porte de Choisy). Service on number 215 is every 10 minutes from 6 am to 11.30 pm. The journey takes 20 minutes, and from Denfert you can link up with regular metro, bus and taxi service. Tickets: 9F.

4. Taxis: Available at the taxi stands (*tête de station*) in front of both terminals 24 hours a day. For fares, see above under Roissy taxis.

5. Driving: From either west or south terminals just follow the signs to Autoroute Orly (A6) heading north into Paris. The A6 ends at the Boulevard Périphérique, which you can take all the way around Paris. The first exits into the city

centre are Porte d'Orléans and Porte d'Italie. From Orléans follow the Avenue du Général Leclerc to Place Denfert-Rochereau, from which you can take several roads into central Paris.

Driving

The road distance between London and Paris is 455 km, which means you can easily drive from city to city within a single day. If there was no water in the way, the drive might take only five hours. Unfortunately, the English Channel intervenes, and this means a delay of at least two hours taking the ferry.

There are dozens of ferries each day operating between the principal English and French Channel ports, so you should never have to wait long. The primary Channel services are offered by:

Sealink UK Ltd: Eversholt House, Eversholt St., London NW1. (tel: 01-828 0007). Ferries from Dover to Calais, Dover to Boulogne, Dover to Dunkerque, Folkestone to Calais, Folkestone to Boulogne, Newhaven to Dieppe and Weymouth to Cherbourg. For 24-hour recorded information on the Dover and Calais sailings telephone 01-828 0007; for Newhaven and Weymouth sailings call 01-828 7603.

Townsend Thoresen: 127 Regent St., London W1; (tel: 01-734 4431 or 01-437 7800). Ferries from Dover to Calais, Southampton to Cherbourg and Southampton to Le Havre.

Hoverspeed Ltd: International Hoverport, Ramsgate, Kent CT12 5HS; (tel: 01-554 7061). Hovercraft from Dover to Calais and Dover to Boulogne.

The most popular crossing is Dover-Calais because this takes the least time, 30 minutes on the hovercraft and 75 minutes by conventional ferry. Prices don't vary much from port to port or from company to company (although Hoverspeed is most expensive). However, the fare will depend on what time of year and time of day you will be

Perhaps the most novel means of travelling between London and Paris is by hovercraft across the Channel, a service which operates from Dover to Calais and Boulogne.

sailing, on how many adults and children there are in your party, and on the weight and length of your vehicle. The lowest seasonal fares are in the winter, the highest in July and August. The lowest daily fares are in the early morning and late at night, highest at midday, in the late afternoon and early evening. Obviously, the more popular sailings are the most expensive. Expect to pay a minimum of £60 for a medium-sized car and two adults if you are crossing the Channel in July or August.

Driving in France isn't that different from driving anywhere else in Europe. Just remember one thing: keep to the right! Prior to 1984 vehicles within roundabouts did not have the right-of-way over other vehicles entering from the side, but French motoring law changed and now whatever vehicle is within the traffic circle has the right-of-way.

Depending on the French Channel port at which you land, there are a number of routes for driving to Paris. If you're short on time take the N43 south east from Calais to Nordausques, where you can pick up the A26 and A1 autoroutes all the way to Paris. The autoroute will be completed all the way to Calais by the end of the 1980s.

A scenic alternative is motoring the N1 south from Calais or Boulogne through the picturesque Picardy countryside. The N1 follows a meandering route through Abbeville, Amiens and Beauvais before merging with the A1 at the Parisian suburb of St Denis.

Parking and petrol stations

Parking can be Paris's biggest headache. If your hotel doesn't have a car park you could be in for an impromptu city tour in search of an empty space. Fortunately, Paris has a number of large public car parks at convenient locations, including the Place de la Concorde, Les Halles, Pompidou Centre, Place du Parvis Notre Dame, Place Vendôme, Place St Germain-des-Prés, Esplanade des Invalides, Champ de Mars, Rond Point Champs-Elysées and the Étoile. There are some 150 underground car parks in Paris and a plan showing these

33

is available from the Syndicat d'Initiative office at the Hôtel de Ville (Town Hall), Place de l'Hôtel de Ville, 4e (metro: Hôtel de Ville).

Paris has a multitude of petrol stations and repair garages, many of them situated within the underground car parks or along major thoroughfares. If it's late at night and your petrol gauge is in the red zone, the following list of petrol stations (listed by arrondissement) may save you a long walk:

1er	BP, 58 Rue du Marché St Honoré
2e	Shell, 83 Rue Reaumur
3e	Antar, 42 Rue Beauborg
4e	Antar, 4 Quai des Celestins
5e	Shell, 93 Rue Monge
6e	BP, Parking St Germain (next to Drugstore)
7e	Shell, 6-10 Blvd Raspail
8e	Total, 20 Blvd Malesherbes
9e	Esso, Parking Anvers, 41 Blvd Rochechouart
10e	Esso, 168 Fauborg St Martin
11e	Elf, 46 Rue Oberkampf
12e	Shell, 123 Blvd Soult
13e	Esso, 32 Blvd de Port Royal
14e	Shell, 110 Rue d'Alésia
15e	Elf, 45 Rue St Charles
16e	Mobil, 26 Ave. Paul Doumer
17e	Antar, 160 Rue Cardinet
18e	Esso, Ave de la Porte St Ouen
19e	Mobil, 39 Ave Simon Bolivar
20e	Mobil, 57 Rue de Bagnolet

Trains

British Rail, in conjunction with Sea Link and SNCF, offers a number of options for travelling between London and Paris. The cheapest is the TransAlpino fare for people under 26: £18.90 single and £30.90 return no matter when you travel. For those of you who no longer qualify on age, the least expensive fare to Paris is a five-day excursion for

£36 return. The standard fare £29 single and £58 return, but the ticket is good for two months and you can take as many stops as you like en route. There are also night fares for £18 single and £36 return. Tack on another £5 single or £10 return any time you use a jetfoil or hovercraft. In addition, there are reduced price tickets for children and senior citizens. These trains depart Victoria Station at least seven times each day, arriving in Paris about 11 hours later at either Gare St Lazare or Gare du Nord.

For more information on the British Rail/Sea Link services call 01-834 2345 from 8 am to 9 pm daily, or dial the recorded 24-hour information line on 01-828 8747.

Another possibility is the British Rail/Hoverspeed service, at five and a half hours the quickest land connection between the capitals. Trains depart Charing Cross station at least twice each day, arriving at Gare du Nord. Standard fares are £33 single £66 return, but there is a five day excursion fare of only £42 return.

Once you have arrived in Paris and you plan on leaving the city via train, then you should familiarize yourself with the destinations served by each of the six major stations. The Gare d'Austerlitz, 13e has trains for central and southwest France (including Bordeaux and the Pays Basque) and Spain; the Gare de l'Est, 10e for eastern France (including Alsace), West Germany and Northern Switzerland; the Gare de Lyon, 12e for southern France (including the Alps and Riviera) and Italy, with the sleek orange TGV trains which will whisk you down to Lyon at 190 miles an hour; the Gare de Montparnasse, 15e for western France (Brittany); the Gare du Nord, 10e for northern France;and the Gare St Lazare 8e for northwest France and Britain.

Station information
The following numbers can be called 8 am to 10 pm daily for general information on arriving and departing trains.
SNCF General Information: 261.50.50.
Gare d'Austerlitz: 584.16.16.
Gare de l'Est: 208.49.90.
Gare de Lyon: 345.92.22.

Gare de Montparnasse: 538.52.29.
Gare du Nord: 208.03.03.
Gare St Lazare: 285.88.00.
TGV Reservations: 345.93.33.

Buses

This is the cheapest form of transport between Paris and the other large cities in Western Europe if you don't have a special rail pass or if you're not eligible for the under-26 TransAlpino fares. But coach travel has its obvious disadvantages: it takes longer than planes or trains, and the ride isn't nearly so comfortable. Two big pluses for coach travel are the rock-bottom prices and the great view of the countryside. As coaches continue to get more sophisticated (i.e. videos, bars and fold-out beds), so will the journey between Paris and other cities get much more comfortable.

Hoverspeed offers the best of coach deals because it combines low price with quick journey via those lumbering hovercraft across the Channel. The London to Paris fare is £19.50 single and £39 return, departing from in front of the Royal National Hotel in Bedford Way (tube: Russell Square) at 8.15 am, 11.30 am and 13.45 pm daily. The trip to Paris takes about nine hours and you are deposited in the middle of town, at the Hoverspeed office in 24, rue de St Quentin (metro: Gare du Nord or Gare de l'Est). For reservations and information in London telephone 01-554 7061; in Paris telephone 208.11.96.

The next best of the bus companies is probably Euroways Express Coaches Ltd. at 52 Grosvenor Gardens, London SW1 (tel: 01-730 8235; tube: Victoria). It's cheaper than Hoverspeed at £18.50 single and £32 return, but the journey takes at least an hour longer because conventional ferries are used to cross the Channel. Departures daily at 9.15 am and 9 pm from Victoria Coach Station.

Other London agencies offering inexpensive coach fares to Paris are The Miracle Bus Company (408 Strand WC1; 01-379 6055) and Supabus (Victoria Coach Station, Buckingham Palace Road SW1; 01-730 0202).

VIA International operates the best network of buses from Paris to other cities on the continent from its bustling little terminal at 8, place de Staringgrad, 19e (tel: 205.12.10; metro: Starlingrad). The company runs coaches to most of the major destinations in Western Europe including Athens, Rome, Madrid, Belgrade, Barcelona, Malaga, Lisbon and Hamburg. All prices are dirt cheap. VIA also books for Euroways in Paris, so this is also where you catch buses back to London. Departures daily at 9.30 am and 10.30 pm, with plenty of time to purchase duty-free goods in Calais.

Hitching

It's a lot easier to hitch into Paris from the provinces than to try and get out, which is true for any big city. When leaving there are two major problems: gaining access to the major roads leading out of Paris and getting far enough out of the city centre so that most of the cars whizzing past you are actually heading for the countryside rather than the next suburb down the line. Hitchers might want to take an RER or SNCF train to far suburban stations which are near the entrance to an autoroute or national highway.

Another possibility is trying Allostop-Provoya, a hitching service at 65, passage Brady, 10e (tel: 246.00.66; metro: Strasbourg-St Denis). They have a listing of drivers looking for riders to help with the cost of petrol and autoroute tolls. Having to pay is a negative for most hitchers, but the advantages of this service are that you will reach your destination quicker than by public transport, you will have a chance to meet other travellers, and the price is much lower than for comparable distances covered by bus or train.

The following is a guide to hitching out of Paris in various directions:

North: England (via Calais), Belgium, Lille. Take the metro to Porte de la Chapelle, where the Autoroute du Nord (A1) starts from the Boulevard Ney. An alternative is taking an

SNCF train the 76 km north to Beauvais and trying to get on the autoroute from there. A scenic alternative is the N1 which rolls through some lovely French countryside to Beauvais, Abbeville, Boulogne and Calais. The N1 also begins from the Porte de la Chapelle, but you can get a head start by taking an SNCF commuter train from the Gare du Nord three stops to Groslay, then walking up the Avenue de la République to the N1.

Northwest: England (via Dieppe or Le Havre), Rouen, Normandy. You want the N14 for this direction, but there are a number of options. It's easiest to take the metro to Porte de Clignancourt, cross Boulevard Ney and walk up the Avenue de la Porte de Clignancourt past the Périphérique road to Avenue Michelet. This is where the N14 begins, but you may wait awhile for a ride. Better still, take bus number 154A to the end of the line in Franconville. This will deposit you right on the N14 in one of Paris's outer suburbs.

West: Normandy, Brittany, Cherbourg, Caen, Brest. Take the metro to Porte d'Auteuil and walk across the square to the Avenue de la Porte d'Auteuil where there is an entrance onto the west-bound Autoroute de l'Ouest (A13). As an alternative, take RER line C7 from the Gare des Invalides or Gare d'Orsay to the end of the line in St Quentin-en-Yvelines, turn left outside the station and walk to the entrance of the A12 (to Brest and south Brittany) about one kilometre. Or take bus 482 from the Porte de Boulogne to Vaucresson suburb, where there is an entrance to the A13 near the SNCF station.

Southwest: Spain (via San Sebastian), Loire Valley, Bordeaux, Tours, Le Mans, Angers, Nantes. Two choices here: you can go for the quick ride on the A10, or the scenic route along the N10. To reach the start of the N10, take the metro to Porte de St Cloud and cross over the Périphérique to the Avenue Edouard Vaillant, or take it all the way to the end of the line at Pont de Sévres. The N10 crosses over the bridge. To get a head start take RER line C7 from Gare des Invalides or Gare d'Orsay to the end of the line at St Quentin-en-Yvelines.

The N10 is right outside the station. The A10 is a bit harder to reach. Take RER line B4 from Chatelet station to Orsay-Ville and walk about one kilometre to the entrance of the N118, which quickly turns into the A10.

South: Italy, Switzerland, the Alps, the French Riviera, Lyon, Avignon, Marseille. Take the metro to Porte d'Orleans or Porte d'Italie and try hitching onto the Boulevard Périphér-ique in the direction of the Autoroute du Sud (A6). If you don't have much luck, take bus 297 from Porte d'Orleans to Chilly-Mazarin, where there is an entrance onto the A6.

East: West Germany, Metz, Strasbourg. Take the metro to Porte de Charenton and walk to Porte de Bercy, the start of Autoroute A4. As an alternative, take RER line A4 to Torcy, then walk about one kilometre via Collegien to the A4 entrance.

Northeast: Luxembourg, Belgium (Liège), West Germany (Cologne), Metz, Reims. Take the metro to Porte de Pantin where the N3 starts, but go under the Périphérique to the Avenue de la Porte de Pantin to begin your hitching. As an alternative, you can take the metro to Eglise de Pantin, then hop on bus 246B or 147A to Livry-Gargan, where it will drop you right on the N3 at the edge of Paris.

CHAPTER THREE

Getting around town

The most delightful means of getting around Paris is to walk, for most of the major museums and tourist sights are in a compact area at the centre of the city. The strolls between the Louvre, the Pompidou Centre and Notre Dame are no more than 15 minutes each (unless you get distracted into the numerous shops and cafés en route). And there is no walking path quite like the quays along the Seine.

But those with tired feet, or who want to range out from the city centre, will find an excellent network of public transport that is amongst the fastest and cheapest in Europe. The nucleus of this network is the marvellous metro, the most romantic (and one of the most efficient) underground systems in the world. The RATP (Régie Autonome des Transports Parisiens) runs the metro in conjunction with its wide-spread bus service, and tickets are inter-changeable between the two systems.

Parisian taxis are not as ubiquitous as the yellow cabs of New York or the black beauties of London, but there are over 15,000 of them racing about town. Those with a little extra cash in the bank might want to try their own limousine. And you can also hire bicycles and motorbikes.

Prefer a little historical narration with your transport? Try the scenic bus or boat tours offered by a number of companies, or a lofty helicopter ride over Paris.

Whichever way you decide to explore Paris it'll be a lot of fun.

Metro and RER

Paris has the best underground transport system in Western Europe if all factors are taken into consideration. The metro may not be as new as Munich's U-Bahn, or as cheap as Madrid's subway, but there is no other system on the continent which can top it for overall performance.

The massive metro network blankets the Paris metropolitan area with over 360 stations. And when the revolutionary Réseau Express Régional (RER) is completed there will be 480 stations, nearly twice the number of London's tube. Only two systems in the world are currently larger — Moscow and Tokyo — and when the final steel pin is driven into the ground Paris may top them both.

It's never a long walk to the metro because no point within the City of Paris is more than 550 metres (about the length of five football fields) away from a station. And when you finally get underground, there is a train an average of every minute and a half. The system is being constantly updated with new rubber-wheeled cars to reduce noise and bounce, and the stations are in a rotational system of renovation. Many of them now have art reproductions to represent the collections at nearby museums. Finally, you can't beat the price of the metro: only 2.30F to go anywhere within the Paris city limits if you purchase a *carnet* of ten tickets.

There are constant comparisons with London's underground, but the metro seems to win every category. The tube has more miles of track and more cars, but the metro has more stations and carries over twice as many passengers each day (more than four and a half million). The metro trains come more often, they run later at night (until 1.15 am) and the maximum fare within Paris is the equivalent of 25 pence if you buy a carnet, compared to a maximum journey of £2.00 on the tube.

Paris got off to a relatively late start in the underground

41

business, following the footsteps of London, New York, Chicago and Budapest, which already had subterranean systems. The first metro line was finished in July of 1900 from Porte Maillot to Porte de Vincennes, just in time for the opening of the Paris World Exhibition at the Grand Palais and Petit Palais. A 46-year-old Breton named Fulgence Bienvenue was given charge of the underground engineering works, while architect and artist Hector Guimard was assigned the task of designing the above-ground portion of the stations.

Guimard developed what is often called the 'noodle' style for the first metro entrances: graceful floral patterns and bold steel grills which foreshadowed the evolution of art nouveau. Only two of Guimard's 141 facades remain — at Abbesses in Montmartre and Porte Dauphine — but his genius will always remain an integral part of the metro's endearing image.

The RER network was started in 1970 to complement the 280 stations which already existed in the system, and to provide a high-speed commuter service for the far suburbs. The RER trains run at 48 km per hour faster than the regular metro trains, and range out a distance of over 75 kms from the city centre to the west, south and east. Ten RER lines are already finished, and at least three additional lines are planned for the northern and southeastern suburbs. The nucleus of the RER system is the giant Chatelet-Les Halles station (the largest underground station in the world), but other important city terminals are Gare du Nord, Gare de Lyon, Gare Austerlitz, Invalides, Etoile, Auber, Denfert-Rochereau and Nation.

The first thing to do when using the metro is to decide where you want to travel. Each station has giant colour maps showing the entire network, with each line represented as a different colour. First you should locate the station where you are standing, marked with a red circle on the map. Then you find the station where you want to go. Trace the route with your finger, noting any change in the colour of the line. The stations where you change from one line to another are marked with black circles. Rather than being assigned with compass-point names like east or west, the metro lines are given the name of the last station in any given direction (i.e. Direction Clignancourt or Direction Porte d'Orléans). If you must change lines, then get off the train and follow the signs saying *correspondance* in the direction you wish to go (i.e. Correspondance Clignancourt or Correspondance Porte d'Orléans).

As an example, say you want to go from Odeon to Etoile. You would board the metro at Odeon station marked 'Direction Clignancourt' and proceed to Chatelet station, where you would get out and follow signs saying 'Correspondance Porte de Neuilly' to the platform marked 'Direction Porte de Neuilly'. You would then hop on the train once again and stay on until Etoile station. Then you follow the signs marked *sortie* (exit) to the surface.

Buying a ticket is just as easy. If you are interested only in a single journey and don't plan on using the metro more than a few times, then purchase a single ticket. If your French needs help, just say the name of the station where you want to get off. Single tickets now cost 3F per ride. A better bargain is the popular *carnet* (car-nay) of ten tickets for 23F second class. These yellow tickets must be inserted into the slot at the front of the electronic gates before you can gain entry to the metro, and you should keep your ticket until getting out of the station at the other end because of spot checks by metro security folks. Most Parisian commuters now have a *Carte Orange* which gives them up to 50 per cent reductions on metro travel for one month. This is a fantastic idea if you plan on staying more than two weeks in Paris. A Carte Orange valid for zones one and two (the inner city with most of the tourist attractions, restaurants and hotels) is 122F second class. You can get various combinations of validity up to a zone one through five Carte Orange for 260F second class which entitles you to use every station in the metro and RER networks.

Yet another possibility is the new Sesame ticket designed especially for tourists, good for periods of two, four and seven days on all metro, RER and RATP bus lines. They issue you with a special magnetic card which must be inserted into the electronic gates of the underground or shown to the bus driver. Two-day Sesame tickets are 35F, four-day tickets 53F and seven-day tickets 88F. They can be purchased at most metro and train stations, the Paris tourist office on the Champs-Elysées, and at certain banks.

If you are not travelling on one of these special cards or tickets, keep in mind that both metro and RER fares rise once you cross from the City of Paris into the suburbs. Price is usually judged by the distance travelled (similar to the London system). The only major difference between the regular metro system and the RER is that you must insert your ticket into an electronic gate at both the start and finish of the trip when using the RER.

Buses

Paris's metropolitan bus service is brought to you by the same folks who operate the metro, the RATP. Thus, metro and bus tickets are one and the same. The Carte Orange and Sesame tickets are also valid on buses. Tickets can be purchased on the bus, in metro stations, at bus kiosks, Tabac stores and at other shops displaying the red RATP sign.

The RATP operates an incredible network of bus services, almost 200 lines covering over 2,000 km. But there are pros and cons to taking the bus as opposed to the metro. On the positive side are the facts that you see a lot more of the Parisian landscape from a bus window, and buses go to places where the metro doesn't penetrate. On the negative side is the complicated nature of the system and the fact that many bus journeys will cost you more than comparable metro rides. Buses are also slower.

Bus rates are based on the number of stages (arrêts or étapes) travelled. Most places within the City of Paris can be reached on only a single ticket, but some distant corners will run you two tickets. Reaching the suburbs takes three or four tickets, so your journey could actually cost 12F before you reach your destination.

The maze of Parisian bus lines is made somewhat simpler

with the great bus route maps available from the RATP. You can pick them up at the Paris Tourist Office at 127, avenue Champs-Elysées, at certain RATP information kiosks in the metro, or the RATP offices at 53 bis, quai des Grandes Augustins, 6e; or Place de la Madeleine, 8e. The red plan is for the 55 Paris city bus routes, the green plan for the more than 100 suburban routes, the brown plan for night buses.

Bus stops are marked by the red and yellow RATP signs, and most stops have all-weather kiosks and route maps. People queue for buses in Paris just like most other big Western cities. Queue-jumping is less tolerated than in Britain. The bus number and destination are marked on the front of each bus. When the bus you want approaches, wave to the driver to make sure he stops. You will get your ticket punched by the conductor or driver, and you must hand it back in at the end of your journey.

Most bus lines operate from 5.30 am to 8.30 pm each day. There are 13 late-night lines *(service assuré en soirée)* which operate from 8.30 pm to 12.30 am each night and 10 all-night lines *(service d'autobus de nuit)* which operate from 1.00 or 1.30 am to 5.00 or 5.30 am. The all-night buses run every hour on the half hour from Chatelet, including one to Rungis for Orly Airport. The cost of the all-night buses is three tickets (9F) per journey within the City of Paris no matter how far the distance, and up to five tickets (15F) per journey for trips to the suburbs.

For more information on Paris buses call the RATP on 346.14.14.

Taxis

Each of the 15,000 or more taxis in Paris has a standard meter on the dashboard which clearly shows the price of the ride. The minimum fare was 8F in 1984, with a standard charge of 1.80F per kilometre. The prices go up considerably for trips from 11 pm to 6.30 am, and for any journeys outside the boundary of the City of Paris (i.e. any of the suburbs or airports). There are also supplementary fees of 1.50F for any luggage which must be carried on the roof or in the boot, and 3F for being picked up or delivered to a train station or racecourse. On top of this, a tip of at least 15 per cent is expected by the drivers.

Taxis are quite easy to find in Paris, for there's always a cluster in front of the train stations, airports, big hotels and major tourist sights. They can also be found at major road junctions and squares, and at special taxi stations marked *tête de station*. The Mairie de Paris also publishes a small leaflet called *Bornes d'Appel des Taxis* (Places to call for a taxi).

If you are off the beaten track you can always telephone a taxi agency on 205.77.77. (Bolivar Taxi), 735.22.22. (Rad Art Taxi), 200.67.89. (Allo Taxi), 203.99.99. (Taxi Radio) or 739.33.33. (Taxi Radio G 7).

Be on the lookout for illegal taxis without meters. Unless you are totally desperate and don't care how much you pay, it's better to refuse their service and wait for a meter taxi.

Car hire

Rental cars can be found at the three Paris airports and at most of the railway stations, as well as the specific agency offices around town. And most hotels above two stars can arrange a rent-a-car for you. A valid driving licence is required wherever you rent a car, and most agencies have minimum age requirements ranging from 18-25 years. Most of them also require a sizeable deposit (usually about 1,000F) or a credit card.

Almost every rental agency has a basic economy car in the 100-150F per day range including the 18.6 per cent value added tax. But remember that this basic price doesn't include petrol, mandatory insurance or delivery/collection away from the agency site.

Following is a list of major car hire firms in Paris, including basic rates and rental qualifications.

Autorent: 196, rue St Jacques, 5e; (tel: 325.88.10; metro:

Luxembourg, Pont Royal). 11, rue Casimir-Perier, 7e; (tel: 555.53.49. metro: Solferino). Cars from 98.60F per day and 1.06F per kilometre, probably the cheapest in Paris.

Avis: 5, rue Bixio, 7e; (tel: 550.32.31; metro: Ecole Militaire). 60, rue Ponthieu, 8e; (tel: 359.03.83; metro: Roosevelt). 12-14, Rond Point des Champs-Elysées, 8e; (tel: 562.18.68; metro: Roosevelt).

Azure: 81, boulevard Gouvion St Cyr, 17e; (tel: 757.14.50; metro: Porte Maillot). Cars from 136.39F per day and 1.33F per kilometre.

Budget: 3, rue Bernoulli, 8e; (tel: 293.02.92; metro: Rome). 4, avenue Franklin D. Roosevelt, 8e; (tel: 225.79.89; metro: Roosevelt). 17, Cour d'Amsterdam in the Gare St Lazare, 8e; (tel: 293.35.67; metro: Gare St Lazare).

Europcar France: 42, avenue de Saxe, 7e; (tel: 273.35.20; metro: Segur). 48, rue de Berri, 8e; (tel: 563.04.27; metro: St Philippe-du-Roule).

Hertz: Aerogate des Invalides, 7e; (tel: 551.20.37; metro: Invalides). 92, rue St Lazare, 9e; (tel: 280.35.45; metro: St Lazare). Cars from 145F per day and 1.70F per kilometre.

Mercedes-Service: 56, rue la Fontaine, 16e; (tel: 380.00.11; metro: Jasmin). Mercedes from 280F per day and 3.90F per kilometre.

Parking and petrol stations are discussed on page 33.

Limousines

Executive Car: 25-27, rue d'Astorg, 8e; (tel: 265.54.20; metro: St Augustin). Affiliate of the International Limousine System. Multi-lingual chauffeurs and guides. Choice of everything from a Rolls Silver Shadow to a Renault minibus.

Limousine-Guide Hans Forster: 202, rue de Rivoli, 1er; (tel: 296.40.02; metro: Tuileries). Wide choice of luxury class cars at 150F per hour unlimited mileage. Minimum three hours hire.

Motorcycles

Autotheque: 80, rue Montmartre, 2e; (tel: 236.87.90; metro: Sentier). Mopeds for hire at 45F per day or 200F per week. Deposit of 800F required. Bring your own helmet (required by law).

Bicycles

Bike rental agencies are listed in the Sports and Recreation section on page 346.

Helicopters

Heli-France: 4, avenue de la Porte de Sèvres, 15e; (tel: 557.53.67; metro: Balard). Paris's premier helicopter service. Three air tours available: 'Paris in the Year 2000' (150F per person), 'Versailles — The National Showcase' (200F), and 'The Sights of Paris' (350F). Flights to all three Paris airports, transportation to anywhere on demand, surveillance missions, promotional and advertising activities, flying school.

Bus tours

Cityrama: Bus terminal at 4, place des Pyramides, 1er; (tel: 260.30.14; metro: Palais Royal). Travel office at 21, rue de la Paix, 2e; (tel: 742.06.47; metro: Opera). Complete city tour hits all the main sights via a double decker bus, with taped commentary in 10 languages but no inside visits: 127F per

Paris Vision is one of several coach companies that run double decker sightseeing buses around all the major monuments in the centre of the city.

person (high season), 115F (low season). Five other city tours, plus visits to Versailles, Malmaison, Chartres, Fontainebleau, the Loire Valley and Barbizon. Paris by Night tours include visits to the Moulin Rouge (495F), Lido (540F) and Folies Bergère (590F HS, 530F LS). Paris 'X' tour to striptease and live sex shows for 420F HS and 380F LS.

Paris Vision: 214, rue de Rivoli, 1er; (tel: 260.30.01; metro: Tuileries). Complete city tour to major points of interest via double decker bus: 115F. Seven other city tours, plus visits to Fontainebleau, Barbizon, Chantilly, Giverny, Versailles, Malmaison, Chartres, Vaux-le-Vicomte, Rheims, Epernay, Champagne, Rouen, Normandy and the Loire Valley. Paris by Night tours include visits to the Nouvelle Eve (340F), Paradise Latin (595F), Lido (505F), and Moulin Rouge (430F). 'Forbidden Paris — Tour X' for 345F.

RATP: Place de la Madeleine, 8e; (metro: Madeleine). Or: 53 bis, quai des Grands-Augustins, 6e; (tel: 346.14.14; metro: St Michel). Paris's rapid transit company offers bus excursions to major sights in the countryside during the summer months, including treks to Chartres, Chantilly, Fontainebleau, the Loire Valley, Mont Saint-Michel, Amiens, Champagne, Orleans and Compiegne.

Boat trips

Bateaux-Mouches: Port de l'Alma, 8e; (tel: 225.96.10. or 359.30.30; metro: Alma). Paris's largest fleet of tourist cruisers. One hour and fifteen minute tours depart every half hour from 10 am to 8.30 pm. The price is 20F and the tour takes you past the Eiffel Tower, Louvre, Notre Dame, Conciergerie, Ile Saint-Louis, Hotel de Ville and many other monuments. There are special lunch cruises at 1.00 p.m. (180F) and dinner cruises at 8.30 pm (350F) every day except Monday. You have a choice of fully enclosed boats, or opened-decked seating for the sunny summer months.

The most romantic way to tour the river Seine is by bateaux-mouches, the glass-topped riverboats that ply between the Eiffel Tower and the Ile Saint-Louis.

Vedettes du Pont Neuf: Square du Vert-Galant, 1er; (tel: 633.98.38. or 329.86.19; metro: Pont Neuf). One-hour cruises depart daily at 10.30, 11.35 and noon, then every half hour from 1.30 to 6.30 pm. From May to October there are special evening cruises at 8, 9.30 and 10.15 pm. The price is 20F, with children under ten at 10F and special rates for groups. The tour follows the same route as the Bateaux-Mouches. Boats are heated in winter.

Vedettes de Paris Ile-de-France: (tel: 705.71.29. or 550.23.79.). Special historical and sightseeing cruises in and around Paris, including tours of the Marne and Seine valleys and a Belle Epoque tour. Departures every half hour from 10 am to 5.30 pm. This company also hires out boats for weddings and other special occasions.

Vedettes Tour Eiffel: Pont d'Iena, 7e; (tel: 551.33.08. or 705.50.00; metro: Trocadero). Typical Seine cruises with all the big sights. Departures from the left bank near the Pont d'Iena every half hour from 9.30 am to 11 pm. Tickets are 20F for adults and 10F for children under age 10.

CHAPTER FOUR

Where to stay

Finding a proper place to stay is a major consideration no matter where you are travelling. Paris is no different. And more than any other topic, the hunt for a hotel should be thoroughly researched before you set off from home, if for no other reason than that you will probably have to make reservations months in advance of when you actually travel to Paris.

There are thousands of hotels, *pensions* and hostels in Paris, a city which sports probably more world-famous hotels than any urban area on this earth. But likewise, Paris probably has more dives and flea-bag joints than any other city. So sorting out the posh from the prunes is vital.

Your first consideration when looking for a Paris hotel is how much money you want to spend. Those who expect impeccable service and international chic will naturally opt for the five-star deluxe hotels like the Inter-Continental and Ritz; while those on a backpacker's or students budget will want the low prices and congenial atmosphere of the youth hostels and one-star hotels. Most visitors, however, will probably want something in between: cheap enough for the entire family, yet tidy enough for you to leave the bug spray at home!

Our 'star' rating system — which roughly corresponds to those issued by the Office de Tourisme de Paris — will help you make the correct choice in terms of your budget: five-star (*****) hotels generally run over 400F (£32) per person but often much more; four-star (****) hotels are generally 300-400F (£24-32) per person; three-star (***) hotels generally 200-300F (£16-24) per person; two-star (**) hotels generally 100-200F (£8-16) per person; and one-star (*) hotels generally 50-100F (£4-8) per person. Youth hostels are usually in the 40-60F (£3.50-4) range, but you will probably be sharing a dormitory-style room with numerous strangers.

There are other charges to consider. Sometimes breakfast (*petit déjeuner*) is included in the price, sometimes it's not. If not, breakfast will cost you an extra 15-20F per day in the medium-range hotels, more in the deluxe and less in the student hostels. And don't expect bacon and eggs, fresh fruit juice and corn flakes. Paris is home of the infamous Continental breakfast, that early morning dread of the Anglo-Saxons: croissants, jam and coffee or tea. Barely enough to get an American or Englishman started, but apparently sufficient for the French.

The 15 per cent service and government taxes are usually included in the room price *(prix tout compris)*. But there are deluxe hotels who might quote you a figure without tax (*prix non compris*) to soften the initial shock of their lofty prices. In that case you will have to add the 15 per cent yourself. In our listings below, the price figures quoted include taxes in every case.

And there's always the problem of tipping, no worry in the cheap hotels but a constant bother in three-stars and above. The porter who brings your bags to the room or takes them back down to the car, the room service waiter and any other staff who do you a substantial service will all be expecting *at least* 10-12F each time they lift a finger. You can halve that sum for the lad who fetches your car from the garage or the doorman who opens the taxi door. Lastly, there is the hall-porter *(concierge),* that superman behind the front desk who can make or break your stay (depending on how demanding you are and how efficient he is). Try 50-60F at the end of your stay to keep him happy, especially if you enjoyed the hotel and plan to return.

Unless you have a major credit card, or you are staying in a big hotel where they already know you, then payment at least one night in advance is generally required. This is especially true of the cheaper hotels, who have been ripped off by early-rising boarders more than once. Most hotels at three stars and above take major credit cards (American Express, Visa, Diners Club, Carte Bleue, Eurocard) but you should check first — never assume they take every credit card even at the Ritz. There is an expanding number of two-star hotels that will take at least one or two major credit cards (American Express is your best bet), but few one-star hotels and no youth hostels which will accept any type of plastic money. It's cash across the counter in these places. The four and five-star hotels will also cash your international traveller's cheques (for a small commission).

Once you have the financing figured out, you can move on to step two: deciding in which part of Paris you want to stay. The luxury hotels are neatly congregated in the wealthiest districts — the 8th arrondissement around the Champs-Elysées and Rue du Faubourg St Honore, and the 1st arrondissement around the Place de Vendôme and Rue de Rivoli. The greatest cluster of medium-priced hotels can be found in the St Germain district of the Left Bank, the 6th and 7th arrondissements. But also try the Ile Saint-Louis. Student hotels abound in the 5th and 6th arrondissements, St Michel and St Germain, because the various branches of the university are situated in this area. The old Marais district, the 4th arrondissement, is also chock full of cheap hotels and the best of Paris's multiple youth hostels. Keep in mind, however, that you can find inexpensive and medium-priced hotels in every district of Paris. The most complete list of these establishments is the *Guide des Hotels — Paris/Ile de France* put out by the Office de Tourisme de Paris. You can pick it up from their headquarters at 127, avenue des Champs-Elysées, 8e.

The third thing to consider when choosing a Paris hotel room is the plumbing, a category which will particularly un-nerve Americans used to spic'n-span bathrooms in every room. Such is not the case in France, or for that matter most of Europe. All the four and five-star hotels have modern bathrooms, but plumbing becomes a real problem at three stars and below. Bluntly stated, the French have never cared much for either a complete or shiny bathroom in their hotels. And at the lower end of the market, many of the rooms don't even have a toilet.

A little terminology is in order. When looking over the official hotel prices (usually posted in the window near the hotel entrance) please take note of the following categories: *chambre, eau-courante* is a room with wash basin only, *chambre, cabinet de toilette* is a room with wash basin and toilet, *chambre, douche + W.C.* is a room with shower and toilet, and *chambre, salle de bains* is a room with a complete bathroom including bathtub. But you can find these in different combinations, for instance a room with a shower but the toilet down the hall. And note that if you have a room without shower or bath, the hotel will often charge 5-10F extra for the use of the facility down the hall.

A few more hotel terms: *chambre simple* is a single, *chambre double* or *chambre deux* is a double, *appartement* is a suite, *duplex* a two-level or townhouse suite, *salon* a sitting room, *lit supplementaire* is the price for an extra bed, say a third bed in a double room.

Two more hotel precautions before we get into the listings. First, Paris is a very noisy city at all hours of the day and night. The city has the highest car theft rate of any urban area in northern Europe, and to combat the robbers, car owners have struck back with alarm systems that seem to go off with amazing regularity at four in the morning (and right outside your hotel window!). Many of the bars and clubs are open until dawn, which means merry revellers and disco beats far into the night. If you can sleep through all of this racket, great. But you light sleepers should request a room away from the street, preferably on the tranquil inner courtyard which is a feature of many hotels. If you simply can't get away from the noise, it's best to switch hotels, or go out and buy some earplugs (*boules de Qwièss*).

Lastly, don't forget those all-important reservations. Paris does have its tourist high season in the summer (when it's virtually impossible to show up on the spot and get a room, unless you want to stay in a youth hostel or far off the beaten track) but the best hotels are jam-packed throughout the year. All it takes is a simple letter, telex, cable or phone call. And if you really want to make sure, send a one night's deposit. Best to make reservations two months in advance for the summer, and one month in advance the rest of the year.

Hotels — an area list

● 1er   Les Halles, Louvre

Grand Hotel de Champagne 17, rue Jean-Lantier; (tel: 261.50.05; metro: Chatelet).   *** Pleasant little hotel on a quiet street near the Seine. Simple, but elegant decor. Rooms: 250-300F. Breakfast: 25F.

Henri IV 25, place Dauphine; (tel: 354.44.53; metro: Pont Neuf).   * Certainly the most romantic of the down market hotels, situated in a 17th century townhouse on a leafy square of the Ile de la Cité. The hotel building dates from 1607, when King Henri IV commissioned a new housing project to be built on land recently reclaimed from the Seine. As you look out your window, you can see old men playing *boules* in the square, or lovers sitting on wooden benches under the massive trees. And to top it off, Yves Montand, the great romancer of the French cinema, lives across the place. The only problem with the Henri IV is the fact that it is mentioned in nearly every guide book published on Paris in the last twenty years, including that bible of the American student abroad *Let's Go Europe,* which ensures a steady flow of clients and almost never a vacant sign. If you know when you're going to be in Paris then it's wise to make reservations several months in advance. Room with washbasin: 56-78F; rooms with washbasin and toilet: 82-104F.

Hotel des Pavillons 14, rue Vauvilliers; (tel: 508.42.92; metro: Les Halles, Louvre). Nothing special about this Right Bank cheapy except the location and the prices. It's adjacent to the massive second-stage development of the Forum des Halles complex, which means it will be next to a tree-filled square when the whole thing is finally complete. Room with washbasin: 40-80F; with washbasin and toilet: 120-140F. Breakfast: 11F.

Inter-Continental 3, rue Castiglione; (tel: 260.37.80; metro: Tuileries). ***** One of the *grandes dames* of Parisian hotels, a luxury-class establishment with all the amenities your heart could desire. Best thing about the Inter-Continental is the location, for it's situated just off the Tuileries, just down the street from the super-posh Place Vendôme, and within walking distance of the Louvre and the Jeu de Paume. The hotel was known as the Continental when it was opened in 1878 at the height of the Belle Epoque, and obviously didn't need much of a name (or style) change when it was purchased and renovated by the deluxe Inter-Continental chain in 1968. The 500 rooms are lavishly decorated with traditional 18th and 19th century French pieces, and the spacious suites are equipped with colour TV and mini-bars. The restaurants are equally elegant, and known for their excellent cuisine, inluding the Café Tuileries, Rotisserie Rivoli and the pleasant Terrasse Fleurie, a flower-filled garden where you can dine outdoors from May to September. There are conference and banquet facilities for groups as large as 1,300, and several of the grand salons are classified as historic monuments because of their sumptuous Napoleon III decors. The hotel also has 24-hour room service. But you will obviously pay for all this luxury. Singles are 880-1175F, doubles 1050-1102F, deluxe rooms 1200-1603F and apartments 1400-6546F. Breakfast: 65-80F.

Lotti 7, rue de Castiglione; (tel: 260.37.34; metro: Tuileries). ***** Another of Castiglione's elegant ladies, a superb luxury-class hotel right next to the Inter-Continental. In fact, the two establishments are now under the same management, so you will find similar amenities and services. But the Lotti is a petite, more intimate version of the big hotel with only 130 rooms, each furnished with love-ly 19th century decor. Singles are 752-938F with service, doubles are 947-1239F with service, and suites 2415-3018F with service. Breakfast: 60F not including service.

Louvre-Concorde Place André Malraux; (tel: 261.56.01; metro: Palais Royal). **** Slightly down-market from the luxury class hotels, but you would hardly notice the slight difference in service or style. The location is perfect for the overseas visitor with a little cash: right on the Place André Malraux facing the Comedie-Française and the Palais Royal, and just around the corner from the Louvre and the Tuileries. Singles are 640-700F, doubles 710-770F. Breakfast: 40F.

Meurice 228, rue de Rivoli; (tel: 260.38.60; metro: Tuileries). ***** Staying at the Hotel Meurice is a bit like visiting Louis XIV at Versailles: you are suddenly plunged into a luxurious atmosphere of incomparable service and sumptuous decor. The 221 rooms are furnished according to lavish 18th century tastes, but each is a little different in its style and taste. The Meurice has been around since 1816, right after the fall of Napoleon, and in many respects it feels like one of the grand palaces of the past. The Galerie des Bijoux is a miniature Hall of Mirrors with its inlaid marble floor, vaulted ceiling and Belle Epoque windows, while the immense Salon des Tuileries resembles an 18th century banquet hall. Meanwhile, the Galerie de Chasse houses paintings and tapestries with representations of the hunt, and one of the hotel lifts is the royal carrying chair of Marie-Antoinette. Also, there are three luxurious bars: the 18th century Salon Pompadour with its chandeliers and piano music, the Victorian-style Copper Bar, and the Art Deco Bar Fontainebleau. Singles are 820-1150F, doubles 1090-1365F, and suites 1890F and up. Breakfast: 75F.

Montpensier 12, rue de Richelieu; (tel: 296.28.50; metro: Palais Royal). **Quiet and comfortable hotel near the Palais Royal on the street where Molière spent his last years. If your room faces the Rue de Richelieu you may have some noise, but most of them look onto a serene inner courtyard which is hidden from the street. There are seven rooms with washbasin only, priced at 100-143F, and 36 renovated rooms with washbasin and toilet at 214-226F. Breakfast is included in the price.

Prince-Albert 5, rue St Hyacinthe; (tel: 261.58.36; metro: Tuileries) ** A tiny hotel on one of the quietest streets in the district, with Le Rubis wine bar just down at the corner in case you get thirsty. The name tells you quite correctly that this is a Parisian version of a Victorian English hotel, and many of the guests are indeed from that island across the Channel. The Prince Albert has all the three 'Cs': comfortable, clean and convenient. Singles are 124-213F, doubles 142-231F including breakfast; 22 of the 36 rooms have private baths.

Ritz 15, place Vendome; (tel: 260.38.30; metro: Tuileries). ***** 'There is no other hotel in the world comparable to the Ritz' say the people who run the place. Full stop. No more said. And how do you begin to describe the hotel that has set standards for luxury throughout the hotel world, that has even gone so far as to inspire an eponym for the word elegant? Cesar Ritz founded the hotel in 1898 to cater to the rich and famous of the world. His formula was simple: superb service, elegantly furnished rooms in the 18th and 19th century French styles, and the first private baths in Paris. Now, the Ritz guest books read like a who's who of the 20th century: Marcel Proust, Charlie Chaplin, Ernest Hemingway, F. Scott Fitzgerald, Rudolph Valentino, Greta Garbo, Winston Churchill, Herman Goering and King Edward VII to name just a few. The hotel underwent a £15 million renovation in 1972 that modernized all of the plumbing and lighting without harming the antique ambience of the 163 rooms. Among the amenities are two bars (including the famous Hemingway Bar where the author supposedly headed upon the liberation of Paris in 1944), two restaurants and three beautiful gardens, plus a huge wine cellar to match any taste. Singles start at 1250F, doubles at

1750F, and suites at 2400F. Continental breakfast: 60F. American breakfast: 110F. But keep in mind that you get what you pay for. The Ritz is indeed ritzy.

Saint-Roch 25, rue St. Roch; (tel: 260.17.91; metro: Tuileries, Pyramides). ** Clean, comfortable and moderately priced hotel just off the rue St Honore. A good bet for tourists who can't afford the Ritz, but who want more than youth hostel spartan. Singles are 160-170F, doubles 170-235F, triples 300F, including breakfast.

Washington-Opera 50, rue de Richelieu; (tel: 296.68.06; metro: Palais Royal) ** The name is a bit misleading because this hotel is nowhere near the Opera. But it is convenient for the Palais Royal and the Louvre. Simple but tidy rooms and good prices. Singles are 96-240F, doubles 123-233F including breakfast.

●2e   Opéra, Bourse

Favart 5, rue Marivaux; (tel: 297.59.83; metro: Richelieu-Drouot). *** Situated on an interesting street just off the Boulevard des Italiens, opposite the Opera Comique. Each room has a washbasin, toilet and showers for those who are fussy about the bathrooms, and Favart also has a bar and restaurant. Singles are 215F, doubles 225F, breakfast 15F,

France d'Antin 22, rue d'Antin; (tel: 742.19.12; metro: 4 Septembre). ** Simple, medium-priced hotel just off the Avenue de l'Opera. Every room has a WC and shower, while some of them also have TVs. There's a bar in the hotel, but Harry's is just down the road on Rue Daunou. Singles are 180-220F, doubles 220-260F, breakfast 14F.

●4e   Marais, Beaubourg

Bretonnerie 22, rue St Croix-Bretonnerie; (tel: 887.77.63; metro: Hotel-de-Ville). ** One of the better medium-range hotels in the Marais, and an excellent location for forays into the historic streets of this neighbourhood or trips to the Pompidou Centre. The place has been renovated in the last decade so the fixtures are fairly modern, and all but two of the 32 rooms now have baths. Singles are 100-240F, doubles 120-295F, breakfast 16F.

Grand Hotel Jeanne d'Arc 3, rue Jarente; (tel: 887.62.11; metro: St Paul). * Situated in the heart of the ancient Marais, near the Place des Vosges and the Hotel Carnavalet. Nothing fancy, but it's certainly quiet and friendly, and the price is right for most backpacking budgets. Of the 44 rooms, half have washbasins only and half have washbasins and toilets. Singles are 59-77F, doubles 107-170F, breakfast 13F.

Grand Hotel Mahler 5, rue Mahler; (tel: 272.60.92; metro: St Paul). * Modest but comfortable hotel in Paris's Jewish district, a good place for those on a tight budget to base their explorations of the Marais. Rooms with washbasin are 42-54F, with toilets and washbasin 65F, with shower 94F, and with shower and toilet 119-154F. Breakfast: 11F.

Nice 42 bis, rue de Rivoli; (tel:278.55.29; metro: St Paul). *West Side Story on the Rive Droit, this little down-and-out hotel is the kind of student and young people's hangout you easily romaticise given the right circumstances. Many of the rooms look down upon the busy rue de Rivoli, always crowded with people both night and day who seem to represent the four corners of the earth. There's a lot of Greeks, Italians, Jews and North Africans in this neighbourhood and they all come together on the Rivoli. The Nice is nothing fancy, but the price is right. Singles 56-130F, doubles 83-135F, breakfast 13F.

Quatrième-Arrondissement 19, rue Bourg-Tibourg; (tel: 278.47.39; metro: St Paul, Hotel-de-Ville). * Don't let the cold facade put you off this little hotel, for this inexpensive place has a lot of charm inside. Singles are 75-125F, doubles 80-182F, breakfast 13F.

Saint-Merry 78, rue Verrerie; (tel: 278.14.15; metro: Chatelet, Hotel-de-Ville).   *** One of the more unusual hotels in Paris and certainly the best up-market hotel on the mainland Marais. The Saint-Merry backs on to the 16th century Gothic church of the same name, thus most of the dozen rooms are incorporated into the majestic flying buttresses of the south side of the church. The rooms are furnished in something of an up-dated Gothic — lots of stone and wood — but the ambience is both warm and friendly. This is also the closest hotel to the Pompidou Centre. Rooms with a washbasin are 180-200F, with a washbasin and WC 300-350F. Breakfast: 17F. Wise to make reservations because this is a Paris favourite.

Vieux Marais 8, rue du Platre; (tel: 278.47.22; metro: Rambuteau).   **Another one of those romantic hide-aways, tucked between ancient buildings on a super-quiet street near the Pompidou. The 30 rooms of the Vieux are indeed old, but they were renovated only five years ago when the hotel changed owners. Moderate prices and fantastic location, plus a management which is both courteous and friendly. Singles are 165-210F, doubles 240-280F, breakfast included. All of the rooms have WC and shower.

● **4e   Ile Saint Louis**

Deux-Iles 59, rue St Louis-en-l'Ile; (tel: 326.13.35; metro: Pont Marie).   *** The most highly recommended of the hotels on the island and probably the best accommodation in the entire Marais. Deux-Iles is a charming and comfortable hotel, a restored 17th century mansion (one of the original townhouses on the island) that has been updated into something of a mini-Raffles. While there are no mysterious Oriental ladies wandering about the lobby, there's a tropical garden in the courtyard and plenty of wicker and bamboo in the light, airy rooms. The downstairs bar is one of the better hotel watering holes in Paris, with its warming fireplace and relaxing chairs. There's also a library for the use of hotel guests. Singles are 265F, doubles 337F, breakfast

22F. Every room has a toilet and shower.

Lutece 65, rue St Louis-en-l'Ile; (tel: 326.23.52; metro: Pont Marie). **** The newest of Roland Buffat's trio of fine hotels on the Ile St Louis (the other two are the Deux-Iles and the St Louis), a bit of a compromise between the modern earthiness of the Deux and the more traditional lines of the Hotel Saint Louis. The 23 rooms are a bit short on space, but each is furnished with antiques, and each is a little different from the others. Downstairs is a cosy lounge with fireplace. Singles are 315-335F, doubles 337-360F, breakfast 22F. And every room has a toilet and shower, despite the lack of space.

Saint-Louis 75, rue St Louis-en-l'Ile; (tel:634.04.80; metro: Pont Marie). *** The largest and least expensive of Buffat's island monopoly, with the same characteristic fine service, impeccable decor and shortness of space as the other two. Likewise, the Saint-Louis is situated in a renovated 17th century townhouse, a relic of the days when this island was Paris's newest and most fashionable housing estate. Rooms with washbasin only are 109F, with washbasin and toilet 190F, with a shower or bathroom and toilet 230-286F. Breakfast: 20F.

● **5e   Saint Michel**

Colbert 7, rue de l'Hotel-Colbert; (tel:325.85.65; metro: St Michel).   **** It's rather impressive for a hotel to have the street outside named after it. Not even the Ritz has that. But such is the case with this elegant, impressive hotel on the Rive Gauche. The stone facade of the Colbert is a bit cold, as is the somewhat chilly attendant at the front desk whose job it is to keep out the usual Saint Michel riffraff. But if you can overcome the initial coolness, the 40 guest rooms are a lavish blend of 18th and 19th century French domestic styles. Some even have television, a bit incongruous in this district of medieval streets and churches. Singles are 228-534F, doubles 353-534F, breakfast 19F. All of the rooms have WC and bathroom.

Esmeralda 4, rue St Julien le Pauvre; (tel: 354.19.20; metro: St Michel). ** St Michel is a bastion of cheap, student-type hotels where you can get a mattress and little more for under 50F a night. Thus, it's a pleasant surprise to find yet another excellent medium-range hotel in the district. The only problem being that the Esmeralda's reputation has spread and it's often booked up months in advance. You could hardly find a better location for a Left Bank hotel: overlooking the Square René Viviani opposite the Ile de la Cité and Notre Dame. The rooms are traditional, if not downright rustic or rural in approach, while the atmosphere of the Esmeralda is calm and relaxed. And this hotel always seems to be full of couples in their 20s and 30s, either on their first or second honeymoon trip to Paris. Get the hint? Esmeralda is also one of the most romantic establishments in town. Singles are 60-150F, doubles 150-270F, triples 255-300F and quads 340F. Breakfast: 19F.

Excelsior 20, rue Cujas; (tel: 634.79.50; metro: Luxembourg). * One of the better one-star hotels on the Left Bank, but its cheap rates and close proximity to the Sorbonne mean the Excelsior is often filled with visiting student groups and academics. With 96 rooms this hotel is large by St Michel standards, but only 21 of them have full bathrooms. Singles are 53.50F, doubles 67.50-167F, triples 125-196.50F. Showers are 10F extra if you don't get one with the room.

Flandre 16, rue Cujas; (tel:354.67.30; metro: Luxembourg). * If the Excelsior is full and you don't feel like walking anymore, try the Flandre just down the road. It isn't nearly as nice, but it's cheaper and more likely to have space. Rooms with washbasin are 55-70F, with toilet and washbasin 62-85F. Breakfast: 11.80F. Showers: 10F.

Grandes Ecoles 75, rue Cardinal-Lemoine; (tel: 326.79.23; metro: Cardinal-Lemoine). * The nearby schools (the

Sorbonne and the Faculté des Sciences) might be grand, but this hotel isn't. Still, it has a great central location, the place is invariably filled with students and foreign backpackers, and the prices are hard to beat. Best of all, the rooms are large and there's a tranquil garden in the courtyard where you can forget about the noise of the streets. Rooms with washbasin are 90F, with washbasin and WC 110-150F, with WC and shower 150-160F, with WC and bathroom 160-200F. The big rooms can sleep three or four, so you could get the price down to 40-50F per person. Breakfast: 15F.

Grand Hotel Saint Michel 19, rue Cujas; (tel: 633.65.03; metro: Luxembourg).   * You can call it the Grand for short. The third of the Left Bank cheapies on Rue Cujas. Not bad for a one-star hotel, and the Grand even has conference facilities. Rooms with WC and washstand are 60-75F, with WC and shower 80-90F, with WC and bathroom 110-180F. And get this: there are even two suites with showers and WC for 140-200F. No breakfast, so you'll have to eat *crêpes* down on the boulevards.

Mont Blanc 28, rue de la Huchette; (tel: 354.49.44; metro: St Michel).   * The most recommended one-star hotel on the Left Bank, situated in the heart of the St Michel pedestrian precinct and just off the Seine. You can't find another hotel in Paris where there's more round-the-clock action taking place in the street outside, which is fantastic for night owls and nightmarish for insomniacs. The Mont Blanc will probably receive its official second star soon, given the upgrading in both services (TVs in some of the rooms) and prices. Singles are 120-195F, doubles are 150-195F, extra persons are 30 per cent extra. Breakfast: 12F.

Notre Dame 1, quai St Michel; (tel:354.20.43; metro: St. Michel).   * Everyone has their first hotel in Paris and this is mine, where I first stayed as a 20-year-old student visiting the capital. My strongest memory is of Bastille Day morning, when I was awakened long before the rest of Paris by the clip-clop of horses in the street below. Looking out the window I caught a quick glimpse of a small group of cavalry dressed in the shiny breast plates and golden helmets of Napoleonic times. No reflection on the hotel, of course, but I've always looked at the Notre Dame through rose-coloured glasses. Ask for a room facing the street when you go to reception in the ground floor café by the same name. It will be a little noisy, but the view from the rooms is superb, looking out over the river to the great western facade of Notre Dame. And the hotel is still cheap after all these years: 52-55F for both singles and doubles. No showers or breakfast.

Saint-Christophe 17, rue Lacepede; (tel: 331.81.54; metro: Monge). * The last of our St Michel cheapies, a simple but very inexpensive hotel with a very good location near the university, the Lutece Arena and the Botanical Gardens. The place is frequented by French students and overseas backpackers. Rooms with a washbasin are 60.70F, with WC and washbasin 72.90-91F, with WC and shower 90.60-117.80F, with WC and bathroom 111.30-144.70F. Breakfast: 14.40F.

● **6e   Saint Germain**

Abbaye Saint-Germain 10, rue Cassette: (tel: 544.38.11; metro: St Sulpice). **** This popular Left Bank hotel is just what the name says, an ancient convent and abbey that was converted into a modern luxury hotel in the 1970s. The central courtyard, where the nuns used to pray, has been renovated into a delightful garden. And the old convent rooms, spartan as they must have been in clerical days, have been transformed into 45 colourful and spacious guest suites, each with a private bath. The clientele is heavy on the Anglos and Americans, businessmen and families who know a good deal when they see one. Almost everyone praises the Abbaye staff and service as among Paris's best. Singles are 320-370F, doubles 320-430F, including breakfast.

Angleterre 44, rue Jacob; (tel: 260.34.72; metro: St Germain). ***If you've ever wanted to stay in a British embassy overseas this is your chance. The 18th century building in which the Angleterre is situated housed the king's ambassador to France until Wellington moved into the Hotel de Charost a week after the Battle of Waterloo. Like many of the old buildings in Saint-Germain, this hotel has a central courtyard which has been converted into a leafy garden. The place has a slightly rustic air, although every room has its own private bath and many of them have been redecorated in the past decade. And in the last year they've installed TVs in some of the rooms. Singles are 180F, doubles 260-350F, with extra persons at 30 per cent more. Breakfast: 20F.

Buci 22, rue de Buci; (tel: 326.89.22; metro: Mabillon).   *
You will pay a bit more than your average flop house, but what you get in return is one of the best cheap hotels in Saint Germain. The Buci is cleaner than your normal one-star, very comfortable for the price, and conveniently located on one of the most action-packed streets in Paris. The Buci street market is right outside your front door, and the nightlife in this region tends to last until the sun comes up. But it can be loud, so if you want early nights then ask for a room away from the street. Rooms with washbasin and toilet are 72-107F, with WC and shower 107-142F. No breakfast.

Danube 58, rue Jacob; (tel: 260.34.70; metro: St Germain).   *** Those with a particular interest in modern art or high fashion might choose the Danube, for it is situated in a neighbourhood of narrow streets and dark alleys that's just saturated with galleries and trendy boutiques. The Danube itself is a bit trendy, both in clientele and decor. And there is that inevitable inner courtyard-cum-garden where you can get away from the hustle and bustle of the Rive Gauche scene. Rooms with washbasin and shower are 190-290F, with WC and shower 320-515F. Breakfast: 18.50F.

Grand Hotel des Balcons 3, rue Casimir-Delavigne; (tel: 634.78.50; metro: Odeon).   ** Perhaps the best of the two-star establishments in Saint-Germain. The location is *très bon*, close to a multitude of inexpensive but tasty restaurants, just off the boulevards and the Place de l'Odeon, and within

68

walking distance of one of Paris's great parks, the Jardin du Luxembourg. The rooms could use a bit of updating here and there (although some of them now have TVs and private baths), but otherwise you get very good value for your money at the Balcons. Rooms with wash basin only are 100F, with shower 130F, with shower and WC 176-210F. Breakfast: 17F.

L'Hotel 13, rue des Beaux-Arts; (tel: 325.27.22; metro: St Germain).   ***** This hotel always reminds me of an Agatha Christie thriller, perhaps because of its romantic and somewhat magical setting, and possibly because the clientele is composed of the wealthy and famous from around the world, just the cast of characters you would expect in a Christie novel. Death on the Seine? Murder on the Metro Express? The building has been around since the 18th century when it was called the Pavillon d'Amour, part of it designed by Louis XVI's court architect Claude-Nicolas Ledoux. It was renovated into the Directory style in the 19th century and called the Hotel d'Allemagne and Hotel d'Alsace. The Alsace is where a destitute Oscar Wilde died in 1900, uttering his famous last words 'I am dying beyond my means'. Actor Guy-Louis Deboucheron bought and renovated the old hotel in 1968, renaming it l'Hotel and quickly gaining a reputation as the best new hotel owner in Paris. Even more than the Ritz, l'Hotel is a bastion of the rich and famous, drawing a clientele of film and show-biz personalities from America and Britain. They come for the 26-room intimacy, the privacy they just cannot get in the big hotels no matter how exclusive, and the hotel's reputation for impeccable service and sophistication. What's more, the guest rooms are individual masterpieces, redesigned and decorated by Texas architect Robin Westbrook. You can sleep in the bed where Oscar Wilde died, if you are thus inclined. Or you can reside in the sumptuous suite furnished with the Art Deco relics of the great French song and dance star Mistinguett. Her bed sits on a frame and headboard of mirrored boxes, looking a bit like Manhattan skyscrapers reaching up into the sky. The basement bar and restaurant (with the expected superb cuisine) are situated in Ledoux's old vaults, and there is a maze-like bar on the top floor filled with little rooms and cubicles. What Deboucheron has managed to create is the most unique and superb hotel in all of Paris, perhaps in all the world. If you can afford to stay in five-star luxury, then l'Hotel is the place to stay. Try to make your reservations several months (or years) in advance. Rooms with a wash basin and shower are 540-650F, with a full bathroom 850-1000F. Suites start at 1500F a night and work their way up to 1900F. Breakfast: 47F.

Michelet-Odeón 6, place de l'Odeon; (tel: 634.27.80; metro: Odeon, Luxembourg).   ** Very good medium-range hotel near the Jardin du Luxembourg, not bad for a family visiting Paris who want to keep within a certain budget. Lots of inexpensive but good eating places in the neighbourhood. Rooms with washbasins are 91F, with shower and WC 179F, with full bathroom 227F, suites 298F. Breakfast: 16F.

Petit Trianon 2, rue de l'Ancienne Comedie; (tel: 354.94.64; metro: Odeon).   * Backpacker's paradise located at the strategic intersection of rues Mazarin, Buci, St André-des-Arts and Ancienne Comedie. The Trianon, run by a charming Frenchwoman and her Brazilian student staff, is always filled with young Americans and Canadians rifling through their copies of *Let's Go Europe*. Nothing fancy, and many of the rooms are downright primitive. But at least the water in the showers is hot, the price is right and you don't have to walk far to Notre Dame or the Louvre. Singles are 57-95F, doubles 120-135F, breakfast 13F. For the hungry or thirsty, there's a good bakery down Ancienne Comedie and a pleasant pavement café on the ground floor.

Recamier 3 bis, place St Sulpice; (tel: 326.04.89; metro: St Sulpice).   ** Pleasant hotel overlooking the leafy Place St Sulpice, just across from the 16th century Church of St Sulpice. The Recamier is a charming piece of old Paris, a bit rustic in design but certainly comfortable. And most of the 30 rooms now have private baths. Rooms with washbasin and WC are 92-120F, with washbasin and shower 165F, with shower and WC 190-300F. Breakfast: 15F.

Regent 61, rue Dauphine; (tel: 326.76.45; metro: Odeon).   *
If you want to stay in the heart of Saint Germain, and the
Petit Trianon and St André-des-Arts are full, try this place.
The rooms are basic, the plumbing in need of modification,
but the Regent is cheap and central. Ask for a room away
from the street, because rue Dauphine is filled with merrymakers until early in the morning. Rooms with washbasin
only are 50-52F, with washbasin and WC 64-83F, with WC
and shower 128-155F. No breakfast.

Relais Christine 3, rue Christine; (tel: 326.71.80; metro:
Odeon).   ***** Saint Germain's other superb establishment
besides l'Hotel, a 17th century cloister which has been converted into a luxury-class hotel. The Relais Christine is a bit
like a French country inn spruced up and transported lock,
stock and barrel to the middle of Paris. The ambience and
decor is definitely rustic, with lots of wood, stone and
antiques. And Relais is one of the few hotels in town to
offer two-level suites. Most rooms open on to the tranquil
central courtyard, and just across the street is the cosy
Photogalerie tea salon and café. Singles or doubles with a
private bath are 580-640F, rooms with a drawing room and
bath are 770F, while a duplex suite with bath will cost you
880-1150F. Breakfast: 35F.

Saint-André-des-Arts 66, rue St André-des-Arts; (tel:
326.96.16; metro: Odeon).   * The best of the one-star hotels
in Saint Germain, with a reputation among overseas
backpackers which extends from Tokyo to Tacoma. The Saint
André is a bit dark, the ceilings a little low, but that adds
to the ancient charm of the place. And both staff and visitors
are always ready to strike up a conversation on their latest
travels and adventures. This is where many of the die-hard
international travellers (not tourists) stay when they visit
Paris. The only negative point about the hotel is its size —
only 32 rooms — which means there is a rush every
morning to snatch any vacancies there might be. So get there

early or call before. Singles are 64F, doubles with a shower 155-190F, doubles with a WC and shower 148-265F, including breakfast.

Scandinavie 27, rue de Tournon; (tel: 329.67.20; metro: Odeon). *** Nothing like a romantic old hotel with a little scandalous history. This is the very building where that great lover Giovanni Casanova lived, and it was the home of poet Clement Marot. The structure dates from the early 18th century during the reign of Louis XIII, and the Scandinavie today is a bit like a museum with its suits of armour, antiques and paintings. It's a two-minute walk from the Jardin du Luxembourg and situated in the midst of trendy boutiques and clothes shops. But there are only 22 rooms and the place is popular, so book early. Singles are 245F, doubles 265F. All rooms have private baths. Breakfast: 15F.

● **7e   Saint Germain, Invalides**

Bourgogne et Montana 3, rue de Bourgogne; (tel: 551.20.22; metro: Chambre-des-Deputés). *** An excellent medium-range hotel just off the lovely Place du Palais Bourbon and opposite the Assemblée Nationale. This is a very good location for overseas diplomats or businessmen who have dealings with the French government, for the Montana is close to most of the ministries and but a five-minute walk from the Air France air terminal at the Gare des Invalides. The ground floor has a bar and restaurant, lounge and study. Singles are 235-318F, doubles 358-450F, triples from 605F. Breakfast: 18F.

Grand Hotel Leveque 29, rue Cler; (tel: 705.49.15; metro: École Militaire). * A real find, for the Leveque is one of the most charming small hotels in Paris. Not only are the prices rock bottom, but the rooms are clean, the staff is friendly (and most speak English), the place is quiet and there's even a daily street market on the rue Cler where you can stock up on the most delicious of French foods. Nearby are the Eiffel Tower, Champ de Mars and Invalides. The only problem with the Leveque is there isn't much nightlife in the area, and you must take the metro to another neighbourhood to find a good restaurant. Singles are 65-170F, doubles 80-130F. Breakfast: 12F.

Lenox 9, rue de l'Université; (tel: 296.10.95; metro: St Germain). *** A slick, chic hotel that looks like a set from a Richard Gere movie. And I wouldn't be surprised to find a few Hollywood types staying at the Lenox. The building dates from the 18th century, but the decor and ambience are late 20th century: clean, modern, polished and posh. Each of the 35 rooms comes with unique furnishings and private bath. The hotel bar on the corner has palm trees and Venetian blinds, just right for a romantic tête-à-tête. Singles are 225F, doubles 235-370F, suites 495F. Breakfast: 20F.

Pont Royal 7, rue de Montalembert; (tel: 544.38.27; metro: Bac). ***** One of the least known of the luxury hotels in Paris, perhaps because it's a bit off the beaten track, tucked away on a tiny street off the Rue du Bac. The Pont-Royal is at the centre of Paris's greatest antiques district, and the traditional lines found in the 80 guest rooms would seem to be taken directly from the 18th and 19th century furnishings found in the nearby galleries. A comfortable bar and a very good restaurant on the ground floor, plus a leafy sidewalk terrace where you can sit and watch the world pass by. As part of its luxury presentation, the Pont-Royal includes television, refrigerator and safe in each room. Singles are 540-1100F, doubles 630-1250F, including breakfast. Children under seven are free. Breakfast for non-guests is 45F.

Quai Voltaire 19, quai Voltaire; (tel: 261.50.91; metro: Bac). *** One of the more romantic hotel venues in Paris, facing on to the Seine, with the Louvre and the Tuileries just across the river. And the Voltaire goes a long way towards exploiting its favourable situation to full advantage: most of the 33 rooms face the Seine and there are huge, double windows which allow an unhindered view of the historic landscape. These windows also ensure that the Voltaire has

73

amongst the sunniest rooms in Paris during the summer. Only drawback is the noise from the traffice on the quay. Many famous names of the past have also been taken by the location of this hotel, among them Richard Wagner, Jean Sibelius and the ever-wandering Oscar Wilde. Great place for a honeymoon, or your own private recreation of *An American in Paris*. Singles are 115-258F, doubles 276-336F, including breakfast. Most of the rooms have private bath.

Saint-Simon 14, rue St Simon; (tel: 548.35.66; metro: Bac).   *** One of the best kept secrets of the Rive Gauche, an exquisite hotel hidden away on a quiet street off the Boulevard St Germain. This place is run by a Swedish couple named the Linqvists, who undertook a complete renovation of the interior and exterior in late 1983. The St Simon is built around a lovely courtyard with flowered terraces, and many of the 34 rooms face onto this miniature botanical garden. The decor is along traditional French 19th century lines, and many of the rooms are furnished with antiques. Plumbing has also been renovated, so that all rooms have complete private baths. Both singles and doubles are 350-500F. Breakfast: 20F.

Solferino 91, rue de Lille; (tel: 705.85.54; metro: Solferino).   ** Charming location on a tranquil street just off the Seine, and opposite the historic Palais de la Legion d'Honneur. And the prices are right, one of the few down-market establishments in this district of high-priced hotels. The Solferino is also clean and comfortable, although a bit simple and airless. Singles are 118-215F, doubles 215-240F, breakfast: 18F. Good value for money.

Université 22, rue de l'Université; (tel: 261.09.39; metro: St Germain).   *** Another of the seventh district's fantastic medium-range hotels, situated in a late 17th century townhouse and furnished with tapestries and antiques. The name derives from a curious legal twist, for the land on which the hotel is built was once the property of the University of Paris. It was expropriated by Queen Marguerite of Valois for

74

her personal use, thus initiating a lengthy legal battle which the University eventually lost. Each room has a modern private bath, and there's a nice inner courtyard with flowers and a fountain. Singles are 170-280F, doubles 300-520F, triples 365-515F, breakfast: 22F.

● 8e   Champs-Elysées

Aguesseau 24, rue Boissy d'Anglas; (tel: 265.91.20; metro: Madeleine).   ** Yes, there are inexpensive hotels in the 8th arrondissement for those who want to live in middle-class poverty amongst all that posh. Try the Hotel d'Aguesseau out for size. This hotel could best be described as utilitarian, but it's tidy and well-situated near the Place de la Concorde and the Madeleine. Singles are 160-190F, doubles 180-240F, breakfast 13F.

Le Bristol 112, rue du Faubourg St Honore; (tel: 266.91.45; metro: Clemenceau).   ***** Frommer's guide calls the Bristol one of the top two or three hotels in Europe, a claim which is hard to dispute. This establishment deals out unabashed luxury, incomparable service and deluxe amenities like few others in Paris. And it's been the home-from-home for foreign diplomats, visiting aristocrats and the global high society since its foundation in 1924. And for a posh hotel, the staff remains unusually friendly to even the scruffiest urchin who may wander through these beautiful swing doors at the entrance. After all, those urchins might be millionaire rock stars. The decor of the 205 guest rooms is decidedly antique, with many original 18th century pieces which might once have resided at Versailles. The public rooms of the Bristol are filled with Gobelin tapestries, paintings by old masters (possibly the best hotel collection in Paris) and signed period furniture. Many of the suites open on to the lovely French garden, with its well-kept trees and shrubs. Le Bristol's cordon bleu restaurant was named the best hotel dining room in Paris in 1982. And to top it off, the Bristol has one of only two swimming pools among the luxury class hotels of the district, a marvellous indoor pond with teak decks, bamboo furniture and a nearby sauna. Singles are 800-1100F, doubles 1100-1500F, and suites from 2100F. Breakfast: 58F. Le Bristol also has its own underground parking garage for those who want to bring the Rolls along.

Claridge-Bellman 37, rue Francois 1er; (tel: 723.54.42; metro: George V, Roosevelt). ***** One of the least conspicuous of the grand hotels around the Champs-Elysées, a smaller (42 rooms) establishment which provides a more intimate service with no drop in the quality or luxury. The Claridge has an attractive blue-grey facade with red verandas, typical of the 18th century French mansions of the neighbourhood. Inside, the Claridge is equally refined in decor and manner. Both public rooms and guest chambers possess a wealth of period furniture, Oriental carpets and valuable tapestries, plus all the fixtures of a 1980s bathroom. There is a pleasant, Victorian-style bar on the ground floor, and a very good restaurant with a pavement terrace. All rooms come with showers, colour television and mini bars, and the Claridge has on-site parking. Singles are 550F, doubles 650F, breakfast 36F.

Crillon 10, place de la Concorde; (tel: 265.24.24; metro: Concorde). ***** There are few hotels in the world with as checkered a history as the fabulous Crillon. The massive granite building with its Greek colonnade was designed by the famous architect Gabriel, as part of a new royal square commissioned by Louis XV to honour the Well Beloved. It took twenty years to finish, from 1755 to 1775, but upon completion it was universally hailed as one of the world's great squares. Just three years later, the building was the site of a historic treaty signed between Louis XVI and Benjamin Franklin, as France recognized the youthful United States of America. The square outside witnessed the most bloody episodes of the French Revolution, for it was the site of the Tribunal's feared guillotine. Louis XVI, Marie-Antoinette, Robespierre, Danton and over 1,300 others were executed on this spot. The building later became the home of the Duke of Crillon, and then in 1909 it was renovated into one

The Crillon Hotel is one of the most historic in Paris, for the square outside witnessed some of the most bloody scenes of the French Revolution and the final battle to liberate Paris from the Nazis.

of the globe's great hotels. Among its distinguished guests in the earlier part of this century were Charlie Chaplin, Gloria Swanson and many of the world's diplomats and heads-of-state. When Paris was liberated from the Nazis, the Place de la Concorde was the scene of a fierce tank battle. You can still see the shell and bullet holes on sections of the Crillon's facade. No less spectacular than the history is the sumptuous interior of this hotel. The entire Crillon seems to be built from marble, from the lavish walls and columns of the foyer, to the bathrooms in the 206 guest rooms. The public galleries are something out of Versailles with their parquet floors, crystal chandeliers, tapestries and period furniture. Particularly gorgeous are the Salon Marie-Antoinette, the Stairway of Honour and the restaurant overlooking the Place de la Concorde. Each of the rooms has its own special ambience, ranging from 18th century traditional to conservative modern. Many of them were decorated by famed designer Sonia Rykiel. Naturally, the prices are as high as the obelisk in the square outside: 862-1150F for a single, 1250-1800F for a double, one-bedroom suites from 2500F and two bedroom suites from 3800F. Breakfast: 60F.

George V 31, avenue George V; (tel: 723.54.00; metro: George V). ***** Another of the 8th arrondissement's sparkling pleasure palaces, which makes it all the harder to choose a luxury class hotel if you don't have a favourite in Paris already. It's hard to fault the George 'Sank' on anything, from the lavish marble-and-mahogany decor, to the impeccable service, to the list of auxiliary services like the Nina Ricci, Cartier and Givenchy boutiques on the ground floor. There is a lush inner courtyard where you can take afternoon tea, a cordon bleu restaurant and one of the most popular hotel bars in Paris. Singles are 1050F, doubles 1350F, one-bedroom suites from 2800F and two-bedroom suites from 4150F. Breakfast: 50F.

Lancaster 7, rue de Berri; (tel: 359.90.43; metro: George V). ***** The Hotel Lancaster has a high opinion of itself;

two lines in the hotel brochure sum up this self-pride: 'The apartments are decorated to make you feel at home, so much so that you will not want to go out. The quality of the service will make it unnecessary for you to go out.' Really? But then, the people who stay at the Lancaster have just as lofty an opinion of the place after they depart. The Lancaster is an old-fashioned hotel, not only in decor and ambience, but also in spirit. It offers 'civilised living' and 'unexpected calm' and the management puts the emphasis on privacy and personal service. The rich and famous respond in loyal hordes, for the Lancaster is a favourite of British and American film stars and celebrities. Singles are 700-820F, doubles 945-1100F, suites from 1500F, breakfast 45F.

Madeleine 6, rue de Surene; (tel: 265.71.61; metro: Madeleine). ** A good inexpensive hotel which tends to get lost among the luxury giants of the district. The Madeleine is excellently situated near the church and square of the same name, and the lavish shops of Faubourg St Honore. You can easily spend the money you save on residing here in the shops down the road. Nearly all the 30 rooms have private baths. Singles are 130-165F, doubles 165-230F. Breakfast: 15F.

Nova-Park Elysées 51, rue Francois 1er; (tel: 562.63.64; metro: George V, Roosevelt). ***** The newest of Paris's luxury class establishments, opened with a flourish in the spring of '82. The Nova-Park bills itself as 'the palace for the international elite' and so far it has been able to attract quite a trendy (and wealthy) crowd. There are only 73 guest rooms, most of which are suites or apartments. But the hotel is full of plenty of other attractions. It has one of only two swimming pools among the delux hotels in this area, plus private parking. There are two excellent restaurants — Le Champagne Club and Les Elysées — and a bistro-style grill. And there are three bars, including jazz in the Musiciens. Those who want to stay in tune with the latest stock prices can visit the Salon Wall Street with its direct-line ticker-tape machines. Singles are 1280-1410F (the most expensive single rooms in Paris), doubles 1475-1620F, suites 1500-2125F, duplex apartments 3000-4250F and the eight presidential suites from 5620F. Breakfast: 49.50F.

Plaza-Athenée 25, avenue Montaigne; (tel: 723.78.33; metro: Alma, Roosevelt).   ***** The plaza likes to think of itself as a businessmen's hotel, offering the widest range of services of any residence in Paris. There are conference rooms, and elegant salons for private luncheons and dinners, translation and secretarial services. The staff will book everything from a seat at the theatre to your plane ticket home. There is room service 24 hours a day, and there are both men's and women's hairdressers in the building. No stone is left unturned to give the overseas visitor the best of treatment. Added to this superb service is an excellent bill of auxiliary facilities: the Bar Anglais with its plush Edwardian decor, the excellent posh Regence Plaza restaurant with its French haute cuisine, the Grill Relais Plaza for a quick meal, the trendy and popular Bar Relais, and the casual and charming setting of the Cour-Jardin, a delightful garden café in the central courtyard. The 218 rooms are no less impressive, for they are furnished with 18th century antiques, marble fireplaces, elegant carpets and countless works of art. The suites on the top floor offer an unobstructed view of the Seine and the nearby Eiffel Tower. Singles are 850F, doubles 1150F, bedsitting rooms 1850F, one bedroom suites from 2150F and two-bedroom suites from 3600F. Breakfast: 55F.

Prince de Galles 33, avenue George V; (tel: 723.55.11; metro: George V).   ***** Same in form and function as the other five star hotels: an opulent international pleasure palace offering sumptuous decor, unmatched service and numerous amenities. What sets the Prince apart from the others is that it tends to be a gathering ground of Parisian high society and an urban residence for the French aristocracy in from the hinterlands on a shopping foray to the big city. Let's not push those noses too high in the air. The 160 rooms are traditional in design, some to the point of being rather boring. But there is a tranquil inner sanctum over which most of the rooms look, and you can sink into an Old World serenity at the Plaza that is now impossible to obtain at many other delux hotels. The Plaza delights in being a slight anachronism, and it's this very formal nature which attracts the loyal guests. The Panache Restaurant serves up (you've guessed it) traditional French haute cuisine, while the Regency Bar provides a conservative, although woodsy place to drink. Singles are 848-1150F, doubles 1090-1365F, suites from 1826F, breakfast for 70F.

Residence Lord Byron 5, rue de Chateaubriand; (tel: 359.89.98; metro: George V). *** One of the best medium-range hotels in the Champs-Elysées region, a midget hotel with only 26 rooms which provides a superb standard of service and comfort for half the price of the delux palaces. In other words, luxury for a reasonable price. The rooms are furnished tastefully with a wide range of antiques, and there is a tranquil inner garden in which you can take quiet refuge from the bright lights of the nearby avenue. In addition, the small but excellent staff is both friendly and helpful. Lord Byron is one of the great secrets of the eighth district. Singles are 265F, doubles 265-450F, breakfast 17F.

● 9e Opéra

Chopin 46, passage Jouffroy; (tel: 770.58.10; metro: Montmartre, Richelieu-Drouot). ** One of Paris's most romantic hotel locations, for the Chopin is a charming little place hidden away in a corner of the Passage Jouffroy, a classic Belle Epoque shopping arcade built over a hundred years ago in 1846. You enter the passage at 10-12 Boulevard Montmartre, and proceed up a lovely row of both curious and interesting shops. The Chopin is heavy on the wood decor, and all 38 rooms have private baths. This is one of the city's great accommodation secrets, perfect for the visitor who wants to stay in an atmosphere of old Paris. Singles are 142-202F, doubles 149-214F. Breakfast: 12F.

Geoffroy Marie 12, rue Geoffroy-Marie; (tel: 770.11.85; metro: Montmartre, Cadet). * A place for the student or backpacker's budget, a pleasant hotel situated on the main street of the 9th district's Jewish neighbourhood. Eleven of the 32 rooms have private baths, while a further 14 have washbasins and WC. The street outside is packed with kosher delicatessens and shops, and there are several other one-star hotels just down the road if the Geoffroy is full. Singles are 61-63F, doubles 86-103F, including breakfast.

Grand Hotel 2, rue Scribe; (tel: 260.33.50; metro: Opera). ***** The Grand Hotel is just that, a massive 583-room facility with everything you could probably want in a luxury class establishment: 24-hour room service, sauna and health club, top flight bars and restaurants, a tranquil inner garden, laundry and valet service, translation and secretarial help for businessmen, and a long and colourful history. It's a city in itself. The Grand began life in the 1870s, designed by the same man (Charles Garnier) but on less flamboyant lines than the adjacent Opera. With such close proximity to the globe's greatest theatre, the Grand quickly became the haunt of stage stars, aristocrats, composers and writers. Its ground floor facilities were favourite hangouts of the expatriate Americans in the '20s and '30s, populated by such legendary figures as Hemingway and Fitzgerald. The Grand underwent an extensive renovation in the 1970s which modernized the plumbing, convention facilities and the like. Today, the hotel offers a good range of both traditional and contemporary decor, so guests who don't like the formality of 18th century France can opt for 20th century surroundings. The Bar Capucines and Foyer Bar Opera are both stylish and popular, while the Ravel Restaurant offers excellent breakfast and lunch menus. But the highlight of the Grand's eating places is the world famous Café de la Paix on the Place de l'Opera side. The Café has two indoor restaurants and a delightful pavement terrace. Singles are 810F, doubles 910F, suites from 1539F. Continental breakfast: 55F, American breakfast: 90F. Dogs: 60F.

Seze 16, rue de Seze; (tel: 742.69.12; metro: Madeleine).
** An excellent medium-range hotel with a superb location
just off the Boulevard des Capucines near the Opera and
the Madeleine, and very close to the hot shopping of the
Place Vendome and Rue Faubourg St Honore. Half of the
25 rooms have private baths, while the decor ranges from
charming antique to bland modern. Rooms with a washbasin
are 65-71F, with washbasin and WC 118F, with washbasin
and shower 173F, with WC and shower 196-230F. Breakfast:
15F. Showers for those who don't have them in the room are
15F extra.

● **14e Montparnasse**

Grand Hotel des Ecoles 15, rue Delambre; (tel: 329.76.50;
metro: Vavin, Edgar Quinet).   ** Nothing fancy but the
prices are right at this well-situated hotel in Montparnasse.
A good place for couples on a shoestring budget. The rue
Delambre is an interesting street filled with exotic restaurants
(Korean and Indian) and rustic little bars like the world-
famous Rosebud. Just up the hill is the wide Boulevard Edgar
Quinet with its fruit and vegetable market, and in the other
direction is the Boulevard du Montparnasse with its cluster
of century-old cafés. Singles and doubles are 64-147F.
Breakfast: 16F. Twenty of the 66 rooms have bathrooms.

Istria 29, rue Campagne-Premiere; (tel: 320.91.82; metro:
Raspail).   * One of the better rock-bottom hotels in Montparnasse. The plumbing needs a bit of updating (only two
of the 30 rooms have private baths), but the Istria is close
to the Montparnasse café and nightclub action, and the street
offers a tranquil repose from the hectic boulevards. Singles
with washbasin are 65F, singles with washbasin and WC 71F,
singles with a shower and WC 130F; doubles with washbasin
and WC 118F, doubles with shower and WC 141F; including
breakfast.

Montparnasse Park Sheraton 19, rue du Comm. Mouchette;
(tel. 320.15.51; metro: Gaîté, Montparnasse). ***** One of

the flashy Americans in Paris, a glistening Montparnasse tower with 995 rooms and superlative amenities. There's that unusual Parisian feature known as the underground car park, plus large-scale convention and conference facilities. It has a cordon bleu restaurant in the Montparnasse 25, a flashy New York-style bar in Le Corail, and an American-style coffee shop in La Ruche. There is an adjacent discotheque, bowling alley and ice skating rink, plus the new Gaîté shopping complex. And the massive Maine-Montparnasse Centre with all its shops and squash club is just down the road. The view from the guest rooms is probably the best of any hotel in Paris, with a panorama of the Eiffel Tower, Invalides, Tour Montparnasse, Notre Dame and the rest of the Left Bank. Singles are 535-755F, doubles 615-865F, breakfast 34F.

Parc 6, rue Jolivet; (tel: 320.95.54; Edgar-Quinet, Montparnasse). * Superb one-star establishment on a little-known square off the Boulevard Edgar Quinet. The Hotel du Parc is dwarfed by the futuristic giants in the neighbourhood, the black hulk of the Tour Montparnasse and the silver flash of the Sheraton. But somehow this hotel and the rue Jolivet retain a 19th century ambience despite the 20th century swank. The square is often filled with school children and pensioners, and nearby is the ancient fruit and vegetable market of the Boulevard Edgar Quinet. Great value for budget guests. Rooms with washbasin are 55F, with washbasin and WC 83-96F, with WC and shower 104-155F. Breakfast: 11F.

PLM Saint-Jacques 17, boulevard St Jacques; (tel: 589.89.80; metro: St Jacques, Glacière). ***** The other luxury giant in Montparnasse, what is often called a French version of the great American businessman's hotel. Baron Rothschild, the developer of the PLM, has done an excellent job of giving traditional French tastes an American theme. The 797 rooms are tastefully decorated, and there is an unusual variety to the auxiliary features found on the ground floor. For eating, you have a choice of superb Japanese dining at Le Jun, or traditional French menus at the Café Français brasserie and bistro. There are American and Polynesian-style bars, a coffee shop, cinema, coiffure and photo shop in the massive complex. The PLM also has extensive underground parking facilities. The only problem with the hotel is that it's a bit off the beaten track, well away from the centre of Montparnasse in a not-too-quaint neighbourhood of council flats and cement gardens. You will need public transport, taxi or a private vehicle to get almost anywhere in town. Singles are 649F, doubles 726F, apartments 900F and suites from 1040F. Breakfast: 32F.

Residence Domance 17, boulevard Edgar Quinet; (tel: 320.63.15; metro: Edgar-Quinet).   * Don't be fooled by the single star or the somewhat shabby facade, for this tiny hotel is among the best Paris has to offer at the lower range of the market. Like the nearby Hotel du Parc, the Domance represents a slice of the past, a charming anachronism in the futuristic ambience of 1985 Montparnasse. You can imagine what poor and starving artists must have stayed at this hotel in the 1920s and 30s. And even though the Tour Montparnasse may block out much of the sunlight, it cannot obscure the patina of bygone days. The furnishings of the Residence Domance look a bit like the pickings of a jumble sale, and the rooms are a bit short on space. But the place is warm and comfortable, and you can hardly beat the prices. What's more, every one of the fourteen rooms has a private bath. Singles are 85-96F, doubles 118-153F, triples 153F. Breakfast: 13F.

● **15e   Eiffel Tower**

Hilton 18, avenue Suffren; (tel. 273.92.00; metro: Bir-Hakeim, Dupleix). ***** The prototype American hotel in Paris, the sort of cool but efficient place for those who can't stand to be without their dry martini or bacon and eggs. The Hilton has all the extras one would expect of a modern five-star establishment: conference facilities, car park, hair salons, post and telegraph service, news kiosk, boutique, closed-circuit television with first-run movies, plus numerous eating places and watering holes. The 11th floor Toit de Paris restaurant and cocktail bar has striking views of the Eiffel Tower and Seine, as well as marvellous French cuisine. Downstairs is Le Western restaurant and grill, with its Wild West ambience and fresh American beef. Le Western Bar is for New York style lounge lizards, while Le Bar Suffren offers a touristy Belle Epoque atmosphere. The guest rooms are spotless, comfortable if somwhat characterless, but many of them offer superb views. Singles are 610-680F, doubles 720-800F, suites from 1450F. Extra guests are 90F per room. Breakfast: 40F. No room charges for children sharing their parents' room.

● 16e   Etoile, Victor Hugo

Metropole 6, avenue Victor Hugo; (tel: 501.79.80; metro: Etoile).   ** Agreeable, comfortable medium-range hotel bang in the middle of all those trendy boutiques on the Avenue Victor Hugo. You can stare out of your window at all of the pretty young things passing below, or partake of the purchasing action yourself. The Arc de Triomphe is a two-minute walk, and the leafy confines of the Avenue Foch (Paris's widest street) are just around the corner. The Metropole is also close to the Parisian bastion of Anglo drinking, the Winston Churchill pub. All of the twenty rooms have private baths. A good cheap hotel in a ritzy neighbourhood. Singles are 151-247F, doubles 287F. Breakfast: 20F.

Le Perouse 40, rue la Perouse; (tel. 500.83.47; metro: Kleber). ***** The Perouse looks a bit like a Romantic painting on first glance, a gorgeous turn-of-the-century facade set at the end of a pretty tree-lined square which evolves into a start-ling flash of reds browns and yellows in autumn. The street is tranquil, almost traffic free, but Le Perouse is just a stone's throw from the bright lights of the Champs-Elysées. This is one of Paris's least-known luxury hotels, an elegant but obscure establishment where the rich and famous can fade into the woodwork and hide away from the hounding press.

Despite recent modernization (every room has a colour TV and mini-bar), the Perouse retains a slow-moving, Old World charm, evoking its most famous resident, General Charles de Gaulle, who lived here for several years after the liberation of Paris. Singles are 675-850F, doubles 950-1300F. Breakfast 40F.

Residence du Bois 16, rue Chalgrin; (tel: 500.50.59; metro: Argentine).   ***** This hotel is a shock to the system, for all you can see on the approach down the rue Chalgrin is the cold stone of the surrounding 19th century blocks. Then out of a dream appears a brilliant 18th century mansion submerged in a verdant patch of trees. The contrast could not be more startling, no subtle nuances here. Residence du Bois is a former private home which has been converted very successfully into a combination hotel and monument to the French Enlightenment. The place drips with Louis XIV and XVI antiques, tapestries and paintings, and the impeccable service is good enough for a king or queen. This tranquil backwater is also a haven for insomniacs, like a country retreat in the heart of Paris. Each of the 20 rooms has a private bathroom, and in 1983 the Bois was upgraded from three to four stars. Rooms are 520-950F, including breakfast.

Residence Chalgrin 10, rue Chalgrin; (tel: 500.19.91; metro: Argentine).   * A real paradise for bargain hunters, a comfortable but inexpensive hotel just off the leafy precincts of the Avenue Foch. The Chalgrin is little used by overseas visitors and almost always has a vacancy. Thirteen of the 17 rooms have private baths, while the other four have washbasin and WC. Rooms with a wash basin are 82F, with washbasin and shower 145F, with WC and shower 176F, with WC, shower and salon 301F. Breakfast: 16F.

● **17e   Palais des Congrès**

Concorde la Fayette 3, place du Gal Koenig; (tel: 758.12.84; metro: Porte Maillot).   ***** The 42-storey centre-piece of the Palais des Congrès, this massive new hotel caters to the international business and convention crowd. The Concorde has direct access to the main conference hall with its 4,300 capacity and the surrounding galaxy of smaller meeting rooms, offices and business suites. All of the typical business facilities are available in the Concorde: translation and secretarial services, international post and telex, excellent service, a multitude of bars and restaurants, ticket service and the like. The immense lobby is almost big enough for a convention itself. The Salon Panoramique on the top floor offers one of Paris's most stunning views looking out toward the Arc de Triomphe, the Eiffel Tower and the Sacré Coeur. Meanwhile, the Bar la Fayette has piano music and jazz from 10 pm to 1 am nightly. The complex also includes two floors of exclusive shops dubbed Les Boutiques du Palais des Congrès, the Vitatop Fitness Club, the Air France Terminal for De Gaulle-Roissy Airport, banks, post office, pharmacy, news agency and cinema. The Bois de Boulogne is just across the Porte Maillot. Singles are 720-840F, doubles 840-900F. Breakfast: 40F.

Meridien 81, boulevard Gouvion Saint-Cyr; (tel. 758.12.30; metro: Porte Maillot). ***** The other five-star wonder off the Porte Maillot. This is the Parisian branch of the world-wide French hotel chain, the elegant and ultra-modern flagship of the line. It's just across the street from the Palais des Congrès, so almost as convenient as the Concorde for convention goers and certainly just as good for the visiting business person. The Meridien has the full range of services to assist the on-the-go business types including stock market reports, translation and secretarial help, travel and entertainment ticket service and meeting facilities for up to 2,000 people. With 1,027 rooms the Meridien is the largest hotel in France, and each of the rooms is furnished with TV, radio, private bath, telephone and air conditioning. Many of them have panoramic views. Lots of after-work distractions too, like Le Patio with its jazz sessions and cocktails, the Ecume des Nuits nightclub, and French, American and Japanese restaurants. And because the Meridien chain is associated with Air France (the Roissy terminal is just across the street), the place is always thronged with pilots and stewardesses. Singles are 785F, doubles 880F, suites 1150-3500F, extra persons 190F. Breakfast: 38F.

Regent's Garden 6, rue Pierre Demours; (tel: 574.07.30; metro: Ternes). **** A bit downmarket from the Concorde and Meridien, but definitely one of the best medium-range hotels in the district. The Regent is a bastion of the Second Empire style, the immediate forerunner to the Belle Epoque with its high ceilings, brass fixtures and ever-present mirrors. The ambience is one of bygone days, a flashy Old World charm that's absent from the modern hotels of the Palais des Congrès. This grand old mansion is now in need of a little restoration, but this slight dilapidation adds to the atmosphere. Parking is in the garden. Singles are 326-420F, doubles 360-480F, suites 400-520F. Breakfast 22F and parking 23F.

● **18e Montmartre**

Commerce 34, rue des Trois Frères; (tel: 264.81.69; metro: Abesses). * Montmartre cheapy on a sultry, somewhat dilapidated street which seems not to have changed much in the past 100 years. The Commerce isn't the cleanest or most comfortable, but the prices are definitely right for the backpacker's budget. Rooms are 40-85F. Close to the bright lights and low life of Pigalle, the climb to Sacré Coeur and the priceless Abesses station.

Prima-Lepic 29, rue Lepic; (tel: 606.44.64; metro: Abesses, Blanche). ** A fantastic little two-star hotel, perhaps the best of the medium-range accommodation in Montmartre. You could easily mistake the Prima for a nursery with its abundance of plants and flowers, plus the prevalent green and white colour scheme of the public rooms. The guest rooms are refreshingly decorated in floral patterns, and each has a private bath and telephone. Fantastic value for money and a great place to base explorations of Montmartre. Singles start at 154F, doubles at 225F. Breakfast: 16.50F.

Terrass 12, rue Joseph de Maistre; (tel: 606.72.85; metro: Clichy, Blanche). **** Montmartre's only four-star hotel, run with high efficiency by the French-based Mapotel chain. The Terrass is situated in a modern six-level tower opposite the Montmartre Cemetery. It's within a minute's walk of the colourful food stalls of the Rue Lepic and Rue des Abbesses, and but a ten-minute stroll through the most charming parts of Montmartre to Sacré Coeur. Both atmosphere and decor are thoroughly modern, and the Terrass is often populated with wealthy German visitors who seem to appreciate this contemporary ambience (notice the 'M', 'HH' and 'F' plates of the Mercedes parked outside: Munich, Hamburg and Frankfurt). There are two excellent restaurants in the Albaron and the Guerlande, and the rooftop terrace café offers one of Paris's most spectacular views. Each of the 108 rooms has a private bath. Singles are 340-400F, doubles 480F, suites 470-610F, including breakfast.

TIM Montmartre 11, place Emile Goudeau; (tel: 255.74.79; metro: Abesses). *** The most charming hotel in Montmartre, at some of the best prices in Paris. The TIM is a tranquil little hotel with a lot of character, for it's located on one of Montmartre's most famous squares. Just around the corner at No.13 Place Emile Goudeau is the Bateau-Lavoir, the renowned artists' studio where the young, struggling Picasso and Braque invented cubism, and where the equally destitute Max Jacob plunged into avant-garde prose. The place itself is a treat with its leafy canopy of trees, wooden benches and Wallace fountain. The TIM underwent a major renovation in 1983 and most of the 63 rooms now have private bath. In addition, each room has direct dial telephone service, TV, radio and video-cinema. And you have a choice of breakfast in bed or in the ground floor dining room. Singles are 73-139F, doubles 82-230F, breakfast 17F.

*The ultimate in Paris romance: the tiny TIM Montmartre
hotel is situated on the leafy Place Emile Goudeau,
right next to the former artists' colony where Picasso
and Braque worked.*

Youth hostels

Paris probably has more student and youth accommodation than any other city in the world, but this massive network of cheap inns is hidden behind a wall of acronyms and rival organizations. There are least 6,000 hostel beds in the Paris metropolitan area, which means even at the peak of summer there should be a place for you. It may take a little perseverance, and trekking from agency to agency, but you will get a bed for the night.

First off, there are no IYHF (International Youth Hostel Federation) hostels within the Paris city limits, only two suburban branches at Choisy-le-Roi and Rueil-Malmaison mostly frequented by French young people. So the most important acronyms to keep in mind for finding a bed in the middle of Paris are AJF (Accueil des Jeunes en France) and UCRIF (Union des Centres de Rencontres Internationales de France). The AJF is Paris's oldest and most popular hostel organization, with booking offices at the Gare du Nord, Pompidou Centre and Hotel de Ville, and nine hostels spread around town, most of them in the historic Marais district. UCRIF is an umbrella organization which books rooms for such ominous-sounding groups as BVJ, FUAJ, CISP, FIAP, CNFA, CREPA and UNESCO. Their main booking office is near the Forum des Halles. One further hostel organization is the OTU-Accueil, which has one hostel in central Paris and six in the suburbs.

Following are two lists: the first gives the central booking offices of the three major hostel organizations, the second lists the actual hostels. Beds can be booked either through the booking offices or by showing up at an individual hostel in person. But, as with hotels, it's a good idea to telephone first to see if anything is available.

Booking offices

AJF Beaubourg 119, rue St Martin, 4e; (tel: 277.87.80; metro: Rambuteau, Châtelet, Les Halles, Hotel-de-Ville). Opposite the Pompidou Centre. Booking for nine hostels. No youth hostel card or student i.d. is required. No age limitations. Beds are 50-55F including breakfast in dormitory accommodation, with WC and showers down the hall. No alcoholic drinks on the hostel premises. The hostels are closed for several hours in the afternoon for cleaning. TransAlpino rail tickets sold at this office for anyone under 26. Open Monday to Saturday 9.30 am to 7 pm.

AJF Gare du Nord Arrival Hall in the Gare du Nord, 10e; (tel: 285.86.19; metro: Gare du Nord). Same service as above, but no TransAlpino tickets. Open daily 8.15 am to 9.30 pm in the summer. Monday to Friday 9.15 am to 6.15 pm the rest of the year.

AJF Hotel-de-Ville 16, rue de Pont Louis-Philippe, 4e; (tel: 278.04.82; metro: Hotel-de-Ville). Same service as above including TransAlpino tickets. Open Monday to Saturday from 9 am to 7 pm in the summer, and Monday to Friday 9.30 am to 6.30 pm the rest of the year.

OTU-Accueil 137, boulevard St Michel, 5e; (tel: 329.12.88; metro: St Michel, Maubert-Mutualité). Headquarters for this nation-wide chain of hostels, which provides students and other young people with cheap accommodation in student residences during the summer. Many of these are single rooms. But to stay in any OTU hostel you must first purchase a voucher book with ten coupons at the OTU head office, or at any branch offices in France. Each voucher is good for one night's stay in a hostel, but they are not refundable if not used. No prior booking is required.

UCRIF 20, rue J.J. Rousseau, 1er; (tel: 236.88.18; metro: Les Halles, Louvre, Palais Royal). Booking information on the 77 UCRIF affiliated hostels in France, including 11 in Paris. Prices for one night are 41-80F depending on the hostel, but in many cases the fees decrease with stays of more than two nights. Most of the hostels also include breakfast in the basic price. Many also provide lunch, dinner and half-board for extra fees.

UCRIF Gare du Nord Arrival Hall in the Gare du Nord, 10e; (tel: 874.68.69; metro: Gare du Nord). Same service as head office.

Hostels

Bastille AJF 151, avenue Ledru Rollin, 11e; (metro: Bastille, Voltaire, Ledru Rollin). A little on the clinical side, but English is spoken and the beds are only 50F a night including breakfast. Dorm rooms. Closed noon to 2 pm each afternoon.

BVJ Louvre 20, rue J.J. Rousseau, 1er; (tel: 236.88.18; metro: Louvre, Les Halles, Palais Royal). Bed and breakfast is 50F a night no matter how many nights you stay. Lunch or dinner are 30F each, half-board is 80F. Good central location. 200 beds. UCRIF affiliate.

BVJ Les Halles 5, rue de Pelican, 1er; (tel: 260.92.45; metro: Louvre, Palais Royal). Same as above. 55 beds. Around the corner from BVJ Louvre.

BVJ Opera 11, rue Therese, 1er; (tel:260.77.23; metro: Pyramides, Palais Royal). Same as above. 68 beds. Near the Molière Fountain and the Palais Royal.

Coubertin AJF 53, rue Lhomond, 5e; (metro: Censier Daubenton). Same prices and conditions as other AJF hostels. In the heart of the university district, near the Mouffetard street market. Many cheap restaurants and bars in this area. Open July and August only.

C.I. Le d'Artagnan 80, rue Vitruve, 20e; (tel: 361.08.75; metro: Porte de Bagnolet). Suburban setting near Pere Lachaise cemetery. Bed and breakfast is 65F for one or two nights, 50F for three or four nights and 45F for five or more nights. Half-board is 82F, lunch and dinner 32F each. Sports facilities. 207 beds. UCRIF affiliate.

CISP Kellermann 17, boulevard Kellermann, 13e; (tel: 580.70.76; metro: Porte d'Italie). The Centre International de Sejour de Paris. Beds are 70F including shower for one or two nights, 50F for three or four nights and 35F for five or more nights. Breakfast is 5-10F, lunch and dinner 15F. Language courses and facilities for the handicapped. There are two large parks nearby, but it's a bit far from the centre of Paris. UCRIF and AJF affiliate.

CISP Ravel 6, avenue Maurice Ravel, 12e; (tel: 343.19.01; metro: Porte de Vincennes). Same room prices and conditions as above, but breakfast is 13F, lunch or dinner 34F. Swimming pool, tennis courts, bicycle hire and language courses. Very near the giant Bois de Vincennes park, but otherwise a long way from central Paris.

Le Fauconnier AJF 11, rue de Fauconnier, 4e; (tel: 274.23.45; metro: St Paul, Pont Marie). Bed and breakfast is 50F a night at Paris's oldest AJF hostel, an ancient renovated building in the middle of the Marais. The structure is exquisite, an 18th century mansion in the French baroque style, on a quiet street near the Seine. Lots of marvellous antique furnishings in the public rooms, which makes this one of life's more elegant youth hostels. 100 beds. Closed in the afternoon for cleaning.

Le Fourcy AJF 6, rue de Fourcy, 4e; (tel: 274.23.45; metro: St Paul). Same prices and conditions as other AJF hostels. The Fourcy is another marvellous 18th century mansion which has been updated into a modern youth hostel. It has a quiet inner courtyard around which the rooms are arranged. Nearby is the restored Marais historic quarter and the busy Rue de Rivoli.

Foyer Internationale d'Accueil de Paris (FIAP) 30, rue Cabanis, 14e; (tel: 589.89.15; metro: Glacière). Paris's super hostel. A high-rise hotel for students and young people run by a private, non-profit organization (FIAP) which goes out of its way to make overseas visitors feel at home. Singles are

61F including shower, doubles 57F without shower and 61F per person with shower. Breakfast is 9.30F, lunch and dinner 31.50F in the FIAP cafeteria. There is also a bar open from 9 to 10.30 pm every night. You must check in on Monday to Friday 9 am to 1 pm and 6 to 9 pm, Saturday and Sunday 9 am to noon and 3 to 9.30 pm. The FIAP Theatre presents a continuous bill of live music, and the organization can also arrange language courses and sightseeing tours. Stamps and maps are available at the reception desk. UCRIF affiliate.

FUAJ Jules Ferry 8, boulevard Jules Ferry, 11e; (tel: 357.55.60; metro: République, Goncourt). Auberge de Jeunesse above the Canal Saint Martin. Bed and breakfast is 41F including a shower no matter how many nights you stay. Half-board is 68F, lunch or dinner 27F. 100 beds. UCRIF affiliate.

Lourmel AJF 29, rue de Lourmel, 15e; (metro: Dupleix). Same prices and conditions as other AJF hostels. Open in July only. Near the Eiffel Tower and the Champ du Mars.

Luxembourg AJF 270, rue St Jacques, 5e; (metro: Luxembourg, Port Royal). Same prices and conditions as other AJF hostels. Open July to September only. Near the Sorbonne and the Jardin du Luxembourg.

Maison des Eleves Ingenieurs 33, boulevard Jourdan, 14e; (tel: 253.51.44; metro: Cité Universitaire). The only OTU hostel in Paris, so you will need a voucher to stay here. Part of the Cité Internationale Universitaire de Paris complex, so it's a bit far from central Paris. But this hostel is very convenient for people using Orly airport, only 15 minutes away via the 215 bus. Open July 1st to September 20th only. You can check in from 4 to 10 pm daily, Breakfast at the hostel dining room, lunch and dinner (17F) at the Restaurant Cité Internationale.

Maison Internationale des Jeunes 4, rue Titon, 11e; (tel:

371.99.21; metro: Faidherbe). Bed and breakfast is 50F no matter how many nights you stay. No lunch or dinner available at the hostel. Rather spartan decor (some would say cement city) and far off the beaten track, but it may have a bed if other hostels are full. UCRIF affiliate.

Maubuisson AJF 12, rue des Barres, 4e; (tel: 272.72.09; metro: St Paul, Hotel-de-Ville). The flagship of the AJF line, situated in a beautifully restored 18th century mansion in the heart of the Marais historic quarter. The 15th century Church of St Gervais and St Protais is opposite, and the Seine is just down the cobble-stone road. Lots of antique furnishings and exposed wood beams, plus a friendly staff who speak English. Bed and breakfast is 50F a night.

UNESCO Glacière 43, rue de la Glacière, 13e; (tel: 336.00.63; metro: Glacière). United Nations hostel near the ugly council flats of the 13th district. But the place has a swimming pool and tennis courts, and there's an avant-garde theatre and cinema in the same complex. Bed and breakfast is 50F no matter how many nights you stay. No lunch or dinner available. Handicapped facilities. UCRIF affiliate.

UNESCO Vaugirard 13, rue de Vaugirard, 6e; (tel: 326.50.78; metro: Odeon, Luxembourg). Another United Nations hostel, close to the action of St Germain and St Michel, and just around the corner from the pleasant Jardin du Luxembourg. Same prices as above. Swimming pool and tennis courts. UCRIF affiliate.

Camping

Camping Champigny Quai de Polangis (Joinville le Pont); (tel: 283.38.24; RER: Joinville). The Touring Club de France facility on the eastern edge of Paris, situated in the massive Champigny park near the Seine. Space for about 1,000 people on 350 sites, plus money exchange and snack bar. Near the A4 Autoroute, but take the N4 into Paris.

Camping Paris-Ouest Allée du Bord de l'Eau, 16e; (tel: 506.14.98). The only place to camp within the city limits of Paris, riverside camping in the Bois de Boulogne. The ground is run by the highly efficient Touring Club de France and there is room for up to 1500 people. But the place is packed out in the summer. Nearby attractions include the Bagatelle gardens, Longchamp race track and the Grande Cascade. A bit hard to get into central Paris unless you want to drive, or walk a few miles to the nearest metro or RER station. There is a bank and snack bar at the ground, and several (expensive) restaurants nearby. Fees are 5F per site and 4.50F per person.

Maisons-Laffitte Foret de St Germain (Maisons-Laffitte); (tel: 962.43.37). Camping next to the beautiful forest of Saint Germain-en-Laye. Take the N308 into Paris, or the SNCF mainline train from Maisons-Laffitte to Gare St Lazare. The magnificent Chateau St Germain, one-time home of Mary Stuart and the deposed James II of England, is nearby.

Neuilly Haute Ile (Neuilly-sur-Marne); (tel: 935.21.21; metro: Porte de Neuilly). Municipal campground situated on an island in the Seine with space for up to 700 campers. Very convenient for exploring Paris. Take N13 or metro into central Paris.

Port Creteil Ile Brise Pain (Creteil); (tel: 207.06.75; RER: St Maur-Creteil; metro: Creteil). Les Cigognes campground on a tiny island in the Marne River. Room for 225 campers. Take N19 into Paris if you are driving, the metro line from Creteil or the RER line from St Maur-Creteil to Chatelet station.

CHAPTER FIVE

Where to eat

From delicious apple crêpes on a streetstand, to a five-course banquet at the Tour d'Argent, Paris is a gastronomic paradise. The perfection of French cooking is world famous, and perhaps there is no other nation in which the art of eating is elevated to such mouth-watering heights.

To most overseas visitors French cooking means traditional haute cuisine, those great French dishes found in cook books for the last 50 years, soufflés, sauces, filet and the like. But when you start to explore the Parisian world of eating you discover that French cooking is much more. One of your first discoveries will be the somewhat oddly named *nouvelle cuisine* or new cooking. But in fact nouvelle cuisine is just a return to the good old basics of French cooking before it became so ornate during the Belle Epoque. Nouvelle cuisine means crispy vegetables, delicious meats and fish, and imaginative desserts.

Your second discovery will possibly be French provincial cooking, which is so sadly ignored overseas. Alsace, with its long German occupation and influence, is a bastion of excellent sauerkraut and sausages. Savoy, tucked away in the Alps next to the Swiss border, is the home of savoury cheeses and fondues. Down in the southwest, in the Basque Country, the cuisine is spicy and exciting, resembling the food of nearby Spain. Brittany is big on seafood, as to be expected of a rocky peninsula which juts out into the Atlantic. And the Auvergne region of central France is known for its hearty country cooking, basic but delicious ingredients and huge helpings. All of these provincial delights are represented by special restaurants in the capital.

But Paris is more than just French cuisine, for its cosmopolitan nature lends perfectly to a demand for exotic tastes from around the world. The latest fad is Brazilian cuisine, heavy on the spice, meat and beans. But it's Paris where you will find the best American food in Europe — steaks, hamburgers, chili, salads and the like — and perhaps the most tasty Vietnamese cuisine this side of the Mekong. In addition, there are countless Chinese, Italian, German, Spanish and Japanese eating houses, and if you look hard enough, even a few spots with English specialities like Yorkshire pudding and roast beef.

The first thing you will encounter in any Parisian restaurant is the menu, usually posted in a window next to the front door. Paris veterans will have no problem, but the tourist rookie will be thoroughly confused. Spread out before you — sometimes in barely legible handwriting — is an array of foreign terms and exotic sounding dishes. You have absolutely no idea where to begin or what to eat.

First you should know that a typical French restaurant meal consists of three or four courses: (1) starter, which can consist of salad, soup, hors d'oeuvres or a variety of other small plates; (2) entrée, an optional second course usually consisting of fish; (3) main course, typically a meat, poultry or fish dish with a delicious French sauce and possibly vegetables on the side; (4) dessert. You will be offered an aperitif drink before dinner, usually a light and tasty drink like sherry or Campari. Wine goes with the meal, although it's also perfectly acceptable to order your vintage for drinking before the meal. The red with meat, white with fish rule no longer holds true, for in this enlightened age of wine and drinking you are encouraged to drink whatever pleases your taste buds. But do remember that even the most flavourful white can be overwhelmed by a heavy meat dish, like drinking a glass of slightly-flavoured water. Coffee comes after dessert, but no one will scream if you order it with your ice cream or cake. If you want cheese, it comes in there between the main course and dessert.

Step number two is figuring out a few basic menu terms. *A la carte* is a fairly universal term meaning from the card or menu. There are items ordered by themselves, not as part of a fixed meal. You get a better selection of dishes this way, but you will pay more. When selecting à la carte, look for the restaurant specialities, house dishes which will un- doubtedly be superb and well worth your money.

Those on a more limited budget or who don't want to flip through their English-French dictionary while glancing over the menu, should look for the set price meals, variously called *menu à prix fixe, menu touriste, menu special, menu exprès, menu conseillé, menu extraordinaire,* or *menu con- ventionne.* This will give you a choice of three or four courses at one price, and within each course you will generally have five to ten selections. Dining is much less adventurous with a fixed price menu, but a hell of a lot easier.

Then there's the pricing system. Some restaurants include taxes and service charge in the à la carte and fixed price menus, while others do not. They just tack it onto the end of the bill, a nice after-dinner shock. Look for the terms *prix nets, service compris* or *s.c.,* which all mean that service is included. Otherwise, be prepared for 15 per cent later. Some fixed price menus will also include drinks, so look for the terms *vin compris* or *boisson compris* or just *b.c.*

Another term you will see on many menus, often hand written, is *plat du jour.* This is the dish of the day, a special course often at a bargain price which is prepared that very day. Grab these up as quickly as you can, for the plats du jour are often fresh fish or game dishes you may not find elsewhere in Paris, and the quality is most often superb.

Our 'star' pricing system is based on how much one per- son will likely spend for a three or four course meal, plus wine and service. But please remember these are just general guidelines: you can often pay much more by ordering à la carte, and in some cases a little less with plats du jour and fixed price menus. Five-star (*****) restaurants are the top of the line at 200F (£16) per person and up, four-star (****) restaurants are 150-200F (£12-16), three-star (***) restaurants are 100-150F (£8-12), two star (**) restaurants 50-100F (£4-8) and one-star (*) restaurants 25-50F (£2-4) per person.

Eating hours in France are generally noon to 3 pm for lunch and 8 to 11 pm for dinner, although there are restaurants open until after midnight for the theatre crowd. No need to worry about tipping unless the service charge is not included in the bill (only likely in some one-star restaurants). In that case leave a standard 10-15 per cent.

Restaurants

● **1er   Les Halles**

Le Bayern Place du Chatelet; (tel: 233.48.44; metro: Chatelet).   ** A quaint little touch of Bavaria in the centre of Paris, good for a quick snack after the theatre or between treks to the Louvre and the Pompidou Centre. Among the delicious house specialities are Munich sauerkraut (50F) and a German wurst plate (38F), topped off with apfelstrudel (20F) for dessert. The menu also includes oysters and seafood. Bavarian orchestra provides the entertainment,and best of all, Le Bayern is open from noon until 3 am.

Caveau des Halles 17, rue des Halles; (tel: 236.16.17; metro: Les Halles).   *** Another of Les Halles good late-night places, open noon until 2.30 pm for lunch and 8 pm until 4 am for dinner. Among the house favourites are Escalope cordon bleu (F49), Selle d'agneau aux cepes (125F for two) and Boeuf cepes et moelle (115F). Menu: 115F.

Chez Didine 5, rue Berger; (metro: Les Halles).   * One of the best crêperies in Paris, whether you pick up something from the stand outside or come inside for a sit down. But the house speciality is Boeuf bourguignon for only 20F. Menus: 20F and 25F. Great for the backpacker's budget.

Aux Deux Saules 91, rue St Denis; (metro: Les Halles). *
Authentic Belle Epoque cafe/restaurant with pleasant outdoor seating and wooden tables on Les Halles' busiest street.
Good for people watching, but the food is excellent and
cheap. Eggs with chips (22-24F), omelette with chips
(16-20F), soups (6-12F) and a *menu promotional* (35F).

L'Escargot Montorgueil 38, rue Montorgueil; (tel: 236.83.51;
metro: Etienne Marcel). **** The famous 'Golden Snail',
a place of pilgrimage for those who delight in molluscs. Open
at the same Les Halles location since 1832. Among the snail
specialities are Escargots à la Bourguignonne (60F),
Escargots au curry, au Roquefort (60F) and Escargots à la
menthe (60F). But the E.M. also serves fish and fowl,
delicious items like Fricasse de lotte (anglerfish) and Turbot
Montorgueil. Other features are the restored Belle Epoque
interior and the superb service. Menu: 240F for two. Closed
Tuesday. Open 12.30 to 2 pm for lunch and 8 pm to midr·ght.

Front Page 56-56, rue St Denis; (tel: 236.98.69; metro: Les
Halles). ** Hang-out for newspaper groupies, old hacks
and homesick Americans. Trans-Atlantic specialities include
Chili con carne (30F), Chicken-in-a-basket (37F), T-bone
steak (60F), Barbecued pork (39.50F) and juicy hamburgers
(25-39.50F), served in an ambience of old newspapers, press
photos and checkered tablecloths. New York-style bar includes cocktails (20F) and Jameson's Irish Coffee (19.75F).
And don't forget the extensive ice cream menu. Open noon
until 2 am.

Mon Bar 3, rue Etienne Marcel; (tel: 236.18.68; metro:
Etienne Marcel). ** A ramshackle old bistro left over from
Les Halles market days, with a picturesque facade and a
classic Belle Epoque interior. The food is marvellous and
not expensive: Terrine of crab (24.50F), Terrine of duck
(17.50F), Beef provincial (45F), Navarin of lamb (51.50F),
Chicken with langoustines (51.50F) and Chitterling sausages
à la moutarde (39F). Menu: 78F. Closed Saturday night and
all day Sunday.

L'Escargot Montorgueil, the famous "Golden Snail" which is a place of pilgrimage for visitors who delight in garlic smothered molluscs.

Mother Earth's 66, rue des Lombards; (tel: 236.35.57; metro: Les Halles). ** The kind of place to make a Greenwich Village or Haite Ashbury dropout feel at home. Casual atmosphere and good Stateside cuisine like spare ribs (40F), meatloaf (39F), barbecued chicken (40F), lamb chops (40F), steak and baked potato (40F), hamburgers (20-39F), tacos (22F) and tostados (25F). For dessert try the apple pie (19F).

Au Petit Ramoneur 74, rue St Denis; (metro: Les Halles). * Casual and modest atmosphere for those on a tight budget, typical French cuisine. Menu: 35.50F.

Pharamond 24, rue de la Grande-Truanderie; (tel: 233.06.72; metro: Etienne Marcel). *** Classic French cuisine, both traditional and nouvelle, in a beautiful Belle Epoque setting. Consistently one of the best medium-priced restaurants in Paris. The house speciality is Tripe à la mode de Caen (actually prepared in Normandy), but other excellent dishes include Rognons d'agneau aux bacon (lamb kidneys with bacon) for 48F, fillet of veal for 60F and fillet of beef at 62F. Open noon to 2.30 pm and 7 to 11 pm. Closed all day Sunday, and Monday afternoon.

Au Pied de Cochon 6, rue Coquillere; (tel: 236.11.75; metro: Les Halles). *** Another of Les Halles' classic old restaurants, a relic of the bygone market days and a temple to the cuisine of pork. The list of pig delights is endless: Grilled pig's trotter in béarnaise sauce (43F), Piglet stew (48F), Stuffed trotter (54F), Stewed tripe (38F), Pig's head in Gribiche sauce (52F), Grilled chitterling sausage (43F) and the pièce de résistance, Tentation de St Antoine, a concoction of pig's tail, snout and trotter (53F)! For those who don't like pork there's also Trout with almonds (38F), Crêpes flambées au Grand-Marnier (51F for two), duck livers (55F) and caviar with toast (141F), plus oysters and other seafood from the stall out front. Fixed price menus: 80F and 105F. Open 24 hours a day, seven days a week.

La Poule au Pot 9, rue Vauvilliers; (tel: 236.32.96; metro:

Les Halles).   ** Late-night hangout in the heart of Les Halles. Fillet of beef à la moelle (70F) and Eggs cocotte à la crème (20F) are among the simple but delicious specialities. Open from 7 pm until 7 am. Closed Monday.

Restaurant Paul 15, place Dauphine; (tel: 354.21.48; metro: Cité, Pt. Neuf).   ** Old neighbourhood-style bistro on a historic square on the Ile de la Cité. Starters will cost you 18-20F and main courses 38-52F, with such specialities as Escalopè of veal à la papillotte (50F) and Quennelles de brochet à la Nantua. Closed Monday.

La Rose de France 24, place Dauphine; (tel: 354.10.12; metro: Cité, Pont Neuf).   ** One of the great new restaurants of Paris, a charming little place on the quiet Place Dauphine with one of the more interesting menus you will see in the city. The delights include Quennelles (fish purée rolls) in Nantua sauce (42F), White pudding roll with truffles served with creamed mushroom mousse (42F), Fresh duckling foie gras (48F), Normandy veal chops with cream sauce and cooked apples (49F), Spring cabbage stuffed with smoked breast of pork (42F) and Veal liver St Pol cooked with raspberry flavoured vinegar sauce and with artichoke puree (48F). A real taste treat; the menu is enough to make your mouth water!

● **1e   Louvre, Vendôme, Palais Royale**

Baryna 8, rue Gomboust; (metro: Pyramides).   *** Russian and Scandinavian delights in a small restaurant off the Place de Marche. Menu includes smoked Norwegian salmon (75F), smoked trout (70F), Iranian caviar (96F), Beef Stroganoff (75F), Chicken Kiev (65F) and Borsch Moscow (35F).

Bistro Hubert 36, place du Marché St Honoré; (tel:260.03.00; metro: Pyramides).   *** Nice little bistro with a big reputation on an old market square. Starters are around 62-110F, main courses 85-190. Among the recommended dishes are Veal escalope and Lobster fricassée. A bastion of nouvelle cuisine in the Belle Epoque atmosphere. Menu: 120F. Open noon to 2 pm for lunch and 7.30 to 10.30 pm. Closed Sunday and Monday.

La Ferme Irlandaise 30, place du Marché St Honoré; (metro: Pyramides). ** One of Paris's great new taste treats, specializing in Irish cuisine. Don't be put off by the bland reputation of Emerald Isle food, for Ferme Irlandaise will break any preconceived notions you have about Irish lack of imagination in the kitchen. Irish smoked salmon (48 and 69F), Potatoes with mushrooms (28F), Chicken with herbs in cream sauce (52F), Steak à la Guinness (60F) and Irish stew (59F), topped off with Irish coffee (30F).

Foujita 41, rue St Roch; (tel: 261.42.93; metro: Pyramides). ** Sushi in Paris? Why not? And what better place than chef Mitsuo Abe's sushi bar in the heart of Paris's rapidly expanding Japanese 'ghetto'. A tiny place with a cosy wooden bar. Sushis range 25-55F, Sashimis 20-50F and the selections include crab, cuttlefish, mackerel, octopus and shrimp. Open noon to 2.30 pm and 7 to 10.30 pm. Closed Sunday.

Grand Vefour 17, rue de Beaujolais; (tel: 296.56.27; metro: Pyramides, Palais Royale, Bourse). ***** Tucked back in one of the dark arcades of the Palais Royale, a Parisian gem in both decor and cuisine. They've been serving food on this spot since the 18th century, but the present establishment was opened in 1948 by super-chef Raymond Oliver. House favourites include Lamb chops Albarine, Red mullet Anne and Frog legs soufflé. Closed Saturday evening and Sunday.

Le Jardin du Louvre 2, place de Palais Royale; (tel: 261.16.00; metro: Palais Royale). ***** Chic, new restaurant in the same building as the Louvre des Antiquaries, thus a perfect place for a meal if the antique shopping starts to get you down. You can dine in the sun garden in the summer months or enjoy the Salon de thé during the afternoon (3 to 6 pm). Menu: 152F. Over 200F if you go à la carte. Open noon to 3 pm for lunch and 8 to midnight for dinner.

Lescure 7, rue de Mondovi; (tel: 260.18.91; metro: Concorde). ** Excellent but uncrowded restaurant on a backwater street off the Rue de Rivoli. On the same spot since 1919, and the prices don't seem to have gone up that much in all these years! Simple but delicious French cooking like Basque chicken (22.50F), Croquettes de volailles (19.30F), and Beef bourguignon (22.50F), plus English haddock (27.80F) for cross Channel types. Menu: 61.90F with service and drinks. Convenient location for visits to the Jeu de Paume or Place de la Concorde. Closed Sunday.

Louis XIV 1b, place des Victoires; (tel: 261.39.44; metro: Louvre, Sentier). *** Perhaps the best lunchtime girl-watching in Paris, thus Louis XIV is packed with stockbrokers, journalists and businessmen who want to get a glimpse of the sweet young things shopping at Kenzo, Thierry Mugler and Tokio Kumagai which are all nearby. The food is good too, Lyonnais specialities like Rabbit à la moutarde (60F), Goose with olives (125F for two), Fillet of turbot (68F), and an excellent selection of Beaujolais wines. Menu: 135F. You can dine in the fashionable upstairs salon or on pavement tables in the square. Open noon to 2.30 and 7 to 10 pm. Closed Saturday, Sunday and August.

Osaka 163, rue St Honoré; (tel: 260.66.01; metro: Palais Royale). ** Another one of Paris's expanding list of sushi bars, this one just off the Place André Malraux. The local Japanese eat here so it must be good. Sushi (65F), Sashimi (50F) and Tempura (50F). Menu: 110F. Open until 1 am.

Prunier 9, rue Duphot; (tel: 260.36.04; metro: Madeleine). ***** The city's most venerated seafood establishment, simple atmosphere but sumptuous cuisine. The house speciality is a bouillabaisse called Marmite Dieppoise, made fresh from the daily English Channel catch. Also on the menu are salmon (50F), scallops St Jacques (80-105F), mussels (35F), oysters (40-120F), Brittany clams (50F) and prawns (50F). Among the excellent non-seafood dishes are chicken curry, stewed duckling and veal chops with lemon. Pricey but superb. Open noon to 2.30 pm and 7 to 11 pm. Closed Monday.

Le Soufflé 36, rue du Mont-Thabor; (tel: 260.27.19; metro: Tuileries, Concorde). *** Reincarnation of the famous André Faure restaurant on this spot, concentrating on traditional French soufflés of just about any type. Among the selection are Escalope salmon soufflé (62F), Duck à l'orange soufflé (59F), Sweetbread of veal soufflé (62F) or simple cheese soufflé (33F). Dessert soufflés are 21-26F including service. Open noon to 3 pm and 7 to 10 pm. Closed Sunday.

● **2e Bourse Opéra**

Le Bistro Romain 9, boulevard des Italiens; (metro: Richelieu Drouot). **Italian nouvelle cuisine from the same folks who bring us the Bistro de la Gare and Assiette au Boeuf, and at rock bottom prices. No à la carte, rather several fixed menu choices including a 37.50F express menu in the afternoon and a regular 46.90 menu at night. Among the items to pick are Italian-style Fillet of duck, Jambon de Parme and a selection of desserts and sorbets by owner-creator Michel Oliver. Open daily from noon until 1 am.

Claude Brissemoret 5, rue St Marc; (tel: 236.91.72; metro: Bourse). ** Exquisite little hideaway near the Bourse frequented by stockbrokers; some of the best value food in Paris. Fixed menu at 60F includes choice of Pork chops with prunes, Chicken in Bordelaise sauce, Fillet of mackerel in mustard sauce, Guinea fowl, Rillons flambés in cognac and Terrine de jambonneau. Closed Saturday and Sunday.

Aux Crus de Bourgogne 2, rue Bachaumont; (tel: 233.48.24; metro: Sentier). ** An excellent selection of Bourgogne specialities at reasonable prices. Starters are 12-15F, main courses 20-55F, wine 40-65F. so you can easily get by on less than 100F. Special dishes include Coq Brouilly, fresh foie gras and Lobster in mayonnaise sauce.

Drouant Place Gaillon; (tel: 742.56.61; metro: 4 Septembre).
***** One of the grand old dames of Paris dining, serving
up haute cuisine for more than 100 years on this spot. The
grill is cheaper than the main dining room, which is less expensive than one of the private dinner salons available to
parties of two to 90. Snooty in a typically Parisian manner,
but you do get first class food for your money. The menu
includes Lobster thermidor (280F), Heart of fillet of beef
(140F), Duck with blueberries (200F for two) and Fresh
bananas in kirschwasser (33F) for dessert. Other dishes
include fillet of sole, sea bass, lamb kidneys and turbot in
a cream sauce. Menus: 120F and 195F. Open noon to 2.30
pm and 7 pm to midnight, every day.

Du Grand Cerf Passage du Grand Cerf at 145, rue St Denis.
(metro: Etienne Marcel).   * The best paella Valenciana this
side of the Pyrenees, and for only 35F! This little, out-of-
the-way restaurant specializes in Franco-Spanish food at
shoestring prices. Starters are 7-9F, plats du jour 12-19F and
a fixed menu 29F. Lots of locals, and starting to catch on
among the international backpacker set.

King Opera 21, rue Daunou; (tel: 260.99.89; metro:
Opera).   ** Brand new American hangout on the same
street as the famous Harry's New York Bar. Triples as an
eating house, show bar and jazz club in trying to recapture
50s America and the era of Elvis, Bogart, Gable and Monroe.
Barbecue spare ribs (52F), Chili con carne (33F), Arizona
lamb shish kebabs (63F), Atlanta barbecued chicken (53F),
plus California corn and T-bone steaks.

Lyonnaise 32, rue St Marc; (tel: 296. 65.04; metro: Bourse,
Richelieu Drouot).   ** The marvellous wooden facade of
this restaurant is a feast for the eye, and the food inside is
pretty good too, modest but delicious provincial cuisine like
pork sausages, tripe, poultry, freshwater fish and fish purée
rolls (quennelles). The speciality of the house is pork cooked in a variety of ways. Menu: 46.90F. Open 11.30 am to 3
pm for lunch (another stockbroker hangout) and 8 pm to

midnight for dinner. Closed Saturday and Sunday.

Le Montorgueil 58 rue Montorgueil; (metro: Sentier, Etienne Marcel). * Neighbourhood restaurant specializing in the cuisine of South West France and the Basque country. Among the delights are snails, paella, tripe, shrimps, mussels and Bayonne ham. The 31F menu makes it perfect for student and budget travellers.

Vaudeville 29, rue Vivienne; (tel: 233.39.31; metro: Bourse). *** The opposite of Louis XIV: perhaps the best man-watching spot in Paris seeing as it's across the street from the Bourse and French Press Association. An art deco-style brasserie which specializes in seafood dishes. Starters are 15-39F, main courses 29-98F. There's a seafood bar outside where you can purchase fresh oysters, scallops and foie gras. Menu: 46.90F. Open daily 11.30 am to 3 pm and 7 pm to 2 am.

Vishnou 11 bis, rue Volney at rue Daunou; (tel: 297.56.54; metro: Opera). ***One of Paris's up-and-coming Indian establishments, run in collaboration with the Centaur Hotel in Bombay. A real taste treat for Asian fans. The house speciality is Tandoori (32-85F), but you can also order Chicken biryana (55F) and various mutton dishes (48-62F), topped off by Lassi (a yoghurt drink with fresh cucumbers and mint), mango ice cream or Darjeeling tea. Menu: 110F. Open noon to 2.30 pm and 7.30 to 11 pm.

● **3e Upper Marais, Temple**

Ambassade d'Auvergne 22, rue du Grenier St Lazare; (tel. 272.31.22; metro: Ramuteau). *** A fantastic introduction to the hearty cooking of mountainous Central France, the Auvergne region, where they specialize in down-to-earth but delicous country cuisine. The menu includes Auvergne soup with cooked cabbage (65F), Stuffed cabbage mijoté (45F), freshwater fish (45F), a lentil and sausage stew called Cassoulet (65F), and a special Auvergne cheese plate (24F).

A choice of four dining salons with different decors. Open noon to 2 pm and 7.30 to 11 pm. Closed Sunday.

Les Jardins du Marais 15, rue Charlot; (tel: 272.08.65; metro: St Sebastian Froissart, Arts et Metiers). *** Bastion of nouvelle cuisine in the heart of the old Marais, and an after-dinner discotheque too. Three fixed menus to choose from at 39F (three course including service), 45F (four course including service) and 75F (four course with service and wine). On the menu are such delights as Rabbit à la catalane, Grilled lamb chops, Preserved duck, Artichoke leaves with prawns and Crab en chemise. Open 11.30 am to 2.30 pm for lunch and 7 pm to 5 am for dinner and dancing. Closed Sunday and August.

Nicoles Flamel 51, rue de Montmorency; (tel.272.07.11; metro: Rambuteau). *** Come for the medieval atmosphere or the excellent food. This auberge is housed in the second oldest (1407) building still standing in Paris, a wonderful old stone mansion that looks as if it could tumble over at any moment. Full of smoky windows, wrought iron, heavy wooden furniture, and beams. The 115F menu includes wine, service and your choice of dishes like Duck à l'orange, Basque scallops, lamb and beef. Huge helpings.

Porto 3, rue Dupuis; (tel:887.98.36; metro: Temple, République). ** Great little neighbourhood restaurant near the Marché du Temple, as yet undiscovered by tourists. Full of locals partaking of the delicious fish specialities like Fillet haddock (39F), Baltic herring (15.50), Russian salmon (49F), Smoked mackerel (14.50F) and Norwegian salmon (57F). Inexpensive wines and chocolate mousse (9F) for dessert. Menu: 36F and 52.50F.

● **4e   Lower Marais, Vosges, Beaubourg**

Bofinger 5, rue de la Bastille; (tel. 272.87.82; metro: Bastille). *** Possibly the most beautiful restaurant in Paris if you enjoy the Belle Epoque style. Bofinger is an authentic Alsatian brasserie founded in the 1860s, still resplendent with wrought iron lace curtains, shiny brass rails and knobs, mirrored walls and a brilliant stained glass ceiling. Visions of Toulouse-Lautrec and Renoir! Chef de cuisine René Schweri has created an excellent menu based on the German-inspired food of the Alsace, which translates into hearty servings and down-to-earth tastes. Try the grilled salmon or sole (both 65F), the Steak tartar, the Pork Strasbourgeoise, or some Choucroute (sauerkraut) with Alsatian sausages. Plats du jour: 52F and 60F. Menu: 115F with wine. New Orleans-style Dixieland jazz several nights a week. Open daily noon to 3 pm and 7.30 pm to 2 am.

Chica 71, rue St Martin; (tel: 887.73.57; metro: Rambuteau, Chatelet). ** One of Paris's quickly expanding list of Brazilian restaurants, a new and unusual taste treat for the gastronomic capital. Best to start with a black bean and meat stew called Feijoada (65F) and then graduate to Xinxin chicken (65F), Tongue of beef (65F) and Angua-a-Bahiana, a concoction of beef heart, liver and kidney (56F). Fish dishes too. Menu: 70F. Brazilian samba and bossa nova.

Coconnas 2 bis, place des Vosges; (tel: 278.58.16; metro: Bastille, St Paul, Chemin Vert). *** Classic French cuisine in Louis XIII surroundings on the oldest square in Paris. Good place to break a tour of the Marais, and the baroque atmosphere alone is worth a visit. Claude Terrail (who also owns the famous Tour d'Argent restaurant) has transformed Coconnas into one of Paris's exquisite dining pleasures. The 150F menu gives you choices like Escargots à la bourguignonne, Duck salad, Panache of chicken with vegetables and beef. Open 12.30 to 2 pm and 7.45 to 10 pm. Closed Monday, Tuesday and Christmas.

Goldenburg 7, rue des Rosiers; (tel: 887.20.16; metro: St Paul). ** Jewish delicatessen and retaurant in the heart of Paris's old Jewish Quarter, the kind of place you find in New York or Vienna. New menu each day with selections like

113

herring, caviar, matsa, foie gras, borsch, goulash, carp, with Israeli wines. Plats du jour: 40F and 50F. Continuous service 11 am to midnight.

Ma Bourgogne 19, place des Vosges; (tel: 278.44.64; metro: Bastille, St Paul, Chemin Vert). ** An old-fashioned café specializing in Burgundy-style food and the excellent wines of both Burgundy and Beaujolais. Pavement tables with a good view of the action in the place. Among menu items are Lamb chops (42F), Sauerkraut (40F), Saucisson (warm sausages) chanel de Beaujolais (40F) and Andouillettes (chitterling sausages) (35F).

Mary's Restaurant 9, rue de Turenne; (tel: 272.67.98; metro: St Paul). ** Vegetarian and health food specialities in a cosy, homely setting. Masterminded by English expatriate Mary, the menu includes delicious vegetable tarts. Dinner or lunch will cost you 40-50F with drinks. Open noon to 2.30 pm and 7 to 10.30 pm. Closed Sunday.

L'Oree de Marais 29, rue des Francs Bourgeois; (tel: 887.81.70; metro: St Paul). ** Fantastic red facade and little wooden tables, an old style brasserie wedged between all those ancient mansions in the heart of the Marais. A local restaurant little patronized by tourists. Choice includes Veal escalope Savoyarde (52F), Chicken flambé à l'Armagnac (52F), Confit of duck (55F) and Baron of lamb (49F). Menu: 47F. Good value for money.

Au Tibourg 29, rue de Bourg Tibourg; (tel: 278.57.44; metro: St Paul, Hotel de Ville). ** An excellent little Greek taverna tucked away on a side street off the Rue de Rivoli; convenient for the cluster of youth hostels located five minutes away. Interesting interior of old posters, gadgets and trophies. Greek feta cheese salad (25F), Moussaka (40F), Beef ribs à la Kalymos (140F), plus retsina wine (40F) to wash it down. Closed Sunday and Monday.

Le Trumilou 84, quai l'Hotel-de-Ville; (tel: 277.63.98; metro:

Hotel de Ville). ** Old fashioned neighbourhood brasserie, bar and café on a busy quay overlooking the Seine. If you sit outside in the summer you can see the central spire of Notre Dame and the Pantheon dome. Don't be fooled by the simple decor, for Le Trumilou's cuisine is anything but plain: Chateaubriand filet de boeuf (58F), Duck with prunes, Entrecote minute (48F), Croquette of rabbit, and veal. Menu: 41.20F and 55F with service.

● 4e   Ile de la Cité, Ile Saint Louis

Brasserie de l'Ile Quai d'Orléans at Rue Jean-du-Bellay; (tel: 354.02.59; metro: Pont Marie).   ** The famous Belle Epoque brasserie and bar just off the Pont St Louis on the tip of Ile St Louis. A sunny, happy place with a regular lunch time crowd. Don't miss 'Big Bertha', the huge, antique coffee machine at the end of the bar. Typical brasserie food like omelettes (13-19F), paté (16-20F) and English haddock (55F). Serves continuously from midday until 1.30 a.m. Closed Wednesday.

La Colombe 4, rue de la Colombe; (tel: 633.37.08; metro: Cité).   **** One of Paris's romantic hideaways, the perfect restaurant for honeymoon couples, dirty weekends in Paris or any people in love. 'The Dove' is located in one of the city's oldest buildings, a Gothic house built in the 13th century and occupied for seven centuries by a tavern. Since 1924 it's been owned by the Valette family who have transformed it into one of the most sumptuous dining experiences in France. Classic French cuisine with menus at 96F and 165F. Eat on the flowered terrace during the summer, or enjoy the Baroque music inside. Open 12.30 to 2.30 pm and 7.30 to midnight. Closed Sunday, at lunchtime on Monday, January 1st to February 23rd and August 11-22nd.

Au Gourmet de l'Isle 42, rue St Louis en l'Ile; (tel: 326.79.27; metro: Pont Marie).   ** Simple but delicious specialities from the Auvergne-Limousin region of central France, dispensed from a cosy 17th century 'cave' setting. A long-time bastion of St Louis locals now being discovered by tourists. You can get fillet fish for 42F, or the house speciality, chitterlings and other sausages, for 42F and up. Menu: 80F. Open noon to 1.45 pm and 7 to 9 pm. Closed Monday, Thursday and August.

Nos Ancêtres les Gaulois 39, rue St Louis en l'Ile; (tel: 633.66.07; metro: Pont Marie). *** For the person with a ravenous appetite; they really feed you at the 'Ancient Gauls'. The fixed price menu of 112F includes service, all the wine you can chug down, and a whopping six courses, two of them all you can eat. One must remember that the ancient Gauls were heavily influenced by the Romans, for whom the term 'orgy' really meant a gargantuan feast. That's exactly what you get here. Specializes in grilled game and delicious lamb dishes. Strolling guitarists for your dinner entertainment. Open 7 pm to 2 am. Closed Christmas and New Year.

● 5e   Left Bank, Latin Quarter

Abelard 1, rue des Grand Degnes; (tel: 329.16.46; metro: Maubert-Mutualité). *** Excellent new bastion of nouvelle cuisine on a tiny street off the Quai de la Tournelle. 'A singularly good restaurant which gives me hope for nouvelle cuisine' according to one food reviewer. Chef Claude Jean and owner Stefan Wenta have created an interesting menu which includes Oriental red mullet, Lamb chops de sisteron, and rhubarb or peach sorbet for dessert. Menus: 65F and 120F for lunch, 59F and 140F for dinner plus 15 per cent service. View of Notre Dame and the Seine from the upstairs windows.

Au Beaujolais 19, quai de la Tournelle; (tel: 033.67.74; metro: Maubert-Mutualité). *** Specializing in the cuisine of Beaujolais and Macon in central France, including good pork and poultry dishes, and house favourites like Veal liver Lyonnaise. Starters about 15-26F, fish courses 22-35F and meat courses 38-90F. Needless to say, a good selection of Beaujolais wines. Closed Monday and August.

116

Auberge 'In' 32, rue de Cardinal Lemoine; (tel: 326.43.51; metro: Cardinal Lemoine). * New expensive vegetarian fare in the heart of student Paris. Among interesting menu items are Andalusian gazpacho, omelettes, vegetable salads and paté, and a good variety of fruit. Menu: 40F. Good for a quick snack in the afternoon. Open 10 am to 3 pm and 6 to 11.30 pm.

Les Balkans 3, rue de la Harpe; (tel: 326.20.96; metro: St Michel). * A comfortable little restaurant in the Latin Quarter's pedestrian area with an emphasis on Hungarian food. Roast lamb (24F), Couscous (32-38F), Shish kebab (29F), and Hungarian goulash (23F). Menu promotional: 35F inc. service. Closed Wednesday.

Dodin Bouffant 25, rue Frederic-Sauton; (tel: 325.25.14; metro: Maubert-Mutualité). **** Chef and owner Jacques Manière has created some of the most unusual and interesting dishes in Paris at this highly regarded house of nouvelle cuisine. The speciality is seafood, kept alive in special seawater tanks in the basement. Among the dishes are Fricasséed salt cod à la Provencale (45F), Roast Breton lobster (price varies according to availability), Sole soufflé with mushrooms (85F), Roast partridge with cabbage (120F) and a frog special called Blanquette de grenouilles (80F). Oysters are available year round. Open 12.30 to 2 pm and 8 pm to 12.45 am. Closed Saturday, Sunday and August.

My Vi 6, rue des Ecoles; (metro: Maubert-Mutualité). * Good Vietnamese food for those on a tight budget. Menus at 24.50F and 34F give you a choice of Crab soup with asparagus, Imperial Vietnamese paté, Vietnamese ravioli, Duck with bananas, Beef curry, Pork with bamboo shoots, Ginger chicken, and lychees. Open for lunch and dinner.

Au Pactole 44, boulevard St Germain; (tel: 633.31.31; metro: Maubert-Mutualité). **** Left Bank standby of classic French cuisine in a romantic atmosphere. A popular Parisian hangout where reservations are a must. Starters run

38-96F, while the main fish and meat courses are in the 80-90F range. Among interesting fare are the lamb tongue salad (Langue d'agneau), goose liver paté (Terrine de foie gras) and duck sausages (Andouillettes de canard). Menu: 135F including service. Open noon to 3 pm and 7.30 to 11 pm. Closed Sunday and for Saturday lunch.

Aux Savoyards 14, rue des Boulangers; (tel: 633.53.78; metro: Jussieu, Cardinal Lemoine).   * Student-style restaurant near the Facultés des Sciences, this modest little bistro concentrates on the fine food of Savoy. The 40F menu includes service, wine and a choice of marvellous dishes like chitterling sausages, potted pork, duck paté and steak de cheval (horse steak — popular in France). Good place for student and shoestring budgets. Open noon to 2.30 pm and 7 to 10.30 pm. Closed Sunday and holidays.

Le Tire-Bouchon 47, rue Descartes; metro: Place Monge).   * Another informal, inexpensive but tasty bistro, popular with students and locals but little known by outsiders. Menus at 38F, 46F and 50F include drinks and choice of items such as paté, crêpes, steak with chips, pork chops and scallops. But the house favourites are the Savoy-style fondues from the French Alps: Fondue bourguignonne (45F) and Fondue savoyarde (42F).

La Tour d'Argent 15, quai de la Tournelle; (tel: 354.23.31; metro: Maubert-Mutualité).   ***** The supreme dining experience of the Left Bank and one of the top five restaurants in Paris. Owner Claude Terrail has transformed the Tour into a bastion of impeccable service, romantic atmosphere (the sixth floor penthouse overlooks Notre Dame and the Seine), sumptuous decor (Dresden china at every table) and fantastic cuisine in the classic French tradition. The house speciality is duck, prepared in 16 different manners including the famous Caneton, or pressed duckling, for which each customer receives a certificate stating the duck's official number! Other dishes include Fricasséed lobster, Fillet of sole Cardinal and Chicken broth soup. Menu: 195F without

118

wine or service. Expect to pay over 400F à la carte. Open 12.30 to 3 pm and 8 to 10.30 pm. Closed Monday.

● 6e Left Bank, Saint Germain, Odeon

Assiette au Boeuf 22, rue Guillaume Apollinaire; (tel: 260.88.44; metro: St Germain). * Yet another of Michel Oliver's chain of fast and fine French cuisine, this one specializing in beef. A somewhat overdone and modernised Belle Epoque decor, which tends to rake in the tourists and turn off the locals. But the food is hard to beat for the price: 37.90F for L'Express and 46.90F for the regular menu. The first and second courses (walnut salad and steak with chips) are fixed, but you have a good selection of Oliver's own creations to choose from for dessert. Don't forget to tack on 15 per cent service and drinks when figuring your dinner budget. Open noon to 3 pm and 6 pm to 1 am. Other Assiettes are at 123, avenue des Champs-Elysées (9e); 720.01.13; metro: Georges V; and at 103, boulevard du Montparnasse (6e); metro: Vavin.

Beaux Arts 11, rue Bonaparte; (tel: 326.92.64; metro: St Germain). * Perhaps the most famous cheap restaurant in Paris, and certainly one of the best. A Rive Gauche landmark under the direction of Chef L. Cochennec. There's a 39.50F set menu which includes wine and service, but be more daring and try some of Beaux-Art's inexpensive à la carte dishes. Chateaubriand (38F), Rabbit (32F), Salmon in hollandaise sauce (34F), Fillet of beef (42F), Escargot (17F or 34F), Sautéd chicken (28F) and Artichoke hearts (13F). Closed Monday and August.

Les Byzantins 33, rue Dauphine; (tel: 326.47.85; metro: Odeon). ** Perhaps the most delicious moussaka and Greek salads in Paris. This is a tiny restaurant and it's always packed, testament to the quality of both service and food. The menu also includes tasty kebabs and lamb dishes, plus other Mediterranean specialities. The kind of place to make you feel like you've wound up in Ios instead of Paris. Be sure to check out the two-headed falcon in the window. Menu: 45F.

Aux Carpentiers 10, rue Mabillon;(tel: 326.30.05; metro: Mabillon).   ** Another St Germain cheapy with excellent cuisine. The ambience is cosy, the food is hearty French country cooking. Among menu items are Roast duckling (38F), Beef à la ficelle (52F), Chitterling sausages (38F), Grilled pigs' trotters à la Ste. Menehould (24F) and Black pudding à l'Artisanal (26F). Plats du jour cost 30-33F. Once a gathering place of workmen, now a student retreat. Open noon to 2.30 pm and 7 pm to midnight. Closed Sunday.

Aux Deux Dragons 24, rue Monsieur Le Prince; (tel: 354.66.73; metro: Odeon).   * Tiny but excellent Chinese and Vietnamese restaurant popular with students and young Parisians. The staff are fast and friendly, the food inexpensive and good. Menu: 35F. Open daily noon to 2.30 pm and 7 to 11 pm.

L'Ecluse 15, quai des Grands Augustin; (tel: 633.58.74; metro: St Michel).   ** You can walk past l'Ecluse without a blink, first because it's got such a narrow facade, second because you are usually gazing up at Notre Dame at this point along the Seine. So tiny, yet so good. What's the old saying: 'Good things come in small packages?' It's a perfect label for this wine bar cum restaurant. Among the fabulous cold plates are Jambon San Daniele (38F), Smoked salmon (65F), Roquefort cheese à la cuillère (25F), Dried sausages (22F) and Dried meat à la Bresaola (38F). Plats du jour: 70-90F. Bordeaux is the house wine and there's an excellent selection. Open noon to 2 am. Closed Sunday.

La Méditerranée 2, place Odeon; (tel: 326.46.75; metro: Odeon).   **** One of the great seafood restaurants of Paris, located opposite the Odeon Theatre on a quiet square. Dine on the romantic outdoor terrace under the blue and white veranda, or in the sumptuous upstairs salon. The clientele has traditionally included many theatre people and jet-setters. They come for both the atmosphere and the exceptional

120

cuisine: Seafood bouillabaisse (160F for two), Escalope of John Dory (90F), Brochette of anglerfish (65F), Haddock Salad (55F), Scallops St Jacques with walnuts (90F), and Seabass garnished with crescent-shaped pastries (90F). Menu: 170F including wine. There is no better Provençal and French Mediterranean restaurant in Paris.

La Nouvelle Marinara 46, rue Dauphine; (tel:326.45.94; metro: Odeon). ** Simple but delicious Italian restaurant with a warm ambience and earthy decor. The service is quick and friendly, the waiters making you feel like you've eaten there every day of your life. A good range of pizzas, spaghetti, salads and other pasta dishes. For a yummy, filling and inexpensive meal, try the Spaghetti carbonara (35F) and the Chef's salad (18F). Menus: 46F and 56F. Open until midnight and usually bustling with after theatre and cinema crowds.

Restaurant Osteria de Passe 20, rue de l'Hirondelle; (tel: 634.14.57; metro: St Michel). *** New and little-known Italian restaurant on a tiny street off the Place Saint Michel, what must surely rate as one of the most romantic of Left Bank dining places. It's very small with simple tables, candlelight and a warm, family atmosphere. The menu features gorgeous Italian haute cuisine dishes and changes daily. Expect to pay 100-150F per person for a full course meal plus wine and service.

Petit Zinc 25, rue de Buci; (tel: 354.79.34; metro: Mabillon). *** A flavour of old Paris, situated in the heart of the Buci market and specializing in seafood. The outdoor terrace offers some of the best people-watching in town, but the 'Little Bar' is even more renowned for its food. Choose from Salmon cru (48F), Anglerfish à la Florentine (65F), Fillet of seabass (65F), Fillet of rascasse (hog-fish) (60F) or tiny Soles meunière, in a sauce of butter, parsley and lemon juice (65F). Petit Zinc also has oysters and foie gras. After dinner head for the Furstemburg jazz and piano bar downstairs. Service is continuous from noon to 3 am, thus

Zinc is a favourite watering hole of the Left Bank late-night crowd. Open every day.

Pizza Navona Trattoria rue St André des Arts at rue Git-le-Coeur; (metro: Odeon). * Even in Paris you get a desire for Italian food and Navona is a great place to find it. Take your choice of pizza for 18.50 to 29F or spaghetti for 20.50 to 25.50F. They also have delicious fetuccine (24.50F) and ravioli (27F), but the speciality of the house is lasagne (25.50F). Italian salads are 12.50 to 25F and there are also fish, eggs and cheese dishes, plus Italian ice cream. Open daily noon to 2.30 pm and 7 pm to midnight.

Polidor 41, rue Monsieur-le-Prince; (tel: 326.95.34; metro: Odeon). * One of the Left Bank's oldest and best bistros, a lovely restaurant frequented by artists, writers and students for half a century. The interior is a sort of neighbourhood Art Deco style. Lots of brass, glass, lace and wood, but far less conspicuous than the Art Deco found along the big boulevards. Polidor is downright homey, the food absolutely superb for the price. For starters try the Escargots (28F per dozen), perhaps the cheapest snails in Paris. Or you might want to sample the extensive list of French cheeses at 6-8F per plate: Brie, Camembert, Bleu de Bresse, Roquefort, Cantal, Chèvre and Blanc, to name just a few. Meat or fish courses around 20-38F. Menu: 33F. Open noon to 2.30 pm and 7 to 10 pm. Closed Sunday, Monday and August.

Le Procope 13, rue de l'Ancienne-Comédie; (tel:633.69.71; metro: Odeon). ** Paris's oldest restaurant and café, operating on the same site since 1686. Procope's clientele has included such notable figures as Napoleon, Voltaire, Victor Hugo, Ben Franklin, Balzac, Robespierre and Danton before their executions, and the great playwright Molière, who lived just down the road on Rue Mazarine. The café's name derives from the Italian who founded the place, while the street is named after Molière's Comédie-Française, which drew crowds until evicted in 1770. Today, Procope sports an

18th century interior of mirrors, gilt woodwork, blood red upholstery and glass chandeliers. A bit antiquated compared to the trendy places on the remainder of Ancienne-Comédie but forgivable given the historical significance of the place. The 65F set menu doesn't include wine or service, but it gives you a choice of mouth-watering dishes like Roast duck with cherries, Lamb kidneys, Brochette of Pork with prunes or Beef bourguignon. If you're not in the mood for food, stop by Procope for coffee or a glass of wine just to soak up some of the history and add your name to the list of famous who have entered here.

Le Texel rue Christine; (metro: Odeon).   * Filling and inexpensive Tunisian food, although the quality does suffer somewhat and the service isn't always great. But what can you expect for the price? The 29F Tunisian menu gives you three courses with several selections in each category. I would recommend the Salad Tunisian followed by a Couscous brochette, with a North African pastry for dessert. Aperitifs are only 6F, while a half litre of wine costs 10F. There is also a 29F French menu for those with less exotic tastes. Guaranteed to fill your tummy!

Au Vieux Paris 2, rue de l'Abbaye; (tel: 326.21.92; metro: St Germain, Mabillon).   ** Popular Greek bistro also known as Chez Nico. You may have to wait awhile for a seat, but you won't be disappointed with the cuisine. Among house favourites are the special Chicken kebab (41F), Donner kebab (45F), Moussaka (40F), Calamari flambés (44F), and Lamb chops (45F). Menu: 43F including wine and service, so Vieux Paris is a real bargain hunter's delight. Closed Monday.

● **7e   Saint Germain, Invalides**

L'Archestrate 84, rue de Varenne; (tel: 551.47.33; metro: Varenne).   ***** An intimate setting on a quiet street near the Musée Rodin. This elegant restaurant is now regarded as the climax of nouvelle cuisine in Paris. Chef and owner Alain Senderens trained at the famous Tour d'Argent and then broke off to form his own eating palace, experimenting with new concepts and dishes which push l'Archestrate into the realm of avante garde dining. Nothing else like it in Paris, but expect to pay at least 400F per person for the extravagance. Among the specialities are Foie gras with cabbage, Asperges sauvages with broad beans, Baked turbot, as well as lobster, scallops, duck, pigeon and beef dishes. Open noon to 2.30 pm and 8 to 10 pm. Closed Saturday, Sunday and three weeks in August.

L'Auberge Basque 51, rue de Verneuil; (tel: 548.51.98; metro: Bac, Solferino). ** Tiny bistro specializing in the food of South West France which makes a good and inexpensive break from shopping in the rue du Bac area. And the Louvre and Tuileries are just across the Pont Royal. On the menu are fresh Salmon à l'oseille (65F), Scallops St Jacques (55F), Anglerfish à l'anis (45F), Crêpes Basquaise (25F) and omelettes with seafood, ham and à la Basque (20-25F).Menu: 75F not including wine or 15% service.

Le Baobab 7, rue de l'Université; (tel: 261.20.88; metro: Bac). ** New African-style restaurant with an interesting and well-rounded menu, serving the nearby international diplomatic quarter. The cuisine seems to represent all of the continent: Senegalese beef (44F), Nigerian curry (46F), Congolese chicken (44F), Couscous (42-48F), Ivory Coast mutton (46F) and Cape Verde rice with seafood (48F).

Le Bistro de Paris 33, rue de Lille; (tel: 261.16.83; metro: Solferino). **** The first and probably the best of Michel Oliver's chain of delightful Parisian bistros. This is the place young Oliver opened after he left the tutelage of his father at the Grand Vefour restaurant at the Palais Royal. The cuisine is a compromise between nouvelle and classic French, which means the best of both worlds, with the menu changing daily to encompass various new Oliver creations. Try any of the various sherbets — another Oliver speciality — for dessert. The wine list is also interesting, featuring a good selection of Beaujolais, Côtes de Brouilly, St Amour,

Château Poujeaux and Châteaux Soutard. Closed Saturday, Sunday and August.

La Chaumière 35, rue de Beaune; (tel: 261.26.09; metro: Bac). *** Pleasant neighbourhood restaurant serving excellent food in what the owners term a 'rustic' atmosphere. You might start off with the rabbit paté and then progress to main dishes like Chateaubriand in Béarnaise sauce (58F), Veal Grenadin with peaches (52F) or Fricasséed scallops with sole à la Chaumiere (60F). Amazing food for the moderate prices. Open noon to 2.15 pm and 7.30 to 10.15 pm. Closed Saturday, Sunday and August.

Chez les Anges 54, boulevard Latour-Maubourg; (tel: 705.89.86; metro: Latour-Maubourg). **** You rarely find great food on the big boulevards, but Chez les Anges is a noteworthy exception. Specializes in the fine food of Burgundy. Chef and owner François Benoist has created an attractive menu which includes Soufflé à la Mirabelle and Soufflé with Cointreau (35F), Pigeon with green cabbage (95F), Entrecote au Mercury (78F) and Canette of seabass with exotic fruits (150F for two). Fresh fish every day including turbot, salmon, scallops and seabass. And as expected, a good selection of Burgundy wines. Menu: 140F not including 15% service. Open noon to 2.30 pm and 7 to 10.30 pm. Closed Sunday afternoon and all day Monday.

Aux Cinq Pains d'Orge 29, rue Surcouf; (tel: 705.86.31; metro: Invalides, Latour-Maubourg). *** Newer restaurant in a quiet area which serves up *grande cuisine française* in intimate surroundings. The house forte is fresh seafood: salmon, anglerfish, turbot, sole, crayfish and especially lobster. But the menu also features Chicken cooked in a whiskey sauce (50F), Veal livers with raisins (60F), plus roast pork and leg of lamb. Extensive dessert list. Menu: 60F and 100F not including wine or 15% service. Open noon to 2.30 pm and 7 pm to midnight. Closed Wednesday.

Chez Germaine 30, rue Pierre Leroux; (metro: Vaneau). *

For those on a backpacker's budget: good, wholesome food in a working class bistro. Main dishes are 15-25F and there's a 25F fixed menu including service. Closed Saturday and Sunday.

Le Petit Laurent 38, rue de Varenne; (tel: 548.79.64; metro: Bac, Sèvres-Babylone). *** Italian haute cuisine by chef Luigi Menegale in a new and popular restaurant off the Rue du Bac. Reservations a must. Possibly the best Italian food in Paris. Among menu delights are Fettucine al basilico e pomodoro (42F), Tagliatelle alle noci (49F), the Ravioloni allo chef (49F) and Zuppa de frutti di mare (42F). Menu: 120F including wine and service. Closed Sunday.

● **8e   Champs-Elysées, Rue Royale**

La Boutique à Sandwiches 12, rue de Colisee; (tel: 359.56.69; metro: Roosevelt).   * If you must eat fast food this is certainly leagues better than the hamburger joints around the corner on the Champs-Elysées. A paradise for sandwich connoisseurs with nearly 50 varieties. The Boutique was first made popular by an article in the Herald Tribune, so it's been an American hangout for the past decade. But the French also crowd in. On the menu are sandwiches of Hungarian salmon, Portuguese tuna, mussels, crevettes, anchovies, veal, pork, ham, chicken, beef, cheese and an Alsatian corned beef called *pickelfleisch*. Prices are 8-10F per sandwich. Try the apflestrudel for dessert. Alsatian owners Claude and Hubert Schich have made this an inexpensive and quick taste treat. Open until 12.30 am. Closed Sunday.

Fouquets 99, avenue des Champs-Elysées; (tel: 723.70.60; metro: George V).   **** Not known so much for its traditional French cuisine as the fabulous history and Belle Epoque decor. Lots of brass, lace curtains and stained glass, as well as a clientele of movie stars, international jet-setters and other celebrity types. Best to dine on the pavement terrace and watch all the world pass by. Expect to pay at least 200F for a full dinner. Open noon to 2 pm and 7 pm to midnight.

Closed Sunday and Monday.

Chez Germain 19, rue Jean-Mermoz; (tel: 359.29.24; metro: Roosevelt, St Philippe)   ** Unpretentious little place in a very pretentious neighbourhood, with the emphasis on hearty home cooking. Among the specials are Veal chops with creamed mushrooms (30F), Grilled mutton chops (28F) and Escalope panée spaghetti (28F). Plats du jour: 30-40F. Open until 11 pm. Closed Sunday.

Chez Vania 25, rue Royale, in the Passage Cité Berryer; (metro: Madeleine).   *** Russian haute cuisine in the exotic atmosphere of a dark passageway off the Rue Royale. The daily specials include Goulash Moscovite (Monday), Paprika St Petersburg (Wednesday), Coqueret Caucasien (Thursday) and Bitoch de Kazan (Saturday). Also on the menu are Borsch à la crème (25F), Pirojoh (30F), Beef stroganoff (70F) and caviar (150F). Menu: 70F not including wine or service. Good value for money. Open until half past midnight for after-theatre meals. Closed Sunday.

Copenhague 142, avenue des Champs-Elysées; (tel: 359.20.41; metro: George V).   */**** Actually two restaurants: the lavish Copenhague indoors and the Flora Danica sandwich boutique in the garden. Together, they offer Paris's best Scandinavian fare. Copenhague offers such delights as smoked fish and Danish duck, with a full meal around 150-250F. Danica has open sandwiches, smorrebrod and Danish beer for under 50F, plus an 85F fixed menu. Both are open noon to 2.30 pm for lunch and begin serving dinner at 7 pm, but Flora Danica closes one hour later than Copenhague at 11.30 pm. Copenhague is closed Sunday and August, but Danica is open seven days a week all year round.

Au Jardin du Printemps 32, rue de Penthievre; (tel: 359.32.91; metro: Miromesnil).   *** Chinese and Vietnamese nouvelle cuisine in a simple but elegant atmosphere. Quickly becoming *the* Asian restaurant on the Right Bank. Crab leg curry (70F), Canton duck (58F), the delicious sounding Poulet ananas, a chicken and pineapple dish (38F) and Sauteed shrimps with shredded mint. Menu: 75F including service but not wine. Open noon to 2.30 pm and 7.30 to 11.30 pm. Closed Sunday.

Lasserre 17, avenue Franklin D Roosevelt; (tel: 359.53.43; metro: Roosevelt Clemenceau).   ***** Another of the Paris top five, a luxurious maison serving the best of French haute cuisine. The most elegant decor in the city, the salons dripping with silk, crystal, porcelain, silver, Rubenesque murals and Louis XVI furnishings. And the roof of the main salon is rolled back in good weather to expose diners to either the afternoon sunshine or the evening stars, a coup de grâce of Paris romance. As expected, service is impeccable and the cuisine is out of this world. Among the house specials are Duck à l'orange, Baked fillet of sole with a crustacean sauce, and Red mullet à la cuisson de moules. Don't expect to get out for under 350F. Piano music for your dining entertainment. Open 12.30 to 2.15 pm and 7.30 to 10.30 pm. Closed Sunday, Monday and August.

Le Moulin du Village 25, rue Royale in the passage Cité Berryer; (tel: 265.08.47; metro: Madeleine).   *** Co-owned by Briton Steve Spurrier and American Chuck Scupham, which makes this a meeting place of the English-speaking community in Paris. It's located on a quiet pedestrian street off the rue Royale, perfect for outdoor dining in the summer or a romantic interlude at any time of year. Cosy and comfortable. Chef Marc Bertin creates an enticing menu which changes daily. Among the specialities are Mussel soup (35F), Haddock salad with walnuts (45F), Escargot à la bourguignonne (45F), Fillet of veal mignon (82F), Sole meunière (84F) and rump steak (78F). The owners also run the Paris Académie de Vin, so you can imagine the extent and variety of the wine list. Could be Paris's best food at a medium price. Closed Sunday and August.

Ma Bourgogne 133, boulevard Haussmann; (tel: 563.50.61; metro: St Augustin, Miromesnil).   ** Sister to the little café in the Place de Vosges, this brasserie and wine bar is popular with the lunchtime business crowd in this area. The daily specials are 50F each and include Beef bourguignon (Monday), Chitterling sausages (Tuesday), Pork stew with cabbage (Wednesday), Coq au vin (Thursday) and Fish purée rolls (Friday). The wine list includes a good selection of Beaujolais, Burgundies and Loire Valley labels. Menu: 90F including service but not wine. Open for lunch and until 8.30 pm in the evening. Closed Saturday and Sunday.

Maxims 3, rue Royale; (tel: 265.27.94; metro: Concorde). ***** Recently described as 'a mind-blowing trip down memory lane', Maxim's is still the most famous restaurant in Paris. The history goes back to the turn-of-the-century when Maxim's was a haunt of Parisian high society and a young Prince of Wales, the future King Edward VII of England. It passed into cinematic history as the location of scenes from *Gigi* and *The Merry Widow*, and even now it's popular with visiting film stars and dignitaries. The decor is still scrupulous Belle Epoque and art nouveau with stained glass ceilings, shiny brass fixtures and floral designs. The food is said to have declined somewhat in the 70s, and Maxim's even lost a star in the Michelin book. But when Pierre Cardin took over in 1981 he changed the focus from traditional French fare to nouvelle cuisine, hired new personnel and once again put Maxim's among the Paris best. Specialities include Fricassee of sole and crayfish, Duckling with raspberry sauce and Crêpes veuve joyeuse. Expect to pay at least 400F per person. Champagne is the house drink, formal wear on Friday and the Maxim's orchestra for entertainment. Open 12.30 to 2.30 pm for lunch and 7.30 pm to 1 am for dinner. Closed Sunday.

Taillevent 15, rue Lamennais; (tel: 561.12.90; metro: George V, Etoile). ***** Yet another bastion of grand nouvelle cuisine in the 8th district, situated in a historic town house off the Avenue Friedland. The building dates from 1862, but the decor is decidedly Louis XVI: posh, pedantic and intimate. This restaurant isn't as well known as others in its

129

class, but word is that Taillevent's food is amongst the best for its price. Main fish courses run 96-206F, the meat courses 78-210F. Among menu items are Duck livers (116F), Lobster with paté fraiche (120F), Pigeon with green cabbage (110F) and Lamb kidneys (210F), as well as a Seafood truffle with pistachio nuts, Lobster à l'estragon and the house speciality, Seabass with blackcurrants. There are over 500 types of wine in the cellars, most notably 1846 vintage Château Laffite-Rothschild. Expect to pay 250-350F per person. Open 12.30 to 2 pm and 7.30 to 10.30 pm. Closed Saturday, Sunday and August.

● 9e Opéra, the Boulevards

Le Bistro de la Gare 38, bouelvard des Italiens; (tel. 246.15.74; metro: Richelieu Drouot).   ** A fastfood version of nouvelle cuisine at prices anyone can afford, thanks once again to the creative imagination of Michel Oliver. The formula is thus: for 37.50F (express menu) or 46.50F you can choose from any one of three entrées and three main courses. But wine will cost you at least 30F extra, and don't forget to add the service charge. The service is fast and good, but the waiters are a little more pedantic than is necessary. Lots of old photos on the walls, but the overall impression is that le Bistro is trying too hard to emulate the Belle Epoque. The house speciality is beef: veal escalope in lemon sauce, entrecot steaks and the like. But I prefer the roast duck with chips. Enormous ice cream and dessert menu (extra money once again) and a few good wines. Overall, great value for price, but too plastic. The other Bistros de la Gare are at 73 Champs-Elysées (8e), 59 Blvd. Montparnasse (6e), and 30 Rue St Denis (1e). Open noon to 3 pm and 6 pm to 1 am, every day.

Café de la Paix Place de l'Opéra at Blvd. des Capucines; (tel: 260.33.50; metro: Opéra).   *****/** One of the most famous cafés on the Right Bank, this old Belle Epoque masterpiece was restored in 1976 and is now listed as a historic monument. The design is by Charles Garnier, the same man who built the nearby Opéra, one of the classic examples of lavish art nouveau. Now the Café is two restaurants catering to two different crowds: the Restaurant Opéra is expensive and top-of-the-line, specializing in haute cuisine; the Relais Capucines serves up *cuisine rapide* for the tourist in a hurry. Expect to pay 250-300F at the Opéra, 80-100F at the Relais, where you can actually get a beer for 12F. Not renowned for its food, so you are basically paying for the atmosphere, and the right to sit at the same pavement tables as Fitzgerald, Hemingway, Oscar Wilde and others who've come this way. The Opéra is open noon to 3 pm and 7 to 11 pm; closed August. The Relais serves continuously from noon to 1.15 am every day of the year.

Cartier 7, rue du Faubourg-Montmartre; (tel: 770.86.29; metro: Rue Montmartre).   * Not to be confused with the diamond people, this Cartier is one of the best cheap restaurants in Paris, perfect for the bargain basement budget. And best of all, you even get to dine in authentic Belle Epoque surroundings from the 19th century. Good variety and excellent food for under 50F. Mecca of American and Canadian backpackers, always busy. Open every day of the year.

Casa Miguel 48, rue St Georges; (tel: 281.09.61; metro: St Georges, Notre Dame de Lorette).   * *Passion* magazine calls this the 'best budget chow' in Paris, a claim that's not hard to dispute when you discover you can get a three-course meal for 5F at Casa Miguel. That's right: 5F. Nothing fancy, and a little out of the way, but who cares at that price. Open noon to 1 am for lunch every day and 7 to 8 pm for dinner every day but Sunday. Get there on time.

Haynes 3, rue Clauzel; (tel: 878.40.63; metro: St Georges).   * Another 9th district cheapy, this time specializing in good old American soul food. The menu includes Southern fried chicken, spare ribs, coleslaw, apple pie, corn on the cob, chili con carne and sweet potato pie. You can easily eat well for under 50F, but reservations are usually a must. Open 8 pm to 1 am. Closed Sunday and Monday.

● 10e   Strasbourg — Saint Denis, Gare du Nord

Brasserie Flo 7, cour des Petites-Ecuries; (tel: 770.13.59;
metro: Château d'Eau).   *** Jean-Paul Bucher's famous
Alsatian brasserie on a tiny market street off the Rue du
Faubourg St Denis, one of the most popular medium range
restaurants in Paris. The brasserie dates from the turn-of-
the-century when it was a well known *traiteur*.

Bucher took over in 1979, renovated the mahogany panels
and leather-bound booths, and transformed Flo into a
habitual loitering place of the chic and famous. The house
special is a mouth-full in both name and content: La for-
midable choucroute Paysanne (85F), a sauerkraut, bacon,
ham and sausage delight for two. For the less hungry there
is the Choucroute spéciale (39.50F), as well as onion soup,
fish with sorrel, foie gras, guinea hen and other Alsatian
dishes. And even if you're not hungry, come in for a Kronenbourg beer (brewed in Alsace) just to check out the
mahogany bar and the Belle Epoque interior. Menu: 96.80F.
Open noon to 3 pm and 7 pm to 1.30 am every day.

Julien 16, rue du Faubourg St Denis; (tel: 770.12.06; metro:
Strasbourg St Denis, Château d'Eau).   *** Another of
Bucher's collection of classic restaurants, this one with
authentic 1890s decor, some of the most amazing art
nouveau in Paris. The cuisine is *francaise bourgeoise* or
home cooking, and Julien is famous for its delicious soups.
But the house special is Cassoulet d'oie à la Castelnaudary,
a bean stew with goose meat and sausage (54F). Also on
the menu are fresh foie gras and scallops. Plats du jour:
45-54F. Great dessert menu. Open noon to 3 pm, 7 pm to
2 am every day.

Terminus Nord 23, rue de Dunkerque, opposite the Gare
du Nord; (tel: 285.05.15; metro. Gare du Nord).   *** Yet
another Bucher masterpiece, this time in the art deco style
of the 1920s with marble walls, mirrors and waiters in

tuxedo and floor-length aprons. A real classic, packed with Parisian commuters and business types. Like Flo, this is an Alsatian style brasserie with specialities like sauerkraut and foie gras. Also known for its seafood, especially the fresh oysters and the Escalope of salmon à l'oseille. Prices similar to Flo and Julien, so expect to pay 100-150F for an à la carte meal. Menu: 80F and 96F. Open from 11 am until 2 am with continuous service.

● 11e   Popincourt

Le Repaire de Cartouche 8, bouelvard des Filles-du-Calvaire; (tel:700.25.86; metro: Filles du Calvaire).   *** A bastion of tasty South West cooking and Basque cuisine in a little-explored neighbourhood just north of the Marais. It's a bit off the beaten track, but worth it for the food. The 70F set menu gives you a choice of Paté Basque à l'armagnac with prunes, Sautéed beef à la moutarde de Meaux, Fillet of chicken forestière, Bayonne ham, Smoked breast of duck and Pyrenees cheese. Inexpensive wines at 22F. A quiet, cosy place in a working class district. Open noon to 2 pm and 7 to 10 pm. Closed Saturday, Sunday and August.

● 12e   Bastille, Gare de Lyon

La Tour d'Argent 6, place de la Bastille; (tel: 344.32.19; metro: Bastille).   ** The other Tour, this one more affordable for the student and backpacker budget. If you're on a budget and want just one delicious splurge in Paris, this is an excellent place. Downstairs is a typical Parisian brasserie and grill, while upstairs is a classic Belle Epoque salon overlooking the square. The speciality is fresh seafood (and you know it's fresh from the seaweed and kelp littering the kitchen floor!) like Mussels in cream (29F), Smoked Norwegian salmon (85F), Salmon with vegetables (38F), trout (41F) and Bouillabaisse (29F), as well as oysters, Fillet of sole meunière and a seafood kebab cooked on a skewer. Service continuous from 11.30 am until 1.30 am. Closed in August.

Le Train Bleu 20, boulevard Diderot at the Gare de Lyon; (tel: 343.09.06; metro: Gare de Lyon). **** Opened in 1899 as the station restaurant for the Gare de Lyon and still considered the classiest railway café in the world. As Train Bleu itself likes to point out: 'dans le decor classé Belle Epoque, le plus somptueux de Paris.' Hard to dispute, and the place is even protected as a national monument. The cuisine is classic Lyonnaise, delights like freshwater fish, poultry, tripe, fish purée rolls, frog legs, sausages and cheese. You'll pay 120-180F for a full meal. For real contrast, dine at Train Bleu before whisking off to Lyon at 300 km/hour (200 mph) on the TGV. Open 11.30 am to 2.30 pm and 6.30 to 10.30 pm every day.

● 13e   Place d'Italie

Chez Francoise 12, rue de la Butte-aux-Cailles; (tel:580.12;02; metro: Place d'Italie, Corvisart). ** Excellent and inexpensive restaurant in a district which is void of good places to eat. The atmosphere is rustic, the cuisine is traditional French. Among the ten house specials are Anglerfish with green peppercorns, Duck cooked in apple cider, and Peaches à la Francoise. Menu: 36F and 69F inc. service. Open noon to 2.30 pm and 7 to 10.30 pm. Closed Sunday, Saturday lunch and August.

● 14e   Montparnasse

La Creole 122, boulevard du Montparnasse; (tel: 320.62.12; metro: Vavin, Edgar-Quinet, Port Royal, Raspail). ** Antilles specialities with live West Indian music. Among the arousing Creole menu items are Langoustines with Chinese sauce (120F), Fricasseed chicken (36F), Antilles-style steak (40F), and Creole-style shrimp (60F). Menu: 55F. Open until 2 am nightly except Sunday.

Crêperie de Pont-Aven 52, rue du Montparnasse; (metro: Edgar-Quinet). * Brittany style crêpes on a little street which is packed with cosy crêperies bretonnes, and surprisingly undiscovered by tourists. The crêpes range from 5-12F, while galettes (flaky pastry puffs) are 5.27F and chocolate mousse 9.50F. If you don't like the menu here try the half dozen other Brittany places up the road. Open noon to 2.30 pm and 6.30 to 1 am.

Kabouki 9, rue de la Gaîté; (tel: 320.04.78; metro: Edgar-Quinet, Gaîté). ** A bit of a surprise to find a fine maison of Japanese cuisine on such a sleazy street. Kabouki is a Japanese restaurant rather than strict sushi bar, which means a greater selection of Oriental delights. It's run by American expatriate ballerina Helene Constantine. Among menu items are Sukiyaki, Shrimp tempura, Sushi, Soy bean curd and Japanese-style eggplant. Expect to pay 30-40F per dish. Open from 7 pm to 1 am. Closed Sunday.

Le Pouilly 96, rue Daguerre; (tel: 322.60.18; metro: Gaîté). * Crowded, rustic neighbourhood bistro near the Montparnasse cemetery. The menu is not extensive — paella, couscous and a few beef items — but the helpings are ample and the prices are right (34-37F for main courses) for the student and backpacker budget. Good value for money, but the place is often packed with locals so get there early. Open until 9 pm. Closed Sunday and August.

Rehana 33, rue Delambre; (tel: 322.63.45; metro: Vavin, Edgar-Quinet). ** The great thing about this Indian restaurant is you can have a fantastic meal and then go and buy all the ingredients at the Rehana-owned store across the street. Specializes in tandooris, curries and kebabs. Main courses run 23-64F. Open for both lunch and dinner. Closed Sunday.

● **15e   Montparnasse**

Olympe 8, rue Nicolas-Charlet; (tel: 734.86.08; metro: Pasteur). ***** Rapidly gaining a reputation as one of the best nouvelle cuisine establishments in Paris. It's run by two women: master brain Eve Ruggieri who comes up with the recipes, and master chef Dominique Nahmias, who is the first female to be awarded three chef's hats by Gault-Millau. Together, they've written four excellent nouvelle cuisine cookbooks including *Une grande cuisine toute simple*. The decor is 1930s Paris, the food simply exquisite. Take a sample: Pigeon with honey (125F), Noisettes of lamb (120F), Veal kidneys with lemons (128F), Smoked duck (115F), Duck soup with chives (135F), Goose liver paté (120F) and Ravioli stuffed with duck and served with broccoli (68F). Open 8 pm to 2 am. Closed Monday.

● **16e   Trocadero, Victor Hugo, Etoile**

L'Ile de France Quayside, 32 avenue de New York; (tel: 723.60.21; metro: Iena, Trocadero). ***** A floating restaurant nestled on the north bank of the Seine between the Pont d'Iena and Pont Debilly. Superb view of the Eiffel Tower and the skyscrapers downstream at Issy. If the weather is nice you can dine on deck. Some of the best (and most expensive) traditional French cuisine in Paris. The menu includes Smoked Baltic salmon (85F), Caviar Ossetra (30 grams for 240F), Filet mignon of veal (72F). Menu: 140F for brunch and 190F for dinner, excluding 15% service.

Vivarois 192, avenue Victor Hugo; (tel: 504.04.31; metro: rue de La Pompe). ***** Not your classical French restaurant in any way, shape or form. Rather, an unobtrusive facade you can easily pass by, ultramodern furnishings and equally contemporary cuisine of the nouvelle variety. In just over 15 years, chef and owner Claude Peyrot has managed to earn three Michelin stars and the respect of food connoisseurs around the world. The menu changes daily with such treats as Bavarois of sweet peppers in a light tomato sauce (66F), Curried oyster chowder (115F), smoked salmon (92F), fresh foie gras (103F), Coq à la Pommard (89F), and Chicken with tarragon à la Bressane. Finish off with one of the wonderful desserts like Mousse de cassis (37F). A full dinner can easily run to 350F per person. Closed Saturday, Sunday and from mid July to end August.

Winston Churchill 5, rue de Presbourg; (tel: 500.75.35; metro: Charles de Gaulle/Etoile). ** Just like the corner pub back home, the Winston Churchill is a meeting place of British tourists and local businessmen. And it's a delicious and inexpensive alternative to the fast food joints along the nearby Champs-Elysées. Dark, woodsy Edwardian interior with outdoor seating in the summer. Best bet is the real English breakfast served daily 8 to 11.30 am which includes corn flakes or porridge, bacon and eggs, toast with marmalade, plus tea, hot chocolate or coffee. For lunch or dinner you can have roast beef (51F), leg of lamb (42F), or English haddock (42F), semolina cake with chocolate, cheddar and Roquefort cheeses with biscuits. If you're in a hurry, you can get any of the food at a special take-away counter. Watney's, Churchill Brown Ale and Winston Red Barrel to wash it all down. Open daily until 12.30 am.

● **16e   Bois de Boulogne**

Auberge de Bonheur Allée de Longchamp, near the Grand Cascade; (tel: 772.40.75; metro: Port Dauphine, Ranelagh). ** A good restaurant in the Bois de Boulogne we common folks can actually afford. Excellent French country cooking, by sunlight and blue sky in the garden for lunch, or by candlelight in the salon for dinner. Mostly grilled items, costing about 50F for lunch and 100F for dinner. Open noon to 2.30 am.

La Grande Cascade Bois de Boulogne, near the Carrefour de Longchamp and the imitation waterfall of the same name; (tel: 506.33.51; metro: Port Dauphine, Ranelagh). **** Grand French cuisine in the confines of a miniature château built by Baron Haussmann as a private hunting lodge for Emperor Napoleon III in the days when the Bois was still the royal hunting preserve. It was converted into an eating place in the 1890s and still retains its fabulous art nouveau interior with stained glass ceiling and wrought iron lamp posts. You also have the choice of eating in the garden to the sound of the nearby Grand Cascade itself. Expect to pay at least 200F for lunch or dinner. Open 12.30 to 2.30 pm for lunch and 7.30 to 10 pm. Closed December 22 to January 23.

Le Pré Catelan-Lenotre Rue de Suresnes, Bois de Boulogne; (tel: 524.55.28; metro: Porte Dauphine).   ***** Nouvelle cuisine served in one of the most romantic and beautiful settings in Paris. The Pré Catelan is a leafy area of huge trees where a famous court minstrel was murdered in the 14th century. The restaurant is run with a superb touch by caterer Gaston Lenotre, who offers such menu items as Goose liver with asparagus. Menu: 200F for lunch and 300F for dinner. You can dine indoors or in the lovely garden terrace. Open noon to 2 pm and 7 to 10 pm. Closed Sunday night and Monday.

● **17e   Maillot, Etoile, Wagram**

L'Etoile Verte 13, rue Brey, (tel: 380.69.34; metro: Ternes, Charles de Gaulle/Etoile).   * An excellent and inexpensive restaurant where you wouldn't expect to find one, on a quiet residential street off the Avenue de Wagram. Frequented by knowing locals but few tourists. The menu runs the gamut: Hungarian goulash, hamburgers, steak, Chinese food, fish, duck, chicken, veal and spaghetti, plus an enormous selection of hors d'oeuvre, desserts and salads. Plats du jour: 22-45F. Menus: 21F with 10% service and 35F with wine. Fantastic value for money. Service continuous from 11 am until midnight. Convenient for those visiting the Arc de Triomphe or the Champs-Elysées.

La Mère Michel 5, rue Rennequin; (tel: 763.59.80; metro: Ternes).   *** A delicious Breton grill known to 17th district locals but few outsiders. The house speciality is fish served with the amazing Beurre blanc Nantais, a white butter sauce (75F). Also on the menu are fresh grilled salmon (80F), Scallops St Jacques (80F), and veal kidneys (78F). The dessert menu is also tasty, things like Banana flambée with Cointreau (27F) and Michel's own soufflés (60F for two). Out of the way, but worth the trek in terms of both culinary

138

and monetary value. Closed Saturday and August.

Relais de Venise 271, boulevard Pereire (metro: Porte Maillot). ** An excellent old standby in Paris's most rapidly expanding visitor area (Palais des Congrès, Hotel Meridien, Hotel Concorde, Air France Terminal). A sunny, comfortable place tucked around a corner from the Gare Maillot. Famous for its ribs, but there's also a good cheese and dessert menu. Menu: 49.50F excluding service and wine. Excellent food for the money, Open for lunch and dinner.

● **18e Montmartre**

Au Grain de Folie 48, rue la Vieuville; (tel: 258.15.57; metro: Abbesses). * Superb little vegetarian restaurant owned and operated by a couple of American expatriates. The atmosphere is San Francisco circa 1968 and the crowd is mostly international (British, American, Scandinavian, Dutch, German). Not too many tables so get there early. The best of the house are the vegetable tarts (spinach, leek or courgette) and the marvellous fruit juices (apple, raisin, orange and carrot). Servings are more than enough to fill, but if you have room for dessert try the apple crumble. Menu: 38F for three courses. A litre of house wine runs 30F extra. Open 7 to 10 pm nightly.

Lionel 26, rue Yvonne-Le-Tac; (tel: 606.20.51; metro: Abbesses). ** 'In praise of an honest menu' says *Passion* magazine of this new restaurant on the Butte, a tiny place with the cosy atmosphere you expect to find in Montmartre. Owner and maître Gilbert Lecointe runs something of a combination between classic French cooking and nouvelle cuisine, nothing fancy, but certainly delicious and great for the price. The 100F set menu gives you a choice of at least four dishes for each course, and among recommended dishes are Veal escalopes à la mandarine, Sauteed Anglerfish, Veal liver in a cider vinegar sauce, and cheese soufflé. Try the chocolate mousse for dessert. Open 7.15 pm to midnight. Closed Sunday.

Au Grain de Folie in Montmartre is one of Paris's best new restaurants, a vegetarian establishment with some of the tastiest meals in town.

Le Vieux Chalet 14 bis, rue Norvins; (tel: 606.21.44; metro: Abbesses). ** An excellent and surprisingly untouristy restaurant in the middle of Montmartre's obnoxious tourist quarter. There's a courtyard and garden in the back where you can dine safely away from all the snapping cameras, portrait artists and postcard hawkers. The Chalet specializes in cuisine provençale from the deep south of France: roast chicken (29F), veal escalope (42F), lamb chops (50F), fillet of beef (55F), Chicken niçoises (42F), and Confit de canard (60F). Menu: 57F inc. service. Plats du jour: 29-60F. Open for lunch and from 7.30 pm for dinner. Closed Sunday evening and Monday.

CHAPTER SIX

Where to drink

Whenever I leave Paris and travel to another city, I always regret the fact that the rest of the civilised world hasn't caught on to the idea of the French café. Sure, the café isn't even a French invention, It was pioneered in baroque Vienna and only accepted by the French at a later date. But no other people have so refined the concept of café, and ultimately turned it into what is perhaps the most civilised institution on earth.

Stated simply and without attention to the subtle nuances, a café is a place to sit around and drink coffee. But in Paris the cafés are much more. They are the city's foremost social institution, the gathering place of neighbours, friends and business associates, a function not unlike that of Britain's pubs or America's bars. They are a place to get a delicious breakfast, a quick lunch (and in some cases a sumptuous full-course meal), have a drink after work or a quick nightcap after the theatre. They are places to watch people, write a postcard, play pinball machines and video games, or even propose marriage. And they are places not only for coffee, but also for cool beer in the heat of July, or hot chocolate in the cold of January. They are all-encompassing, and they are everywhere — hundreds spread throughout Paris on seemingly every street corner!

Everyone wants to go to the famous cafés — places like

the Deux Magots and Café de la Paix — on their first visit to Paris. That's fine, but you will pay a lot more for the same drink, the same ambience and often inferior service compared with the little neighbourhood cafés without an overseas reputation. There is also a scale of prices according to where you decide to plant yourself in the café. You pay less at the bar than at tables, and less at the indoor tables than those on the pavements. And proper café etiquette is to run up a bill and then pay as you leave. Usually a 15 per cent service charge is added, but if not leave 10-15 per cent on the table for the waiter.

The food at Parisian cafés ranges from downright horrid to cordon bleu. Those which open for breakfast will have a selection of fresh-baked croissants and other pastries, plus jam, butter, fresh fruit juice, hot chocolate, coffee and tea. Those who want coffee should take care: if you want milk with your cup say *café au lait*. Otherwise you will get straight black coffee of the expresso variety. Many cafés also offer crêpes in the morning.

Lunches are a bit more adventurous on the café scene. Some of the famous establishments offer excellent three-course meals, tourist menus and plats du jour. But every café has at least open sandwiches, paté and cheese. Lunch is served between noon and 3 pm, so if you get there late forget the food.

But some people go to cafés for the drinks. There's the usual run of coffee, tea, chocolate, milk and soft drinks. Or you can opt for the ever-popular beer or wine. French beer has taken a lot of flack in the past for being amongst the worst in Europe. However, this situation has been largely remedied by Kronenbourg, the blond-coloured beer from Alsace, a province which used to belong to Germany and which has obviously picked up the Teutonic skill for brewing beer. The house wines are generally average, but most cafés also stock a selection of vintage bottles.

There are also aperitifs and liqueurs like Cognac, Campari, Dubonnet, Calvados (apple brandy), Pernod and the liquorice-flavoured Pastis, which is often consumed with water and ice as a kind of French version of ouzo.

The best thing about cafés, however, is the fact you can stay forever. Even if you buy only a cup of coffee or a simple beer, the waiter will not disturb you all day. Now that is civilised!

Paris's second most popular drinking establishment is the bar, something adapted from the Americans, although not necessarily what you might find on the other side of the Atlantic. Many of Paris's bars advertise themselves straight out as a classic 'bar Americain', which means they serve up stiff drinks and good doses of American-style cocktails in an atmosphere of dark wood and shiny leather. Many of the best bars in Paris — like the world-famous Harry's — were actually started by and for expatriate Americans. But the Parisians themselves have become American bar fanatics, and many of the city's rich and trendy have their regular watering holes. American bars have actually hit Paris in three ways: the old wave of the 1920s and 30s with such classic places as Harry's and Rosebud; the middle wave of the 1950s and 60s which saw a flowering of slicker-type establishments like Joe Allen's and Conway's; and the new wave of the 1980s with its earthy Californian-Mexican bars like Cactus Charly and Mother Earth's.

The other great bar fad in Paris is the wine bar, something that the wine-drinking French also had to import from overseas, in this case from the English. These are establishments which specialize in certain types of wine, and in which you can actually purchase wine by the glass rather than the bottle, as is customary in France. The advantage is obvious, for you can taste many types of wine in one session, perfect for people with a rudimentary education in wine who have no idea what varieties they might enjoy. Paris's wine bars have quickly become 'très trendy', especially with young up-and-coming professionals. And the casual, friendly ambience makes the wine bars easier for meeting people than the more formal cafés and American bars.

Paris also has its fair share of British-style pubs, mostly for students and expatriates. Most of them have at least one British beer on draught (usually Guinness) and many have a good selection of traditional British bar food.

Another of the drinking place fads to hit Paris in the past decade is the *salon de thé* (tea room). But unless you go to W.H. Smith's, don't expect anything like Victorian high tea. These are an outgrowth of the earthy sixties, the flowerchild culture which put such great emphasis on natural teas and healthy food. But most of the tea salons are far cries from Fortnums or Haight-Ashbury. They offer a variety of delicious teas, pastries and other sweets, served up in a casual and comfortable ambience that might remind you of your grandmother's sitting room. Prices are moderate to cheap, and many of the goodies are on sale for your later consumption at home.

Lastly, for you sweet-tooths, we have listed some of Paris's better ice cream establishments. The French are less famous for their milk-based ice cream than for their *sorbet* or sherbet; tasty fruit-based water ices in a variety of interesting flavours.

Bars

● Right Bank: Les Halles

A La Cloche des Halles 28, rue Coquilliere, 1er; (tel: 236.93.89; metro: Les Halles). Under the big bell (hence the name) at the intersection of Rue du Louvre, a wine bar and café specializing in the grapes of Beaujolais, Burgundy and the Loire. Great corner location for people-watching.

Conway's New York Bar 73, rue St Denis, 1er; (tel: 233.22.86; metro: Les Halles). Traditional American-style bar and restaurant with cocktails, beer, wine and spirits, plus yummy Yank food like spare ribs, burgers and baked potatoes. Casual atmosphere and friendly crowd. Sunday brunch for 70F, one of the best trans-Atlantic breakfasts in town. Open nightly until 2 am.

Le Diable des Lombards 64, rue des Lombards, 1er; (tel: 233.81.84; metro: Les Halles). Neon and palm tree decor, with

145

a trendy (some say plastic) clientele. A 90F menu and burgers for 31-38F. Good for a late afternoon rendezvous, but bring your agent and business manager. The kind of place for a serious discussion over a piña colada. Service continual from noon until 12.30 am.

Front Page 56-58, rue St Denis, 1er; (tel: 236.98.69; metro: Les Halles). The least precocious of Les Halles American bars, with a casual, friendly clientele and hometown atmosphere. You can watch the crowds on St Denis from the terrace outside, or enjoy your drink from the long bar inside. A wide range of cocktails and whiskies for 20F a go, draught Guinness at 14.35F and Jameson's Irish Coffee for 19.75F. For those who get hungry there are burgers (25-39.50F), chili con carne (30F), t-bone steaks (60F), barbecued pork chops (39.50F), chicken in a basket (37F), and an extensive ice cream menu. Best of all, you can get food or drink continuously from noon to 2 am.

Joe Allen 30, rue Pierre-Lescot, 1er; (tel: 236.70.13; metro: Les Halles, Etienne Marcel). Don't be put off by the rather cool facade. Joe's is perhaps the most American of Paris's American bars in terms of atmosphere, clientele and reputation. There's a long, wooden New York-style bar, red and white checkered table cloths and celebrity photos on the walls. The customers are chic, trendy and usually rich, out to make a score or a reputation. And the drink prices are naturally sky-high. Typical American bar food (burgers, salads, ribs, etc.) at higher prices than Les Halles other US hangouts. Open nightly until 1 am. Lounge lizards will feel at home.

Kouikett's 35, rue Etienne Marcel, 1er; (metro: Etienne Marcel). Casual and unpresumptuous wine bar and salon de thé left over from the old Les Halles market days. Mostly frequented by local business types, traders and workmen. Not many trendies or tourists at Kouikett's. Aperitifs are 6-25F, liqueurs 22-40F and cocktails 25-30F.

Blue Fox Bar is run by a dynamic duo of American and English wine experts, which makes it a natural Anglo-American meeting place, but the local French are also starting to catch on to its delights.

● Right Bank: Louvre, Opéra, Madeleine

Le Blue Fox Bar 25, rue Royale in the Cité Berryer passage, 8e; (tel: 265.08.47; metro: Madeleine). One of the best new wine bars in Paris, run by Briton Steve Spurrier and American Chuck Scupham in conjunction with Le Moulin du Village restaurant next door. This dynamic duo also own the Académie de Vin, where you can learn the ins and outs of the grape business and purchase some of the wines you sample at Blue Fox. No wine bar on earth could have a more romantic location: a quiet passage off the Rue Royale with quaint wooden tables and well-worn cobblestones. Blue Fox was an instant Anglo-American gathering place, but the French are starting to catch on! Blue Fox serves 15 wines by the glass and there are four daily specials. Service is continuous from 11 am to 10 pm. Closed Saturday evening, all Sunday and August.

Harry's New York Bar 5, rue Daunou, 2e; (tel: 261.71.14; metro: Opéra). Paris's most famous bar, dispensing from 'sank roo doe noo' since 1911. In the 1920s and 30s Harry's was a staunch American hangout frequented by diplomats, musicians, actors, playboys and literary types. And among the clients have been George Gershwin, F. Scott Fitzgerald, and Ernest Hemingway, who is largely responsible for Harry's world-wide reputation. The decor is straight out of the American heartland: college football pennants, sports and celebrity photos, long wooden bar and the ubiquitous piano. The kind of place where you wanna buy a round of drinks for the boys and shout out 'Play it again Sam!' Harry's is the headquarters of the International Bar Flies, and the place where such cocktails as the Bloody Mary (1921) and Sidecar (1931) were invented. The cable address, in fact, is 'Cocktail Paris'. Open every day of the year except Christmas from 10.30 am to 4 am, but eat before you go to Harry's because they only serve hotdogs.

Le Jeroboam 8, rue Monsigny, 2e; (tel: 261.21.71; metro: 4 Septembre). The place with the burgundy facade, as if you

148

couldn't tell this was a wine bar by the aroma drifting down the street. Bordeaux red wines are the house speciality, but there's also a good selection of Beaujolais, Côtes du Rhone, Loire, Alsace, Bourgogne, Champagne, Bordeaux whites, port and sherry. A good place for beginners to experiment and taste. Lunchtime watering hole for stockbrokers and journalists. Closed Saturday and Sunday.

Le Rubis 10, rue du Marché St Honoré, 1er; (metro: Pyramides, Tuileries). Universally hailed as the finest wine bar in Paris, a fixture at the corner of Marché St Honoré and St Hyacinthe since 1949. Wine bars must also get better with age, for Le Rubis has a warm and friendly atmosphere which is lacking in some of the city's newer establishments. The place is packed with local workers at lunch and after office hours, insiders who know the excellence of Le Rubis's wines and food. House specialities are Beaujolais, Bordeaux, Muscadet and Sancerre. Serves from 7 am to 10 pm. Closed Sunday, Saturday and August.

Le Twenty One 21, rue Daunou, 2e; (tel: 260.40.51; metro: Opéra). A promising new American bar and jazz club in conjunction with the King Opera Restaurant next door. Le Twenty One features continuous music, including live sessions by American and Brazilian jazz musicians. If you get hungry, there's always a dish like chili con carne (33F), barbecued spare ribs (52F) or lamb shish kebabs (63F). Open from 9 pm to sunrise.

Willi's 13, rue des Petits-Champs, 1er; (tel: 296.37.86; metro: Bourse, Palais Royale). 18, rue des Halles, 1er; metro: Les Halles). A new, cosy, neighbourhood-style wine bar run by young Englishman Mark Williamson (alias Willi). He specializes in Côtes du Rhone, but offers over 150 varieties including Bordeaux reds and whites, Alsatian, Vallée de la Loire, Provence, Beaujolais, Bourgogne reds and whites, Cognac and even a few good Californian wines. Prices range from 42F for a bottle of Cabernet de Touraine 1981 to 400F for a Château St Pierre 1970. Simple, rural decor heavy on the wood; a clientele composed of stockbrokers, journalists and Anglo-Americans. Open from noon to 9 pm.

● **Right Bank: Marais, Beaubourg, Ile de la Cité**

Cave Dégustation 1, rue Théodore Roussel, 11e; metro: Ledru Rollin). A true neighbourhood wine bar and cellar unknown to most of those outside the 11th arrondissement. The place reeks of old oak barrels and fermenting wine, and you can hardly get in the front door given all the casks.

Guinness Tavern 31, rue des Lombards, 1er; (metro: Chatelet). Why be Guinnless in Paris? At this British style pub, just off the Boulevard de Sebastopol near Les Halles and the Pompidou Centre, there's piano music nightly, plus live folk, jazz and rock from America and Britain on Monday, Tuesday and Thursday nights. Needless to say, the Tavern has Guinness on draught. The right place to make a forlorn English or Irish traveller feel at home. Open 6 pm to 4 am.

Helium 3, rue des Haudriettes, 3e; (tel: 272.81.10; metro: Rambuteau). It's hard to categorize Helium. Half the time it looks like it isn't open, the other half it's bursting with people. The weekend brunch (three course; 11 am to 3 pm) puts it firmly in the American category. But the afternoon (3 to 7 pm) tea-time gives it an English flavour. And there's music and video entertainment every night. Something for everyone. The brunch is 49F and includes a choice of such un-Parisian delights as bacon and eggs, corn flakes, eggs Benedict, tuna and potato salads and bagels with cream cheese. Tea includes pastries, chocolates, ice cream and finger sandwiches. And there's a good selection of the usual wines and spirits. Finally, the occasional photo exhibit gives Helium a gallery touch. Helium's lip-licking cocktail list includes strawberry and banana daiquiris, piña coladas, strawberry margaritas, mezcalito mandarines and brandy Alexanders.

Henry IV 13, place du Pont-Neuf, 1er; (tel: 354.27.90; metro: Pont Neuf). One of Paris's oldest and most famous wine bars, situated on a sunny corner of the Place du Pont-Neuf. It's named after King Henri IV, who commissioned the nearby Place Dauphine in 1607 and who laid the final stones of the Pont Neuf (the oldest surviving bridge in Paris) in 1604. There is a bronze equestrian statue of Henri IV across the street, and the building in which the tavern is located dates from that 1607 project. Henri's wine list includes Beaujolais, Muscat, Bordeaux, Val de Loire, Bourgogne and Champagne, and there's a good choice of cold foods at lunch. Everything is very reasonably priced, and Henri IV is perhaps the best wine bar for students and shoestring travellers. Open 11.30 am to 9.30 pm. Closed Saturday, Sunday and August.

La Tartine 24, rue de Rivoli, 4e; (metro: St Paul). Another of Paris's old time wine bars, heavy on the Belle Epoque decor and famous for its wide selection of fine wines. This part of the Marais is a heavy ethnic neighbourhood, and many of the local Italian and Greek immigrants drop by for a drink of La Tartine. And before the war, Tartine was a meeting place of young and hungry political exiles like Lenin, Trotsky and Tito. The future of European Communism was mapped from its dark and dusky interior. Check out the gas lamps, porcelain and the fine wooden panels. The wine lists includes just about everything produced in France: Beaujolais, Bordeaux, Bourgogne, Loire, Champagne to name just a few. Pavement tables provide good people-watching along Rivoli. Hot and cold food available. Open 7 am to 10 pm. Closed Monday and August.

● **Right Bank: Champs-Elysées, Etoile**

Bidou Bar 12, rue Anatole-de-la-Forge, 17e; (tel: 380.09.18; metro: Argentine). A typical neighbourhood bar just off the Avenue de la Grand Armée, filled with local office workers and traders at lunch. You won't find too many internationals here, indeed a very French bar. Aperitifs are 20F, beer 15F and mixed drinks 30-35F. Cold food at lunch. Open until

2 am. Closed Saturday and Sunday.

Cactus Charly 68, rue de Ponthieu, 8e; (tel: 562.01.77; metro: Roosevelt). A member of the third wave of American-style bars (Harry's representing the first wave, Joe Allen's the second wave) to hit Paris, unabashedly in the California mould. Charly's features your favourite Stateside cocktails and mixed drinks, plus Mexican beers, guacamole, nachos, chili con carne and burgers. There's live music every night, either country & western or soft rock (Eagles etc). And if you're in Paris on the 31st of October, Charly's throws a huge Halloween costume ball with prizes for the best entries and a special 'Witches Brew' punch. The kind of place to let your hair down. Open until dawn. Closed Sunday.

Winston Churchill 5, rue de Presbourg, 16e; (tel: 500.75.35; metro: Etoile, Kleber). And just to round off the Champs-Elysées scene, how about an authentic English pub? Churchill's is probably the best British import to Paris in terms of atmosphere, decor, cuisine and that all-important category of booze. The interior is elegant Edwardian with wooden panels and booths, polished brass, frosted windows and mirrors. They have Watney's Red Barrel in draught, 30-year-old Ballantine's whiskey, champagne cocktails and gin and tonics, served in your choice of a salon bar, public bar or the pavement terrace. Real English breakfast (porridge, bacon and eggs, toast with marmalade, tea, etc.) is served daily from 8 to 11.30 am. For lunch there's roast beef with Yorkshire pud (51F), leg of lamb (42F), haddock (42F), and other Anglo delights.

● **Left Bank: Saint Germain**

Bedford Arms 17, rue Princesse, 6e; (tel: 633.43.54; metro: Mabillon). An English-style 'Free House' opposite the Birdland jazz club on a dark back street off the Rue du Four. Darts and Guinness gives you a clue to the atmosphere and clientele. The whiskey list includes Cutty Sark, Ballantine, Haig, Johnny Walker, Jameson and Jack Daniels. Also

Pimms, Cinzano and the always-present (at English bars) gin and tonics. Open every night until sunrise.

L'Ecluse 15, quai des Grands-Augustins, 6e; (tel: 633.58.74; metro: St Michel). Another nominee for the best wine bar in Paris. Easy to miss because l'Ecluse's green facade is squeezed between two larger and more elaborate cafés. But don't be mistaken by this demure nature: the ambience might be suburban simple but the wines and food are first class. L'Ecluse was opened just seven years ago, in 1978, as the first of a new wave of Parisian wine bars offering the best quality French wines to an up-and-coming clientele. Founder Georges Bardawil offered wine by the glass rather than the bottle to entice his customers to taste as many varieties as possible. It was a revolutionary concept for Paris at the time, but the idea quickly caught on and L'Ecluse became a chic gathering place of the French jet set and 'in' crowd. As Bardawil explained in a magazine article, L'Ecluse is 'a snobbish place for simple people, or a simple place for snobbish people'. Bardawil's good idea soon had its imitators, places like the Blue Fox Bar and Willi's Wine Bar. All the wine found at L'Ecluse is from Bordeaux, but the cellar covers nearly everything bottled in that region. The plats du jour are 70-90F, the entrées 24-65F. Among the kitchen specials are Jambon San Daniele (38F), dried sausages (22F), salmon (65F) and Roquefort cheese (25F). Open noon to 2 am. Closed Sunday.

Furstemberg 25, rue de Buci, 6e; (tel: 354.79.51; metro: Mabillon). Intimate, comfortable jazz club and piano bar below the Petit Zinc restaurant. Nothing fancy, but great music.

La Pinte 13, carrefour de l'Odeon, 6e; (tel: 326.26.15; metro: Odeon). Small, unobtrusive place on the tiny square off the Boulevard St Germain. Guinness, Tuborg and John Courage beer among many others. Piano and jazz most nights. The crowd is mostly student, artist or intellectual. Good for a quick drink or after the cinema. Open nightly until 2 am.

Pub Saint-Germain-des-Prés 17, rue de l'Ancienne-Comédie, 6e; (tel: 329.38.70; metro: Odeon). The most popular bar on the Left Bank, a rowdy mixing ground of students, tourists, office workers and other assorted night creatures. Open and serving drinks 24 hours a day, every day of the year. And with seven halls, this could well be the largest bar in Paris. There's enough space to pack in over 500 seated customers and countless standing drinkers. If you go after midnight be prepared to wait, for there's usually a line outside the front door. St Germain offers 16 draught beers, 250 international bottled beers and 100 whiskies. Among the selection are Whitbread Light Ale, Bass Pale Ale, Campbell Scotch Ale, Black and Tan Shandy, Douglas Scotch Ale, Martin's Pale Ale, Mackeson's Gold Label, Final Selection, McEwan's Lager and Guinness. Wow! Hot food available for lunch and dinner, cold snacks available 24 hours. The place to go when everything else is closed.

Le Taverne d'Aesle 32, rue Dauphine, 6e; (metro: Odéon). The place with all the international flags waving from the facade. A rival to the Pub St Germain with 320 types of international bottled beer, plus an American style bar with cocktails and mixed drinks. Less crowded than St Germain, fewer tourists and more locals. Open all night.

● **Left Bank: Saint Michel, Monge**

Mayflower Pub 49, rue Descartes, 5e; (tel: 354.56.47; metro: Cardinal Lemoine, Place Monge). Heavy on the students, a mild-mannered bar at the corner of Descartes and Thouin in the heart of the university residential district. Beers from Belgium, Britain, France, Denmark, Czechoslovakia, Germany, Holland and Russia and including Watney's, Guinness and John Courage 1787. Open all night.

Les Trois Maillets 56, rue Galande, 5e; (tel: 354.00.79; metro: St Michel, Maubert-Mutualité). Named the best piano bar in Paris by *Passion* magazine, an old-fashioned place with a polished bar and wooden seats. Situated in a 700-year-old building where Paris's stone masons once gathered (hence the name: 'The Three Mallets') after a hard day's work pounding away on Notre Dame or Saint Severin church. The music these days ranges from straight piano tunes to American-style jazz. Open all night, but get there early if you want a seat. Still no cover charge after all these years. The Medieval stone masons would approve.

● **Left Bank: Sèvres-Babylone**

Au Sauvignon 80, rue des St Pères, 7e; (metro: Sèvres-Babylone). A quaint little neighbourhood wine bar that's a lot less trendy and expensive than the shops in this high-fashion district. And stamp collectors will love it: those aren't your usual first day covers up on the wall. Famed for its Beaujolais and Burgundy. The outdoor terrace is great for a little summer sunshine, or people watching along Saint Pères or Sèvres. Open 9 am to 11 pm. Closed Sunday and August.

The Twickenham Rue des St Pères at Rue de Grenelle, 7e; (tel: 222.96.85; metro: St Sulpice, Sèvres-Babylone). As the name suggests, a monument to the game of rugby. It even has the national rugger emblems of England, Scotland, France and Wales painted on the windows. So if you're in town for a big international, Twickers is the place to drink before the match. Definitive English-style pub with lots of wood and brass. The bar stocks Guinness, Bass, Irish whisky, Wilde Turkey, Ballantines and grog. If you're not in an alcoholic mood, try a Twickenham salad (22F) with Earl Grey tea. Closed Sunday.

● **Left Bank: Montparnasse**

Bar American 56th floor, Tour Monatparnasse, 15e; (tel: 538.32.32; metro: Montparnasse). 'The latest sunset in Paris by 38 seconds' and an evening view of city lights to be matched by no bar in town. At plus 200 metres (650 feet) this is the highest bar in France and Europe. Naturally, the

The outdoor cafe is a Paris institution, especially in the Left Bank districts of Saint Michel and St. Germain, where students and artists have integrated the cafés into their avant-garde ways of life.

drink prices tend to be sky-high. The bar also functions as a salon de thé, brasserie and ice cream parlour for those without an alcoholic urge. But first you will have to pay 19F even to get to the 56th floor. If you can afford the cash, take a window seat and enjoy a satellite view of the Eiffel Tower, Notre Dame, Invalides, Sacré Coeur and all the rest. Open daily until 10 pm.

Rosebud 11 bis, rue Delambre, 14e; (tel: 326.95.28; metro: Vavin, Edgar-Quinet). Most of the bars of old Montparnasse have passed away to urban renewal projects on the Main-Montparnasse Complex, ground into dust and splinters. But Rosebud remains as a bastion of the artistic and intellectual spirit of pre-war Montparnasse, when the district played home to Hemingway, Modigliani, Chagall, Picasso, Foujita, Stravinsky, Leger, Lenin and Trotsky among others. No doubt, they may have all taken a drink over some serious conversation at Rosebud. The bar still continues to attract an intellectual and artistic crowd, mixed with Anglo-American businessmen and the occasional tourist. American-type bar food is available. Open to 2 am.

Cafés

● **Right Bank: Les Halles**

Café la Fontaine des Innocents Rue Berger at Rue St Denis, 1er; (tel: 236.37.15; metro: Les Halles). The ultimate in people-watching. An outward facing terrace on the fascinating Place des Innocents (the fountain is in the middle of the square), gathering ground of punks and tourists, school-girls and musicians. This is one of Paris's greatest street hangouts. And the café faces south, with unobstructed sun until late in the afternoon. It's the sunniest outdoor seating in Les Halles. Coffee, tea, wine, beer, spirits, ice cream and brasserie food available.

Aux Deux Saules 91, rue St Denis, 1er; (metro: Les Halles). A real gem. Belle Epoque decor, big wooden tables and lots of plants at the intersection of St Denis and Rambuteau. The usual run of coffee, tea, beer, wine and aperitifs, plus great café food like omelettes with chips (16-22F), soups (6-12F) and eggs (22-24F). Deux Saules has a casual, unpretentious ambience which is equally enjoyable to both Parisians and visitors. Good for an afternoon break from shopping or touring.

● **Right Bank: Opéra, Louvre**

Café de la Paix Place de l'Opéra, 9e; (tel: 260.33.50; metro: Opéra). A Paris landmark for over 100 years and now listed by the government as a historic monument. This classic Belle Epoque café is still one of the most elegant establishments in the city. The location is superb: on the Place de l'Opéra at the corner of Boulevard des Capucines and Rue Auber, which makes the café convenient for the Opera, the traveller's cheque offices, department stores and a number of big theatres and cinemas. The resident Americans in Paris (Hemingway, Fitzgerald, Stein and Company) always loved this one. But unfortunately the ambience was ruined somewhat by a major renovation in 1976. De la Paix is still as spectacular, but it no longer has the feeling of old Paris. In fact, the café has been split in two: the super-chic Restaurant Opéra (250-300F per person) and the downmarket Relais Capucines with its outdoor terrace. Expect to pay at least 12F for a beer and 14.50F for a glass of wine. Plats du jour can be had at 55-62F, full lunch or dinner for 80-100F. Open from noon to 1.15 am.

Rue l'Univers 159, rue St Honoré, 1er; (tel: 260.31.57; metro: Palais Royale). Convenient meeting place and rest stop near the Louvre, Tuileries, Palais Royal and Comédie Française Good for people-watching too, as it commands a corner on the Place André Malraux and Place Colette, one of the busiest intersections in Paris. Ruc is a 1930s style brasserie, café and salon de thé with a somewhat updated art deco interior. A full meal will cost you about 100F, but cheaper snacks are also available. Open daily noon until 1.30 am. Closed in August.

● **Right Bank: Marais, Beaubourg, Ile de la Cité**

Café du Square Trousseau Rue Theodore Roussel at rue A. Vollen, 11e; (tel: 343.06.00; metro: Ledru Rollin). A real blue collar café in a working class district. Tourists and trendy Parisians rarely stray this far east, so this café is filled with real people. The interior is a marvel of classic Belle Epoque with lots of wood, brass, glass and delicate plaster ceilings. Not much English spoken so bring your phrase book. Lunch menu at 55F. A genuine touch of turn-of-the-century Paris.

Ma Bourgogne 19, place des Vosges, 4c; (tel: 278.44.64; metro: St Paul). There is perhaps no more pleasant location for a café in all of Paris, for Ma Bourgogne is nestled on a strategic corner of the historic Place des Vosges, at the point where the square intersects with the Rue des Francs Bourgeois. The place is dripping with Parisian history. Cardinal Richelieu lived next door at No. 21 for 12 years before moving to Luxembourg Palace and No. 6 was the home of Victor Hugo for 15 years in the mid 19th century. The arcade in which Ma Bourgogne is situated dates from 1612 when the square was the centre of royal social life under Henri IV. It's best to sip a glass of wine or an expresso at the wooden tables under the arcade, and then choose a snack from a delicious menu which includes lamb chops (42F), Alsatian-style sauerkraut (40F), chitterling sausages (35F) or hot Beaujolais sausages (40F). Open daily until 8.30 pm.

Pacific Palisades 51, rue Quincampoix, 4e; (tel: 275.01.17; metro: Rambuteau, Les Halles). New, super-trendy café on a back street near the Pompidou. The clientele is très chic, the decor Southern California mod (the café is named after a Los Angeles beach district where Ronald Reagan lived before moving into the White House). In its two years of life, Palisades has played host to such luminaries as Mick

Jagger, Richard Gere and Roman Polanski. Bring your American Express card because the prices are as famous as the customers. The menu ranges through California salads, American burgers and Japanese tempura with a few French dishes thrown in for good measure. Expect to pay 150-200F for a full meal. But you can always stick to a cup of coffee or glass of vino and some mini-binoculars to spot the celebrities. Open daily noon to 3 pm and 8 pm to 2 am.

Relais Beaubourg Rue St Merri at rue St Martin, 4e; (tel: 278.77.16; metro: Rambuteau). Nothing spectacular about this café except the location: on a strategic corner opposite the Pompidou Centre in the heart of the Beaubourg walking district. In the summer it's virtually impossible to get an outdoor seat at Relais, but if you're lucky and snatch a table you will have an unbridled view of the passing hordes, the street musicians and the various impromptu entertainments.

Aux Tours de Notre Dame Rue du Cloître Notre-Dame at rue d'Arcole, 4e; (tel: 325.97.27; metro: Cité). Another strategic location, this time on a corner opposite Notre Dame. A bit touristy perhaps but great for sitting outside in the summer and watching the circus in the Parvis. Usual run of coffee, beer, wine, soft drinks and cold sandwiches.

● **Right Bank: Champs-Elysées**

Fouquet'a 99, avenue des Champs-Elysées, 8e; (tel: 723.70.60; metro: George V). There are many cafés along the grand avenue, but none with a history or elegance to match Fouquet's. It represents a bygone Champs-Elysées style which has faded away in favour of hamburger joints and neon lights. But naturally you will have to pay a bit more to enjoy this bastion of luxury. Fouquet's is still a meeting place of Paris's old money: the cinema stars of two or three decades ago, the wealthy industrialist and cabinet ministers, high-ranking diplomats and what is left of the French aristocracy. Dinner will cost you at least 200F, but the cuisine is better than your average café fare. Open noon to 2 pm and 7 pm to midnight. Closed Sunday and Monday.

● **Left Bank: Saint Michel, Monge**

Café de Cluny boulevard St Germain at boulevard St Michel, 5e; (tel: 326.68.24; metro: St Michel). At the crossroads of the Left Bank, the meeting place of the two famous boulevards. Cluny is a straight forward, no frills café which offers typical window seats, long bar, speedy waiters and tiny tables. But the clientele tends to be a bit more diverse than usual because Cluny is *the* big meeting point of the Left Bank. There's a great news stand outside with a large foreign press selection if you want some reading material with your coffee. Service from 6.30 am (for early birds) to 2 am.

La Chope Café 2, place de la Contrescarpe, 5e; (tel: 326.51.26; metro: Monge, Cardinal Lemoine). Sunny pavement tables on a pleasant little square in a district populated with students and workers. And those are the people who frequent this typical neighbourhood café. Not many tourists get as far off the track as Contrescarpe. Prices are considerably lower than the bouelvard cafés, but the snacks and food are just as good.

La Gentilhommière Rue St Andrés des Arts at Place St Andrés des Arts, 6e; (tel: 325.67.38; metro: St Michel). Inconspicuous and unpretentious café just off the Place St Michel. A quiet little place which is good for conversations, reading or writing postcards. The terrace seats give you a view of the trees, tourists, pigeons and clochards who inhabit the square.

Notre Dame Quai St Michel at rue Jacques, 5e; (tel: 354.20.43; metro: St Michel). Advantageous location near the Pont St Michel opposite Notre Dame. With a magnificent view of the cathedral facade, this is one of St Michel's more romantic cafés. Surprisingly, it tends to be filled more with locals than tourists, which says something about the

161

food, drinks and prices. There's a little bar annex around the corner on St Jacques where you can get a quick Kronenbourg. Notre Dame lends itself as a perfect point of rendezvous.

● Left Bank: Saint Germain

Deux Magots 170, boulevard St Germain, 6e; (tel: 548.55.25; metro: St Germain). The birthplace of French Existentialism during the 1920s and 30s, Deux Magots has played host to Jean-Paul Sartre, Albert Camus and Madame de Beauvoir, as well as up-and-coming artists like Picasso and Chagall. The famous names are gone, but the café is still a meeting place of students, artists and intellectuals, as well as the occasional tourist. The outdoor terrace is always packed during the daytime. The coffee, hot chocolate and ice cream are recommended, and there's a good selection of wine, beer and aperitifs. Prices a bit on the high side. Service from 9 am to 2 am.

Café de Flore 172, boulevard St Germain, 6e; (tel: 548.55.26; metro: St Germain). Right next to the Deux Magots, a traditional rival in both spirit and trade. This is where all the great French thinkers were drinking when they weren't at the Deux. Flore is older and a bit more elegant than Deux Magots, with an interior of exquisite Belle Epoque rather than later art deco. The café has lost most of its intellectual clientele, but it's still the haunt of beautiful women and their equally striking companions. Open daily until 2 am.

Brasserie Lipp 151, boulevard St Germain, 6e; (tel: 548.53.91; metro: St Germain). The third of the famous cafés clustered around the Place St Germain des Prés. Lipp is both a typical Alsatian brasserie featuring sauerkraut and dried sausages, and a typical Left Bank café with great coffee, hot chocolate, wines and beer. It was founded by an Alsatian refugee named Lippman in 1870 and has been a Left Bank fixture ever since, attracting many of the famous names from Deux Magots and Flore across the street. Legend has it that

Paris's cafés tend to be gathering places for the entire population, be it senior citizens or teenage students, for they serve as places of relaxation, conversation or just quiet contemplation.

Hemingway was the first customer after Paris was liberated in 1944 (a distinction also claimed by the Ritz Hotel Bar). Check out the turn-of-the-century decor of the ground and first floors, or take a terrace seat and watch the world walk past. The place is always packed to the seams, and in the evening and at lunch you'll probably have to wait for a table. A full meal is around 120-150F, but there are plats du jour for under 100F. Service from noon to 12.45 am. Closed Monday and July.

● Left Bank: Montparnasse

La Coupole 102, boulevard du Montparnasse, 14e; (tel: 320.14.20; metro: Vavin). This place tries to do everything: café, brasserie, American bar and dance hall. Coupole first became popular in the 1920s when it was a gathering place of Montparnasse artists, writers and intellectuals like Picasso, Chagall, Leger and Modigliani. The reputation has faded a bit with the decades, and today La Coupole has something of an anachronistic air. The old folks come here to dance (4.30 to 7 pm and 9.30 pm to 2 am daily) to the tunes of the 20s, 30s and 40s. But there aren't too many Cubists or Surrealists left these days. And a heartless renovation has left La Coupole sterile and plastic. The food is still quite good, however, under the direction of Chef Galois. There are 79F and 99F set menus, while à la carte will cost you about 100F per person. House specialities include seafood, grilled meats and pastries. Open 8 am to 2 am. Closed August.

Le Dome 108, boulevard du Montparnasse, 14e; (tel: 222.65.27; metro: Vavin). Another Montparnasse landmark. Le Dome was also a hang-out of French and American artists and writers in the 1920s, but like the other cafés in the neighbourhood it's lost some of its spirit and flavour. The creative types are gone, replaced by less colourful businessmen and tourists. But unlike Coupole, the Belle Epoque interior hasn't been ruined by renovation. Hot meals available inside, including a recommended seafood bouillabaisse (90F). Drinks only on the terrace, but it's still great for people-watching after all these years. Open until 2 am.

Le Select 99, boulevard Montparnasse, 6e; (tel: 222.65.27; metro: Vavin). The third and least-known of the famous old cafés situated at the Montparnasse-Raspail crossroads. Select retains its marvellous art deco interior (it opened in 1923), and because it has always remained something of a neighbourhood café it still attracts the young artists and thinkers from the nearby university districts. Less flashy and lower prices than the Dome or the Coupole, the right bracket for students and backpackers visiting Paris who want to indulge in the café life. Service from 7.30 am to 3 am daily.

Tea salons

● **Right Bank: Rivoli**

Angelina 226, rue de Rivoli, 1er; (tel: 280.75.34; metro: Tuileries). Brings to mind visions of aged French ladies with fur coats and neatly clipped French poodles. Angelina's (also known as the Maison de l'Afrique) was founded in 1903 under the lovely Rivoli arcade and has been a meeting place of Parisian high society and French aristocrats ever since. Perhaps Astrid Hustvedt pegged Angelina right in an article on the 'in' places to eat in Paris: 'provides its upwardly mobile clientele a place to while away their idle afternoons'. But you don't only find rich widows here, for Angelina's is also a gathering spot for the French version of Sloane Rangers (the BC/BGs). Lots of fancy cakes and pastries to go with the fancy people, plus ice cream and cheeses and numerous varieties of tea. The turn-of-the-century decor is well preserved and Angelina will remind you of bygone days along the Rivoli. The terrace tables provide excellent views of the strolling masses and the lovely Tuileries across the road. Bring your bank roll. Open daily noon to 7 pm.

Les Bouchons 19, rue des Halles, 1er; (tel: 233.28.73; metro: Les Halles). One of the great shop facades of Paris. In lesser places this building might serve as the city hall or court house. But, alas, in a city filled with marvellous architecture, this classic example of the art nouveau style is relegated to the position of a salon de thé! But all the better for tea drinkers. The name translates into 'the corks' but *bouchon* is also a slang term given to simple wine bars in rural France. Thus, Les Bouchons also functions as a wine bar, brasserie and piano bar. There's brunch from noon on Saturday and Sunday, and piano jazz in the bar after 10 pm each night. Open daily noon to 2 am.

Café Verlet 256, rue St Honore, 1er; (metro: Pyramides, Tuileries, Palais Royal). Comfortable and friendly salon de thé which serves as a good rest and recuperation point along this busy shopping street. Over 50 varieties of tea for you connoisseurs. But Verlet is more than just a tea room, for it also serves up fantastic coffee (two dozen kinds from such diverse places as New Guinea, Kenya and Colombia), jams, shortbread, maple syrup and delicious sandwiches. Prices are very reasonable and everything is available for take-away sale in neat little packages. The kind of café your grandmother would like. Open noon to 6.30 pm. Closed Saturday and Sunday (Easter to October 1) or Sunday and Monday (October 1 to Easter).

Le Jardin du Louvre 2, place de Palais Royal; (tel: 261.16.00; metro. Palais Royal). Swank, new salon de thé in the same building as the Louvre des Antiquaries antique market. The location and prices lend themselves to an up-market crowd: wealthy tourists in search of antiques, fashion models, rock stars and the like. During the sunny summer months you can sip your tea outside in a lovely terrace. Serving tea and cakes from 2 to 6.30 pm. Closed Sunday and Monday. A perfect break from long hours at the Louvre.

W.H. Smith 248, rue de Rivoli, 1er; (tel: 260.37.97; metro: Tuileries). The ultimate English tea room in Paris, serving no less than 'high tea' in the late afternoon. The best Darjeeling, Earl Grey and Souchong come with crumpets, tea cakes, muffins, fruit cakes, marmalade and honey. For the really hungry there are club sandwiches too. Be sure to buy *The Times* downstairs in the bookstore. Or if you really want to get into some British colonial ambience, try a Graham Greene over tea and bikkies. The English Tea Room is open 10.15 am to 6 pm, but high tea is 3 to 6 pm. Closed Sunday and from July 26 to August 1.

● Right Bank: Bourse

A Priori Thé 35-37, Galerie Vivienne, 2e; (tel: 297.48.75; metro: Bourse). Ambience supreme, the best location for a salon de thé in Paris. Priori is located in a beautiful shopping arcade built in the early 19th century, a place of high, vaulted ceilings with glass plates, wood-panelled shop facades, tiled pavements and spiral stairways. So authentic is Galerie Vivienne that it's often used to film period scenes for movies and advertisements. Gentlemen in bowler hats and ladies in Victorian gowns are not an unusual sight. Because the Galerie is totally enclosed, the Priori has some of the only terrace tables where you can enjoy a sip of tea despite a blizzard or a downpour. A young and happy crowd, great tea and snacks. Open noon to 7 pm. Closed Sunday.

● Right Bank: Marais

L'Ebouillante 6, rue des Barrès, 4e; (tel: 278.48.62; metro: Pont Marie, Hotel de Ville). A pint-sized salon in a recently renovated walking district of the old Marais. There's a good view of the 17th century Church of St Gervais and St Protais out the front window, and the salon is just down the road from the beautifully restored Accueil des Jeunes (youth hostel) at No. 12 Barrès. Even on a frozen winter day, l'Ebouillante has a warm, comfortable look about it. The windows are frosted over, but there's an orange glow and the sound of laughter and conversation from inside. The salon is always packed — there are only a half dozen tables — but the excellent tea and cakes make a wait tolerable. And for those cold days there's plenty of home-made soup. Open Wednesday to Saturday noon to 7 pm and Sunday 2 to 7 pm. Closed Monday and Tuesday.

Eurydice 10, place des Vosges, 4e; (tel: 277.77.99; metro: St Paul, Chemin Vert). Simple decor and a casual atmosphere pervade this new salon under the archways of the Place des Vosges. Eurydice is run by two friendly women who have given it a family-style ambience which attracts a mixed clientele of tourists, local debutants and Marais pensioners. There's even a big, furry dog to pet. The cakes and pastries are exquisite, and the Sunday brunch is highly recommended at only 41F. Tasty vegetable or fruit dishes are also available. A spot to flake out on a sweltering summer day. Open Wednesday to Saturday noon to 10 pm and Sunday noon to 7 pm. Closed Monday and Tuesday.

● Ile de la Cité, Ile Saint Louis

Fanny Tea 20, place Dauphine, 1er; (tel: 325.83.67; metro: Pont Neuf). Inconspicuous tea salon next to La Rose de France restaurant on what is certainly one of Paris's loveliest squares. The land on which Fanny sits was once Patriarch's Isle, a marshland filled with water birds and reeds downstream from the Ile de la Cité. King Henri III had the shallow inlets filled at the end of the 16th century, making both Patriarch's and Jews' islands part of the Cité. His successor, Henri IV, commissioned a housing project for the renewed land, known as the Place Dauphine. And it's the ground floor of one of these 1608 townhouses in which Fanny is located. The salon is packed at lunch, not only because of its warm ambience, but because of an excellent selection of teas and food. The menu includes various egg dishes, salads, pastries and ice creams. Open Tuesday to Saturday 1 to 8 pm and Sunday 3.30 to 8 pm. Closed Monday.

168

Le Flore en L'Ile 6, quai d'Orleans, 4e; (tel: 540.94.30; metro: Pont Marie). A combination salon de thé, ice cream parlour, café and restaurant that tends to be overpriced and full of the strident type of tourist. But the drinks and food are excellent, and you could hardly beat the location: the tip of Ile Saint Louis opposite Notre Dame. Barges float past on the muddy Seine and light breezes rustle through the quayside trees. Romantic indeed, if you can shut your mind to the almost constant banter and repartee which fills this most French of tea salons. The big treat is exquisite Bertillon ice cream (17F) from down the island, but the menu also offers fruit and vegetable juices (10-14.90F) and hot chocolate (14.90 . . . but it's about the best in Paris). A cuppa will cost you 11.60F, with a selection that includes Earl Grey, Ceylon, jasmine and China red. Breakfast/brunch served every morning. Open 11 am to 1.45 am every day but Christmas and New Year's Day.

Le Jardin de Thé 81, rue St Louis en l'Ile, 4e; (tel: 329.81.52; metro: Pont Marie). Where the Saint Louis locals gather for a snack and quick cup of tea. A newer establishment with an antique look: lots of wood, dusty windows and aged islanders with chisled faces and black berets. The food is superb: salads, eggs, cheese and desserts, plus crumpets, muffins, scones and English buns and pastries to eat with your tea. The house specials include quiche lorraine (26F), roast beef (30F) and tortellini (30F). Le Jardin does an excellent job of recreating a bygone Parisian atmosphere. Open noon to midnight every day.

● **Left Bank: Saint Michel**

La Bucherie 41, rue de la Bucherie, 5e; (tel: 354.78.06; metro: St Michel). The only tea room with a view of Notre Dame's west facade. which is the real attraction of La Bucherie. Comfortable terrace seats which face onto a tiny green square inhabited by pensioners and pre-schoolers. This salon has the usual range of teas and cakes, plus a 125F lunch or dinner menu. The food is highly recommended. La Bucherie serves as a good rendezvous for thirsty travellers.

La Passion du Fruit 71, quai de la Tournelle, 5e; (tel. 306.76.56; metro: Maubert-Mutualité). New and enticing tea salon where Rue Maurice Albert meets the Seine. The tiny outdoor tables, shaded by the huge trees along the quai, give an excellent view of the rear of Notre Dame, the Pont de l'Archevêché and the park at the end of the Ile de la Cité. Tea, coffee and hot chocolate are available, but what's best about Passion is the food. The menu includes fresh fruit and vegetable salads, white cheeses, various egg dishes, ice creams and sherbets. For hot days there's lemonade and a Super petit déjeuner (breakfast) for 63F. The best new salon on the Left Bank. Open 11.30 am to 3 pm and 6 pm to 2 am.

Tea Caddy 14, rue St Julien le Pauvre, 5e; (tel: 354.15.56; metro: St Michel. A cosy, warm salon with frosted windows and wooden tables that brings to mind visions of granny's sitting room. And, not surprisingly, Tea Caddy is often filled with sprightly dressed and grey-haired French ladies who are, no doubt, someone's grandmother! Tea Caddy is also a quiet, tranquil refuge from the hustle and bustle of the rest of St Michel district. Open noon to 7 pm on Monday to Saturday, 2 to 7 pm on Sunday. Closed Tuesday.

● **Left Bank: Saint Germain**

La Photogalerie 2, rue Christine, 6e; (tel: 329.01.76; metro: Odeon). As the name suggests, this comfortable salon doubles as a photo gallery. Heavy on the wood, with big tables and polished floors. The clientele is a good mix of students, art gallery groupies and resident foreigners. A rainy day hang out, or a general place to while away a lazy afternoon. Open noon to 3 pm for drinks or lunch, 5 to 6.30 pm for tea and snacks, 8 pm to 12.30 am for dinner. Closed Sunday.

The Village Voice 6, rue Princesse, 6e; (tel. 633.36.47; metro: Mabillon). Avant-garde bookstore and tea salon that's reminiscent of Greenwich Village or Haite-Ashbury in the 1960s. The Voice is run by expatriate Americans and has a decidedly Stateside air. Good selection of teas and fantastic coffee. But according to chief chef Sue Herman the best thing about the Voice is the food: chocolate chip cookies, chocolate brownies, salads and sandwiches in the best American mould. This is the type of salon I could easily get hooked on if I lived in Paris for long. Open 11 am to 10 pm. Closed Sunday.

Ice cream parlours

Le Bac Glaces 109, rue du Bac, 7e; (metro: Bac). Paris's most exotic ice cream collection. A veritable trip around the world with frozen delights such as the Seychelles, with mango, pineapple and cocoa sherbets; the Bahamas, with passion fruit and apricot sorbets; the Bermuda, with banana, lemon and cassis sherbets; and the Fiji, with vanilla, rum and pistachio ice creams. Tea, coffee and hot chocolate too.

Bertillon 31, rue St Louis en l'Ile. 4e; (metro: Pont Marie). The most famous ice creams and sherbets in Paris are served in this ancient establishment which draws Parisians and visitors alike with its mouth-watering scoops. Bertillon actually makes the ice creams and sorbets and ships them out to various restaurants and cafés around the city, so you can't go wrong with the factory itself. Coffee, tea and hot chocolate to wash it all down. Open 10 am to 8 pm. Closed Monday and Tuesday.

Le Glacier 13, rue Brantome, 3e; (tel: 271.67.21; metro: Rambuteau). A flashy new ice cream parlour and tea salon tucked away on a quiet plaza of the Quartier de l'Horloge project opposite the Pompidou Centre. But the excellent desserts have already ranked Glacier among Paris's top ten ice cream establishments. Homemade ice cream and sorbet, plus banana splits, sundaes, peach melba and fresh strawberries with cream. Modest prices. Open noon to 11 pm.

Le Paradis du Fruit 27, quai des Grands-Augustins, 6e; (metro: St Michel). Among the best milkshakes in Paris, made from fresh fruit, real milk and ice. A number of flavours to choose from, with the price 17.50F for a single flavour or 20F for a double. Left Bank students know this place intimately. Open 11 am to 2 am. Closed Tuesday.

Le Passion du Fruit 71, quai de la Tournelle, 5e; (tel: 306.76.56; metro: Maubert-Mutualité). Previously mentioned salon de thé with wonderful ice cream and sherbet. Fresh fruit for the topping, plus hot chocolate or lemonade to wash it down. Open 11.30 am to 3 pm and 6 pm to 2 am.

La Sorbetière de St Sulpice 27, rue St Sulpice, 6e; (tel: 633.38.26; metro: Mabillon). A mouth-full in both name and menu. An extensive range of ice creams and sorbets (including peach and apricot), plus lots of tasty teas. Open 10 am to 6.30 pm. Closed Sunday and Monday.

CHAPTER SEVEN

Performing arts

Paris is the world nucleus for French culture, and there are few cities in the world which offer a more colourful palette of performing arts. There are two operas, five national theatres, over 100 independent theatres offering both traditional and avant-garde fare, classical music and organ recitals performed in the unmatched ambience of a Gothic church, ballet and modern dance performances, outrageously funny circuses, and that oh so French art of the marionettes.

But there is one major factor which might put a damper on all this culture for the English-speaking visitor: the language. Unless your school French is very, very good, you might as well forget any theatre performed in the French language, for you will miss both the dramatic nuances and the subtle jokes. The one saving grace for theatre buffs is Galerie 55, The English Theatre of Paris, which presents an excellent bill of shows in the Anglo-Saxon tongue.

Otherwise, the language barrier is no problem. Operas are usually in German or Italian, and you're there for the music and pomp anyway. Likewise, classical music and dance transcend the language gap and can be enjoyed by anyone. And all you need is a youngster to tell you that Parisian circus or marionettes are just as entertaining as the shows back home.

Paris is also a popular venue for many of the world's great entertainers and artists — everyone from Placido Domingo to Vladimir Ashkenazy, and many of the most outstanding musical and dance groups. Many of these famous names perform in the cavernous music halls and arenas of Paris, where you may need a good set of binoculars to see the stage. But on other special occasions you might also catch these stars performing in the warm intimacy of the Salle Pleyel or one of the other small concert halls.

To find out about current happenings in the Paris culture scene pick up a copy of the weekly *Pariscope* magazine or the monthly *Passion* magazine, available at most news-stands. *Pariscope* is in French, *Passion* in English, but they will both give you a categorized listing with synopsis, times and ticket prices.

It's much cheaper to purchase your tickets from the theatre or concert hall box office than from independent ticket agencies who will charge you a hefty commission on top of the ticket price. And when you get to the show, don't forget to give a few francs to the person who shows you to the seats.

Parisians traditionally eat dinner after the theatre or concert, and many of the best restaurants in the city are open until one or two in the morning precisely for this purpose. But if you've dined before the show, there is always a bar or café nearby for a nightcap.

Theatre

● **National theatres**

Chaillot Place du Trocadero, 16e; (tel: 727.81.15; metro: Trocadero). The exciting, dynamic theatre located in the Palais de Chaillot, opposite the Eiffel Tower and overlooking the Seine at one of its most beautiful points. The Palais is a masterpiece of the art deco style of the 1930s with its bold horizontal lines and sweeping vertical colonnade. Below the immense terrace, with its world-famous views of the

The Chaillot Theatre beneath the Place du Trocadero as seen from the top of the Eiffel Tower; this huge auditorium plays host to a wide variety of stage productions from Shakespeare to Chekhov.

Trocadero Fountains and the Eiffel Tower, is the 1,800-seat Chaillot National Theatre. From 1951 to 1972 it function-ed as the Theatre National Populaire (TNP), but then the premises were renovated and the name changed to its present form. The associate Theatre Gemier was built below the northeast face of the terrace in 1966 to accommodate less-traditional works. The Chaillot presents a wide variety of European plays, ranging in the 1983-84 season from Shakespeare's *Hamlet* to Chekhov's *The Seagull* and Swift's *The Travels of Gulliver*. Other recent productions have in-cluded Handke, Axionov, Kagel, Voyet, Bayen, Gom-browicz, Byland, Kasapoglu, Janacek, Moraly and Turba. Prices range from 21F to 60F. Tickets can be purchased up to 14 days in advance from the box office, open daily 11 am to 7 pm, and Sunday 11 am to 5 pm. The Chaillot has a restaurant, salon de thé and bar.

Comédie-Française 2, rue de Richelieu, 1er; (tel: 296.10.20; metro: Palais Royal). The most famous playhouse in Paris, and one of the world's oldest established theatre groups. The Comédie's roots go back to the 1640s when a young Parisian called Poquelin changed his name to Molière and became an actor. He formed a small theatre company on the Left Bank which played in converted indoor tennis courts until a permanent facility was built, the now-demolished Théatre Guenegaud in Rue Mazarine. After Molière's death, King Louis XIV combined the Guenegaud troupe with the players from the Hotel de Bourgogne to form the Comédie-Française. It later moved to a location in the Rue de l'Ancienne-Comédie opposite the Café Procope, then in 1770 to the Palais des Tuileries. By 1782 the Comédie had moved once again, this time into the new Theatre de l'Odeon. The troupe settled at its present location in 1792 when the actor Talma captured the Palais Royal with a group of other revolutionary players. Napoleon made the Comédie-Française a national theatre with state financial aid in 1812. Since that time, the Comedie has grown into a stately pillar of French theatre, presenting only works by the great names of the past, in particular Molière, Racine and Corneille. In 1985, the Comedie entered its 305th season as the globe's oldest repertory company. The state subsidy has grown to over £8 million. But changes may be in store. An avant-garde stage director named Jean-Pierre Vincent (former director of the National Theatre of Strasbourg) took over as administrator of the Comedie in 1983 and quickly stated he would like to see at least a third of the company's productions given over to new playwrights or controversial themes. There will also be a likely overhaul of classic productions such as Molière's *The Miser,* which has played nearly 3,000 times in 15 years. Experimentation and change are not beyond the limits of the Comédie-Française — it was the first Parisian theatre to champion the works of Victor Hugo in the 1830s. But it will no doubt remain a bastion of the French classics, the house which Molière built. Prices range from 16-83F. Tickets can be purchased seven days in advance from the box office, open daily 11 am to 6 pm.

Odeon 1, place Paul Claudel, 6e; (tel: 325.70.32; metro: Odeon). Now hosting the premier season of Giorgio Strehler's long-awaited Théatre de l'Europe, a grand scheme to produce some of the continent's greatest works on a spectacular scale. Each production is staged in conjunction with a visiting theatre group and the play is done in the home language of that troupe. For instance, the Piccolo Theatre of Milan presented Shakespeare's *The Tempest* in Italian, and the Bochumer Ensemble presented Karge's *Jacke Wie Hose* in German. In between Strehler's productions are regular Odeon appearances by the Theatre National Populaire and the Comédie-Française, mostly French classics. The Odeon was erected in 1782 for the Comédie-Française under the name Théatre Française, but the troupe moved into the Palais Royal during the Revolution. The Odeon struggled through low attendances, failed companies and two major fires through the next 150 years. It wasn't until after World War II, when the theatre switched to contemporary plays, that it became a Parisian success story. Jean-Louis Barrault and Madeleine Renaud directed the Odeon through its resurrection of the 1950s and 60s. The smaller Petit Odeon next door hosts modern and experimental plays. Prices range from 29-60F. Tickets are available two weeks in advance from the box office, open daily 11 am to 6.30 pm.

Théatre de l'Est Parisien 159, avenue Gambetta, 20e; (tel: 364.80.80; metro: Pelleport, St Fargeau). Petit TEP at 17, rue Malte Brun (20e). Newer, less staid national theatre presenting a varied selection of plays, poetry readings and cinema. The TEP is particularly known for its historical productions, and in the last year it has presented *The Death of Danton* by Georg Buchner and the classic silent film *Bonaparte and the Revolution* by Able Gance. The Petit TEP specializes in avant-garde theatre. Single tickets are 61F, but TEP offers special group reductions and two season ticket plans, the 'Carnet Theatre' and the 'Carte TEP'. Box office open 11 am to 7 pm daily.

Théatre de la Ville 2, place du Chatelet, 4e; (tel: 274.22.77; metro: Chatelet). A general house of Parisian culture that's an upmarket version of the TEP. The theatre is a twin of the Chatelet across the square, both built by Davioud in 1862. A decade later it was destroyed by fire and rebuilt to its present form. Until after World War II it was called the Theatre Sarah Bernhardt. The 1,000-seat auditorium hosts plays, ballet, opera, concerts, lectures and art exhibits. Tickets range from 46 to 72F with reductions for groups. The box office is open daily 11 am to 7 pm.

● **Independent theatres**

American Centre 261, boulevard Raspail, 14e; (tel: 321.42.20; metro: Raspail). Works by both American and French playwrights.

Antoine 14, boulevard de Strasbourg, 10e; (tel: 208.77.71; metro: Strasbourg St Denis). Popular comedies and drama in a 810-seat auditorium. Tickets: 45-140F. Box office: 15-day advanced booking; open daily 11 am to 7 pm.

Arts-Herbertot 78 bis, boulevard des Batignolles, 17e; (tel: 387.23.23; metro: Rome, Villiers). Bastion of French classics and a recent rival of the Comédie-Française. Jean-Laurent Cochet runs the Arts with substantial subsidy from the right-wing Paris city council (the Comédie gets its money from the left-wing national government) to stage works by Molière, Becque, Marivaux and others. Many a disgruntled Comédie actor now performs at the Arts, so the quality of the productions is not to be underestimated. Tickets: 50-130F on Saturday; 40-65F all other evenings. Box office: daily 11 am to 7 pm.

Atelier Place Charles-Dullin, 18e; (tel: 606.49.24; metro: Anvers). Pierre Franck's theatre which presented the much-applauded *Cocteau Marais* by Jean Marais and Jean-Luc Tardieu in 1983. Built in 1822 and now one of the oldest independent companies in Paris. Tickets: 20-120F. Box office: 13-day advance sale; open 11 am to 9 pm daily.

Athenée 4, square de l'Opera Louis Jouvet, 9e; (tel: 742.67.27; metro: Opera). Mixed bag of classical performances and popular stage plays, mostly comedy and drama. The recently renovated Athenée has been split into the Salle Louis Jouvet and the smaller Salle Christian Berard. Recent productions have included Chekhov's *The Strange Animal* starring Marie-Christine Barrault, the avant-garde *La Guerre de Cent Ans* by the Theatre-Groupe 4 Litres 12, and Strindberg's *The Pelican.* Tickets: 25-35F in the Salle Berard, 35-55F in the Salle Jouvet. Box office: Monday to Saturday 11 am to 6 pm.

Bouffes du Nord 37 bis, boulevard de la Chapelle, 10e; (tel: 239.34.50; metro: La Chapelle). Experimental, avant-garde and futuristic productions in the somewhat incongruous ambience of a Belle Epoque music hall. Tickets: 40-65F. Box office: Monday to Saturday 10 am to 7 pm.

Bouffes Parisiens 4, rue Monsigny, 2e; (tel: 296.60.24; metro: 4 Septembre). Mostly modern plays, with a little Molière thrown in for good measure. Tickets: 20-120F. Box office: 14-day advanced booking, open 11 am to 7 pm daily.

Cité Internationale Universitaire 21, boulevard Jourdan, 14e; (tel. 589.38.69; metro: Cité Universitaire). Excellent productions by the university theatre troupe. The complex includes the 600-seat Grand Theatre, 150-seat La Galerie and 130-seat La Resserre. The plays range from Euripides' classic *The Trojans* to Adamov's *The Parody*. Tickets: 22-45F.

Comédie des Champs-Elysées 15, avenue Montaigne, 8e; (tel: 723.37.21; metro: Alma). Revamped playhouse which has become one of the major mixed-media centres in Paris over the last decade. The bill includes theatre, ballet, symphony, jazz, opera and modern dance. The plays range from modern classics to avante-garde. Tickets: 50-150F. Box office: 14-day advanced booking; open daily 11 am to 8 pm.

Daunou 7, rue Daunou, 2e; (tel. 261.69.14; metro: Opera). The theatre is worth a look for its 1930s neo-Egyptian facade. Inside you'll find mostly French popular comedies. Have a drink at Harry's after the show. Tickets: 35-120F. Box office: 11.30 am to 7 pm daily.

Dix Heures 36, boulevard de Clichy, 18e; (tel: 606.07.48; metro: Pigalle). Home of the Comédiens de l'Orangerie, a company which seems to specialize in updated biographies. In 1983 they presented works on Jean Cocteau and Marcel Proust. Tickets: 50F or 80F for two shows; 45F for students. Box office: 14-day advance sale.

Edouard VII 10, place Edouard VII, 9e; (tel: 742.57.49; metro: Opera). Interesting location: a tiny square with a statue of the Duke of Windsor, the former King Edward VIII of England. The theatre's big '83 production was Strindberg's *Mademoiselle Julie*. Tickets: 55-150F. Box office: Monday to Saturday 11 am to 6 pm.

Eldorado 4, boulevard de Strasbourg, 10e; (tel: 208.23.50;
180

metro: Strasbourg St Denis). With 1,100 seats one of the largest playhouses in Paris. The bill features popular comedies and drama. Tickets: 60-130F.

Elysée Montmartre 72, boulevard Rochechouart, 18e; (tel: 252.25.15; metro: Anvers). Another 1,000-seat house which attracts the big name French stars. Elysée's 1983 success was *Love in Tahiti* by Francis Lopez. Tickets: 40-130F. Box office: 13-day advance sales, open daily 11 am to 7 pm.

L'Escalier d'Or 18, rue d'Enghien, 10e; (tel: 523.15.10; metro: Chateau d'Eau). A beautiful old theatre built in 1878 and renovated in 1982. The management has also been overhauled, so the company is now run by a youthful and dynamic team of two Parisian women and two Algerian-born Frenchmen. The productions are most often new, controversial works by little-known or young playwrights, ranging from a tribute to feminists Emma Goldman and Louise Michel, to the French Canadian-inspired *Lingue D'Improvisation Francais.* And yes, there is a golden stairwell. Tickets: 40-100F.

Fontaine 10, rue Fontaine, 9e; (tel: 874.82.34; metro: Blanche). The French classics: Molière, Victor Hugo, Alphonse Daudet, and Jean de la Fontaine, among others, plus modern comedies and drama. Tickets: 70-95F, students 50F. Box office: 10 am to 6 pm daily except Sunday.

Galerie 55 — The English Theatre of Paris 55, rue de Seine, 6e; (tel: 326.63.51; metro: Odeon). The only theatre in Paris presenting every show in English, thus a gathering place of students, diplomats, tourists and business types. Only 85 seats so book early. Tickets: 50-65F, students 35-50F. Box office: Tuesday to Saturday 11 am to 7 pm.

Huchette 23, rue de la Huchette, 5e; (tel: 326.38.99; metro: St Michel). Eugene Ionesco's *La Cantatrice Chauve* (The Bald Singer) has been playing the Huchette since 1957. You might call this the Paris equivalent to London's *The Mouse*

Trap. A second Ionesco work is presented during the late show. Tickets: 100F for one show and 120F for two, students 60F for one show and 80F for two. Box office: 5 to 9 pm except Sunday.

Lucernaire Forum 53, rue Notre-Dame-des-Champs, 6e; (tel: 544.57.34; metro: Vavin, Notre Dame des Champs). Another multi-media centre with three theatres (Noire, Rouge and Petite), two cinemas, an art gallery and restaurant. The menu includes comedy, drama, tragedy, romance and psychodrama. Tickets: 80F, students 45F; Monday: 45F, students 40F; 6.30 pm shows: 50F, students 35F. Box office: 2 to 7.30 pm daily.

Marais 37, rue Volta, 3e; (tel: 278.50.27; metro: Arts-et-Metiers). Home of the Company Jacques Manclair, a small (80-seat) theatre which presents Ionesco and other French classics. Tickets: 70F, students 50F. Box office: 13-day advance bookings, open 11 am to 7 pm Tuesday to Saturday.

Marigny Carre Marigny, 8e; (tel: 256.04.41; metro: Clemenceau). Annex to the Comédie-Française built in 1850. The Marigny has two venues: the 1,000-seat Grande Salle and the 311-seat Salle Gabriel. Productions are less classic than the Comédie, bordering on fringe and avant-garde at times. Last year the Marigny presented Thierry Le Luron's satirical look at French politics from De Gaulle to Mitterrand. Tickets: 40-150F for the Grande Salle, 60-100F for the Salle Gabriel. Box office: three weeks advance booking for the Grande Salle, 13 days for the Salle Gabriel; open 11 am to 8 pm except Sunday.

Mathurins 36, rue des Mathurins, 8e; (tel: 256.90.00; metro: Havre-Caumartin). Popular comedies and drama. This theatre did a big Amnesty International benefit in 1983. Tickets: 35-140F. Box office: 11 am to 7 pm daily.

Michodiere 4 bis, rue de la Michodiere, 2e; (tel: 742.95.22; metro: 4 Septembre). Musical and romantic comedies.

Tickets: 30-130F. Box office: 14-day advance booking, open 11 am to 6 pm daily.

Mogador 25, rue de Mogador, 9e; (tel: 285.45.30; metro: Trinité). This huge, 1,700-seat theatre exploded to the Parisian forefront last year with a brilliant production of Edmond Rostand's *Cyrano de Bergerac*. Tickets: 40-160F. Box office: 11 am to 7 pm daily.

Montparnasse 31, rue de la Gaîté, 14e; (tel: 320.89.90; metro: Edgar-Quinet). A marvellous hang-over from old Montparnasse, when the hill was the haunt of Parisian high society and poor artists. The neo-classic facade is crumbling, but it's still a fine example of Belle Epoque architecture. The Montparnasse today is split into the 715-seat Grand Salle and the 150-seat Petite Salle around the back. Both host romantic comedies. The Petit Bar du Theatre on the corner is a good place for an after-show drink. Tickets: 40-140F in the Grande Salle, 70F (35F for students) in the Petite Salle. Box office: 11 am to 7 pm except Sunday.

Oeuvre 55, rue de Clichy, 9e; (tel: 874.42.52; metro: Place Clichy). Georges Herbert's excellent house of modern French comedies and drama. Among the recent productions was the highly-regarded *The Extravagant Mr Wilde* by John Gay. Tickets: 40-110F. Box office: 11 am to 6 pm except Sunday.

Palais-Royal 38, rue Montpensier, 1er; (tel: 297.59.81; metro: Bourse, Palais Royal). Among Paris's oldest theatres, the Palais Royale was commissioned by Duke Philippe of Orleans in 1786 and built by the famous architect Louis, who was also responsible for the nearby Comédie-Français. It first served as a marionnette theatre, but in the 19th century it was rebuilt and transformed into a vaudeville house. Today, the Palais Royal stages mostly comedies and drama. Tickets: 19-150F. Box office: 28-day advance booking, open 11 am to 7.30 pm daily.

Porte Saint-Martin 16, boulevard St Martin, 10e; (tel:

607.37.53; metro: Strasbourg St Denis). Staged Georges Wilson's brilliant *K2* last year, starring Claude Rich and Bernard Giraudeau as two climbers stranded on a snowbound mountain. A beautiful playhouse built in the 1870s. Tickets: 25-150F. Box office: 20-day advance bookings, 11 am to 7 pm daily.

Renaissance 20, boulevard St Martin, 10e; (tel: 208.18.50; metro: Strasbourg St Denis). Next door neighbour to the Porte St Martin, built in the same year with the same art nouveau overtones. Presents the Theatre de Bouvard, a series of sketches and improvisations. Tickets: 55F, 35F for students. Box office: 11 am to 7 pm daily.

Théatre de Paris 15, rue Blanche, 9e; (tel: 874.10.75; metro: Trinité). Another Belle Epoque playhouse, but this time a multi-media centre presenting traditional drama and comedies, plus ballet and international dance. Tickets: 70-100F. Box office: 11 am to 8 pm daily.

Théatre de la Plaine 13, rue du General-Guillaumat, 15e; (tel: 250.15.65; metro: Porte de Versailles). The official theatre of the 15th arrondissement since 1973, presenting a mixed bag of theatre, musical spectaculars, modern dance, adult marionnette shows and children's theatre, plus a special programme of classical concerts. The building has an interesting futuristic design. Tickets: prices vary greatly according to the type of performance; children's theatre is 20F for adults and 15F for children, while adult drama productions are 50F for over 25s and 30F for under 25s. Box office: open 2 to 7 pm daily except Sunday.

Théatre du Rond-Point Avenue Franklin Roosevelt, 8e; (tel: 250.70.80; metro: Roosevelt). Revamped theatre under Renaud-Barrault direction which includes the 920-seat Grande Salle and the 190-seat Petit-Rond-Point. Presents contemporary drama, comedy and musicals. Tickets: 35-90F, 35F for students in the Grande Salle; 70F, 35F for students in the Petit-Rond-Point. Box office: 20-day advance booking, open 11 am to 6 pm daily.

Le Théatre du Tourtour 20, rue Quincampoix, 4e; (tel: 887.82.48; metro: Rambuteau). Small but dynamic playhouse in the Beaubourg with a menu that varies from Offenbach comic operas to Jean Cocteau romances and special shows of humour and fantasy. Tickets: 60-80F, students 45-50F depending on the production. Box office: 1 to 9 pm daily.

Variétés 7, boulevard Montmartre, 2e; (tel: 233.09.92; metro: Montmartre, Bourse.) A lovely remnant of Napoleonic days, built in 1807. Today the theatre is directed by Jean-Michel Rouzière and presents a mixed bill of comedy, drama, music and operetta. Tickets: 20-150F. Box office: 11 am to 8 pm daily.

● **Avant-garde theatres**

Bastille 76, rue de la Roquette, 11e; (tel: 357.42.14; metro: Bastille). Paris's cutting edge in modern theatre. The Bastille scored points last year with Kafka's *Le Gardien de Tombeau* and a tribute to Lillian Gish called *The Other Side of the Moon*. Drew equal attention (though not necessarily favourable) from an art expo on sodomy and fellatio. Tickets: 60F.

Café de la Gare 41, rue du Temple, 4e; (tel: 278.52.51; metro: Hotel-de-Ville). One of the oldest and most famous experimental theatres in Paris. The Gare has launched many a theatre star with past productions like *Graphique de Boscop* and *Les Robots*. Tickets: 50-70F. Box office: 2.30 to 7 pm Tuesday to Saturday.

Cartoucherie Avenue de la Pyramide in the Bois de Vincennes, 12e; (tel: 808.39.74 (Atelier), 328.36.36 (Tempête), 374.24.08 (Soleil); metro: Chateau-de-Vincennes). Three excellent experimental theatres in the same complex: the Atelier de l'Epée de Bois, the Théatre de la Tempête and the Théatre du Soleil. Each playhouse represents an entirely different company, like the Scarface Ensemble of the Tempête. Tickets: in the 40-60F range depending on the theatre and the production.

La Forge 18-20, rue la Forge-Royale, 11e; (tel. 371.71.89; metro: Ledru-Rollin). Edgardo Lusi's tiny theatre for training and developing young actors, with occasional performances by the resident artists. Staged the International Music, Theatre and Dance Connections in 1984.

Edgar 58, boulevard Edgar-Quinet and 3, impasse de la Gaîté, 14e; (tel: 320.85.11; metro: Edgar-Quinet). A veritable circus of off-beat and avant-garde entertainment spread over three theatres. The bill of fare includes drama, comedy, satire and music, plus special shows for children at the Edgar II. Tickets: 45F, students 35F; children's theatre: 20F for adults and 12F for children. Box office: 2.30 to 7.30 pm daily.

Tai Théatre d'Essai 37, rue Vieille-du-Temple, 4e; (tel: 278.10.79; metro: St Paul). Trendy Marais theatre with everything from abstract expressionism to French classics, Molière to Sartre. Tickets: 30-45F. Box office: 11 am to 6 pm daily.

La Tanière 45 bis, rue de la Glacière, 13e; (tel: 337.74.39; metro: Glacière). Avant-garde theatre, music and dance, plus French and foreign folk music. Part of the UNESCO Club complex. Tickets: 20-30F.

Théatre 13 24, rue Daviel, 13e; (tel: 588.16.30; metro: Glacière). A modern cement block theatre in the midst of a council-type housing estate, presenting equally futuristic and unusual programmes. Run in conjunction with the Centre de Jeunesse et de Loisirs. Tickets: 40-50F. Box office: 2.30 to 8 pm daily.

Théatre 14 20, avenue Marc Sangnier, 14e; (tel: 545.49.77; metro: Porte Vanves). The official theatre of the 14th arrondissement, presenting an eclectic collection of both modern and classical plays by the Théatre de la Jeune Lune troupe. The company is a bizarre amalgamation of Parisian and American mid western styles, founded in 1978 by three Frenchmen and a fellow from Minneapolis. Théatre 14 gets a regular subsidy from the City of Paris. Tickets: 60F, students 40F.

Théatre Essaion de Paris 6, rue Pierre-au-Lard, 4e; (tel: 278.46.42; metro: Rambuteau). Another new avant-garde playhouse, connected both physically and emotionally with the Café de la Gare. The menu ranges from Samuel Beckett to Jean Tardieu. Tickets: 35-85F.

● **Café theatres**

Au Bec Fin 6, rue Therese, 1er; (tel: 296.29.35; metro: Palais-Royal). Tickets: 45F, students 35F, dinner and two shows 150F.

Blancs-Manteaux, 15, rue des Blancs-Manteaux, 4e; (tel: 887.15.84; metro: Hotel-de-Ville, Rambuteau). Drinks only. Six different shows each night. Tickets: 35-45F.

Café de la Gare 41, rue du Temple, 4e; (tel: 278.52.51; Metro: Hotel-de-Ville). Soup and drinks only. Three different shows each night. Tickets: 0-70F depending on your luck at spinning the wheel of fortune.

Edgar 58, boulevard Edgar-Quinet and 3, impasse de la Gaîté, 14e; (tel: 320.85.11; metro: Edgar-Quinet). No food or drinks. Five to eight shows nightly, in three halls. Tickets: 30-60F.

Le P'tit Quebec 101, rue de la Croix-Nivert, 15e; (tel: 828.31.88; metro: Commerce). French Canadian singers and sketches. Tickets: 80F with dinner, and 30F without dinner.

Point Virgule 7, rue St Croix de la Bretonnerie, 4e; (tel: 278.67.03; metro: Hotel-de-Ville). Tea only. Three different shows each night. Tickets: 35-45F.

Le Sentier des Halles 50, rue d'Aboukir, 2e; (tel: 236.37.27; metro: Sentier). Two different shows nightly. Tickets: 45F, 35F for students and 70F for two shows.

Le Tintamarre 10, rue des Lombards, 4e; (tel: 887.33.82; metro: Chatelet, Les Halles). New café-theatre in the Beaubourg walking district which rose to fame in 1983 with the popular *Apocalypse Now* Three different shows each night. Tickets: 35-45F.

La Vieille Grille 1, rue du Puits de l'Ermite, 5e; (tel: 707.60.93; metro: Monge). Oldest café-theatre in Paris. Two different shows nightly. Tickets: 55F for show and one drink.

Music halls, Arenas

These huge modern auditoriums present a year-round bill of almost every form of entertainment and performing arts: opera, classical music, ballet, theatre, circus, ice shows, rock and jazz concerts and the like, the Parisian versions of the Albert Hall or Madison Square Garden. Naturally, with big audiences these halls get the big international stars too. The current shows are usually well-advertised around Paris.

Palais des Congrès Place de la Porte Maillot, 17e; (tel: 758.13.33; metro: Porte Maillot). The 4,300-seat main auditorium has the best acoustics of the big arenas. Concerts, dance, theatre and home of the National Orchestra.

Palais de Glaces 37, rue du Faubourg du Temple, 10e; (tel: 607.49.93; metro: Republique). Mostly music in this 700-seat auditorium. *Chanson* (see page 210) and theatre too.

Palais des Sports Porte de Versailles, 15e; (tel: 828.40.10; or 40.48; metro: Porte de Versailles). Giant theatre productions, ballet, rock and jazz concerts, sporting events etc. 4,500 seats in modern setting.

Pavillon de Paris — Hippodrome 209, avenue Jean-Jaures, 19e; (tel: 205.25.68; metro: Porte de Pantin).

Music

● **Opera**

Théatre National de l'Opéra Place de l'Opéra, 9e; (tel: 742.57.50; metro: Opera). A Paris institution since 1875 and one of the most magnificent opera houses in the world. This neo-Classical masterpiece was designed by Charles Garnier, an unknown architect until his plan was chosen from amongst 170 others in an international competition. The Opera seats 1,991, which makes it one of the biggest theatre auditoriums in the world, and its opening in September is still one of the highlights of the Paris social season. The spectacle tops any Hollywood movie premier, a glittering parade of government ministers, diplomats, business and industrial leaders and entertainment stars who march in their furs and diamonds up the sweeping staircase into the main hall. Most of the great classics been presented here, the works of Puccini, Strauss, Wagner, Mozart and others. But in recent years the Opera has been turning more and more to avant-garde and futuristic interpretations. In 1982, for instance, the Opera staged Gertrude Stein's *Dr. Faustus Lights the Lights* under the direction of avant-garde American Richard Foreman. The annual programme also includes ballet and classical music concerts. Tickets: 35-380F. Box office: 14-day advance booking, open 11 am to 6.30 pm daily.

Théatre National de l'Opéra Comique 5, rue Favart, 2e; (tel: 296.06.11; metro: Richelieu-Drouot). Downmarket, lighter and more traditional version of Big Daddy Opera up the road. The Opera Comique has actually been around longer than the Opera, since 1782, when the Duke of Choiseul com-

The September opening of the Théâtre National de l'Opéra is still one of the highlights of the Paris social season, a flamboyant affair attended by politicians and diplomats, international celebrities and corporate heads.

missioned a theatre for a new troupe called 'Les Italiens' in an effort to attract new residents to a housing estate he had just developed. The place burned to the ground in the 1880s, after which the present Salle Favart was built. Today, the Opera Comique specializes in light opera and operettas, with a particular emphasis on Beethoven, Offenbach, Mozart and Strauss. Tickets: 20-230F. Box office: 14-day advance booking, open 11 am to 6.30 pm daily except Sunday.

Théatre de la Ville Place du Chatelet, 4e; (tel: 274.22.77; metro: Chatelet). Occasional forays into the realm of opera. Last year it presented Robert Wilson's controversial and inspiring *the CIVIL warS,* an avante-garde American opera in 12 languages over 12 hours, starring Jessye Norman, Hildegarde Behrens and David Bowie. Tickets: prices vary with performance. Box office: 11 am to 7 pm daily.

● **Classical music**

American Centre 261, boulevard Raspail, 14e; (tel: 321.42.20; metro: Raspail).

Athenne-Louis Jouvet 4, square de l'Opera Louis Jouvet, 9e; (tel: 742.67.27; metro: Opera). A hefty schedule of big-name opera and symphonic stars from around the world including Dame Kiri te Kanawa and Grace Bumbry. Tickets: 40-200F.

Canadian Culture Centre 5, rue de Constantine, 7e; (tel: 551.35.73; metro: Invalides).

Chaillot Place du Trocadero, 16e; (tel: 727.81.15; metro: Trocadero). Occasional concerts in the intimacy of the 1,800-seat national theatre next to the Seine. Tickets: 30-60F.

Chapelle St Louis de la Salpetrière 47, boulevard de l'Hopital, 13e; (metro: St Marcel). Organ and voice concerts under the octagonal dome of St Louis Chapel in the middle of the old Salpetrière Hospital, founded by Louis XIV in 1656 for Paris's poor and destitute. The chapel dates from 1670.

Chatelet Place du Chatelet, 1er; (tel: 261.81.23; metro: Chatelet). Davioud's neo-Classical masterpiece built in 1862, one of the largest auditoriums in Paris and now the home of the Theatre Musical de Paris. Concerts by well-known soloists like Zoltan Kocsis and Bruno Rigutto, or visiting symphonies like the Israeli Philharmonic, the Orchestre de l'Ile de France and the famous Radio Stuttgart Orchestra. Tickets: 35-175F. Box office: 14-day advance booking; open 11 am to 6 pm except Sunday.

Conciergerie 4, boulevard du Palais, 4e; (metro: Cité) The ultimate in mood music: classical concerts in the spooky confines of Paris's medieval prison. Music ranges from the Middle Ages to 20th century.

Eglise des Billettes 24, rue des Archives, 4e; (metro: Hotel-de-Ville). Sunday organ concerts in the Marais's Lutheran church, built in 1756 by Carmelite Brothers. Next door is Paris's only remaining medieval cloister. Entrance free.

Eglise Notre-Dame du Liban 15, rue d'Ulm, 5e; (metro: Luxembourg). Classical soloists. Tickets: 35-45F.

Eglise St Germain des Pres Place St Germain des Prés, 6e; (metro: St Germain). Sunday evening concerts in the Left Bank's most famous church, first built in 542 by King Childebert and now the oldest house of worship in the city. Most of the present structure dates from the 11th and 12th centuries. Entrance free.

Eglise St Georges 7, rue Auguste-Vacquerie, 16e; (metro: Etoile, Kleber). Works by Handel, Telemann and others. Tickets: 20-30F.

Eglise St Julien-Le-Pauvre Quai Montebello, 5e; (tel: 665.19.95; metro: St Michel, Maubert-Mutualité). Classical works on ancient instruments in the ambience of a medieval chapel built at the same time as Notre Dame. Tickets: 30-40F.

Eglise St Medard 146, rue Mouffetard, 5e; (tel: 331.14.96; metro: Monge). Occasional concerts by the Student Orchestra of the National Conservatory of Paris, under the direction of Jean-Sebastien Bereau. St Medard offers a good example of late Gothic architecture. Tickets: 40F.

Eglise St Merri 76, rue de la Verrerie, 4e; (metro: Hotel-de-Ville). Home of the Accueil Musical St Merri which offers a continuing bill of classical, organ, piano and saxophone concerts, plus chamber music. The church dates from the 15th century, while the organ loft was built in the 17th century. Entrance free.

Eglise St Roch 296, rue St Honoré, 1er; (tel: 261.93.26; metro: Tuileries, Pyramides). The Parisian church which offers the greatest menu of classical concerts, under the direction of the Music Opera Sacra (MOS). The annual Grand Concert series includes works by Brahms, Verdi, Vivaldi, Bach, Mozart, Berlioz, Schubert, Stravinsky, Beethoven, Handel, Rossini and others performed by a rich variety of guest conductors, artists and orchestras. The church was built in the 17th and 18th centuries and houses many valuable works of art. Tickets: 30-80F for concerts, 40-120F for operas.

Ensemble Orchestral de Paris 15, avenue Montaigne, 8e; (tel: 720.67.37; metro: Alma-Marceau). Jean-Pierre Wallez's excellent group which performs the classics at various venues around Paris including the Chatelet, Salle Gaveau, Salle Pleyel and Theatre des Champs-Elysées. Frequent appearances by famous directors and soloists from around the world. Tickets: 25-110F, available from the various theatre box offices or the EOP office.

Foyer Internationale d'Accueil de Paris 30, rue Cabanis, 14e; (tel: 589.89.15; metro: Glacière). Continuous bill of classical music in the theatre of Paris's largest hostel.

Hotel Herouet 14, rue des Francs-Bourgeois, 3e; (tel:

278.62.60; metro: Rambuteau, St Paul). Occasional concerts by well-known soloists, mostly the classics. The Hotel was built in 1510 and was once the home of Louis XII's treasurer. Tickets: 28-40F.

Lucernaire Forum 54, rue Notre-Dame-des-Champs, 6e; (tel: 544.57.34; metro: Vavin). Classical sounds in the concert hall of this famous Left Bank multi-media centre. Tickets: 35-50F. Box office: 2 to 7.30 pm.

Maison de la Radio 116, avenue du Kennedy, 16e; (tel: 524.15.16; metro: Ranelagh). The famous home of the Choeurs de Radio France and the Nouvel Orchestre Philharmonique, an ultra-modern structure built in 1963 by Henry Bernard.

Madeleine Place de la Madeleine, 8e; (tel: 265.52.17; metro: Madeleine). Classical concerts including the annual 'One Hour of Music in the Madeleine' under the direction of Joachim Havard de la Montagne. Particularly moving are Vivaldi's *Gloria* and Saint-Saens *Oratorio de Noel* performed just before Christmas. The Madeleine church was commissioned by Napoleon as a tribute to his Grand Army, built in 1806 and modelled after the Parthenon in Athens. Tickets: 20-25F.

Musée Carnavalet 23, rue de Sevigne, 3e; (tel: 277.92.26; metro: St Paul). Occasional performances of classical and baroque music in the quarters of Paris's most fabulous Renaissance mansion, built in 1544. Entrance free.

Orchestre Colonne 2, rue Edouard Colonne, 1er; (tel: 233.72.89; metro. Chatelet). A Paris musical landmark since 1873, under the leadership of Pierre Dervaux for the last 26 years. The Colonne sticks mainly to the classics, but will often play works by lesser-known composers like Xenakis and Lalo. And there is at least one concert each year featuring the works of contemporary composers. The orchestra plays the Chatelet, Salle Pleyel and Eglise de la Trinité, often with notable guest soloists. Tickets: 25-100F available from the Orchestre Colonne office or the various theatre box offices.

Orchestre de Paris 252, rue du Faubourg St Honoré, 8e; (tel: 561.07.96; metro: Ternes). The premier symphony group in Paris, a world-class orchestra which attracts guests like Vladimir Ashkenazy, Itzhak Perlman, Zubin Mehta, Claudio Abbado, Luciano Pavarotti, Isaac Stern, Yehudi Menuhin, Jessye Norman and Kiri Te Kanawa, to name just a few. Daniel Barenboim directs the orchestra from the Salle Pleyel in a spectacular season which runs from September to April. Tickets: 35-150F. Box office 1 to 5 pm daily except Sunday.

Palais des Congrès Place de la Porte Maillot, 17e; (tel: 758.13.33; metro: Porte Maillot). The ultra-modern home of the National Orchestra of France in a 4,300-seat auditorium which is supposed to have the best acoustics of any big hall in Paris. The complex also includes two smaller halls. Tickets: 90-160F.

Saint Chapelle 4, boulevard du Palais, 4e; (tel: 296.14.33 (FNAC); metro: Cité). The city's most famous classical concert hall, a priceless medieval chapel built by St Louis in the 13th century. The tunes are classical, often performed by famous soloists. Tickets: 60-80F.

Salle Gaveau 45, rue de la Boetie, 8e; (tel: 563.20.30; metro: Miromesnil). Continual bill of classical concerts by guest artist from around the globe and Parisian groups like the famous Ensemble Orchestral de Paris. Tickets: 35-110F depending on the performers. Box office: 11 am to 6 pm daily.

Salle Pleyel 252, rue du Faubourg St Honoré, 8e; (tel: 563.88.73; metro: Ternes). The Centre Artistique de Paris, a modern concert complex which includes the 2,300-seat Salle Pleyel, the 470-seat Salle Chopin, the 120-seat Salle Debussy, numerous music and dance studios and a bar-cafeteria. Pleyel has a year-round schedule of concerts featuring the greatest artists and directors in the world, plus dance performances, lectures, films and classes. It's the permanent home of the world-famous Orchestre de Paris and there are often guest visits by such groups as the Ensemble Orchestral de Paris, the Orchestre Colonne, the Nouvel Orchestre Philharmonique, the Orchestre National de France, the London Philharmonic and the English Chamber Orchestra. Tickets: 35-200F depending on the performers. Box office: 11am to 8 pm daily except Sunday.

Temple de Pentemont 106, rue de Grenell, 7e; (tel: 353.29.83; metro: Bac, Solferino). Occasional classical concerts, plus the annual Festival of Ancient Instruments under the direction of Jean-Louis Charbonnier every March. Tickets: 35-50F.

Théatre des Champs-Elysées 15, avenue Montaigne, 8e; (tel: 723.47.77; metro: Alma-Marceau). Home base of the Ensemble Orchestre de Paris and the scene of a diverse schedule of fine arts performances which lasts the entire year. There's the annual International Festival of Dance each October, now in its 22nd year, plus festivals to the music of particular composers such as Gershwin, Wagner, Mozart, and particular countries like Russia, Spain and France. Among solo artists who have recently given recitals at the Champs-Elysées are Placido Domingo, Teresa Berganza and Christopher Hogwood. Also, there are frequent visits by the Radio France Orchestre National de France and Nouvel Orchestre Philharmonique and the Théatre National Opéra de Paris. Tickets: 12-200F depending on the performer. Box office: 14-day advance booking, open 11 am to 5.30 pm daily except Sunday.

Théatre de la Plaine 13, rue du General Guillaumat, 15e; (tel: 250.15.65; metro: Porte Vanves). Once-a-month classical concerts by an excellent cast of visiting orchestras and soloists in the confines of this futuristic multi-media centre on the outskirts of Paris. Tickets: 25-40F. Box office: 2 to 7 pm daily except Sunday.

Experimental music

IRCAM 31, rue St Merri, 4e; (tel: 277.12.33; metro: Rambuteau). The Institute for Research and Co-ordination of Acoustics and Music (IRCAM) at the Pompidou Centre is a place as futuristic as the name is long and as controversial as the Pompidou itself. In short, it brings together avant-garde musicians and composers interested in creating and spreading music. What the general public sees are the myriad concerts, workshops, seminars and publications put out by IRCAM. What the people don't see is the electronic wizardry and computer tinkering that goes on behind the scenes. The director is Pierre Boulez, the former musical director of the New York Philharmonic and a bold advocate of unconventional styles. Someone once asked him what should be done with opera. 'Blow up the opera house!' was his quick comeback. And while Boulez hasn't physically attacked traditional modes of music, he has blown away many preconceived notions of what music and sound should be. His staff of fifty are spending a seven-million-pound-a-year endowment from the French government on throwing off the shackles of the past and forging into the future. They have the world's most advanced synthesisers and computers at work trying to modify conventional instruments, develop new ones and dissect the essential properties of sound. IRCAM presents an interesting bill of public concerts in conjunction with its resident group, the Ensemble Inter-Contemporain representing musical personalities as antipodal as Frank Zappa and Igor Stravinsky.

Dance

American Centre 261, boulevard Raspail, 14e; (tel: 321.42.20; metro: Raspail). Performances and workshops in modern dance, jazz dance, Latin dance and ballet.

Au Forum du Mouvement (AFM) 31, avenue Parmentier, 11e; (tel: 806.68.01; metro: Parmentier). Chris Pages's extensive centre of dance for both adults and children. AFM offers classes and performances in modern, jazz, tap, Latin American and other forms, plus auxiliary dance skills like mime, song and theatre.

Carre Silvia Monfort 106, rue Brancion, 15e; (tel: 531.28.34; metro: Porte Vanves). Occasional performances by Asian and Third World dance troupes. Tickets: 60-80F.

Chatelet Place du Chatelet, 1er; (tel:261.81.23; metro: Chatelet). The big names in international dance, people like the New York City Ballet, the Netherlands Dance Theatre and the Grand Ballet Classic of Moscow, plus more contemporary themes like an Argentine Tango Festival in 1983. Tickets: 35-175F. Box office: 11 am to 6 pm daily except Sunday.

Dance Theatre du Marais 41, rue du Temple, 4e; (metro: Hotel-de-Ville). *Fame* and *Flashdance* à la Parisienne. Courses and performances in jazz, tap, classical and modern dance, plus the associate Ballet Studio du Marais. Home base of tomorrow's French dance stars.

Espace Cardin 1, avenue Gabriel, 8e; (tel: 266.17.30; metro: Roosevelt). Modern dance and ballet by international artists.

Maison des Arts André-Malraux Place Salvador-Allende, Creteil; (tel: 899.94.50; metro: Creteil). Home of Maugy Marin and the innovative Ballet Théatre de l'Arche, spearheads in modern French dance.

Musée Carnavalet 23, rue de Sevigne, 3e; (tel: 277.92.26; metro: St Paul). Hosted the Mairie de Paris Theatre, Music and Dance Festival in 1983.

Salle Pleyel 252, rue du Faubourg St Honoré, 8e; (tel: 561.06.30; metro: Ternes). The Centre Artistique de Paris's extensive programme of dance classes and performances, including modern, jazz, Hindu, Spanish, classic and tap dancing. There are at least two dozen dance teachers in residence.

Théatre de Paris 15, rue Blanche, 9e; (tel: 280.01.30; metro: Trinité). Occasional performance by national ballet troupes and other well-known dance groups. Tickets: 60-120F.

Théatre des Champs-Elysées 15, avenue Montaigne, 8e; (tel: 723.47.77; metro: Alma-Marceau). Paris's International Festival of Dance, now in its 22nd year, takes place here every October, featuring universal stars and choreographers like Joyce Trisler and Alfonso Cata. There are also performances by ballet company of the Théatre National Opéra de Paris. Tickets: 25-180F. Box office: 14-day advance booking, open 11 am to 5 pm daily except Sunday.

Théatre de la Plaine 13, rue du General Guillaumat, 15e; (tel: 250.15.65; metro: Porte de Vanves). Modern dance performances by the Company Anne Dreyfus and others. Tickets: 30-50F. Box office: 2 to 7 pm daily except Sunday.

Théatre du Rond-Point Avenue Franklin Roosevelt, 8e; (tel: 256.70.80; metro: Roosevelt, Clemenceau). Performances by national ballet and dance companies and other well-known groups. Tickets: 35-90F. Box office: 11 am to 6 pm daily.

Théatre de la Ville Place du Chatelet, 4e; (tel: 274.22.77; metro: Chatelet). Mostly big name dance troupes and national companies, but the Ville does host the annual GRCOP, a festival of new choreographers.

Circus

Cirque Gruss Parc de la Villette, 19e; (tel: 245.85.85; metro: Porte de Pantin). National circus which performs for several months each year in temporary quarters in the Parc de la Villette.

Cirque d'Hiver Bouglione 110, rue Amelot, 11e; (tel: 700.12.25; metro: Filles du Calvaire). Paris's oldest and most famous circus, situated in a bizarre Belle Epoque auditorium off the Boulevard du Temple. The Hiver was started by Napoleon III and has now been run by three generations of the Bouglione family. The show includes famed clowns Eddy Sosman and Petit Gougoux. Tickets: 40-90F.

Cirque de Paris 60, boulevard Lefebvre, 15e; (tel: 250.92.00; metro: Porte de Vanves, Porte de Versailles). Francis and Danielle Schoeller's *Spectacle de cirque* in the Square du Docteur-Calmette.

Marionettes

A Dejazet 41, boulevard du Temple, 3e; (tel: 887.97.34; metro: République, Filles du Calvaire). Co-hosts the Marionnettes de Paris festival each November with the Théatre des Templiers, attracting famous Italian companies like Teatro delle Briciole and Fratelli Napoli, and well-known French puppeteers like Compagnie Philippe Genty, Marionnettes Dougnac and Théatre Caroube. Tickets: 12-45F.

Centre National des Marionnettes 5, rue des Colonnes du Trone, 12e; (tel: 345.02.29; metro: Nation). Organizers of the Marionnettes de Paris and other puppet festivals and shows, funded with grants from the City of Paris and the Minister of Culture.

Champ de Mars (metro: École Militaire). Marionette shows at 3.15 and 4.15 pm every Wednesday, Saturday and Sunday during the summer months.

Marionnettes de Montsouris Parc Montsouris at Avenue Reille/Rue Gazan, 14e; (tel: 665.45.95; metro: Cité Universitaire). Children's marionette theatre in a big park. Tickets: 5.50F.

Théatre de la Plaine 13, rue du General Guillaumat, 15e; (tel: 250.15.65; metro: Porte de Vanves, Porte de Versailles). Adult marionette shows by the Compagnie Griffoul and others. But don't mistake 'adult' for sex shows, these are intellectual comedies. Tickets: 30-50F. Box office: 2 to 7 pm daily except Sunday.

CHAPTER EIGHT

Nightlife

No doubt about it, the best thing about Paris nightlife is its perpetual motion. The cafés stay open until after midnight, many of the bars, discos and clubs until dawn. In neighbourhoods like Saint-Germain, the Champs-Elysées and Pigalle there are crowds on the streets from sundown to sunrise, merrymakers from a hundred nations and every French province. There is an electric excitement which descends upon Paris as soon as the sun has dipped below the Eiffel Tower, and other than New York, there is no city which lives up to and then surpasses its billing as a nightlife mecca.

Parisian nightlife roughly takes on two natures: traditional French entertainment like cabaret and *chansons*, and foreign imports like jazz, disco, cinema and rock. Much of this latter group is American derived, for the French have long been secret admirers of American popular culture. The jazz is straight out of Harlem in the 50s, the cinemas pumped full of classic Hollywood films from every era, the discos just a Continental version of the best New York dance clubs. But the massive colonial influx into Paris from all parts of the world has introduced a new genre in the last decade: Third World sounds and dance. Paris now bops to the tunes of Brazilian samba and bossa nova, West African tribal rhythms and fast-paced Latin jazz.

202

However, Paris is perhaps best known for good, old-fashioned *cabaret*. The term has taken a lot of beating in recent decades, and is now applied to about any kind of nightclub. But cabaret in its purest French form is a theatre show with a lively orchestra, a few acrobats or comedians, and a chorus line of pretty girls waving a bit of flesh about. Nothing too saucy, of course. Unfortunately, there aren't too many of these places left, maybe just the Folies Bergères, the Moulin Rouge and the Lido, and these shows are largely for the benefit of tourists. More likely, the word cabaret today is used to describe a nude revue or tit-and-feather show – big on flesh and small on old Parisian ambience. Some of the cabarets are down-and-out sex shows. So you have to be quite choosy in looking for a cabaret.

Chanson translates into 'song' in English, and a chanson is a club where traditional French ballads or modern folk songs are performed. Many of these are lampoons and political ballads, and you will miss the jokes if your French is sub-standard. But you can enjoy the classic provincial harmonies in any language, and chansons offer some of the friendliest atmospheres in Paris.

Paris's discothèques can be divided into two categories: privately-owned clubs which have limited entry, and open clubs which let everyone in. To get into the innumerable private clubs you will need to be recognized at the front door, either as a club member, international celebrity or someone interesting or wealthy enough to entertain the other clients. Overseas visitors like Mick Jagger or Diana Ross can get in just about anywhere, no such luck for the rest of us. Almost all clubs have a standard cover charge of 50F or more per person. They usually serve a wide variety of drinks and cocktails at extortionate prices. And they are generally in action from 10 or 11 o'clock to dawn. But you can find this international chic scene in any big city: it's not unique to Paris.

Jazz, rock and Third World venues also have a standard cover charge of about 50F, and in the case of outright concerts they may print and sell tickets beforehand at various prices. Paris jazz scene is the most exciting in Europe, and there are often guest appearances by famous American jazz-men. The rock scene is no longer so prosperous, and French rock'n'roll takes some getting used to when compared to its British and American compatriots. The French are still into heavy metal, so don't be surprised if you encounter Francophile versions of Led Zeppelin or Van Halen. The big international pop stars visit Paris on their regular European tours, but as is to be expected they play the huge sports arenas and outdoor stadiums. Among top acts to hit Paris in recent years were the Rolling Stones, Super Tramp and David Bowie.

That brings us to the Paris sex scene, what seems to be the premier attraction of half the German visitors to the city. We have listed a few of the more prominent erotic theatre clubs here, places where you can pay your cash and see strip-tease, live sex shows, bondage and domination, lesbian acts and many other forms of naughty subversion. Paris has dozens, if not hundreds of these types of shows, plus the peep shows, porno shops and erotic books stores that go hand-in-hand. The prices are high and the action not all that different from Amsterdam or Soho.

Paris is justly famous for its prostitutes. The big question facing male visitors (especially those who have been to Bangkok and found them crawling over every inch of the hotel) is where to find a good hooker. I'm no expert, but I can point you in the right direction in a geographic sense. The most centrally situated hookers are in Les Halles, and a good corner to try is Rue St Denis at Rue de la Ferronnerie (metro: Chatelet or Les Halles). The occasional girl is also found on back streets around the Sebastopol-St Denis intersection (metro: Strasbourg St Denis). Two other popular hang-outs are the Avenue Foch and the backstreets of the neighbourhood between the Opera and the Madeleine (but would ex-prostitute Mary Magdalene approve?).

The most famous venue for prostitution, however, is the Bois de Boulogne. They are usually standing boldly along the Allée de Longchamp or the Route de la Reine Marguerite. The Bois also gives you much more than straight female prostitutes: French and Brazilian transvestites, male prostitutes for women, homosexual hookers and exhibitionists to name just a few. It's a regular sexual menagerie at night. If you are really hot to explore the Bois sex scene, pick up a copy of the invaluable *Le Plan du Sexe au Bois de Boulogne* by Mark Turlock, available for 39F at many bookstores and news-stands. It contains a map, plus descriptions of the various activities in English and French, and prices and times.

Another means of meeting a possible sexual partner is the *club de rencontres* or meeting club (sounds more sensual in French). Most of these are straight clubs, where men can meet women or couples can swap partners. But there are a number of gay meeting clubs, like Rencontres Gay (tel: 225.33.47.) for both homosexual men and lesbians. A complete listing of clubs de rencontres can be found in either the weekly *Pariscope* or *'Allo Paris* magazines found at most news-stands. There is usually a cover charge for all clients, but a few clubs let women in for nothing.

There seems to be an endless variety of sexual rendezvous in Paris. For example, there are *hotesses* clubs where men can find the lady of their choice for a steep price; *mixte* or mixed saunas open to both sexes; *relax* centres with sauna and massage for men or women; and the classified ad section of the International Herald Tribune, where call girls and female escorts are listed with unabashed enthusiasm.

Lastly, there is Paris's gay scene. We have already discussed the possibilities of the Bois de Boulogne and the Rencontres Gay. But there are a number of other possibilities for meeting French gays. The men's clubs cluster along the Rue Ste Anne of the first district (metro: Pyramides), while the major lesbian clubs are found in the Rue Ste Anne, or the Rues Bernard-Palissy and Vieux-Colombier of the St Germain area (metro: St Germain).

Cabaret

L'air de Paris 10, rue du Jour, 1er; (tel: 508.17.58; metro: Les Halles). Female impersonation at a private restaurant

205

club. Dinner and dancing to a live orchestra Thursday to Saturday at 11.30 pm. Supper and show: 200F.

Alcazar 62, rue Mazarin, 6e. (tel: 329.02.20; metro: Odeon). Tit-and-feather dinner show with a disco afterwards. Dinner from 8.30 pm nightly, spectacle at 10.30 pm. Choice of show and either a half bottle of champagne or two drinks for 255F, menu tourist without drinks for 230F, or menu prestige with caviar, vodka, chateaubriand, cheese and dessert for 500F.

La Belle Epoque 36, rue des Petits-Champs, 2e; (tel: 296.33.33; metro: Pyramides). Vaudeville à la Parisienne. Traditional French cabaret and comedy acts, chansons and dancers, in authentic art nouveau decor. Dinner, show and dancing for 250F including drinks and service; dinner with champagne for 375F, show only for 100F. Starts at 8.30 pm nightly.

Casino de Paris 16, rue de Clichy, 9e; (tel: 504.16.76; metro: Trinité). Re-styled music hall and theatre which presents a wide variety of events, from traditional cabaret and tits-and-feather, to chansons and classical music.

Chez Hippolyte 23, avenue du Maine, 15e; (tel: 544.64.13; metro: Montparnasse). Not your typical Paris cabaret in any sense of the word. The waiters are attired in gorgeous Napoleonic coats, but they go zipping about the place on rollerskates, perhaps the best balancing act in town when you consider what they must deliver to the tables. The stage show is a typical tit-and-feather spectacular, with dancing afterwards. Dinner, show and dancing for 185F; 65F minimum per person for the show only. Closed Tuesday.

Chez Moune 54, rue Pigalle, 9e; (tel: 526.64.64; metro: Pigalle). Famous lesbian cabaret in the heart of seedy Pigalle. Strip tease and other attractions, plus dancing after the show. From 10 pm Monday to Saturday, from 4.30 pm on Sunday and holidays.

Crazy Horse 12, avenue George V, 8e; (tel: 723.32.32; metro: Alma-Marceau). 'Far and away the best nude show in the universe' as the Crazy Horse likes to bill itself, and not many would disagree. For years this has been regarded as the best tit-and-feather show in Paris, with probably the best-looking girls. But the show also includes good singing and comedy acts, so you get more than enough for your money at this cabaret. The clientele over the last 30 years is almost as famous as the girls, the likes of John F. Kennedy, William Randolph Hearst and George McGovern. Shows start at 9.25 and 11.45 each night, while on Friday and Saturday there's an extra show added at 12.50 am. Seats are 310F including two drinks and 15 per cent service, but it's only 200F (including two drinks) if you want to stand at the bar.

Don Camilo 10, rue des St Pères, 7e; (tel: 260.25.46; metro: St Germain). Classy cabaret and dinner club in the old style, featuring an excellent bill of chanson singers, comedians and other variety acts. And the cuisine by chef Guy Girard is among the best you'll find at Parisian cabarets, sumptuous dishes like smoked salmon, Escargot Bourgogne, Calamari, Foie gras de canard and Jambon de Parme. Dinner and show 268F on Sunday to Thursday, 318F on Friday and Saturday including wine. Shows at 8.30 pm and 1.30 am.

Elephant Bleu 12, rue Marignan, 8e; (tel: 359.58.64; metro: Clemenceau). Featuring *Tahiti mon Paradis*, a tit-and-feather revue with lots of beautiful bodies from the South Pacific. But it's not all nude bodies, for there's also fine singing from the likes of Philippe Norman and Jean Davis. Dinner and show is 250F on weekdays, 300F on Friday, Saturday and holidays; show only is 150F. Dinner from 9 pm, spectacle starts at 10.30 pm.

Folies-Bergères 32, rue Richer, 9e; (tel: 246.77.11; metro: Montmartre, Cadet). A Paris landmark since 1914, one of the original tit-and-feather spectacles which at one time made this city the nude revue capital of the world. And

Folies hasn't compromised a bit despite competition from seedy sex shows in Les Halles and Pigalle. The girls still wear fantastic costumes and the show includes a bill of excellent variety entertainment between all those breasts. The current spectacle is *Folies de Paris* by Michel Gyarmathy, an eclectic revue which includes dancing, music and singing to a wide variety of styles including disco, samba, cancan and waltz. Prices ranges from 58F for standing to 275F for the *'Fauteuils Club'*. Shows start at 8.45 pm nightly except Monday and tickets are available 21 days in advance from the box office. There's also a special wine and cheese party at 7.30 pm each evening for only 90F, featuring 'all the cheeses of France'. Folies-Bergères is still one of Paris's top nightlife treats. Don't miss it. And be sure to check out the art deco facade.

Lido 116 bis, avenue des Champs-Elyseés, 8e; (tel: 563.11.61; metro: George V). From one Paris legend to another, this time the legendary Lido Café Normandie on the Champs-Elysées. The place is a bit touristy these days, but the show is still a spectacular combination of tit-and-feather dancers (the Blue Bell Girls), singers, comedians and acrobats. Dinner, dancing, champagne and show is 370F, champagne and show 255F, not including service. The action starts nightly at 8 pm, with shows at 10.30 pm and 12.30 am.

Madame Arthur 75 bis, rue des Martyers, 18e; (tel: 264.48.27; metro: Abbesses, Pigalle). A transvestite show called *La Cage aux Folles*. A great place if you're into female impersonation, but a bit weird if you are anything approaching straight. AC-DC in both the audience and on the stage. Dinner and show is 195F, show with first drink is 110F, and the regular bar minimum is 43F. Dinner at 8.30 each night, shows at 10.30 pm and 12.30 am.

Main au Panier 3, rue de Poissy, 5e; (tel: 633.33.63; metro: Maubert-Mutualité). One of the few worthy cabarets on the Rive Gauche, a dinner spectacle under the direction of Pascal

Oliver featuring song, comedy and other attractions. Dinner and show is 90F including a half bottle of wine and service. Shows at 8 pm and 1 am nightly except Sunday.

Michou 80, rue des Martyrs, 18e; (tel: 606.16.04; metro: Abessess, Pigalle). Another Pigalle transvestite show with a heavy gay clientele. The current revue is *Folies Folles*, a burlesque parody. Dinner and show is 185F including wine and service. Open from 9 pm nightly.

Milliardaire 68, rue Pierre-Charron, 8e; (tel: 225.25.17; metro: George V, Roosevelt). Tit-and-feather cabaret with lots of beautiful blondes, musicians, magicians, Muppet-like creatures and flashing lights. Sometimes it seems like a bad hangover from the 1960s, but the girls are fabulous. There's dancing after the show with the Charly Delsart Band. Shows every night at 10.30 pm, 12.30 am and 2 am.

Moulin Rouge Place Blanche, 9e; (tel: 606.00.19; metro: Blanche). The third of Paris's famous cabarets, the place made famous by Toulouse-Lautrec and his magic brush. But, unfortunately, the Red Windmill is no longer the bastion of the French cancan. These days the emphasis is on tits-and-feathers (what else?). The tour buses line up outside and the Americans and Germans flock into the Moulin Rouge to see the nudes, plus the supporting bill of chansons, acrobats, magicians and comedians. A bit on the tacky side, but most of the clientele doesn't seem to care. Dinner, dancing, champagne and revue is 370F, champagne and revue only 255F. Dinner from 8 pm nightly, shows at 10 pm and midnight.

Paradis Latin 28, rue du Cardinal Lemoine, 5e; (tel: 325.28.28; metro: Cardinal Lemoine). Jean-Marie Rivière's famous cabaret in St Michel. The latest revue is called *Paradisiac*, a spectacle of song, dance and pretty girls by Francis Morane and Molly Moloy. *Paradis* is considered one of the classier cabarets in Paris. Dinner and revue is 370F, revue and champagne 255F. Dinner is served from 8 pm, while the show starts at 10.30 pm.

Ville d'Este 4, rue Arsene-Houssaye, 8e; (tel: 359.78.44; metro: Etoile). Cabaret and dinner show in the old style featuring top French and international night club stars. The bill usually includes a variety of singers, comedians, acrobats, magicians and pretty girls. Dinner, show and dancing is 170F on Sunday to Thursday, 200F on Friday and Saturday, not including drinks or service. Dinner and dancing from 8.30 pm, spectacle at 10.30 pm.

Chanson

Au Lapin Agile 22, rue des Saules, 18e; (tel: 606.85.87; metro: Lamarck). Paris's most famous chansonnier, a ramshackle little place perched on the north side of Montmartre facing out toward Saint Denis. The 'Agile Rabbit' is little more than a country cottage, but much of the creative history of 19th and 20th century Paris has transpired from within its crumbling walls. This was Picasso's home-from-home, and the gathering place of Montmartre's poor but aspiring group of avant-garde artists and writers. They came for the song, the drink and the conversation, often paying their tabs with works of art now worth thousands of times what the bill of that day might have been. The atmosphere is still rustic, with simple plaster walls, huge wooden tables and dim lighting. The nightly shows haven't changed much through the century, still a joyous mixture of traditional French folk songs, poetry readings, humour and light cabaret. There are two shows nightly except Monday, at 9 pm and 2 am. Entrance and one drink is 55F.

Bateau Ivre 40, rue Descartes, 5e; (tel: 325.25.40; metro: Cardinal Lemoine). An evening of chanson ballads, poetry and guitar music frequented by students and intellectuals from the Left Bank. A tiny place with a huge reputation. Dinner and show 45F or 65F including wine and service; show only 40F. Starts nightly at 10.30 pm.

Bobino 20, rue de la Gaîté, 14e; (tel: 322.74.84; metro: Gaîté, Edgar-Quinet). Ancient music hall which features famous chanson stars from around France. Tickets are 60-110F. Shows start at 10.45 each night, with a 4 pm matinee on Sunday. Box office open daily 11 am to 8 pm.

Caveau de la Bolée 25, rue de l'Hirondelle, 6e; (tel: 633.33.64; metro: St Michel). A dark and mysterious place on a backwater alley off the Place St Michel. It looks like nothing in the daytime, just a crusty wooden door with playing cards painted on the panels. The Caveau is all that remains of a 14th century abbey, and you would swear by the ambience that the place hasn't been redecorated in all those years. Typical chanson music with lots of students and few tourists. Open Wednesday to Saturday from 7 pm.

Caveau des Oubliettes 11, rue St Julien-le-Pauvre, 5e; (tel: 354.94.97; metro: St Michel). This place is a real gem for overseas visitors, a popular chanson located in the remains of a 12th century prison next to the St Julien-le-Pauvre church. The chanson has only been here since 1920, but to keep the medieval atmosphere alive the players wear period costumes and sing only ancient French songs. The current revue is *Epic of the Crusades*, and just to add a bit more to the ambience, the cellar is still damp and dark. A bit touristy (it's hard to find Parisians in the audience), but certainly a lot of fun. Entry is 55F, and there are shows at 9 pm and 2 am every night.

Caveau de la Republique 1, boulevard St Martin, 3e; (tel: 278.44.45; metro: Republique). Unlike the other two Caveaux, this is not an authentic cellar, rather a 480-seat music hall which features top-flight French chanson singers. Tickets are 70F, shows at 9 pm each night with a 3.30 matinee on Sunday.

Chez Ma Cousine 12, rue Norvins, 18e; (tel: 606.49.35; metro: Abesses). Old-style chansonnier on a pedestrian street off the Place du Tertre, right in the middle of the old Montmartre. The Cousine bills itself as a *cabaret artistique*, a rather loose term which includes not only chanson singers, but magicians, mimes, dancers and an excellent political cartoonist. Catering to the tourist market, the show is in both French and English. Try the Brittany crêpes while you're watching. Dinner and show is 200F including wine.

Chez Georges 11, rue des Canettes, 6e; (tel: 326.79.15; metro: St Sulpice, Mabillon). Well-known chanson hall and bar in Saint Germain featuring top folk singers and guitarists. A lot of locals at this place, which gives it an authentic Parisian ambience rather than a glossy, touristy air. Shows at 10.30 Tuesday to Saturday. Entry and first drink is 40F.

Pot de Terre 22, rue du Pot de Terre, 5e; (tel: 331.15.51; metro: Monge). Chanson and guitar music nightly, plus a very good restaurant. Menus at 95F, 110F, 130F, 150F and 165F.

Cinema

It used to be a major struggle finding an English-language (un-dubbed) movie in France. And while it's still next to impossible in the provinces, at least in Paris they're catching on to the idea of original versions. Which is fantastic news for visiting cinema addicts from Britain, America and the colonies.

What's more, English-language movies are easy to find. Just pick up a copy of any major newspaper, or the weekly entertainment publications *Pariscope, 'Allo-Paris* or *Officiel des Spectacles*, and look for 'V.O.' at the end of the movie listing. That stands for *version originale*, which means an English movie in English, German movie in German and so on. The 'V.F.' movies are *version française*. The more detailed listings will also give you the year the film was made, the length, who the stars and director are, a brief synopsis of the plot and the cinemas at which it is currently playing.

The newspapers tend to compile their cinema listings by theatre and arrondissement rather than by the name of the film, so you will have to pick through all of the listings to find what you want. *Pariscope* and the other weeklies are far better, for they have an alphabetical listing by film, split into *films nouveaux* (new releases), *films en première exclusive* (first run films out for more than one week) and *reprises* (re-releases and revivals). And *Pariscope* has a further listing which breaks the films down into adventures, comedies, dramatic comedies, musical comedies, animated, documentaries, psychological dramas, erotic, fantasy, historic, musicals, horror, martial arts, detective and police, science fiction and westerns. How detailed can you get?

Cinema prices in Paris are usually in the 20-30F range for either first runs or revivals. But almost every cinema has a *tarif unique* or reduced price time, either for every show on Monday or matinees during the week. Depending on the theatre, there are also reductions for students with I.D.C.V., children under 18 or people over 60 *(cartes vermeilles)*, large families *(familles nombreuses)* or people out of work *(chomeurs)*. Many of these reductions are only available at certain times on weekdays, but they can reduce the price to as little as 10F.

As with elsewhere in continental Europe, the cinema-goer is expected to tip the usherette. In Paris this amounts to only one or two frances, even though the usherette does little more than tear your ticket and show you the way into the hall. This is because the usherettes aren't paid in France and make their salary entirely off the tips.

The French also have a rating system to protect the innocents from nasty movies. *Interdit aux moins de 18 ans* means no entry to anyone under 18, while *peut être vu par les enfants* means suitable for the entire family. Finally, there is no smoking allowed in any French cinema.

Following is a short list of Paris cinemas which show a continual bill of English-language films. It is by no ways complete (out of the 400 plus cinemas in Paris at least 67 now show English films), so you will have to check the newspapers or weeklies for the full selection.

Filming comes to the film museum: a scene from a movie being shot outside the entrance to the Cinematheque in the Palais de Chaillot.

214

Action Ecoles 23, rue des Ecoles, 5e; (tel: 325.72.07; metro: Maubert-Mutualité). Revival house which stages a different English-language film festival each week, i.e. Festival Marx Brothers or Festival Woody Allen. 18-25F.

Cine Beaubourg les Halles Piazza Beaubourg at 50, rue Rambuteau, 3e; (tel: 271.52.36; metro: Rambuteau). New cinema in the Quartier de l'Horloge development with five halls showing both first runs and revivals. 15-29F.

Cinematheque Palais de Chaillot, 16e; (tel: 704.24.24; metro: Trocadero). Centre Georges Pompidou, 4e; (tel: 278.35.57; metro: Rambuteau). Henry Langloise's famous Musée du Cinema at two spectacular locations: the Chaillot Palace and the Pompidou Centre. There are four different classic films each day at both locations.

Cinoche Carrefour de l'Odeon, 6e; (tel: 633.10.82; metro: Odeon). Small and stuffy cinema, but they show great films. 17-25F.

Elysees Lincoln 14, rue Lincoln, 8e; (tel: 359.36.14; metro: George V). First run films in three halls. 19-28F.

Gaumont les Halles Etage — 3 Forum des Halles, 1er; (tel: 297.49.70; metro: Les Halles). Paris premiers and first run movies in six halls. The place is packed on Friday and Saturday nights. 20-29F.

Les Forums Orient-Express Etage — 4 Forum des Halles, 1er; (tel: 233.42.26; metro: Les Halles). Deep in the bowels of the massive shopping complex, a new cinema with six halls showing premiers and first run films. You can find more obscure English and American movies here. 21-30F.

Marignan-Concorde Pathé 27-33, avenue des Champs-Elysées, 8e; (tel: 359.92.82; metro: Roosevelt). Seven halls showing first run, big name films. 19-30F.

Quintette Pathé 6-10, rue de la Harpe, 5e; (tel: 633.79.38; metro: St Michel). First run films in five halls. 19-28F.

Studio de la Harpe 13, rue St Severin, 5e (tel: 634.25.52; metro: St Michel). Excellent little independent cinema showing first run flicks. 19-28F.

Ballroom dancing

Balajo 9, rue de Lappe, 11e; (tel: 700.07.87; metro: Bastille). They shoot horses, even in Paris. Ballroom dancing straight out of the 1930s, but unfortunately no Jane Fonda to dance with. Matinée orchestra from 3 to 6.30 pm every day; the price is 40F, but there's a discount for women to 30F on Tuesday, Wednesday and Thursday. Bal de Nuit from 10 pm to 4.30 pm every Saturday night for 60F.

La Coupole 102, boulevard du Montparnasse, 14e; (tel: 320.14.20; metro: Vavin). Where Parisian high society danced in the 1920s and 30s, now the haunt of older folks who like to remember the good old days. Two orchestras and two sessions daily: 4.30 to 7 pm and 9.30 pm to 2 am.

Le Tango 11, rue au Mairie, 3e; (metro: Arts et Metiers). The last tango in Paris, a Latin dancing club which has been around since the turn of the century. It's in one of the seedier sections of the Marais, the type of street where you would expect to see a younger Marlon Brando in *On the Waterfront*. But the action is still fast and furious. You can tango daily from 2.30 to 6.30 pm. The price before 3 pm is 15F, after 20F.

Clubs and discos

L'Aventure 4, avenue Victor Hugo, 16e; (tel: 501.73.48; metro: Victor Hugo, Etoile). A chic private club where the beautiful people gather. Entry by recognition, which means

216

either they know you already or they've seen your face on some magazine cover.

Les Bains Douches 7, rue du Bourg-l'Abbé, 3e; (tel: 887.34.40; metro: Etienne Marcel). Disco, rock and punk club on the premises of an ancient steambath (hence the name) called the Bains Guerbois. The clientele is a bizarre mix of Paris trendy, old hippies, punk and fringe depending on the music at hand. There's both piped-in tunes and live bands. Restaurant on the first floor with dancing in the basement. Entry: 55F. The action starts at 11 pm every night except Monday.

Balajo 9, rue de Lappe, 11e; (tel: 700.07.87; metro: Bastille). The thirties dance hall transforms itself into a disco from 10 pm to 4.30 am every Friday night. Very young audience. Entry: 50F.

Bronx 9, rue Ste Anne, 1er; (metro: Pyramides). Gay disco on Paris's men-only street. Bring your leather.

Bus Palladium 6, rue Fontaine, 9e; (tel: 874.54.99; metro: Blanche). Famous disco and rock club with occasional live concerts by well-known groups.

Cameleon 57, rue St Andre-des-Arts, 6e; (tel: 326.64.40; metro: Odeon). Over 3,000 records played on request, plus live bands in the cellar. The music ranges through jazz, reggae, rock, funk, salsa and disco. Wednesday to Saturday only starting at 10 pm. Entry: 40F on Wednesday to Friday, 50F on Saturday.

Club Saint-Germain 13, rue St Benoit, 6e; (tel: 222.51.09; metro: Odeon). One of Paris's oldest private clubs, founded in 1901, and over the years frequented by many great artists, intellectuals, politicians and film stars. The clientele is no less noteworthy today. Upstairs there's the Bilboquet Restaurant and chanson singer Robert Martin; downstairs is the jazz club and piano bar, a dark and smoky place which has become legendary in the annals of Parisian jazz.

Deux Plus Deux 10, rue de l'Arbalete, 5e; (tel: 707.25.81; metro: Censier Daubenton). The famous 2 + 2 Ecole Buissonniere. For those with poor French, that means playing truant from school. And what mischief these pupils get into, for Deux Plus Deux is an unabashed swingers club. This is a disco and restaurant where couples can meet and exchange partners if they desire. But the emphasis is firmly on 'meet' for no action is allowed in the club itself. The food is served from 9 pm, while the disco starts at 11 pm. Closed Sunday and Monday.

Elysée Matignon 2, avenue Matignon, 8e; (tel: 359.81.10; metro: Roosevelt). Super-chic private club off the Champs-Elysées with a snobbish (and famous) clientele. The noses are as high as the prices. Entry by recognition only: if you're Mick Jagger come right on in, if you're Joe Bloggs forget it.

Elysée Montmartre 12, boulevard de Rochechouart, 12e; (tel: 252.25.15; metro: Anvers). Rock venue and disco club at the bottom of Montmartre hill.

Gibus 18, rue du Faubourg-du-Temple, 10e; (tel: 700.78.88; metro: Republique). Disco and live music venue. Some of the best live rock, jazz, reggae and funk can be found at Gibus. Soirée Speciale every Wednesday, an evening of dancing to the latest disco and rock tunes. Clientele depends on the night's music, but ranges from rasta-men to ex-hippies.

Golf Drouot 2, rue Drouot, 9e; (tel: 770.47.25; metro: Richelieu-Drouot). Paris's most famous rock'n'roll venue since the 1960s, a legendary counter-culture hang-out where over 6,500 groups have performed. Live music every Friday and Saturday night.

Incognito 43, rue Dauphine, 6e; (tel: 326.76.87; metro: Odeon). All-night disco where almost anyone can get in.

Nothing fancy, no stars, but at least we common people can go. Open nightly 11 pm to 5 am. Entry: 50F on Friday and Saturday, 40F on all other nights.

Katmandou 21, rue du Vieux-Colombier, 6e; (tel: 548.12.96; metro: St Sulpice). The Left Bank's top lesbian bar and disco, but no men allowed.

King Club 17, rue de l'Echaude, 6e; (tel: 633.00.24; metro: Mabillon). Private club with a disco and restaurant, plus the extra added distractions of billiards and video games. The customers are less outrageous than other private clubs, and the place is easier to get into if you're not a club member. Cocktails are 85F, mixed drinks 80F, a bottle of whiskey 720F.

Le Krypton Club Rue du Comm. Mouchotte, 14e; (tel: 321.48.96; metro: Montparnasse). A brand new disco and night club under the towering Montparnasse Park Hotel. The action kicks off at 11 pm on Sunday and week nights, at 10.30 pm on Friday and Saturday. Entry: 100F on Friday and Saturday, 80F all other nights.

New Jimmy's 124, boulevard du Montparnasse, 14e; (tel: 326.74.14; metro: Vavin, Montparnasse). Left Bank branch of the famous Regines with an equally chic and snobbish clientele. Another one of those elitist recognition only places, so forget trying to get in unless you wave a 500F note under the doorman's nose or you're related by marriage to the royal house of Monaco.

Opera Night 30, rue Gramont, 2e; (tel: 296.62.56; metro: Richelieu-Drouot). Where Paris's trendy blacks dance the night away. But this is no elitist joint and anyone can enjoy the fun. The music ranges through funk, reggae, Afro-jazz, salsa and traditional West Indian, and there's also videos and lasers. Dancing from 11 pm every night but Monday and Tuesday.

Le Palace 8, rue Faubourg Montmartre, 9e; (tel: 246.10.87; metro: Montmartre). The people's dance hall, and possibly the epitome of the classic discotheque. Le Palace has been Paris's most popular and outstanding disco in the last decade, drawing both the common folks and the stars, the chic and the mundane, and the place always seems to keep up with current trends in fashion and music (it underwent another renovation in late 1983). Best of all, anyone can get in. No private club elitism here. The 80F cover charge buys you the first drink and opens you into a world of mirrors, flashing lights, videos and a bizarre assortment of people. Don't forget to check out the roller skating in the basement (they hire out skates). Open every night from 11 pm until dawn.

Regine's 49, rue de Ponthieu, 8e; (tel: 359.21.13; metro: Roosevelt). The original snob city, Paris's second most famous disco after Le Palace. Home of the young French aristocrats (what's left of them), the Saint Tropez set and other assorted elitist groups. The elegantly-attired storm troopers at the front door will not let you in unless you are rich or famous or both. But a fascinating place for people-watching if you do gain entry.

Salle Wagram 39, avenue de Wagram, 17e; (tel: 380.30.03; metro: Ternes, Etoile). 'Le nouvelle discotheque de Paris', a giant music hall which was renovated from a thirties-style dance pavilion into a huge disco in 1983. You might call it the Paris version of the Lyceum. Dancing from 10 pm until dawn every Friday and Saturday night. Entry 60F including first drink.

Le Sept 7, rue Ste Anne, 1er; (tel: 296.47.05; metro: Pyramides). Popular disco and nightclub on Paris's main gay street — but many of the customers are straight. The restaurant has a reputation for excellent cuisine, but prices for both food and drinks are steep.

Le Tabou 33, rue Dauphine, 6e; (tel: 325.66.33; metro:

Odeon). All-night disco club open to everyone. The action lasts from around 9.30 pm until dawn every night. Entry is 50F including first drink on Friday and Saturday, 30F every other night.

Who's 13, rue du Petit-Pont, 5e; (tel: 325.13.14; metro: St Michel). New disco and bar on a busy nightlife street near the Seine. Dancing from 10 pm until dawn every night except Monday and Tuesday. Entry is 60F on Friday, Saturday and holidays, 40F on Wednesday and Thursday, and 35F on Sunday when all drinks are 25 per cent off. Open to everyone.

Wonder Club 38, rue du Dragon, 6e; (tel: 548.90.32; metro: St Germain, St Sulpice). Downbeat disco and jazz club in the heart of St Germain's trendy clothes market. Dancing from 10.30 pm nightly except Monday. Entry is 60F including first drink.

Zed 2, rue des Anglais, 5e; (tel: 354.93.78; metro: Maubert-Mutualité). Student hangout on the Left Bank. Open from 10.30 pm until dawn every night except Monday and Tuesday. Entry is 70F including one drink. Open to everyone.

Jazz venues

American Centre 261, boulevard Raspail, 14e; (tel: 321.42.20; metro: Raspail). 'Jazz on a Sunday Afternoon' at 4.30 pm each week, plus assorted other jazz concerts by American and French artists.

Le Bilboquet 13, rue St Benoit, 6e; (tel: 222.51.09; metro: St Germain). A Left Bank landmark since 1901 and still one of the top jazz clubs in Paris. Restaurant with live music on the first floor, bar and live music in the basement (also called the Club St Germain). 'Paris Blues' was filmed here.

Birdland 20, rue Princesse, 6e; (tel: 326.97.59; metro:

Mabillon). Famous jazz club on a dark street of Saint Germain.

Les Bouchons 19, rue des Halles, 1er; (tel: 233.28.73; metro: Les Halles). Low key, traditional jazz in the bar from 10 pm to 2 am each night. Good selection of wines and brasserie food to go along with the tunes.

Cambridge 17, avenue de Wagram, 17e; (tel: 380.34.12; metro: Etoile). Dinner and jazz club with traditional sounds, ranging through New Orleans, swing and boogie-woogie. Music and food until 2 am every night but Sunday.

Caveau de la Bolée 25, rue de l'Hirondelle, 6e; (tel: 354.64.20; metro: St Michel). A chanson club which gives over to fine jazz on occasions. The atmosphere is superb: a dim and smoky cellar which is all that remains of a 14th century abbey. Music from 11 pm nightly except Sunday. Entry: 30F.

Caveau de la Huchette 7, rue de la Huchette, 5e; (tel: 326.65.05; metro: St Michel). The Left Bank's top jazz club, an ancient cellar which fills each night with some of the best music in Paris. Huchette specializes in Dixieland, but there's often a good range of other forms of jazz. A different band each night and a dance floor to let it all hang out. Open from 9.30 pm nightly, until 4 am on Saturdays and holidays, until 3 am on Friday and until 2.30 am all other nights. Entry: 45F on Friday, Saturday and holidays; 40F all other nights.

Cameleon 57, rue St Andrés-des-Arts, 6e; (tel: 326.64.40; metro: Odéon). Live jazz bands in the basement, plus a selection of over 3,000 records played on request. Music from 10 pm on Wednesday to Saturday. Entry: 50F on Saturday, 40F on all other nights.

Dunois 28, rue Dunois, 13e; (tel: 584.72.00; metro: Chevaleret). Popular French jazz club in the 13th district.

L'Ecume 99, rue de l'Ouest, 14e; (tel: 542.71.16; metro: Pernety). A seedy little place in an even shabbier part of the 14th district, what used to be the heart of the artists' and writers' colony but is now about to be knocked down as part of the massive Montparnasse urban renewal project. How much longer this club will be dispensing its excellent American and Latin jazz is anybody's guess, so get there while you still can. Many visiting American artists stop in at l'Ecume for a session. Shows at 8.30 and 10 pm every night. Entry: 25-30F.

Le Furstemburg 25, rue de Buci, 6e; (tel: 354.79.51; metro: Odeon). Piano bar and jazz venue beneath the Petit Zinc restaurant. The music tends to consist of traditional quartets, trios and solo artists. A low key place with a comfortable atmosphere.

Le New Morning 7-9, rue des Petites-Ecuries, 10e; (tel: 523.51.41; metro: Chateau d'Eau). American-style jazz seven nights a week by such artists as The Lounge Lizards, Archie Shepp and Eddy Louiss. Latin jazz too. Entry: 40F.

Petit Journal 71, boulevard St Michel, 5e; (tel: 326.28.59; metro: St Michel, Luxembourg). Popular student jazz hangout near the Sorbonne. Closed Sunday, but otherwise jazz every night from groups like the Tin Pan Stompers.

Le Petit Opportun 15, rue des Lavandières, 1er; (tel: 236.01.36; metro: Chatelet-Les Halles). One of the few decent jazz bars on the Rive Droit. Music from 11 pm to 3 am every night. No cover charge, but beer runs 20-25F, soft drinks 20F and cocktails 35F.

La Resserve aux Diables 94, rue St Martin, 4e; (tel: 272.01.73; metro: Rambuteau). New jazz club around the corner from the Pompidou Centre. Sessions Tuesday to Saturday from 10 pm. Entry: 60F including drink.

Slow Club 130, rue de Rivoli, 1er; (tel: 233.84.30; metro:

Louvre, Pont Neuf). A Right Bank jazz landmark for many years. The resident sextet is still lead by Claude Luter, one of the grand old names of French jazz. Visiting artists also feature. The emphasis is on New Orleans and Dixieland styles. Sessions at 9.30 pm and 2.30 am every night, with an extra session at 3 am on Friday and 4 am on Saturday. Closed Sunday and Monday. Entry: Friday and Saturday 50F, all other nights 45F.

Le Savoy 15, place de la République, 3e; (tel: 277.86.88; metro: République). The big names in modern French jazz in concert nightly from 10.30 pm.

Théâtre de la Ville 2, place du Chatelet, 4e; (tel: 274.22.77; metro: Chatelet). The huge music hall which hosts the Festival de Jazz de la Ville every October with big name jazz bands and soloists from around the world. This is Paris's biggest jazz bash every year and a must for serious listeners. Other venues for the festival are the Théâtre Musical de Paris across the square, the Museum of Modern Art of the City of Paris (16e) at 14, quai de New York; (metro: Alma). Tickets are 33-95F.

Twenty-One 21, rue Daunou, 2e; (tel: 261.12.27; metro: Opéra). New American-style piano bar and jazz venue next to the King Opera restaurant. Also features Brazilian jazz. Sessions every night from 10.30 until dawn.

Rock and pop venues

Les Bains-Douches 7, rue du Bourg l'Abbé, 3e; (tel: 887.34.40; metro: Etienne Marcel). Rock, pop and punk concerts in the ambience of ancient steam baths. Restaurant on the first floor and a disco in the basement. Entry: 55F.

Bus Palladium 6, rue Fontaine, 9e; (tel: 874.54.99; metro: Blanche). Popular rock and pop venue in Pigalle which functions as a disco on non-concert nights.

Hippodrome – Pavillon de Paris 211, avenue Jean-Jaures, 19e; (tel: 205.25.68; metro: Porte de Pantin). Huge concert venue popular with big name international rock groups in the sixties and seventies, but little used of late.

Olympia 28, boulevard des Capucines, 9e; (tel: 742.52.86; metro: Madeleine, Opéra). Old 2,000-seat music hall which occasionally books big name rock and pop acts. Tickets: 70-160F. Box office: 9 am to 7 pm daily except Sunday.

Palais des Congrès Porte Maillot, 17e; (tel: 758.13.33; metro: Porte Maillot). Only the biggest international rock and pop stars in this ultra-modern, acoustically constructed auditorium. Tickets: 90-160F.

Palais des Glaces 37, rue du Faubourg du Temple, 10e; (tel: 607.49.93; metro: République). Smaller (700-seat) rock venue which also books jazz, Third World acts and chanson acts. Not too many international rock stars anymore. Tickets: 50-90F. Box office: 1 to 7 pm daily except Sunday.

Palais des Sports Porte de Versailles, 15e; (tel: 828.40.10 or 40.48; metro: Porte de Versailles). Paris's favourite venue for the biggest in international pop and rock stars (those who aren't yet big enough to book an outdoor venue like David Bowie or the Stones). Holds 4,500.

Rock 'n' Roll Circus 6, rue Caumartin, 9e; (tel: 268.05.20; metro: Havre-Caumartin). Top French rock and pop bands in a smaller venue, renovated in 1983.

Studio Gabriel 9, avenue Gabriel, 8e; (tel: 265.58.00; metro: Concorde). Well-known American, British and French acts in a concert setting. The music ranges from hard rock to jazz funk.

Third World venues

Chapelle des Lombards 19, rue de Lappe, 11e; (tel: 357.24.24; metro: Bastille). Salsa, French West Indies music and other Latin sounds. Sessions every night from 10.30 pm to 4 am.

Chica 71, rue St Martin, 4e; (tel: 887.73.57; metro: Chatelet, Rambuteau). Brazilian restaurant with live samba, bossa nova and other distinctly Brazilian tunes.

Chez Felix 23, rue Mouffetard, 5e; (tel: 707.68.78; metro: Monge, Censier). Paris's top venue for the Brazilian sound: jazz, samba, and bossa nova, plus comedy and cabaret. Disco dancing after the show. Shows Tuesday to Saturday at 10.30. Dinner and show is 180F on Tuesday to Thursday, 200F on Friday and Saturday including wine and 15 per cent service. Show only is 40-60F on Tuesday to Thursday, 100-400F on Friday and Saturday.

Discophage 11, passage du Clos-Bruneau, 5e; (tel: 326.31.41; metro: Maubert-Mutualité). Yet another of Paris's expanding number of Brazilian clubs and cabarets. The dinner show is 115F on Friday, Saturday and holidays, 105F all other nights, including wine and 15 per cent service. Show without dinner is 60F on Friday, Saturday and holidays, 55F on other nights. Closed Sunday.

L'Ecume 99 bis, rue de l'Ouest, 14e; (tel: 542.71.16; metro: Pernety). Out-of-the-way but popular jazz club which presents a good selection of Latin and African artists. Sessions at 8.30 and 10 pm nightly. Entry: 25-30F.

Petit Forum des Halles Estage −3 Forum des Halles, 1er; (tel: 297.53.47; metro: Les Halles). Excellent bill of Latin American and African artists in a concert setting. Tickets: 40-60F.

El Rancho Guarani 31, rue Descartes, 5e; (metro: Cardinal

Lemoine). Latin American folk music, particularly Argentine sounds in a rustic, cosy setting. Sangria and soft drinks at 48F, beer at 49F and hard liquor for 56F, but no cover charge. Closed Sunday and Monday.

Erotic theatre

Love in Paris 7, rue Fontaine, 9e; (tel: 280.23.16; metro: Pigalle). Live sex shows Hamburg style including strip-tease, lesbian shows, bondage and sado-masochism. Continuous shows from 2 pm to midnight. And they even take VISA and American Express. What is the sex business coming to? Tickets: 200-250F.

Lolita Club 73, rue Pigalle, 9e; (tel: 526.30.31; metro: Pigalle). Strip-tease, lesbian shows and live couples on stage from 2 pm until after midnight. The 12.15 am show each night is recommended only for 'experienced couples', while there is a special 'Exhibition Erotique' on Friday and Saturday. Tickets: 170-230F.

Les Nouveaux Innocents 4, rue de la Ferronnerie, 1er; (tel: 233.59.59; metro: Les Halles). Afternoon session from 2 to 8 pm, then non-stop 'Paris-Sex' on stage from 8.30 pm to 2 am, including live shows between couples, lesbians and groups, strip-tease and X-rated films. Tickets: 120F in the afternoon, 190F at night.

Théatre des Deux Boules 28, rue des Ecoles, 5e; (tel: 325.43.28; metro: Odéon, Maubert-Mutualité). Famous sex club on the Left Bank with live sex shows by a couple suspended in a net several metres above your head, plus erotic French cancans. Sessions nightly at 8.30, 9.30, 11 and 12.30. Tickets: 190F.

CHAPTER NINE

Sightseeing

The great sights of Paris are the stuff of legend. What arm-chair traveller has not dreamed of climbing to the top of the Eiffel Tower and gazing down upon the City of Lights, of pacing the inlaid floors of the Hall of Mirrors at Versailles, of exploring every nook and cranny of the Louvre, or of lighting a votive candle in that great Gothic masterpiece of Notre Dame? These images of Paris are firmly imprinted on every traveller's mind, and you are rarely disappointed when finally setting foot inside this dream city. For Paris becomes a compelling habit, like a drug addiction: you start with just a small dose, then yearn for much more, and finally you're hooked. You have to keep coming back again and again for the rest of your life.

There are few cities which are as visually striking as Paris, and the architects and city planners of Paris over the centuries have gone out of their ways to make this a reality. Whereas the banks of the Thames in London were filled with the dark factories and grey warehouses of the Industrial Revolution, the Seine's quays have always been host to elegant royal palaces and fabulous parks. And while Rome has always retained its jumbled medieval core, Paris very early exploded into a futuristic city of wide avenues and bustling squares.

Paris is now a city of weight and balance: the Greek columns of the Madeleine balance perfectly with those of the National Assembly across the Seine, the immense facade of the Hotel des Invalides is a foil for the gargantuan Place de la Concorde, and the symmetry of that huge corridor from the Louvre Palace to La Defense can boggle the mortal mind. Who else but the Parisians could construct a leafy path which includes the Tuileries Gardens, the Champs-Elysées and the Avenue de la Grande Armée right through the middle of their city?

The city is best explored on foot, with one of those marvellous Michelin Green Guides which gives you a blow-by-blow description of every palace, church and museum. And if you are staying in Paris for at least a week, then perhaps it's best to split your sightseeing into distinct sections for each day, say the islands on Day One, the Marais on Day Two and so on. But you can never really give accurate time allotments to this city, for during the course of your explorations you will undoubtedly find many little interesting buildings and museums you had never even heard of before. That's the beauty of Paris, the fact that no matter how many months, weeks or years you spend here, there seems always to be something more to see.

Buildings and monuments

Arc de Triomphe Place Charles de Gaulle-Etoile, 16-17-8e; (metro: Etoile). Napoleon's grand triumphal arch at the top of the Champs-Elysées, commissioned by the Emperor in 1806 as a tribute to his army, but not completed until 1836 under Louis-Philippe. The sculpture on each face represents the great victories of Napoleon's career. The Arc has been the scene of many a grand victory procession in its days: the Allied armies in 1919, the Nazis in 1940 and the French in 1944 after De Gaulle had liberated the city from the Germans. The viewing platform on top offers a superb view down the Champs-Elysées to the Place de la Concorde, and up the Avenue de la Grande Armée to La Defense. Open daily 10 am to 5 pm. Entrance: 11F.

The Arc de Triomphe on a cold winter morning, as seen through the 19th century wrought-iron gates of Park Monceau.

Assemblée Nationale Quai Anatole France, 7e; (metro: Chambre-des-Deputés). France's version of Parliament or Congress is housed in the 18th century Palais Bourbon on the Seine. Known as the National Assembly or Chamber of Deputies, this is the legislative home of the President of France and the 491 elected representatives from all over the land. To visit the building or to attend sessions of the Assembly, you must apply in writing to the Administrative Office, 126, rue de l'Université, 75355 Paris.

Bastille Place de la Bastille, 4-11-12e; (metro: Bastille). Almost 200 years since its fall, the Bastille still symbolizes the French Revolution. But all that remains of this infamous citadel today is the Place de la Bastille, a giant traffic circle with a 52-metre high column in the middle. The Bastille was stormed in July 1789 and immediately torn apart stone by stone, thus initiating the Revolution and the quick downfall of King Louis XVI.

Bourse Place de la Bourse, 2e; (metro: Bourse). Paris's stock exchange since 1826. The public gallery is open Monday to Friday noon to 4 pm; guided tours on the same days every half hour from 11 am to 1 pm. Gallery: free. Tours: 6F.

Catacombs 2 bis, place Denfert-Rochereau, 14e; (tel: 321.58.00; metro: Denfert). The macabre side of Paris sightseeing, a huge underground complex of tunnels and rooms that has served as a cemetery since 1785. It's estimated that over seven million people are now buried in the catacombs, but there will never be an exact count. They were used as a hiding place by the Resistance during World War II. The long galleries of skulls and cross bones make interesting photos. Open Tuesday to Friday from 2-4 pm and Saturday and Sunday from 9-11 am and 2-4 pm. Entrance: 9F. Bring a torch or flashlight.

Château de Vincennes Avenue de Paris, Vincennes; (tel: 808.13.00; metro: Château de Vincennes). A classic medieval castle with thick defence walls, perimeter towers, keep, dungeon and moat that was constructed by the Valois Dynasty in the 12th century. In subsequent centuries it served as a royal hunting lodge, prison, governor's residence, arsenal, porcelain factory and royal palace. Vincennes has been restored nicely since the retreating Germans almost destroyed it during World War II. Open daily 10 am to 4.15 pm (5.15 pm in the summer). Entrance 5F.

Conciergerie Quai de l'Horloge, 1er; (metro: Cité). France's most notorious prison. You can still see the cell in which Queen Marie-Antoinette spent several months of captivity before her date at the executioner's block, right next to the cell where Danton and Robespierre were later detained before their executions. Nearby is the Chapel of the Girondists, where 22 moderate revolutionaries of that name spent their last night singing and dancing around the body of a dead comrade. The chapel is now a museum with relics of Marie-Antoinette, detention and execution orders, and an authentic guillotine blade. The Conciergerie is the only surviving portion of the medieval royal palace. Open daily 10 am to 5 pm. Entrance 11F normal, 5.50F on Sunday.

Eiffel Tower Champ de Mars, 15e; (metro: Bir Hakeim, Champ de Mars). The endearing symbol of the City of Paris since 1889, when it was built for the Paris World Exhibition. The 300-metre (985-foot) cast-iron edifice is perhaps the greatest symbol of the 19th century Industrial Revolution, evoking the spirit of discovery and invention which characterized those times. The tower was almost universally panned after its construction, but over the decades its dramatic silhouette has crept into the hearts and souls of the French people. The tower underwent a major renovation in 1983 in which new restaurants and lifts were installed, and a tourist information centre built on the first level. Open daily 9.30 am to 11 pm. Entrance: 10F (green ticket) to the first level, 20F (white ticket) to the second level, 34F (ochre ticket) to the third level; 50 per cent reduction for children under seven. You can walk to the first and second levels for only 7F.

Hotel de Ville Place de l'Hotel de Ville, 4e; (metro: Hotel de Ville). Paris's City Hall. The present structure dates from the 1870s, a beautiful Neo-Renaissance palace which arose from the ashes of the old city hall, burnt to the ground by rampaging Federalists in 1871. Paris's municipal government has rested on this spot since 1357. Guided tours on Monday only, 10.30 am.

Invalides Place des Invalides, 7e; (tel: 555.92.30; metro: Latour, Maubourg, Varenne). A 300-year-old Renaissance masterpiece built by Louis XIV as a retirement home for his invalid soldiers, constructed in 1671-76 by the court architect Liberal Bruand. Over 4,000 veterans lived here at one time, but now there are only a few dozen. The bodies of Napoleon and a number of his top generals rest in the Eglise du Dome (Dome Church), but the major part of this massive complex is now taken up by the Museum of the Army. Open daily 10 am to 5 pm (6 pm in summer). 13F normal; 6.50F students (good for two consecutive days).

Luxembourg Palace Jardin du Luxembourg, 6e; (metro: Odéon, Luxembourg). A delightful Renaissance palace set in the lush confines of the Luxembourg Garden, commissioned in 1615 by Maria de Medici to remind her of her Italian birthplace. It later served as a monastery and prison, but since the Revolution it has housed the Senate, the 283-member Upper House of the French Congress. Guided tours of the entire palace on Sundays only, 9.30 to 11 am and 2.30 to 6 pm. But the art gallery is open daily (except Monday) from 11 am to 6 pm. Entrance: 11F.

Palais de Justice Boulevard du Palais, 1er; (metro: Cité). Today this massive complex plays host to the national law courts of France. But this building has a long and checkered history. Under its foundations lie the remains of the Roman and medieval palaces from which Paris was administered. Hugues Capet, Louis IV and Philippe Auguste made France the greatest nation state in Europe from their secure base in the palace, and its Great Chamber is where the young

233

Egypt no, Paris yes. The famous Sphinx Fountain in the Place du Châtélet, with the baroque dome of the Palais de Justice in the background.

Louis XIV uttered his most famous phrase: 'I am the State.' But this old royal abode became the seat of the feared Revolutionary Tribunal in the 1790s, an impromptu court which sent hundreds of people to their deaths at the guillotine at the Place de Grève just across the river. About all that remains of the medieval palace are the exquisite Sainte Chapelle and the evil Conciergerie prison. Thus, the Palais de Justice represents various French architectural forms over the past thousand years. Most of the courts and galleries can be visited by the general public on Monday to Friday from 9 am to 6 pm. Entrance: free.

Panthéon Place du Panthéon, 5e; (tel: 354.34.51; metro: Cardinal Lemoine, Luxembourg). The grand dome of the Left Bank. This masterpiece of the French Baroque style served as the Church of St Genevieve Abbey from 1789-91, but after only two years of life the Revolution intervened and it was transformed into the Panthéon, a burial place for great Frenchmen. Among those now resting within are Victor Hugo, Voltaire, Rousseau, Mirabeau and Emile Zola. Open daily 10 am to 5 pm. Guided tours in French every half hour from 10.30 am to 4 pm. Entrance: 11F normal, 5.50 on Sunday.

Place Vendôme Place Vendôme, 1er; (metro: Tuileries, Opéra). Sumptuous Renaissance square, commissioned by Louis XIV and completed in 1685. But Vendôme is most associated with Napoleon, for it is the Little Corporal who stands atop the great victory column in the middle of the square (Paris's version of Nelson's Column). The original statue and the column were made from the bronze of 1,200 Austrian cannon captured at the Battle of Austerlitz in 1805. Place Vendôme today plays host to the city's poshest jewellers and the world famous Ritz Hotel.

Place des Vosges Place des Vosges, 3-4e; (metro: St Paul, Bastille, Chemin Vert). Often considered Paris's most beautiful square, and the nucleus of the historic Marais district. Vosges was commissioned by Henri IV in the early

17th century as a combined Royal Palace and centre for court social activities like parties, parades and festivals. The place is a perfect square, with Renaissance arcades along each flank and a neat French garden in the middle. It was originally known as the Place Royale. Among the famous people who have lived on the square are Victor Hugo and Cardinal Richelieu.

Pompidou Centre Rue du Renard and Place Georges Pompidou, 4e; (tel: 277.12.33; metro: Rambuteau). There are not too many who would dispute that the Georges Pompidou Centre for Art and Culture is downright ugly. And there is little doubt that it fits into the surrounding neighbourhood, the oldest in Paris, like the proverbial bull in the china shop. But, equally, there is little doubt that the Pompidou Centre has become the success story of contemporary Paris. In seven years it has drawn over 35 million visitors, more than the Louvre and Eiffel Tower combined. It has revitalized the old slum district in which it sits. And it has carried a little of the contemporary art monopoly away from New York and back to Paris where it began 80 years ago. The entire complex is supported by and suspended from a giant steel scaffolding that resembles a child's building set. The guts of the building – pipes, ducts and wiring which are usually hidden from view – are wrapped around the Centre in full and often startling view. A caterpillar-like escalator snakes its way up the six levels of the western facade, its plexiglass tubes giving excellent views of Paris and the action in the plaza below. Inside this maze of supports and services is the core building, which contains the National Museum of Modern Art, the Public Information Library (BPI), the Centre for Industrial Creation (CCI), the Henry Langlois Cinematheque, the Institute for Research and Coordination of Acoustics and Music (IRCAM), the Children's Workshop and much more. And the cobblestone piazza outside has become Paris's biggest gathering place of street performers and musicians. The Pompidou Centre is open daily (except Tuesday) noon to 10 pm. The giant main gallery, viewing platforms and library are always free of charge, while the other components have various entrance charges.

Sewers Entrance at No. 93, quai d'Orsay, 7e; (tel: 705.10.29; metro: Alma). The famous *égouts* or sewers of Paris. The entrance is near where the Pont de l'Alma meets the Left Bank at the Quai d'Orsay. Open Monday, Wednesday and the last Saturday of each month (except public holidays and the days right before and after holidays) 2 to 5 pm. Not open during heavy rain storms or when the Seine is flooding (for obvious reasons). Entrance: 8F.

Tour Montparnasse Place Raoul Dautry, 15e; (tel: 538.52.56; metro: Montparnasse). The most controversial structure in Paris, surpassing even the Pompidou Centre in volume of hate mail. This giant black monolith is the highest office building in Europe at a staggering 210 metres (699 feet) and 59 storeys. If the Tour had been built in the suburbs, probably no one would have complained. But much of the historic and colourful Montparnasse district was bulldozed to make this ulta-modern complex a reality. It dominates the skyline of the district and is generally regarded as a blight upon the Paris skyline. But here it will remain. The main interest for visitors is the viewing platforms on the 56th and 59th levels which offer unmatched panoramas of the city. In fact, the tower offers the latest sunset in Paris by 38 seconds! There is an open-air terrace on the 59th floor; restaurant, bar, souvenir shop, exposition gallery and snack shop on the 56th floor. Open daily 9.30 am to 11.30 pm. Entrance: 25F normal and 16.50F students to the 59th floor; 20F normal and 11.50F students to the 56th floor.

Versailles Place d'Armes, Versailles; (tel: 950.58.32; RER: Versailles). Louis XIV's incomparable château in suburban Versailles, the world's greatest palace and the model for countless other royal abodes throughout Europe. Versailles is the epitome of royal excess and flamboyance, with its sumptuous decor, massive gardens, countless fountains and priceless works of art. Louis moved his entire court to Ver-

237

sailles – over 20,000 people – in order keep a close watch on the French nobles and aristocrats that represented the only true threat to his crown. And the idea worked, for Louis was the first of the Renaissance kings to drag his domain from the dregs of the feudal system into a modern, centralized nation-state. The high points of a visit to Versailles are the famous Hall of Mirrors and Royal Chapel by Mansart, the Royal Opera by Gabriel, and the marvellous State Apartments by Le Vau, plus a tour of the expansive gardens by Le Notre. Open daily (except Monday) 9.45 am to 5.30 pm. Entrance is free on Wednesdays but otherwise is: 13F to the main palace, 9F to the Grand Trianon, 6F to the Petit Trianon. Free entrance to the gardens and the King's Hamlet. There are significant discounts for people under 25 and over 60. To reach Versailles take RER Line C5 from the Gare d'Orsay. Cost is 16.80F return second class and 25.20F first class, and it runs every 10-15 minutes from 5.39 am (5.54 am on weekends and holidays) to 11.54 pm.

Churches

Notre Dame Place du Parvis Notre-Dame, 4e; (tel: 326.07.39; metro: Cité). Called the greatest masterpiece of the Middle Ages, perhaps the most famous church on earth. Notre Dame is the grand old lady of the Ile de la Cité, so dominating in its medieval bulk and Gothic power, yet so vulnerable in the delicate lines of its rose windows and flying buttresses. The cathedral is as much a symbol of Paris as any building in the city, the picture on a thousand postcards, the holy temple of ten million Parisian souls and the mecca of countless tourists. It was the first of the great medieval cathedrals of Europe, but although it is called the epitome of the Gothic church, Notre Dame is in fact a combination of two very distinct styles. The rounded columns of the interior betray the Romanesque touch, while the pointed arches and buttresses are definitely Gothic. It is at once heavy and brooding in the Romanesque style, and then

238

Notre Dame is often called a masterpiece of the Gothic style and perhaps the most fabulous church on earth, for the cathedral is as much a symbol of Paris as any building in the city.

light and airy in the Gothic manner. In the final analysis, however, Notre Dame must be considered one of the foremost statements of Gothic because its construction extended nearly 200 years into that period. Notre Dame's double towers soar 63 metres into the Parisian sky, and the giant bell in the south tower tips the scales at 15 tonnes. The interior of the cathedral is 130 metres long and 35 metres high, with 37 chapels and 75 giant stone pillars. If statistics alone are not enough to impress you, the atmosphere of the place certainly will, for there are few more moving religious monuments in the world. Bishop Maurice de Sully was almost singlehandedly responsible for getting the cathedral underway. He decided that two adjacent older churches should be demolished and that a great place of worship should rise on their site. Sully drew the ground plan, drummed up support, organized the workers and somehow got construction started in 1163. But Notre Dame wasn't finished until 1330, some 170 years later. The cathedral and precincts can keep visitors busy for an entire morning, for not only is there the giant nave and apse to visit, but also the Treasury with all its medieval relics, the climb up the south tower for one of Paris's best views, and a special audio-visual show on the history of Notre Dame; plus Roman ruins in the vaults below the square in front of the church. The main part of the cathedral is open daily 8 am to 6.45 pm, while the Treasury is open 10 am to 5 pm (except Sundays, and holidays), and the towers 10 am to 4.30 pm (except Tuesday). Entrance: free to the main church, 11F to the towers, 10F to the Treasury. Free organ recitals on Sunday at 5.45 pm. Guided tours in English on Saturday 2.30 pm and Sunday 2 pm throughout the year, and every day during the summer.

Sacré-Coeur Basilica Top of the Square Willette, 18e; (tel: 254.17.02; metro: Abbesses, Anvers). This crowning jewel of Montmartre looks to be one of Paris's oldest churches, but in fact it's one of the newest. Sacré-Coeur was constructed in 1876-1910 in an updated Byzantine style by the architect Abadie. Its great white onion domes give the skyline a mystical proportion as they soar upward in graceful, sinuous lines, almost appearing to float above the rest of the city. The expansive interior of Sacré-Coeur is famous for its modern mosaics. You can climb to the top of Sacré-Coeur's dome for one of the most spectacular views in Paris, or descend into the crypt to see the treasure and a video on the history of the church. The main part of the basilica is open daily 6 am to 10 pm, while the dome and crypt are open daily 9 am to noon and 2 to 5 pm. Entrance: free to the main church, 5F to the dome and crypt. You can take the funicular railway from the bottom of the hill.

Sainte Chapelle Inside the Palais de Justice in the Boulevard du Palais, 1er; (tel: 354.30.09; metro: Cité). The Ile de la Cité's other Gothic masterpiece, the royal chapel of the French kings built by St Louis in the 13th century to house the holy relics he had just purchased in the Middle East. If Notre Dame is 'primitive Gothic' then Ste Chapelle is surely 'ultimate Gothic', for there are few more inspiring works of medieval architecture in France. It is a magical statement of the period with its slender flying buttresses, sumptuous woodwork and 1300 stained glass panels, most of them the 13th century originals. The walls of the upper chapel are sheets of coloured glass. Open daily 10 am to 4.45 pm (5.45 in the summer). Entrance: 14F.

Saint-Denis Basilica Rue de Strasbourg, St Denis; (tel: 243.33.55). St Denis has served as the burial chamber of French kings and queens for twelve centuries, but the present basilica was finished only in 1267. Like Notre Dame, it is a combination of both Romanesque and Gothic styles and today St Denis is considered one of France's greatest treasures of medieval art and architecture. Its rose windows were the first of any church, and its religious sculpture is among the best to be found anywhere. The royal corpses were removed during the Revolution, but the ornate tombs remain, including those of Charles Martel, François I, Louis XIV and XVI, Henri IV and Marie-Antoinette. The basilica also contains the relics of St Denis, St Eleutherius and St

Rusticus. Open daily 10 am to 4 pm (5.30 pm in summer). Guided tours every half hour from 10 am to noon and 1.30 to 4 pm (1 April to 30 September only). Entrance: free to church, 11F to transept, chancel and crypt.

Saint-Eustache Rue du Jour at Rue Rambuteau, 1er; (tel: 236.31.05; metro: Les Halles). This moving church is much seen but little visited by tourists, who are more attracted by the Forum des Halles next door. But this combination of Gothic and Renaissance styles produces one of Paris's most historic and beautiful churches. And when the second stage of the Les Halles project is completed in the late 1980s, St Eustache will be flanked by a gorgeous tree-filled square. Presently, however, the church tends to be overwhelmed by the giant construction cranes and the riveting noise of the Les Halles site. St Eustache has had its fair share of historical scenarios since it was finished in 1637, among them the baptisms of Molière, Richelieu and Madame de Pompadour, the baptism of future Sun King, Louis XIV and the funeral of Molière. Open daily 8 am to 6 pm. Entrance: free.

Saint-Germain-des-Prés Place St Germain-des-Prés, 6e; (metro: St Germain). The parish church that has given its name to the Left Bank's most famous district and boulevard, and to a square and metro station. But the importance of St Germain-des-Prés is not only in the name, for it is one of Paris's oldest and most sumptuous Gothic shrines. The church was begun in the middle 6th century, but many later renovations and additions extended the construction period into the late 13th century, transforming St Germain into a classic Gothic church. It was once the nucleus of a giant Benedictine abbey, and for nearly a century it was the burial place of French royalty. St Germain is not so important in church affairs as it once was, but the square outside is one of Paris's most important café locales. Open daily 8 am to 6 pm. Entrance: free.

Saint-Marie-Madeleine Place de la Madeleine, 8e; (tel: 265.52.17; metro: Madeleine). One of the great landmarks of the Right Bank, an exquisite Neo-Classical chapel modelled on the Parthenon in Athens. The present structure was commissioned by Napoleon in 1806 as a shrine to his Grande Armée, but it wasn't consecrated until 1842. Many concerts and recitals are given in the Madeleine today. Open daily 8 am to 7 pm. Entrance: free.

Saint-Severin Rue des Prêtres St Severin, 5e; (metro: St Michel). Many a young backpacker has eaten lunch while leaning up against the aged Gothic walls of St Severin, one of many little chapels situated in the back streets of the St Michel district. The church is named after a 6th century hermit who lived upon this spot, and who was later canonized as a saint. The present structure dates from the 13th century and is considered a supreme example of the Flamboyant Gothic style with its famous ambulatory chapel, rose window and intricate decorations. Open daily 8 am to 6 pm. Entrance: free.

Parks and gardens

Bois de Boulogne 16e; (metro: Porte Maillot, Porte Dauphine, Porte d'Auteuil). Paris's greatest green space, 2,224 verdant acres stretching from Neuilly to Boulogne-Billancourt along the Seine. And the park has enough attractions to keep you busy for a month: the famous Longchamp and Auteuil horse-racing tracks, Grand Prix tennis at Stade Roland Garros, polo at the Club de Paris, the National Museum of Popular Arts and Traditions, the gorgeous Bagatelle Gardens, the Pré Catelan forest, the City of Paris Floral Garden, the Grand Cascade waterfall and a huge children's amusement park known as the Jardin d'Acclimatation. There are miles of walking, cycling and equestrian paths, and among the other recreational amenities are the Paris Bowling Alley, boating on the Lac Inférieur and various team sports at the Terrains de Sports. A number of roads in the Bois are also the haunts of Paris's famous prostitutes. In medieval times the forest was hunted for wild game like deer, bear and boar, and until the middle of the 19th century it was still an official royal domain and hunting ground. Baron Haussmann transformed the Bois into a leafy public park modelled on London's Hyde Park.

Bois de Vincennes 12e; (metro: Porte Dorée, Porte de Charenton, Château de Vincennes, Berault). As if to balance the map of Paris, the expansive Bois de Vincennes lies at the eastern edge of the city as a perfect balance to the western Bois de Boulogne. Its greatest attractions are the incomparable Château de Vincennes, the epitome of a medieval castle, and the Paris Zoological Gardens. But there is also the massive Paris Floral Garden with its greenhouses and gardens (the Paris version of Kew Gardens), row-boating on the Lac des Minimes and Lac Daumesnil, the Tropical Garden and Buddhist Centre. Near to the Porte Dorée entrance are the interesting Museums of Transport and African and Oceanic Art. Among recreational amenities are the Paris Vélodrome (cycling), numerous sports fields, and miles of walking, riding and cycling paths. The Bois was a royal hunting ground and private park until 1860, when Napoleon III gave it to the City of Paris.

Champ-de-Mars 7e; (metro: Champ-de-Mars, Bir-Hakeim, Ecole Militaire). The Field of Mars, the pleasant French garden which lies between the Eiffel Tower and the Ecole Militaire. It started life in the 18th century as a military parade ground for the school and has been the scene of numerous historical moments over the last 200 years, including famous balloon flights and a number of Revolution demonstrations. The Champ-de-Mars was converted into its present formal form in the early part of this century, and now ranks as a perfect place for an early morning jog or late afternoon stroll. Marionettes on Wednesday, Saturday and Sunday at 3.15 and 4.15.

Jardin du Luxembourg 6e; (metro: Luxembourg, Odéon, Port Royal). Many people believe the Luxembourg Garden is Paris's most gorgeous park, a claim that's hard to dispute after a single visit. This park is a bastion of students from the nearby Sorbonne and the many old people who live in this neighbourhood. They sun themselves on the wooden benches of the Terrasse, or take to the leafy alleys of the Ancienne Pepinière for a quiet stroll. The Bassin in front of the Palais de Luxembourg (France's Senate House) is a favourite haunt of young yachtsmen, who launch their toy boats on the reflective waters of the tiny pond. There are public tennis courts and a marionette theatre.

Jardin des Plantes 5e; (metro: Monge, Jussieu, Gare d'Austerlitz). Paris's ancient and venerable Botanical Gardens, often overlooked by tourists but certainly one of the most interesting of the city's green spaces. This place is a must for plant lovers and amateur botanists, for within the precinct are over 10,000 species including a 300-year-old false acacia which is deemed to be the city's oldest tree. Among the special features are a herb garden, ecological park, aquatic garden, Buffon's maze, a winter garden (Jardin d'Hiver) with desert and tropical plants, and an Alpine garden (Jardin Alpin) with arctic and high altitude plants. There is also a small zoo and five galleries dedicated to natural history and science. The garden proper is open daily 7 am to 6 pm, the zoo daily 9 am to 5 pm, and the museums at different times (usually 1 to 5 pm daily except Tuesday). Enter from the Place Valhubert or the rues Cuvier and Buffon. Entrance: 8-15F to the galleries and 13F to the zoo, with reductions for students.

Jardin des Tuileries 1er; (metro: Concorde, Tuileries, Palais Royal). More overseas visitors tramp through the Tuileries than any other park in Paris, although few pause to contemplate their French formality. This is because the Tuileries lie on the direct line from Paris's top two art museums, the Louvre and the Jeu de Paume. The garden was laid out in the 17th century by the great architect Le Notre (who was also responsible for much of Versailles's green space) and stretched from the Place de la Concorde to the Tuileries Palace (which later burned down). Today, the eastern

The Jardin des Tuileries lies at the heart of tourist Paris, yet few visitors bother to contemplate the leafy confines of this pleasant park. Instead, the Tuileries are left largely to the tranquility seeking Parisians.

perimeter is marked by the Place du Carrousel, with Napoleon's triumphal arch, and the massive Louvre Palace. The Tuileries has a number of important sculptures and two impressive fountains, as well as numerous comfortable benches. Small carnivals and circuses are sometimes held in the park during the summer months.

Parc des Buttes-Chaumont 19e; (metro: Buttes-Chaumont, Botzaris). This large park is a bit off the beaten track for most tourists, but from the Butte are incomparable views of north and east Paris, particularly Montmartre and the Marais. You can even make out St Denis Basilica in the far north. There's a small lake and many leafy avenues. Baron Haussmann laid out the Buttes-Chaumont in the 1860s on the order of Napoleon III.

Parc Monceau 8e; (metro: Monceau, Courcelles, Villiers). This has to rate as Paris's weirdest park, an offbeat green space mostly frequented by locals. Monceau began life in the 18th century as a gorgeous Rococo garden belonging to the Duke of Orleans. But the landscape architect went a bit mad, designing a combination French, English and German garden with numerous curiosities like an Oriental pagoda, miniature Egyptian pyramid, fake Roman ruins and Dutch windmills. You might say it was the Disneyland of its day.

Cemeteries

All of Paris's burial grounds are open 7.30 am to 6 pm (16 March to 15 November), 8.30 am to 5 pm (16 November to 15 January) and 8 am to 5.30 pm (16 January to 15 March). Entrance is free.

Montmartre 20, avenue Rachel, 18e; (tel: 387.64.24; metro: Blanche, La Tourche). The burial ground of Montmartre's famous since 1798. Among those interred here are Dégas, Offenbach, Berlioz, Emile Zola, Alexandre Dumas and Stendhal.

Monument to French Jews who died at the hands of the Nazis during the Second World War, just one of many striking memorials in the huge Père-Lachaise cemetery in northeast Paris.

Montparnasse 3, boulevard Edgar-Quinet, 14e; (tel: 320.68.52; metro: Edgar-Quinet, Gaîté, Raspail). Great views of the Tour Montparnasse and more famous names, including the sculptor Zadline, industrialist André Citroen, the writer Guy de Maupassant, poet Baudelaire and composer César-Frank.

Père-Lachaise Boulevard de Menilmontant, 20e; (tel: 370.70.33; metro: Père-Lachaise). Paris's largest cemetery and one of the most famous burial grounds in Europe. If you are going to visit only one cemetery in Paris, then it should be Père-Lachaise. The famous buried within are almost too many to list: Chopin, Oscar Wilde, Balzac, Rossini, David, Edith Piaf, Sarah Bernhardt, Baron Haussmann, Molière, Marshal Ney, Delacroix, Marcel Proust, Modigliani, Bellini, Murat and many more. But oddly, the most popular grave in recent years has been that of a 20th century star: lead singer Jim Morrison of the old American rock group The Doors, who died in Paris in the early 1970s under mysterious circumstances.

Zoos

Jardin d'Acclimatation Rue du Mahatma Gandhi in the Bois de Boulogne, 16e; (tel: 624.10.80; metro: Porte Maillot, Sablons). Small children's zoo that is part of a much larger amusement park for kids, including marionettes, miniature golf, pony rides, roller skating, carnival rides, children's theatre, miniature railway and car tracks, giant doll's house and the Musée en Herbe, a special art collection and workshop for kids. Open daily 9 am to 5.30 pm. Entrance: 4F.

Jardin des Plantes – Menagerie 57, rue Cuvier, 5e; (tel: 336.14.41; metro: Monge, Jussieu, Gare d'Austerlitz). Paris's oldest zoo, created in the 1790s when the Revolutionary Tribunal ordered the royal animal collection from Versailles to the Jardin des Plantes and then opened the collection to the public. Most of the animals were eaten by the starved residents of Paris during the Prussian siege of 1870, but the Menagerie was gradually restocked once the trouble subsided. This zoo still has a somewhat archaic atmosphere, and it could do with more than a little renovation. Among the attractions are the elephant, monkey, and lion and tiger houses, the great aviary, aquarium, reptile enclosure and vivarium. Open 9 am to 5 pm daily. Entrance: 13F normal, 3.50F students.

Parc Zoologique 53, avenue de St Maurice in the Bois de Vincennes, 12e; (tel: 343.84.95; metro: Porte Dorée). Paris's big, modern zoo with thousands of animals from hundreds of species housed in natural surroundings. There's an artificial butte at the centre which you can climb for a fantastic view of the zoo and park. Open daily 9 am to 5 pm (6 pm in summer). Entrance: 16F.

Above Paris

The ten best views of the city are:
1 Eiffel Tower:
Still the best after all these years, but also the most expensive (30F) if you take the high-speed lift to the third level. But oh-la-la, what a view! Height: 274 metres (899 feet) at the third level. See page 232 for times and prices.

2 Tour Montparnasse (56th Floor):
Not the favourite building of Parisians, but quickly becoming recognized as a superior view. There is no higher belvedere in the city, and the panorama is particularly good at sunset. There's also a brasserie, snack shop and the Bar American at the top. Height: 210 metres (688 feet), but the Tour already sits atop a hill. See page 237 for times and prices.

3 Notre Dame Cathedral (South Tower):
The oldest of the great Paris panoramas, and the most cen-

tral. But there are no lifts, so you will have to walk the innumerable Gothic steps of the North Tower, cross over the immense facade and then trek up yet another flight of stairs to the top of the South Tower. But the view is superb, looking out over the Ile de la Cité, Seine, Left Bank and Marais. And you can easily see most of the other major monuments of the city including the Eiffel Tower. Height: 69 metres (226 feet). See page 238 for details.

4 Sacré-Coeur Basilica (dome):
The view from in front of the church at the top of the Square Willette is superb, but for something even more spectacular try the dome atop this famous church. You have old Montmartre spread out before your feet, St Denis to the north, and the remainder of Paris in an impressive arc to the south. Height: only 80 metres (262 feet) but it sits atop Paris's highest hill. See page 240 for details.

5 Arc de Triomphe (viewing platform):
Napoleon's contribution to Paris's panoramas, with a magnificent view straight down the Champs-Elysées to the Place de la Concorde and the Louvre, and up the Avenue de la Grande Armée to the ultra-modern towers of La Defense. Good for watching traffic wars in the Etoile. Height: 50 metres (150 feet). See page 229 for details.

6 Le Samaritaine Department Store (top floor terrace):
One of the most under-rated of great Paris views. The open-air café and tea-room atop the famous store looks directly down upon the Seine, the tip of the Ile de la Cité and across to the Left Bank. You can easily spot the spires of Notre Dame and Sainte-Chapelle, plus the Invalides dome and the Eiffel Tower in the distance. See page 282 for details.

7 Concorde-La Fayette Hotel (42nd floor):
The giant new hotel at the Palais des Congrès is topped by the Salon Panoramique Bar and Restaurant, which lives up to its lofty name. Great views of the Bois de Boulogne, Champs-Elysées and La Defense. See page 87 for details.

8 Pompidou Centre (top floor):
Take the caterpillar escalator to the sixth level and check out this fantastic view. The street players down in the piazza look like energetic ants, but don't forget to look upward toward Sacré-Coeur and Notre Dame. Bar and restaurant for interludes between viewing. See page 236 for details.

9 Hilton Hotel (top floor restaurant):
The Hilton is not renowned as one of Paris's great viewing points, but it offers an unusual panorama of the Eiffel Tower, Champ-de-Mars and Palais de Chaillot that's hard to get anywhere else. This view makes the Eiffel Tower look absolutely gargantuan. See page 85 for details.

10 Parc des Buttes-Chaumont (The Temple):
The place is a bit tacky − a fake temple in the middle of a fake island − but it commands a superb view of Montmartre and the Marais, the only good view of Paris from the northeast. See page 247 for details.

Illuminations

Paris is known as the City of Lights, and there is no better way to soak up some of that famous Parisian romance than seeing the city when it's floodlit at night. Four buildings − Notre Dame, the Arc de Triomphe, Hôtel de Ville and the Place de la Concorde − are illuminated nightly from sunset to midnight in summer, and from sunset to 11 pm in winter. The other famous buildings and churches are floodlit nightly from 10 to 11.30 pm in summer, and on weekend nights and holidays from 8 to 10.30 pm in winter. The famous Renaissance and Baroque mansions of the Marais district have their own illumination schedule: nightly 10.30 to 11.30 pm from 1 April to 30 September (until midnight from 1 June to 1 August). Paris's fountains are floodlit in summer nights from 10 to 11.30 pm (to midnight from 1 June to 1 August) and in the autumn (1 October to 30 December) from 8 to 10.30 pm.

For those who like 'son et lumière' (sound and light) shows, the history of Paris is told in the excellent 'Shades of Glory' in the main courtyard of the Hôtel des Invalides. Shows in English at 11.15 pm nightly from mid-April to mid-October.

Museums

African and Oceanic Art 293, avenue Daumesnil, 12e; (tel: 343.14.54; metro: Porte Dorée). Interesting collection of native arts mostly from former French colonies in Africa and the Pacific, including masks, wood sculpture, pottery and jewellery. Recently the museum had a fascinating exhibit on bark painting. Tropical aquarium in the basement. Open daily (except Tuesday) 9.45 am to 12 noon and 1.30 to 5 pm. Entrance: 9F normal, 4.50F on Sunday.

Air Travel (Musée de l'Air) 8, rue des Vertugadins, Meudon; (RER Meudon – Val Fleury). Displays and artifacts on the Age of Flight, from the rudimentary flying machine of the turn-of-the-century to jet power. Open daily (except Monday) 10 am to 5 pm. Entrance: 10F.

Armenian Art 59, avenue Foch, 16e; (tel: 924.66.40; metro: Porte Dauphine). Religious and secular art from the lost nation of Armenia, now divided between Turkey, Iran and the Soviet Union. Open Saturday and Sunday 1 to 4 pm. Entrance: free.

Army Hotel des Invalides, 7e; (tel: 555.92.30; metro: Varenne, Latour-Maubourg). A massive collection devoted to the military man and the weapons he's fought with, tracing the history of warfare from prehistoric to modern times. This is one of the premier military museums in the world, and the three floors of exhibits include uniforms, armour, swords, cannons, firearms, flags, musical instruments, maps, films, documents and much more. The museum is particularly strong on Napoleonic relics, including the

253

Emperor's famous hat, overcoat, sword and campaign medals. The ticket for the Musée de l'Armée is good for two consecutive days, and also includes admission to Napoleon's Tomb and the Museum of Relief Maps and Plans in the same complex. A must for military freaks. Open daily 10 am to 6 pm (until 5 pm from 1 October to 31 March). Entrance: 13F normal, 6.50F students.

Baccarat 30 bis, rue de Paradis, 10e; (tel: 770.64.30; metro: Gare de l'Est). Tiny museum displaying the precious works of the adjacent Baccarat glassmakers. Open Monday to Friday 9 am to 5 pm.

Balzac 47, rue Raynouard, 16e; (tel: 224.56.38; metro: Passy, Muette). The house where Balzac lived from 1840-47, now filled with mementoes of the great writer's life including manuscripts, letters, books, caricatures, paintings and more. Adjacent library, plus a beautiful garden. Balzac finished *The Human Comedy* here. Open daily (except Monday) 10 am to 5.45 pm. Entrance: 7F normal, 3.50F on Sunday.

Bibliothèque Nationale 58, rue de Richelieu, 2e; (tel: 261.82.83; metro: Bourse). France's National Library, one of the world's greatest collections, housing a treasure of books, manuscripts, periodicals, newspapers, maps, engravings, photographs and music since 1720. There are now close to 10 million works in the collection, representing the breadth of French literature, journalism, cartography and music from the Middle Ages to present. Among the priceless relics are two Gutenberg Bibles, the manuscripts of Victor Hugo and Charlemagne's Gospel. Open daily noon to 6 pm. Entrance to special exhibitions: 8F.

Bourdelle 16, rue Antoine Bourdelle, 15e; (tel: 548.67.27; metro: Montparnasse). The former mansion of the sculptor Antoine Bourdelle, a pupil of Rodin who was famed for his huge bronze statues and busts. He lived in this house from 1884 until his death in 1929. The high point of the collection are the 21 Beethoven busts. Open daily (except Monday) 10 am to 5.40 pm. Entrance: 7F (free on Sunday).

Carnavalet 23, rue de Sevigne, 3e; (tel: 272.21.13; metro: St Paul). The Musée de l'Historie de Paris, housed in a marvellous 16th century mansion known as the Hôtel Carnavalet, one of the best examples of French Renaissance architecture in Paris. The mansion is a joy in itself, but inside are kept mementoes on Parisian history from medieval to modern times. Particularly strong on the Revolution. Open daily (except Monday) 10 am to 5.40 pm. Entrance: 9F normal, 4.50 students, free for people over 65 and for everyone on Sunday.

Cernuschi 7, avenue Velasquez, 8e; (tel: 563.50.75; metro: Villiers, Monceau). The mansion of the 19th century banker Cernuschi, converted into a museum to house his large collection of ancient Chinese art, plus exhibits on modern Chinese paintings and sculpture. Open daily (except Monday) 10 am to 5.40 pm. Entrance: 7F normal, 3.50 students, free for over 65s and on Sunday.

Cinéma Palais de Chaillot, 16e; (tel: 704.24.24; metro: Trocadero). Henri Langlois's excellent little movie museum includes historic photos, posters, costumes, scripts, stage sets, personal effects and landmark equipment like Thomas Edison's kineoscope and the Lumière brothers' kinematograph. The museum comprises the entire north wing of the Palais de Chaillot (built in 1937) and includes the famous Cinematheque film library with over 50,000 movies. A number of classic films are shown each day: at 3, 7 and 9 pm on Tuesday, Wednesday, Thursday and Sunday; and at 3, 5, 7 and 9 pm on Friday and Saturday. There are guided tours of the museum daily (except Monday) at 10 and 11 am, 2, 3 and 4 pm. Entrance: 9F.

Clemenceau 8, rue Franklin, 16e; (tel: 520.53.41; metro: Trocadero, Passy). Where the great statesman Georges Clemenceau lived from 1895 until his death in 1929. He was the overwhelming personality and power in France at the beginning of this century, helping to pen the Treaty of Versailles and serving as the Premier of France. Clemenceau was also a journalist, novelist and avid art collector. Open daily (except Monday and Friday) 2 to 5 pm. Entrance: 4F.

Cognacq-Jay 25, boulevard des Capucines, 2e; (tel: 261.94.54; metro: Opéra). An exquisite temple to the Age of Enlightenment in 18th century France. This interesting collection of furniture, paintings and ornaments was amassed by Eugène Cognacq-Jay, the man who founded La Samaritaine department store in the 19th century. This priceless collection shows just how far the one-time street merchant progressed in life. Open daily (except Monday) 10 am to 5.40 pm. Entrance 7F normal, free on Sunday.

Counterfeit (Musée de la Contrefaçon) 16, rue de la Faisanderie, 16e; (metro: Porte Dauphine). Fraud and deception through the centuries, a museum devoted to forgeries, false advertising and counterfeiting from medieval to modern times. Open Monday to Friday 8.30 am to 5 pm.

Decorative Arts 107, rue de Rivoli, 1er; (tel: 260.32.14; metro: Louvre, Tuileries, Palais Royal). Massive collection (over 50,000 objects) illustrating the development of French furniture, tapestries, woodwork, musical instruments, dining ware, sculpture and painting from the Middle Ages to modern times. The Musée des Arts Decoratifs also houses a research library, and there are usually temporary displays and exhibits like 1983's 'L'Expo des Expos'. Open daily (except Tuesday) 1.30 to 5 pm; special exhibits are open 11 am to 6 pm on Saturday and Sunday, 2 to 6 pm on all other days but Tuesday. Entrance: 15F normal, 8F for people under 25 and over 65.

Delacroix 6, rue de Furstemberg, 6e; (tel: 354.04.87; metro: Mabillon). The former apartment and studio of the greatest artist of the French Revolution and First Empire. It now houses many of his paintings, sketches and mementoes, including his palette and death bed. Open daily (except Tuesday) 9.45 am to 5.15 pm. Entrance 6F normal, 3F on Sunday.

Ennery 59, avenue Foch, 16e; (tel: 924.66.40; metro: Porte Dauphine). Small museum of Oriental art, antiques and jewellery. Open Friday and Sunday 2 to 5 pm. Entrance: Free.

Fashions and Costume (Musée de la Mode et du Costume) Palais Galliera, 10, avenue Pierre 1er de Serbie, 16e; (tel: 720.85.46; metro: Iena). New museum opened in 1977 and filled with some 20,000 outfits and costumes showing the evolution of French fashion from the 18th century to the present time. Open daily (except Monday) 10 am to 5.40 pm. Entrance: 9F normal, 4.50F students, free for over 65s and on Sunday.

French Monuments Palais de Chaillot, 16e; (tel: 727.35.74; metro: Trocadero). Reproductions of the great art and architecture of France, tracing the evolution of monumental design from the Romanesque period to the 20th century. This museum is particularly strong on medieval frescoes and Gothic sculpture. Open daily (except Tuesday) 9.45 am to 12.30 pm and 2 to 5.30 pm. Entrance: 9F normal, 4.50F students, free for over 65s and on Sunday.

Gobelins 42, avenue des Gobelins, 13e; (tel: 570.12.60; metro: Gobelins). Fascinating guided tours of the famous Gobelins tapestry works and the factory chapel. Gobelins has been churning out gorgeous carpets and tapestries for the French royalty and government for three centuries, and they are generally regarded as the best tapestry makers on earth. Open Wednesday to Friday only, with tours at 2.30, 3.15 and 3.30 pm. Entrance: 8F.

Grand Palais Avenue Winston Churchill, 8e; (tel: 261.54.10; metro: Clemenceau). Belle Epoque monolith of concrete and steel in which large touring exhibits are housed. Among past exhibitions were Tutankhamen, Rembrandt, Russian painting, the Art of the Cyclades, Pompeii frescoes and 1983's hugely successful Turner show. Opening times vary with each exhibit, but it is generally 10 am to 8 pm daily (except Tuesday). Entrance: 16F normal, 12F on Saturday.

Grevin 10, boulevard Montmartre, 9e; (tel: 770.85.05; metro: Montmartre). Estage − 1 in the Forum des Halles (1er); metro: Les Halles. Paris's premier wax museums. The Boulevard Montmartre waxworks takes in general subjects, many well-known people, while the Forum des Halles museum concentrates on the Belle Epoque period. Montmartre is open daily 2 to 7 pm; Forum des Halles Monday to Saturday 10.30 am to 9.30 pm and Sunday 1 to 8 pm. Entrance: 26F normal, 16F for under 15s.

Guimet 6, place d'Iena, 16e; (tel: 723.61.65; metro: Iena). Fascinating collection of over 50,000 Asian objects including paintings, sculpture, photographs, books, ornaments and costumes. This is an all-encompassing museum which takes in the art of China, Japan, India, Tibet, Indochina, Nepal, Pakistan, Korea and Afghanistan. One of the finest selections of its kind in Europe. Open daily (except Tuesday) 9.45 am to noon and 1.30 to 5.15 pm. Entrance: 9F (4.50F on Sunday).

Henner 43, avenue des Villiers, 17e; (tel: 763.42.73; metro: Malsherbes). Small museum dedicated to the works of 19th century Alsatian artist Jean-Jacques Henner. Open daily (except Monday) 10 am to noon and 2 to 5 pm. Entrance: 6F normal, 3F on Sunday.

Historial de Montmartre 11, rue Poulbot, 18e; (tel: 606.78.92; metro: Abbesses). Small wax museum showing the history of Montmartre. Always packed with tourists in the summer and on weekends. Open 10.30 am to 1 pm and 2 to 6 pm. Entrance: 6F.

History Museum of France (Archives Nationales) 60, rue des Francs-Bourgeois, 3e; (tel: 277.11.30; metro: Rambuteau). The National Archives of France, housed in the beautiful 16th century Soubise Palace and Hotel de Rohan. There are over six billion papers and documents including the Edict of Nantes, its Revocation signed by Louis XIV, the Revolutionary letters of Louis XVI, Marie-Antoinette and Robespierre, and many papers dating from the Napoleonic era. Open daily (except Tuesday) 2 to 5 pm. Entrance: 4F normal, 2F on Sunday, free on Wednesday.

Holography Estage − 1 in the Forum des Halles, 1er; (tel: 296.96.05; metro: Les Halles). New museum with displays and demonstrations on the 21st century art of holography − art via the laser beam. Buck Rogers here we come. Open Monday to Saturday 11 am to 7 pm and Sunday 2 to 7 pm. Entrance: 18F normal, 15F students.

Hôtel de Cluny 6, place Paul-Painleve, 5e; (tel: 325.62.00; metro: Maubert-Mutualité, St Michel). A bit of very old Paris. This highly interesting compound includes the ruins of a Roman bath, and a 15th century mansion which was once the residence of the Abbots of Cluny. Among the exhibits are medieval arts and crafts, Roman sculptures, and the famous tapestry known as The Lady and the Unicorn. One of Paris's best small museums. Open daily (except Tuesday) 9.45 am to 12.30 pm and 2 to 5.15 pm. Entrance: 9F (free on Wednesday).

Hunting and Nature (Musée de la Chasse et de la Nature) 66, rue des Archives, 3e; (tel: 277.12.33; metro: Rambuteau). Excellent displays on the sport of hunting housed in an 18th century mansion, the Hotel Guenegaud. Among the exhibits are weapons, costumes, stuffed animals and paintings by such masters as Rembrandt and Rubens. Open daily (except Tuesday) 10 am to 5.30 pm. Entrance: 12F.

Jacquemart-André 158, boulevard Haussmann, 8e; (tel: 562.39.94; metro: St Philippe du Roule). Fairly large array of 15th-18th century European artwork and antiques situated in a sizeable 19th century mansion. Strong on the

Italian Renaissance and the Louis XIV period in France. Among the big names are Rembrandt, Titian, Murillo, Botticelli and Donatello. Open Wednesday to Sunday 1.30 to 5.30 pm. Closed August. Entrance: 8F normal, 4F students.

Jardin des Plantes (Botanical Gardens) Rue Buffon at Rue G. St Hilaire, 5e; (tel: 336.14.41; metro: Gare d'Austerlitz). Paris's natural history centre, with separate galleries dedicated to zoology, botany, mineralogy, palaeontology and palaeobotany. The entire complex has an appropriate archaic air, and it needs more than a bit of renovation. But the Institute of Natural History is trying its best, especially with the interesting temporary exhibits. The palaeontology hall is about the only place in Paris to see dinosaur skeletons. The galleries are open daily (except Tuesday) 1.30 to 5 pm and Sunday 10 am to 5 pm, but there may be special times for the temporary exhibits. Entrance: 8.15F per gallery with reductions for students.

Jeu de Paume Place de la Concorde, 1er; (tel: 260.12.07; metro: Concorde). Perhaps the most popular museum in Paris per square metre. Forget trying to go in the summer unless you want to stand for at least an hour in that long line full of American students which winds its way down into the Place de la Concorde. But the collection is 'très magnifique': the cream of 19th and 20th century Impressionism including the great masters Van Gogh, Gauguin, Renoir, Manet, Toulouse-Lautrec, Rousseau, Dégas, Monet, Seurat and Pissarro. The second best art museum in Paris after the Louvre, and the most important Impressionist collection in the world. Open daily (except Tuesday) 9.45 am to 5.15 pm, but get there by 9 am to join the queue. Entrance: 13F normal, 6F for students and on Sunday. Guided tours in English every day at 3 pm.

Jewish Art (Musée de l'Art Juif) 42, rue des Saules, 18e; (tel: 257.84.15; metro: Lamarck). Small collection of Jewish paintings and religious objects, plus models of famous synagogues. Open Tuesday, Thursday and Sunday 3 to 6 pm. Entrance: 4F.

Legion of Honour 2, rue de Bellechasse, 7e; (tel: 555.95.16; metro: Solferino). A unique museum dedicated to Napoleon's Legion of Honour and the older orders of Chevalerie. The collection includes medals and decorations, weapons, uniforms, documents and paintings from the various military orders. Many Napoleonic mementoes. Open daily (except Monday) 2 to 5 pm. Entrance: 10F normal, free on Sunday.

Locks and Keys (Musée de la Serrure). 1, rue de la Perle, 3e; (metro: St Paul). A new collection which explores the history of the lock and key from Roman times to the 20th century, housed in a 17th century mansion called the Hôtel Libéral-Bruand. Also included are a number of interesting metalwork art pieces from the famous Bricard studios. Open Tuesday to Saturday 10 am to noon and 2 to 5 pm. Entrance: 5F.

Louvre Place du Carrousel, 1er; (tel: 260.39.26; metro: Palais Royal, Louvre). The world's foremost collection of pre-20th century art, situated in the expansive Louvre Palace along the Seine. Entry is from the square adjacent to the Place du Carrousel. It would take an entire book to catalogue the contents of the fabulous Louvre collection. But needless to say, it contains more priceless masterpieces than any other museum: legendary works of art like the Venus de Milo, the Winged Victory of Samothrace and the incomparable Mona Lisa by Leonardo da Vinci. The Louvre is comprehensive, covering all major forms of Western art from Egyptian antiquities to the Second Empire period. The palace itself is a hotch-potch of French styles spanning more than three centuries, from the reign of François I (who started the art collection in the 16th century) to that of Napoleon III in the 19th century; but in total, the Louvre is a statement of the French Renaissance. The museum owes the richness of its collection to France's great monarchs, for it was the likes of Louis XIV and Napoleon, in particular,

Visitors queue in the early morning to gain entrance to the popular Jeu de Paume, the Impressionist wing of the Louvre which contains a wealth of paintings by Van Gogh, Renoir, Degas, Toulouse-Latrec and many others.

who expanded the treasure with tribute from conquered lands, or by outright purchases with royal funds. Indeed, much blood has been spilled to make the Louvre what it is today. Open daily (except Tuesday) 9.45 am to 6.30 pm. Guided tours in English are given at 10.30 am and 3 pm daily (except Sunday). Entrance: 13F normal, 6F for people 18-25 and over 65, free for people under 18 and teachers with a professional card. Free on Sunday. Tripods: 5F.

Luxembourg 19, rue de Vaugirard, 6e; (tel: 234.25.95; metro: Luxembourg, Odéon). Newly relocated in its original home in the Luxembourg Palace, this is a small but important collection of art, known as the Luxembourg Museum, which has in past years been housed in the Orangery and the Palais de Tokyo. Open daily (except Monday) 11 am to 6 pm. Entrance: 11F normal, 8F on Saturday.

Malmaison Rue Charles Floquet, Malmaison; (tel: 749.20.07; RER: Rueil-Malmaison). A place of pilgrimage for Napoleon aficionados, a museum dedicated to Bonaparte and Josephine in the old Malmaison Château. Included in the expansive collection are Napoleon's bedroom and drawing room, Josephine's harp, and many historic paintings of the Little Corporal. Open daily (except Tuesday) 10 am to 12.30 pm and 1.30 to 5 pm (4.30 pm in winter). Entrance: 10F normal, 6F on Sunday and holidays.

Man (Musée de l'Homme) Palais de Chaillot, 16e; (tel: 505.70.60; metro: Trocadero). Extensive but somewhat antiquated museum devoted to the history of man, including important displays on anthropology, archaeology and ethnology. The museum traces the development of our species from neolithic to modern times with a chronological sequence that includes artwork, religion, clothing, weapons, tools, jewellery and burial rites. Very strong on pre-Columbian Aztec and Maya art, and African, Arctic and Asian cultures. Open daily (except Tuesday) 9.45 am to 5.15 pm (5 pm in the winter). Entrance: 12F.

Maritime (Musée de la Marine) Palais de Chaillot, 16e; (tel: 553.31.70; metro: Trocadero). A shrine to shipping and all those brave men who have sailed the seven seas. This museum contains a wealth of old navigational instruments, maritime artwork and the models of historic ships, plus interesting displays which trace the history of seagoing man from the barges of ancient Egypt to the super tankers of the 1970s. Special galleries on fishing boats, naval warfare and underwater exploration. Open daily (except Tuesday) 10 am to 6 pm. Entrance: 11F normal, 5F for disabled people and students in a group, free for military personnel in uniform.

Marmottan 2, rue Louis Boilly, 16e; (tel: 224.07.02; metro: Muette). Another mouth-watering collection for Impressionist freaks. The nucleus of this fantastic collection is 75 works by Claude Monet, given by his son to the City of Paris. But there are also works by Renoir, Manet, Pissarro and lesser known Impressionists. The collection is situated in the former home of art historian Paul Marmottan and also includes much of his extensive Empire art and antiques. Open daily (except Monday) 10 am to 6 pm. Entrance: 15F normal, 6F students.

Military Health (Musée de Service de Santé Militaire) 277 bis, rue St Jacques, 5e; (metro: Port-Royal). Displays on famous army physicians and the history of battlefield medicine from Napoleonic to modern times, including the Crimean War, colonial wars, and Second and First World Wars. Part of the giant Val de Grace complex, a former 17th century abbey and cloister which is now a premier medical school and military hospital. Open Monday to Friday 10 am to noon and 2 to 5 pm.

Mineralogy 5, rue des Fosses St Bernard, 5e; (metro: Jussieu). Small but important collection of rocks and minerals situated in Tower 15 of the Université Pierre et Marie Curie (Faculté des Sciences). Open Wednesday and Saturday 3 to 5 pm, but only when the university is in session. Entrance: 10F normal; free for students.

Mining (Ecole Supérieure des Mines) 60, boulevard St Michel, 6e; (tel: 329.21.05; metro: Luxembourg). One of the best collections on mining and minerals you will see. Part of the School of Advanced Mining Engineering and housed in a 19th century mansion just outside the Jardin du Luxembourg. Open Tuesday to Saturday 2.30 to 5 pm.

Mint (Musée de la Monnaie) 11, quai de Conti, 6e; (tel: 329.12.49; metro: Odéon, Pont-Neuf). Everything you always wanted to know about coins and money, from Roman to modern times, plus guided tours of the French national mint (no samples allowed). Naturally, the tour ends in the mint shop, where for hefty sums you can purchase the latest line of commemorative coins and medals. The museum is open daily (except Sunday) 11 am to 5 pm; guided tours on Monday and Wednesday only at 2.15 and 3.15 pm. Entrance: Free.

Montmartre (Musée du Vieux Montmartre) 17, rue St Vincent, 18e; (tel: 606.61.11; metro: Abbesses). A trip into the romantic past of this most famous of Paris's hills, via a fascinating array of old photos, paintings, recreated rooms and other mementoes. Renoir had one of his many studios in this building. Open daily 2.30 to 5.30 pm, Sunday 11 am to 5.30 pm. Entrance: 10F normal, 5F students.

Moreau 14, rue de la Rochefoucauld, 9e; (tel: 874.38.50; metro: Trinité). The former house and studio of artist Gustave Moreau, the man generally regarded as the founder and forerunner of the Surrealist movement. Over 10,000 of his paintings and sketches. Open Wednesday to Sunday 10 am to 1 pm and 2 to 5 pm. Entrance: 9F normal; 4.50F on Sunday.

Musical Instruments (Conservatoire National de Musique) 14, rue de Madrid, 8e; (tel: 292.15.20; metro: Europe). Several thousand historic and antique instruments, including

265

Marie-Antoinette's harp, Beethoven's clavichord and the piano on which the Marseillaise was composed. There's also an important musical library with historic scores. Open Wednesday to Saturday 2 to 6 pm.

National Museum of Antiquities Place Charles de Gaulle, St Germain-en-Laye; (tel: 451.53.65; RER: St Germain-en-Laye). Huge museum of French archaeological treasures from the Stone Age to the Middle Ages, housed in the Renaissance château of François I. The collection covers the Palaeolithic, Neolithic, Bronze and Iron Ages, Roman occupation and Merovingian empire. Open daily (except Tuesday) 9.45 to noon and 1.30 to 5.15 pm. Entrance: 9F normal: 4.50F for students, people over 65, and for everyone on Sunday.

National Museum of Modern Art (Pompidou Centre) Rue Renard or Place Georges Pompidou, 4e; (tel: 277.12.33; metro: Rambuteau). The crown jewels of the Pompidou Centre. Rambling over the fifth and sixth floors and the space of four football pitches, this museum displays more than 800 works of art from cubism to hyper-realism, the world's largest and most important collection of 20th century art. It's twice the size of the second most important collection, the Museum of Modern Art in New York. The content runs the gamut, both in terms of medium (painting, sculpture, engraving, photography and film) and exhibitors (Chagall, Picasso, Kandinsky, Ernst, Dali, Calder and Matisse to name just a few). K G Pontus Hulten, the former director of Sweden's Moderna Musset, runs the Pompidou museum with a brilliant and creative hand. He is a life-long promoter of avant-garde experiments in modern art, and he is set on bringing the museum's collection to the masses. Hulten's plan is spearheaded by the giant special exhibitions for which the Pompidou is now famous, especially the landmark expos mapping the cultural relationship between Paris and three other centres of 20th century culture: New York, Berlin and Moscow. Open daily (except Tuesday) noon to 10 pm, Saturday and Sunday 10 am to 10 pm. Entrance:

13F normal, 8F for people 18-25, free for people under 18 and over 65. Free for everyone on Wednesday, Sunday and holidays. Entrance to special exhibits is an extra 12F (Grande Galerie) or 6F (Galeries Contemporaines). One day pass good for all exhibits: 21F.

Nissim de Camondo 63, rue de Monceau, 17e; (tel: 563.26.32; metro: Villiers, Monceau). Interesting collection of 18th century art and antiques given to the City of Paris by the Count de Camondo. The museum includes valuable paintings, sculpture, tapestries, carpets, furniture and other artifacts of the Age of Enlightenment. Open Wednesday to Sunday 10 am to noon and 2 to 5 pm. Entrance: 12F.

Optics (Musée des Lunettes et Lorgnettes) 2, avenue Mozart, 16e; (metro: Clemenceau). New museum with displays on eye glasses, telescopes, microscopes and other optical instruments. Open Tuesday to Saturday 10 am to 6 pm. Entrance: free.

Order of the Liberation 51 bis, boulevard de Latour-Maubourg, 7e; (tel: 705.35.15; metro: Latour-Maubourg). Small museum dedicated to the men who helped to free France from the Nazi occupation. Includes exhibits on the Resistance, the Deportation and the major Allied military operations, plus the manuscripts and papers of General Charles de Gaulle, who founded the Order in 1940. Open daily (except Sunday) 2 to 5 pm. Entrance: 5F.

Orsay Quai Anatole France, 7e; (metro: Solferino). A museum for future visitors to Paris. The old Gare d'Orsay is being renovated into the Museum of Art and Civilization of the 19th century, a massive complex which will tell the story of French culture in one of its greatest ages. Included in the collection will be the First and Second Empires, plus the marvellous Belle Epoque. Look for lots of Romantic and Impressonist artwork, as well as Art Nouveau design. The museum was commissioned by the national government in 1977 and scheduled for completion in 1983, but work has now ground to a snail's pace and the complex won't be open until at least 1987.

Palais de Tokyo 13, avenue du President Wilson, 16e; (tel: 723.61.27; metro: Alma, Iena). Home of the Museum of Modern Art of the City of Paris and the temporary quarters of the Orsay Museum until its Gare d'Orsay location is finished. This is the most important collection of 20th century art in France after the Pompidou Centre, with a treasure that includes Picasso, Matisse, Braque, Utrillo, Gauguin, Modigliani, Leger and many others. It tries to bridge the gap between pure Impressionism and more modern forms like Cubism. There are many special exhibits. Open daily (except Tuesday) 9.45 am to 5.15 pm. Entrance: 9F normal: 4.50F on Sunday.

Pasteur 25, rue du Dr Roux, 15e; (tel: 541.52.6; metro: Pasteur). The former apartment of Louis Pasteur, the 19th century chemist and biologist who gave the world pasteurized milk and many vaccination processes. His tomb is in the crypt of this building, now called the Pasteur Institute. Open Monday to Friday 2.30 to 5 pm.

Petit Palais Avenue Winston Churchill, 8e; (tel: 265.12.73; metro: Clemenceau). Many special exhibits, plus a permanent collection which represents just about every school of Western artwork from Classical to modern times. Strong on Greek, Roman and Egyptian antiquities, medieval religious art, Renaissance painting and furniture, and Impressionism. Open daily (except Monday) 10 am to 5.40 pm. Entrance: 9F normal, 4.50F students, free on Sunday.

Picasso (Hotel Sale) 5, rue de Thorigny, 3e; (metro: St Sebastian). A yet-to-be-completed museum which will display many of the works and mementoes of the great Pablo Picasso, the Spanish master who made his name in Paris as one of the founders of Cubism. The Hotel Sale is an 18th century Marais mansion built by a wealthy salt tax collector. Due to open in the mid-1980s.

Popular Arts and Traditions (Musée des Arts et Traditions Populaires) 6, route de Mahatma Gandhi in the Bois de Boulogne, 16e; (tel: 747.69.80; metro: Sablons, Porte Maillot). A superb folk art museum which shows how man has manipulated his natural environment in the evolution of culture. Displays on agriculture, religion, folklore, arts and crafts and much more. Open daily (except Tuesday) 10 am to 5 pm. Entrance: 9F normal, 4.50F on Sunday and holidays.

Post and Stamps (Musée de la Poste) 34, boulevard de Vaugirard, 15e; (tel: 320.15.30; metro: Montparnasse). Everything for the avid stamp collector and postal freak: models of mail transport from carriages to planes, machines for printing stamps and sorting post, antique mail boxes, the complete history of post through the ages, every stamp ever issued in France, and the collections of many other countries. Also, there's a stamp library, photo collection, philatelist workshop and stamp sales counter. Perhaps the finest museum of its kind in the world. Open daily (except Sunday and holidays) 10 am to 5 pm. Entrance: 5F normal; 2.50F for people 18-25 and over 65, free for under 18's.

Posters (Musée de l'Affiche) 18, rue de Paradis, 10e; (tel: 246.13.09; metro: Château d'Eau, Gare de l'Est). Recently opened museum housing over 70,000 posters from all over the world, including movie and advertising posters. There are also temporary exhibits of various kinds. Open daily (except Tuesday) noon to 6 pm. Entrance: 15F normal, 7.50F students.

Public Assistance 47, quai de la Tournelle, 5e; (tel: 633.01.43; metro: St Michel, Maubert-Mutualité). Paris's newest museum, opened in late 1983 and dedicated to the hospitals and medical personnel of France. Open Wednesday to Sunday 10 am to 5 pm. Entrance: 5F.

Radio France 116, avenue du President Kennedy, 16e; (tel: 230.21.80; metro: Ranelagh). The home of the ORTF (Office de Radio Télévision Française) since 1963, an ultra-modern round building which is the largest single structure in France. Guided tours daily (except Monday) 10 am to noon and 2 to 5 pm. Entrance: 6.50F normal, 3.50F students.

Rodin 77, rue de Varenne, 7e; (tel: 705.01.34; metro: Varenne). Quickly becoming one of the most popular art museums in Paris. The Rodin collection is housed in the Hotel Biron, an 18th century mansion where Rodin lived and worked. The house and garden contain many of his inspiring sculptures, including The Thinker. Open daily (except Tuesday) 10 am to 5 pm. Entrance; 9F normal, 4.50F on Sunday, free on Monday.

Science (Palais de la Découverte) Avenue Franklin D Roosevelt, 8e; (tel: 359.16.65; metro: Roosevelt). Fascinating galleries on the history of scientific discovery, including astronomy, biology, chemistry, physics, mathematics, medicine, geology and more. There are special halls on nuclear energy and colour television, plus a library, cinema and planetarium. A great place to take the kids on a rainy day. Open daily (except Monday) 10 am to 6 pm. Entrance: 10F normal, 18F including the planetarium, with reductions for students.

Sèvres Porcelain (Musée National de Céramique) 4, grande rue, Sèvres; (tel: 534.99.05; metro: Pont Sèvres). The world's greatest porcelain collection, with items from nearly every school and period including Sèvres, Delft, Vienna, Dresden, Wedgwood and China. The world famous Sèvres National Porcelain Factory is in the same complex. The museum is open daily (except Tuesday) 9.30 am to noon and 1.30 to 5.15 pm. Guided tours of the factory on the first and third Thursday of each month at 2 and 3.30 pm (except July and August). Entrance: 9F normal, 4.50F on Sunday.

Technology (Musée National des Techniques) 270, rue St Martin, 3e; (tel: 271.24.14; metro: Reaumur-Sebastopol).

Science and industry collection housed in the former Church of St Martin des Champs, adjacent to the national institute for technical instruction. The museum covers a wide variety of disciplines including electronics, astronomy, agriculture, railways, energy, domestic industry and flight. Lots of historic specimens and models. Open daily (except Monday) 1 to 5.30 pm, Sunday 10 am to 5.15 pm. Entrance: 9F normal, 4.50F students.

Tobacco (Musée du Tabac) 12, rue Surcouf, 7e; (tel: 555.91.50; metro: Invalides, Latour-Maubourg). New museum with displays on the fine art of growing and smoking tobacco. Open daily (except Sunday and holidays) 11 am to 6 pm.

Transportation (Musée des Transports Urbains) 60, avenue Ste Marie, Saint-Mandé; (tel: 271.24.14; metro: Porte Dorée). Fine selection on the history of public transportation, including vintage buses, locomotives, carriages, metro cars and the like. Open Saturday, Sunday and holidays from May to October 2.30 to 6 pm. Entrance: 12F.

Victor Hugo 6, place des Vosges, 4e; (tel: 272.10.16; metro: St Paul, Bastille). The home of the great writer Victor Hugo from 1832-48 now displays a collection of his manuscripts, plus his own paintings, illustrations and craftwork. This is the former Hotel de Rohan-Guemenée, a beautiful 17th century mansion that was part of Henri IV's original Place Royale. Open daily (except Monday) 10 am to 5.40 pm. Entrance: 7F (free on Sunday).

Wine (Musée du Vin) Rue des Eaux, 16e; (tel: 525.63.26; metro: Passy). Another of Paris's new museums, opened in 1983 in the ancient Caves de la Tour Eiffel on the Right Bank of the Seine. Includes wax dioramas of the history of wine making in France, audio-visual programmes and documentation on vine growing in the various regions of France. Open daily 2 to 6 pm. Entrance: 18F, including wine tasting.

CHAPTER TEN

Shopping

One of the exciting things about shopping in Paris is that the city retains much of its medieval trade heritage. Paris still has particular streets or districts given over to very specific arts and crafts.

There is a section of the seventh arrondissement, bounded roughly by the Rue Saints-Pères, Boulevard Saint-Germain, Rue du Bac and the Seine which houses perhaps a hundred antique shops, ranging in stock from medieval monastic furniture to nautical equipment and hunting trophies. Nearby is one of Paris's richest shopping districts: Saint-Germain-des-Prés. This district can be divided into two neat sections by the boulevard of the same name — trendy fashion shops to the south and modern art galleries to the north. Paris's bookstore neighbourhood is situated further down Boulevard St Germain, in the Saint-Michel district near the Sorbonne.

This situation is no different on the Right Bank, where you find the super-plush Rue du Faubourg Saint-Honoré in the eighth arrondissement. This road is the famous home of many of the capital's great fashion houses and luxury shops. The Avenue Montaigne nearby is the site of many of the *haute couture* salons — the folks who will make you a custom-tailored outfit for a few thousand pounds! The Place Vendôme and the Rue de la Paix are known for their fabulous jewellery and watch stores. Les Halles is the ancient market district of Paris, and while most of the food operations have moved to new quarters near Orly airport, a number of gourmet food shops remain along the Rues Montmartre and Montorgueil.

Construction of the Pompidou Centre has revived the Beaubourg into a neighbourhood of art galleries and trendy fashion shops. And way out there in the twelfth district, along the Rue du Faubourg Saint-Antoine, you will find the great carpentry factories and furniture outlets of the city.

Likewise, the multitude of street markets found throughout Paris are also a survival from medieval days. The most famous is the giant flea market at Porte de Clignancourt, but every district and neighbourhood has its own miniature food and flea markets where even greater bargains can be had. Check out the second-hand and discount clothes of the Marché du Temple, the flower and pet market of the Place Louis Lepine on the Ile de la Cité, or the colourful postal stock of the Marché des Timbres on the Champs-Elysées.

The Parisians have a bad reputation as shopkeepers — how they refuse to speak a word of anything but French or how they are downright rude to foreign customers! But these rumours, while they must have a basis in fact, are largely unfounded today. Money is tight in France, and the merchants want as much business as they can get, which means more often than not that you will find entrepreneurs willing to speak English and sales people who actually smile and are helpful. The Japanese fashion outlets in Paris have the greatest reputation for courtesy, but then the Japanese are the most polite folks on this earth. But the French have learned from their Asian counterparts, and this cheerful, bi-lingual attitude is trickling down into the French shops.

Even if you should stumble into a shop in which the sales people don't speak a word of English, it's as easy to do business in Paris as any other Continental city. Prices are usually well-marked, people very willing to help, and international hand signals easily understood. And it's often while shopping around the language barrier that you have the most fun.

Another question always asked by overseas visitors is whether things in Paris are actually as expensive as they always imagined? The answer is usually yes, if it's Cartier diamonds or Dior fashions they are inquiring about. Luxury items are expensive everywhere. But there is the distinct advantage of being in the home city of so many of these famous names: Yves-Saint-Laurent-anything, be it clothes or perfume, is cheaper in Paris than back home in Kansas City or Luton. This is true of all the luxury dealers, so if you really have a fancy for French chic then Paris is the place to save money.

The best means of saving money is taking advantage of Paris's tax free outlets. There are expansive duty free shops at both Orly and Roissy airports (often cheaper than their British or American counterparts), and a good selection of duty free shops in the middle of Paris where an automatic 20 per cent is taken off the top. The best of these are probably the Benelux shop in the Rue de Rivoli and Eiffel Shopping near the tower of the same name.

Overseas visitors are also eligible for a refund on sales tax for anything they purchase inside France and then take home. To qualify you must buy at least 690F (Common Market visitors) or 400F (non-Common Market visitors) of goods from any one shop. Not every shop in Paris offers tourist discount, so ask before buying. And your actual refund will be anywhere from 15-20 per cent depending on how much in 'carrying charges' a particular shop decides to skim off your savings.

The problem is actually getting your refund. The special duty-free shops and department stores give you receipts you can present at airport banks before departing to claim your refund. Most of the smaller shops are not so well organized, so it's best to demand your refund on the spot. If they simply refuse, then your only option is to wait for your refund in the post. It does involve a certain risk, and in some cases you will never see that discount, but it may be your only choice. The store will give you a personal receipt, and two customs receipts to hand in at the airport or Channel port as you depart from France. Theoretically, you will receive your refund cheque in the mail at some later date (don't hold your breath). You can always contact the French government if you don't receive the refund, for those little slips you turn into the customs people are proof that you are entitled to a discount.

Lastly, a few words on shopping hours in Paris. There is only one set rule: most shops are open from 9 am to 7 pm Monday to Saturday, usually with an hour or so off for lunch in mid-afternoon. But some are open in the evenings, some on Sundays, some don't close for lunch, some take two or three hour lunches, and some may take Monday, Tuesday or both off. Crazy, but at least there's always something open to catch your interest (and money).

Shopping centres

Le Claridge 74, avenue des Champs-Elysées, 8e; (metro: Roosevelt). Big money centre representing the finest names in haute couture, ready-to-wear, perfumes and accessories. The rest of us can window shop. On the site of the former Claridge Hotel which gives its name to the complex. Open daily 10 am to 9 pm.

Le Centre Gaîté 68-80, avenue du Maine, 14e; (metro: Gaîté, Montparnasse). A new shopping complex next to the Gare Montparnasse. Three floors of varied shops and offices including the Patinoire curling and ice-skating rink, a huge bowling alley, Le Krypton Club nightclub and the huge Montparnasse Park Hotel.

Le Forum des Halles Rue Pierre Lescot, 1er; (metro: Les Halles). The ultra-modern, inspiring hole in the ground on the site of the old Les Halles market pavilions. This huge complex is now the most popular and famous shopping centre in Paris after only four years of operation, attracting an estimated 30 million customers a year. The five floors of Les Halles include over 200 shops, fifteen restaurants, a dozen cinemas and a music hall, museums of the Belle Epoque and holography, an art gallery, a cultural information centre, two photo galleries and an FNAC department store. It's also one of Paris's largest transportation hubs, sitting at the intersection of four metro lines, eleven bus routes and an RER line. And the Châtelet-Les Halles metro station is now the largest underground station in the world. The central courtyard features several outdoor cafés and it's a summer gathering place for the city's colourful street musicians and players. The Forum now rivals the nearby Pompidou Centre as a trendy hangout for Paris's youth and students. What more could you want from a shopping complex? The French have done it once again!

Maine-Montparnasse Centre Boulevard du Montparnasse at Place du 18ème Juin 1940, 15e; (metro: Montparnasse). The southside version of Les Halles, a gigantic complex which sprawls across three floors from the Place du 18ème Juin to Raoul Dautry in front of the Gare Montparnasse. The most obvious feature is the Tour Montparnasse, a controversial black skyscraper of 59 storeys which is the tallest office block in Europe. At the top is a restaurant, bar and observation deck. The centre also contains over 100 shops, a public swimming pool, squash complex, and Galeries-Lafayette, C & A and Habitat department stores. The old Gare Montparnasse was located on this site until 1967, and the signing of the Nazi surrender of Paris on 25th August 1944 took place in the old station. As with Les Halles, the Maine-Montparnasse Centre is a transportation hub with four metro lines, an RER commuter route and numerous bus lines.

Palais des Congrès Place de la Porte Maillot and Place Gal Koenig, 17e: (metro: Porte Maillot). Massive new centre which contains the Hotel Concorde LaFayette, the Air France Terminal for Charles De Gaulle Airport, the Palace of Congress convention and entertainment complex and two levels of upmarket shops. Among the selection are Charles Jourdan, Chanel, Ted Lapidus, Guy Laroche, Pierre

The striking modern lines of the Forum des Halles, a massive new shopping complex on the Right Bank which has over 200 shops, fifteen restaurants and a dozen cinemas.

277

Cardin (junior shop), Christian Dior, Van Sheen jewellery, Eiffel Shopping (tax free) and Jean Lemière. There is also a branch of the Japanese department store Diamaru, plus a post and telegraph office, bank, tabac shop and news stand. The indoor terrace of Le Drugstore is a good place for a break and a bite to eat. Inside the Hotel Concorde are Avon and Cartier boutiques, a fitness salon and on the 34th floor is the aptly-named Panoramique Bar with a fine view down the Avenue de la Grand Armée to the Arc de Triomphe.

Department stores

Au Bon Marché Rue de Sèvres at Rue du Bac, 7e; (tel: 260.33.45; metro: Sèvres-Babylone, Vaneau). The grand old dame of Paris's department stores, a revolutionary store in both marketing techniques and employee relations founded by country boy Aristide Boucicaut in 1852. The 'Good Deal' was the first store to have fixed prices, free entrance, item exchange, the concept of large volume at low profit margin and January white sales. And Boucicaut was among the first employers to offer paid vacations, pensions, medical service and a six-day work week for staff. Which all goes to show how much we take for granted in the commercial world after only 130 years. The building itself is a Belle Epoque masterpiece. Today's Bon Marché is a bastion of middle class, middle-of-the-road shopping. Nothing fancy, nothing too expensive, nothing too trendy, just good quality merchandise at moderate prices for the masses. But surprisingly, Bon Marché has an excellent selection of antiques. Open 9.30 am to 6.45 pm. Closed Sunday.

Bazar de L'Hotel de Ville (BHV) 52-64, rue de Rivoli, 4e; (tel: 274.90.00; metro: Hotel de Ville). The least known of Paris's big department stores, but the most profitable store per square metre. BHV is not your usual department store and don't expect to find your haute couture and Cartier diamonds here. The accent is firmly on home and garden with an inventory that includes hardware, work tools, lawnmowers and garden implements, lawn furniture, washing machines, refrigerators, cameras, stereos, televisions and multiple electronic appliances. In fact, BHV is often called a man's department store. Open 9 am to 6.30 pm (to 10 pm on Wednesday). Closed Sunday.

Les Drugstores 149, boulevard St Germain, 6e; (metro: St Germain). 133, avenue des Champs-Elysées, 8e; (metro: Etoile). 1, avenue Matignon, 8e; (metro: Roosevelt). 6, boulevard des Capucines, 9e; (metro: Opéra). Estage 1, Palais des Congrès, 17e; (metro: Porte Maillot). Not really department stores, but where else do you fit in these late-night purveyors of just about everything you could possibly want at 2 am? Les Drugstores are the ultimate in the corner store, or for you Yanks in the audience, the super 7-11. Among the available items are cigarettes and cigars, newspapers and magazines, books, film, liquor and wine, matches and lighters, records and tapes, postcards and greeting cards, sunglasses, cosmetics, shampoo and soap, toothpaste and take-away foods. They also contain cafés where you can snatch a quick drink or snack, plus public telephones for both domestic and international calls. The Opéra Drugstore has a bureau de change open 10.30 am to 7.20 pm. And naturally, Les Drugstores are also late-night pharmacies for those in need of medications. Open daily until 2 am.

FNAC Forum des Halles, 1er; (tel: 261.81.18; metro: Les Halles, Châtelet). 26, avenue de Wagram, 8e; (metro: Etoile, Ternes). 136, rue de Rennes, 6e; (metro: Montparnasse, St Placide). Paris's newest department store chain, a good selection of clothes, household and kitchen items, electronic equipment, gifts and gadgets. The Forum FNAC has a huge photo-video-cinema shop and a record department with over 150,000 labels.

Galeries Lafayette 40, boulevard Haussmann, 9e; (tel: 282.34.56; metro: Chaussée-d'Antin). Main-Montparnasse

Centre, 15e; (tel: 538.52.87; metro: Montparnasse). The main store on Boulevard Haussmann has been a Parisian landmark since 1896 when it was founded by Théophile Bader. It's been a well-run family business ever since, other than the four years of Nazi occupation when the Germans forced ownership into the hands of a non-Jew. Superb Belle Epoque interior with lots of glass, gilt and curls. Among the Lafayette fortés are high fashion for both men and women, junior clothes, perfumes, household and gift items. Famous names represented include Yves St Laurent, Christian Dior, Ted Lapidus, Sonia Rykiel, Dorothée Bis, Louis Feraud and Castelbajac in fashion; Van Cleef, Lanvin St Laurent, Jean Patou, Guy Laroche, Rochas, Chanel, Paco Rabanne, Nina Ricci, Gres and Gallet in perfume. Special services for foreign visitors including interpreters (nine languages), multi-lingual aid phones and guides. And a bureau de change and theatre booking office too. Lafayette's famous 3-J sale is every October, same month as the new 'Festival de la Mode' fashion show for both established and new designers from around the world. Open 9.30 am to 6.30 pm. Closed Sunday.

Marks and Spencer 35, boulevard Haussmann, 9e; (tel: 742.42.91; metro: Opéra). British visitors might not be impressed by the presence of a 'Marks and Sparks' in Paris, but the Americans and other colonials will delight in this trans-Channel branch of the famous London department store. Great food and clothing departments, plus lots of interesting British gadgets and gifts. Like Bon Marché, this store is known for good quality and medium prices rather than flashy high-priced items.

Le Printemps 64, boulevard Haussman, 9e; (tel: 285.22.22; metro: Havre-Caumartin). 'The Most Parisian Department Store' as Le Printemps likes to bill itself, but Bon Marché and la Samaritaine would certainly have something to say about that. And Le Printemps is the arch-enemy of Galeries Lafayette which is right next door. Founded in 1865 by Bon Marché graduate Jules Jaluzot, who used funds from his wife's dowry to establish a massive store near the Gare St Lazare. Jaluzot ruled Printemps with an iron grip until 1904 and in that time he gained a reputation as a brilliant innovator in advertising, marketing and presentation. Printemps was the first department store in the world to install electric elevators and lights, and their vivid ad campaigns have always drawn compliments and applause. This is the most upmarket of the big stores, rivaling Galeries Lafayette in the number of big names under contract and breaking through into avant-garde designs that Lafayette might not touch. Among the designers represented are Thierry Mugler, Cerruti, Miyake, Damikage, Gautier, Koskino and Shimada. The building is a Belle Epoque dream and goes a long way to enhancing the elegant image Le Printemps attempts to foster. Brummel, the special Printemps men's shop, is down the street at 112, rue de Provence, 9e. January is Le Printemps big month with the annual White Sale and the new 'Fête du Livre' book fair. Don't miss the restaurant on the top floor with its lovely stained-glass dome, or the outdoor terrace with its fine view of central Paris. Open 9.30 am to 6.30 pm. Closed Sunday. Less sumptuous branches at Place d'Italie, 13e and at 21, Cour de Vincennes, 12e.

La Samaritaine 75, rue de Rivoli, 1er; (tel: 508.33.33; metro: Pont Neuf, Châtelet, Louvre). This huge store (Paris's largest) is worth a visit even if you don't plan to buy, to look at the classic Art Nouveau facade and to enjoy the magnificent view of the Seine and Left Bank from the 5th floor terrace. Another Paris landmark, the biggest thing on the river front between the Louvre and Notre Dame, established in 1870 by the now-legendary Ernest Cognacq. The young Frenchman struggled through his teens and twenties in dire poverty, but saved enough from his small stall under the Pont Neuf to found his dream store at the age of 30. Cognacq soon married Bon Marché graduate Louise Jay and the couple exploited their own hardwork and genius to make La Samaritaine a success. The name, by the way, derives from a statue of Jesus meeting the Good Samaritan

La Samaritaine department store is the largest in Paris, a spectacular Art Nouveau building established in 1870 by the legendary Ernest Cognacq, a one-time street vendor who became one of the richest entrepreneurs in France.

which once stood on the Pont Neuf. By 1984 La Samaritaine was sprawling across three city blocks, 63,000 square metres, with over 5,000 personnel. The store caters for the middle and working class rather than the upper end of the market, and La Samaritaine's long-standing reputation is to offer anything you might ever want to buy at a department store. Good selection of clothes, kitchen equipment and pets. Open 9 am to 6.30 pm (until 10 pm on Wednesday and 7 pm on Saturday). Closed Sunday.

Aux Trois Quartiers 17, boulevard de la Madeleine, 1er; (tel: 260.39.30; metro: Madeleine). Another grand old dame of the Parisian scene, on the periphery of the first, second and eight arrondissments. This is the most upmarket of the big stores with a reputation for fine luxury items and accompanying high prices. Known for its clothes, perfumes, accessories. Madelios, the men's store, is across the street at 10, place de la Madeleine.

Street markets

Aligre Place and Rue d'Aligre, 12e; (metro: Ledru Rollin). General clothes, household and appliance market sprawling across a lovely shaded square and up a busy market street. The local North and West Africans add an exotic flavour and you might even find a few unusual African curios for sale. Daily.

Bastille Centre divider on Avenue Richard Lenoir, 11e; (metro: Bastille). Little known but interesting clothes and household market frequented mostly by locals. Daily.

Bicetre Avenue Eugène-Thomas at Paul-Vaillant-Couturier, Gentilly; metro: Gentilly RER). Small but interesting flea market in suburban Gentilly, just south of the Cité University. Sunday only.

Clignancourt/Saint-Ouen Avenue Michelet at Rue des

Rosiers, St Ouen; (metro: Porte Clignancourt). The incomparable Marché aux Puces in suburban St Ouen, Paris's most famous, and the world's largest, flea market. The Clignancourt market sprawls across four square miles encompassing an area roughly bounded by Avenue Michelet, Rue Jean-Henri-Fabré, Rue Jules Valles and Rue L. Dain, with Rue des Rosiers running straight up the middle. On a given weekend there are anything from 1,000 to 3,000 stalls in the market selling every imaginable item. This flea market was founded in the late 19th century at the height of the Belle Epoque, and by the 1920s it had exploded into Paris's largest bargain centre. Most convenient for buyers is the fact that Clignancourt is actually subdivided into six smaller markets specializing in various items. Marché Biron has 18th and 19th century antiques and furniture; Marché Cambo has furniture and paintings; Jules-Valles has French country and provincial furnishings; Malik sells old and new clothes, records and tapes, spectacles and sunglasses; Marché Paul-Bert has china, ironwork and Art Nouveau and Art Deco items; Marché Vernaison sells ornaments, books, pottery, period furniture, old photographs and linen. For a quick snack or a shopping break, try the Chez Louisette bistro in the Marché Vernaison. Saturday, Sunday and Monday only; the market stalls are generally open 9 am to 7 pm, but go early or on Monday for the best bargains.

Grenier de France Place de la Porte de Pantin, 19e; (metro: Porte Pantin). New flea market featuring household items, art and antiques. A bit far out but good prices make the long trek worthwhile. Saturday, Sunday and Monday.

Kremlin-Bicetre Avenue Paul-Vaillant-Couturier at Eugène-Thomas, le Kremlin-Bicetre; (metro: Porte d'Italie; bus: no. 47). The clochard's market of Paris, just outside the city boundaries in the south, where the bums and winos come three times a week to sell the junk they've collected in the rubbish bins and trash heaps of Paris. Their stock includes just about everything: furniture and antiques, old clothes, kitchen equipment, old books and magazines, records and tapes. Some of the best buys in Paris and great for photos. Sunday, Tuesdays and Thursdays from 7 am to 1 pm.

Marché aux Fleurs Place Louis Lepine, 4e; (metro: Cité). The famous flower and plant market on the Ile de la Cité, the perfect place for a romantic stroll after lunch. This is where many of the retail dealers of Paris purchase their flowers, and if home is but a day's airline flight away then the market is great for a living souvenir of the city. Bring your camera. Monday to Saturday.

Marché aux Oiseaux Place Louis-Lepine, 4e; (metro: Cité). Takes over from the flower market every Sunday. Once a bird market but now a display of all sorts of pets and accessories. Among the animals are rabbits, kittens, puppies, hamsters, guinea pigs, mice, parrots, canaries, finches, budgies, chickens, ducks and the occasional snake or lizard. And for those who have already purchased a furry or feathery little friend, the market also features bird and animal food, toys, cages, leads and collars, books, food dispensers and containers (ie, dog bowls) and much more. Great for kids and even better for photographers (who sometimes outnumber the animals). Sunday only.

Marché aux Timbres Avenue Champs-Elysées at Avenue de Marigny, 8e; (metro: Champs-Elysées, Roosevelt). Outdoor stamp market on the north side of Place Clemenceau. Both new and ancient issues, first-day covers, etc. Thursday, Saturday and Sunday only.

Porte Didot Avenue Georges Lafenestre, 14e; (metro: Porte de Vanves). Tiny market on the southern edge of Paris specializing in antiques, furniture, artwork and glassware. Walk down Boulevard Brune to Avenue G. Lafenestre from the Porte de Vanves metro station. Saturday and Sunday only.

Porte des Lilas Avenue Gambetta at Boulevard Mortier, 20e; (metro: Porte des Lilas). Small and little-known flea market on the eastern edge of Paris. Frequented mostly by locals. Sunday only.

Porte de Montreuil Place de la Porte de Montreuil, 20e; (metro: Porte de Montreuil). Large selection of household items and kitchen wares on the giant overpass of the Periphérique just before Paris turns into Montreuil Sous-Bois. A favourite of smart Parisian bargain hunters and antique buyers. Saturday and Sunday only.

Quai de la Megisserie Quai de la Megisserie between the Louvre and Châtelet, 1er; (metro: Pont Neuf, Châtelet). The permanent home of Paris's pet and accessories market, a series of tiny shops which spill out onto the pavement along the Seine. Everything from tropical fish to chickens, bunny rabbits to pussy cats. Monday to Saturday.

Saint-Pierre Place Saint-Pierre, 18e; (metro: Anvers, Abbesses). New and used clothes market in the shadow of Sacré Coeur, at the base of the Montmartre hill and cableway. Lots of old Parisian atmosphere even though they sell blue jeans and T-shirts. Monday to Saturday.

Temple Rue Eugène-Spuller, 3e; (metro: Temple). Huge new and used clothes market off the Square du Temple. Housed in the massive Carreau du Temple, a beautiful iron and glass pavilion reminiscent of the old Les Halles market, constructed in 1857 by Baron Haussmann. The market is on the site of the notorious Templar Tower prison, demolished in 1808 and replaced by the first clothes market. Among former residents of the tower were Marie Antoinette and her husband, King Louis XVI, before they were transferred to the Conciergerie and their deaths at the guillotine. Today's market sells everything from fur coats to Levis. Tuesday to Sunday.

Vanves Place de la Porte de Vanves, 14e; (metro: Porte de Vanves). The south side's most famous and largest flea market. Among the varied items are old clothes, antiques, books and vintage cameras and electronic equipment. Saturday and Sunday only.

Womenswear

● **Faubourg Saint Honoré**

Pierre Cardin 59 and 83, rue du Faubourg St Honoré, 8e; (tel: 266.62.94; metro: Clemenceau). Haute couture at no. 59 including the famous Cardin silk evening gowns. Ready-to-wear knits and sportswear at no. 83, and at a dozen other locations around Paris including the Palais des Congrès, 17e, Galerie du Claridge in the Champs-Elysées, 8e, and at 185, boulevard St Germain, 6e.

Jean-Charles de Castelbajac 31, place du Marché St Honoré, 1er; (tel: 260.78.40; metro: Pyramides). Colourful and comfortable collection of cotton and woollen knitwear, on the old market square off the Rue St Honoré.

Chanel 31, rue Cambon, 1er; (tel: 261.83.35; metro: Madeleine). The city's most elegant and famous boutique, a Paris landmark for half a century. The inspiring Chanel haute couture on the first floor, ready-to-wear by the trendy German Karl Lagerfeld on the ground floor. Plus all your favourite Chanel scents.

Chloe 60, rue du Faubourg St Honoré, 8e; (tel: 266.01.39; metro: Madeleine). The fabulous Herr Lagerfeld once again, this time designing ready-to-wear for Chloe. His cuts are nothing less than daring, but along more traditional lines than the super avant-garde Japanese designers. Both evening dresses and business suits for the woman-on-the-go, plus perfume, bags, belts, shoes and hats.

Cocon 255, rue St Honoré, 1er; (tel: 260.08.63; metro: Madeleine). The most sensual leatherwear in Paris, at both prices and styles to deter the most ardent punk or skinhead.

Cocon is leather at its most luxurious: neat business suits and mouth-watering evening wear for the woman who really wants to stand out in that crowd. Plus an equally sensual collection of silk blouses and suede coats. Also at 22, rue du Vieux-Colombier, 6e and 25, rue Quentin-Bauchart, 8e.

Courrèges 40, rue François 1er, 8e; (tel: 720.70.44; metro: George V). Tasteful evening wear and some of the freshest sportswear fashions in Paris from that energetic Basque, André Courrèges. Natural fabrics like silk, cotton and wool add to the attraction of the Courrèges line. For those with a smaller bank account who still appreciate these sleek lines, try the Courrèges Soldes boutique at 7, rue de Turbigo (1er), where last year's clothes are sold at half price. And those with a special interest in sportswear (ie, the kind of clothes you actually wear while playing sports) should pop into Courrèges Sport Futur at 113, avenue Victor-Hugo (16e), where André displays his chic line of tennis, skiing, golf and running wear, designed with the aid of athletes and sports technicians.

Christian Dior 30, avenue Montaigne, 8e; (tel: 723.54.44; metro: Roosevelt). Often described as a 'supermarket for the rich', the incomparable Dior offers something for everyone (with a hefty Swiss bank account). There is the famous haute couture for women, plus special ready-to-wear boutiques for women, men and children. In addition, you can also purchase the Dior lines of perfume, cosmetics, shoes, bags and belts, costume jewellery, spectacles, porcelain, lighters and writing pens. New Dior boutique in the Palais des Congrès (17e). Bring your credit cards and armoured car.

Louis Féraud 88, rue du Faubourg St Honoré, 8e; (tel: 265.27.29; metro: Clemenceau). Women's and men's ready-to-wear from the cheerful Louis Féraud. Other boutiques at 265, rue St Honoré (1er), 26, avenue des Champs-Elysées (8e) and in the Palais des Congrès (17e).

Givenchy 1, avenue George V, 8e; (tel: 723.80.05; metro: George V). Both haute couture and ready-to-wear by the quickly emerging Hubert de Givenchy, one of the most talented designers to make a name on the Parisian scene in the last decade. Givenchy's lines are more classic than trendy, much more appealing to the over 30s women. Lots of black and reds in 1983. Also at 66, avenue Victor-Hugo, 16e.

Tan Giudicelli 36, rue du Faubourg St Honoré, 8e; (tel: 265.32.33; metro: Concorde, Madeleine). Reputed to be the most daring (and expensive) cocktail dresses and evening gowns in Paris. The perfect boutique to buy your costume for the next Andy Warhol party.

Lanvin 22, rue du Faubourg St Honoré, 8e; (tel: 265.14.40; metro: Concorde, Madeleine). Classic haute couture on the first floor, elegant ready-to-wear on the ground floor. Traditional lines and warm colours. Nothing too far out.

Hanae Mori 17-19, avenue Montaigne, 8e; (tel: 723.52.03; metro: Alma). Striking Japanese designs along more traditional lines than Kenzo or Miyake. Mori clothes are known for their refinement of movement and graceful ease.

Nina Ricci 39, avenue Montaigne, 8e; (tel: 723.78.88; metro: Roosevelt). Large selection of Ricci's elegant haute couture and ready-to-wear designs.

Jean-Louis Scherrer 51, avenue Montaigne, 8e; (tel: 359.55.39; metro: Roosevelt, Alma). Super-elegant haute couture for the woman who no longer wants to look like a teenager. Chic evening gowns are the speciality, but Scherrer also turns out a luxurious selection of satin blouses, leather overcoats and perfume. Scherrer also turned to the Eastern look in '83, with its exciting (and sensual) collection of Oriental dresses in sumptuous blues and purples. Other boutiques at 90, rue du Faubourg St Honoré, 8e; 14, avenue Victor-Hugo, 16e and 31, rue de Tournon, 6e.

Emanuel Ungaro 2, avenue Montaigne, 8e; (tel: 723.61.94; metro: Roosevelt). Don't let anyone fool you, silk and sable are a girl's best friend, and you can find both at Ungaro's ultra-luxurious boutique. Haute couture for the *haute société*.

Valentino 19, avenue Montaigne, 8e; (tel: 723.64.61; metro: Roosevelt). The Italian designs which drive the young girls in London crazy. Super chic and super expensive, but oh so elegant.

● **Saint Germain**

Giorgio Armani 31, rue du Four, 6e; (tel: 354.87.98; metro: Mabillon). Striking ready-to-wear sports clothes in natural fabrics, from the famous Italian designer.

Benetton 47, rue Bonaparte, 6e; (tel: 326.39.74; metro: St Germain). Warm, luscious sweaters and pullovers in a million delightful colours, plus knitted trousers and skirts to match. The fabrics are natural, including imported cashmere and lambswool. And the prices are inside anyone's budget. Other Benetton boutiques at the Forum des Halles, 1er, 82, avenue Victor-Hugo, 16e and at the corner of the rues St Martin and Rambuteau opposite the Pompidou Centre, 4e.

Anne-Marie Beretta 24, rue St Sulpice, 6e; (tel: 326.99.30; metro: Odéon). Original ready-to-wear designs in vibrant colours and warm, natural fabrics.

Biba 18, rue de Sèvres, 7e; (tel: 548.89.18; metro: Sèvres-Babylone). Trendy ready-to-wear from Claude Montana and others. For the young and young at heart.

Burberry's 55, rue de Rennes, 6e; (tel: 548.52.71; metro: St Sulpice). London's Sloanes need not apply, for they will already have their Burberry raincoat. This is Sloanwear for the French and visiting colonials.

Dorothée Bis 33, rue de Sèvres, 6e; (tel: 222.00.45; metro: Sèvres-Babylone). A good place on a cold day, for Dorothée stocks some of the city's most desirable sweaters and jackets, plus lots of slinky ready-to-wear knits. Designs by Corinne and Jacqueline Jacobson.

Emmanuelle Khanh 2, rue de Tournon, 6e; (tel: 633.41.03; metro: Odéon). Embroidered blouses, skirts, jackets and woollen suits. Where the fashion conscious business-women shop.

Michel Klein 39, rue de Grenelle, 6e; (tel: 548.37.34; metro: Sèvres-Babylone). A Left Bank trend setter who is slowly gaining a world-wide reputation. At 28, Michel Klein is one of the youngest of Paris's fashion giants and who knows what he can do in the four decades. His striking designs range from chic leather jackets and berets, to soft cotton blouses and skirts inspired by African and Japanese prints and the free-form colour of hippy days.

Issey Miyake 201, boulevard St Germain, 7e; (tel: 548.10.44; metro: Bac, St Germain). Miyake has exploded onto the international fashion scene in the last few years with his bold, imaginative designs. And it would not be brash to suggest he is the globe's most exciting new designer at present. Miyake is avant-garde with a capital 'A' and so striking are some of his styles that they were featured in a special touring exhibit of American *art* museums in the fall of 1983. His speciality is baggy, furry knitwear made from a combination of cotton and wool, including skirts, jackets, capes, scarves and trousers. And Miyake also throws in a bit of daring leather. Just to browse, the boutique is a treat in itself.

Paco Rabanne 7, rue du Cherche-Midi, 6e; (tel: 222.87.80; metro: St Sulpice). The ultimate in avant-garde from the man who brought the world aluminium evening gowns and the plastic dress. Rabanne's clothes are no less exciting and imaginative today than they were in the experimental 1960s, and his advertising is also on the cutting edge of commercial design.

River Bop 7, rue de St André-des-Arts, 6e; (metro: Odéon). Trendy knitwear in many colours, by Takara, Moderate prices.

Sonia Rykiel 4-6, rue de Grenelle, 6e; (tel: 222.43.22; metro: Sèvres-Babylone). Ultra-chic business and evening wear from the 'Master of Knitting' Sonia Rykiel. Her famous 'black on black' look is among the most graceful in Paris, while Vogue goes so far as to call the Rykiel look 'otherworldly'. Ms Rykiel herself is rather striking, with her flaming red hair and flowing black robes. Also at 70, rue du Faubourg St Honoré, 8e.

Chantal Thomas 11, rue Madame, 6e; (tel: 544.57.13; metro: St Sulpice). Clothes for the sensual women by the imaginative Ms. Thomas. Actually two boutiques: one for ultra-sexy lingerie and nightwear, the other for slinky business suits and evening wear. Don't forget to check out the angora sweaters. Lots of blacks and whites, proof that basic is often best.

Tiffany 10-12 rue de Sèvres, 7e; (tel: 222.81.82; metro: Sèvres-Babylone). Simple, but pleasing designs at moderate prices. Tiffany's forte is elegant clothing for the mature woman, the styles of the 1930s and 40s updated to contemporary lines. And Tiffany also has a good selection of the 'tartan' look from Scotland.

Yves Saint-Laurent Rive Gauche 6, place St Sulpice, 6e; (tel: 329.43.00; metro: St Sulpice). The biggest name in contemporary Paris fashion, a giant in the world of design, and the only man who has managed to earn a retrospective at New York's Modern Museum of Art while still alive. St Laurent has been in the business 25 years now, and in that time he has managed to dress most of the world's most elegant (and richest) women, everyone from Diana Vreeland to Catherine Deneuve. The numerous Rive Gauche stores (this is the only one that's actually on the Left Bank) feature elegant, timeless ready-to-wear knits and sportswear. Others are situated in the Forum des Halles, 1er, 38, rue du Faubourg St Honoré, 8e, 88 avenue des Champs-Elysées, 8e and 7, avenue Victor-Hugo, 16e. You cannot find better quality for the price.

● **Les Halles Beaubourg**

Agnes B 3, rue du Jour, 1er; (tel: 233.04.13; metro: Les Halles). Comfortable and colourful ready-to-wear collection with prices that make it popular with young Parisians.

France Andrevie 2, place des Victoires, 1er; (tel: 261.52.72; metro: Sentier, Palais Royal). Chic and expensive clothes for young girls who want to impress other young girls.

Cacharel 49, rue Etienne-Marcel, 1er; (tel: 508.12.73; metro: Sentier, Les Halles). Classic ready-to-wear along traditional French lines, more appealing to the mature woman than the young trendsetter. Good value for money plus timeless designs. Also at 30, rue de Buci, 6e, 34, rue Tronchet, 9e, the Palais des Congrès, 17e and the Galerie du Claridge in the Champs-Elysées, 8e.

Fiorucci 34, rue St Denis, 1er; (tel: 233.85.08; metro: Les Halles). Trendy city. Four floors of teenage girls trying on the latest in Italian playwear. Prices to suit the masses.

Kenzo 3, place des Victoires, 1er; (tel: 236.81.41; metro: Sentier, Palais Royal). This place is more of a circus than a store. Kenzo was the first of the Japanese designers to make a name on the Parisian scene, and the popularity of his trendy, avant-garde clothes is shown by the masses of patrons who adoringly cluster around his shop. Can you slash your way through the cordon of teenage girls (all aspiring models) at the front door? Or will you accidentally trip over one of the Japanese tourists, who for some unexplained reason are taking photos of the facade of a store that's a household name back home? A bit like the English taking a picture of Marks & Sparks in Paris! As for the Kenzo clothes, they're frilly and fun.

Tokio Kumagai 52, rue Croix-des-Petits-Champs, 1er; (tel: 236.08.01; metro: Sentier, Palais Royal). Right around the corner from Kenzo, more trendy clothes and accessories in the avant-garde Japanese mould. Where the *Bon-Chic-Bon-Genre* (the smart set) buy their black patent leather shoes.

Thierry Mugler 10, place des Victoires, 2e; (tel: 260.06.37; metro: Sentier). *Passion* magazine puts it best: 'Vital pit-stop for the well-dressed space cadet'. The French response to all that Japanese trendy chic on the other side of the square.

Ton Sur Ton Estage −1, Forum des Halles, 1er; (tel: 296.48.17; metro: Les Halles). New wave Japanese designs for trendsetters under 21. Also at 84, avenue des Champs-Elysées, 8e.

Uranium 5, passage de l'Horloge, 3e; (tel: 274.73.98; metro: Rambuteau). American and Japanese trendy in a brand new shopping passage which is chock full of fun boutiques. Uranium's house brand is the comfortable and casual UCLA sportswear.

Victoire 10-12, place des Victoires, 2e; (tel: 508.53.29; metro: Sentier). French trendy from a bevy of young 'in' designers, including the popular Claude Montana and Azzedine Alaia. Like Kenzo across the square, you will have to push your way through the Parisian teenagers to get at the racks.

● **Avenue Victor Hugo**

Laura Ashley 95, avenue Raymond-Poincaré, 16e; (tel: 501.24.73; metro: Victor-Hugo). The Parisian branch of England's great bastion of Sloanedom, where the *Bon-Chic-*

Bon-Genre (BCBGs) try and dress like the Princess of Wales. Rangers will find this old hat, but the colonials might be interested in the traditional Ashley designs. Lots of 100 per cent cotton, and you can even buy a dress to match your wallpaper.

Cerruti 1881 15, place Madeleine, 8e; (tel: 742.10.78; metro: Victor-Hugo). Famous line of Italian knits and sportswear and lofty prices.

Lacoste 82, avenue Victor-Hugo, 16e; (tel: 553.39.49; metro: Victor-Hugo). Fine sportswear from the people who brought us the alligator shirt. Where energetic women can pick up their tennis or golf outfits. Also at 37, boulevard des Capucines, 2e and 44, rue St Placide, 6e.

Ted Lapidus 6, place Victor-Hugo, 16e; (tel: 500.88.11; metro: Victor-Hugo). Haute couture and ready-to-wear along classic Parisian lines, but Lapidus has recently ventured into the realm of the avant-garde to squash thoughts that his clothes were somewhat unimaginative and old-fashioned. Wild selection of hats, what you might term the Truman Capote look. Also at 37, avenue Pierre 1er de Serbie, 8e, 23 rue du Faubourg St Honoré, 8e, 52, rue Bonaparte, 6e, and in the Palais des Congrès, 17e.

Guy Laroche 9, avenue Victor-Hugo, 16e; (tel: 501.66.05; metro: Victor-Hugo). Haute couture and ready-to-wear along traditional French lines. Also at 47, rue de Rennes, 6e, 30, rue du Faubourg St Honoré, 8e, 29, avenue Montaigne, 8e, and in the Palais des Congrès 17e.

Georges Rech 23, avenue Victor-Hugo, 16e; (tel: 500.83.19; metro: Victor-Hugo). Classic lines but casual comfort is the trademark of this outstanding ready-to-wear designer.

Women's accessories

La Bagagerie 41, rue du Four, 6e; (tel: 548.85.88; metro: Mabillon). Wide selection of handbags and belts at a wide selection of prices. Every colour of the rainbow.

Bottega Veneta 48, avenue Victor-Hugo, 16e; (tel: 501.70.58; metro: Victor-Hugo). 'When your own initials are enough' is the motto of this famous Italian house of leather. This elegant collection includes bags, belts, shoes and luggage. The prices are high, but the quality is superb.

Carel 41, boulevard des Capucines, 2e; (tel: 354.11.69; metro: Opéra). 12, rue du Four, 6e; (metro: Mabillon). Chic Parisian footwear ranging from the traditional to the trendy, for both work and play.

Maud Frizon 81-83, rue des Sts Pères, 6e; (tel: 222.06.93; metro: Sèvres-Babylone). Trendy footwear, plus matching bags, belts and suitcases. The collection includes both lizard and snakeskin shoes. This is where the Bon Chic buy their heels.

Gucci 2, rue du Faubourg St Honoré, 8e; (tel: 742.90.27; metro: Concorde, Madeleine). Be it Rome, London or Beverly Hills, Gucci always try to bowl you over with their sumptuous locations. And the new Paris store is no different, situated in a marble masterpiece near the Rue Royale. All the famous Gucci leather is there: handbags, belts, wallets, purses, luggage and more.

Hermès 24, rue du Faubourg St Honoré, 8e; (tel: 265.21.60; metro: Concorde, Madeleine). 18, avenue du Suffren, 15e; (tel: 566.89.29; metro: Bir-Hakeim). Paris's most reputable house of fine leather goods. You're not only paying for the golden Hermès emblem, but also the superb quality. The range includes gloves, handbags, belts, saddles, riding boots and other tack. Hermès is where the aristocracy buy their riding equipment, and where the BCBGs pick up their ubiquitous Hermès bags. And London's Sloanes (as well as thousands of tourists from around the world) are liable to stop off at Hermès for one of their famous silk scarves. Don't forget the Hermès scents, for both men and women. Hermès is to Paris what Gucci is to Beverly Hills: the ultimate in status symbols.

Charles Jourdan 86, avenue des Champs-Elysées, 8e; (tel: 562.29.28; metro: George V). Another of Paris's famous names in leather, featuring high quality bags, belts, hats, shoes and boots. The workmanship is impeccable, the quality superb. Also in the Forum des Halles, 1er, 5, boulevard de la Madeleine, 1er, 12, rue du Faubourg St Honoré, 8e, and at the Galerie du Claridge in the Champs-Elysées, 8e.

Laurent Mercadel 3, place des Victoires, 1er; (tel: 508.84.44; metro: Sentier, Palais Royal). Trendy shoes, bags and other accessories in many shapes and sizes.

Le Nouveau Maroquinier Estage −1 in the Forum des Halles, 1er; (metro: Les Halles). Stylish, high-quality leather handbags and belts from North Africa. Very reasonable prices, but no bargaining like in the bazaars.

Roots rue du Jour, 1er; (tel: 508.09.84; metro: Les Halles). 20, rue St Sulpice, 6e; (tel: 354.78.66; metro: Mabillon). North Americans know this place well, the store that brought us the trendy 'earth shoes' of the early 1970s. But Roots is pretty new on the Parisian scene, and the French are just taking to their rustic, lumberjack styles. The selection includes the famous Roots shoes and boots, plus handbags, belts and other leather goods. Also featured are men's, women's and children's clothes, and Wayfarer Ray Ban sunglasses for those of you who want to look like the Blues Brothers. A refreshing breath of Canadian air in the somewhat stuffy atmosphere of French fashion.

Sacha 15, rue de Turbigo, 2e; (tel: 508.13.15; metro: Etienne-Marcel). Wide selection of trendy but inexpensive shoes, mostly made in Italy. Great for a Kenzo outfit, but not so much for the older ladies.

Walter Steiger 5, rue de Tournon, 6e; (tel: 633.01.45; metro: Odéon). The grand old master of Parisian shoes. Steiger has been around for ages, dispensing footwear to those who want timeless elegance rather than throw-away flash. The place to buy shoes for the Opera, or your forthcoming audience with the Queen. Also at 49, rue du Faubourg St Honoré, 8e.

Tokio Kumagai 52, rue Croix-des-Petits-Champs, 1er; (tel: 236.08.01; metro: Sentier, Palais Royal). Black patent leather shoes and other exciting numbers to go with that trendy outfit you've just spent a fortune on at Kenzo or Thierry Mugler. Animal lovers might want to stay away from the snake and lizard skin designs.

La Tournelle 33, quai de la Tournelle, 5e; (metro: Maubert-Mutualité). Gorgeous silk scarves and shirts in a multitude of vibrant colours. The place is a charm to browse in even if you don't buy.

Lingerie and nightwear

Cadolle 14, rue de Cambon, 1er; (tel: 260.94.94; metro: Tuileries). High-fashion undies in sensual blacks and whites. English spoken. Open Monday to Saturday 9.30 am to 1 pm and 2 to 7 pm.

Chantal Thomas 11, rue Madame, 6e; (tel: 544.57.13; metro: St Sulpice). Ultra-sexy lingerie for the sensual woman. Paris's most famous purveyor of stylish women's nightwear.

Janique 41, boulevard des Capucines, 2e; (tel: 261.11.37; metro: Opéra). Stylish ladies' underwear and dressing gowns at reasonable prices.

Pascale Madonna 7, rue des Quatre-Vents, 6e; (tel: 325.54.64; metro: Odéon). A rather irreverent name for a very sensual store. The 'Easter Madonna' has lingerie to seduce your man with, lace and silk undies that are guaranteed to turn the head of any male.

Les Trois Marchés 1, rue Guisarde, 6e; (tel: 354.74.18; metro: Mabillon). Antique petticoats, corsets, brassières and girdles for those romantic ladies with Victorian mores.

Bridal wear

France Favery 79, rue des Sts Pères, 6e; (tel: 222.04.29; metro: St Germain). Paris's specialist in robes de mariage including gorgeous dresses, shoes, gloves and handbags. Everything a girl needs to plan her wedding.

Menswear

● **Rue du Faubourg Saint Honoré**

Camps de Luca 11, place de la Madeleine, 8e; (tel: 265.42.15; metro: Madeleine). World famous custom-cut suits. The name De Luca stands for impeccable workmanship and the finest quality fabrics, and it's doubtful you could find a finer suit anywhere in the world.

Pierre Cardin 35, avenue George V, 8e; (tel: 723.73.44; metro: Madeleine, Concorde). Famous Cardin suits for the macho businessman, plus all those lovely Cardin accessories. The price tags are guaranteed to make a dent in your Pierre Cardin wallet.

Jean-Charles des Castelbajac 31, place du Marché St Honoré, 1er; (tel: 260.78.40; metro: Pyramides). Fantastic range of ready-to-wear knits and imaginative jackets.

Cerruti 1881 15, place de la Madeleine, 8e; (tel: 742.10.78; metro: Madeleine). Classy three-piece suits and sportswear from one of the top Italian designers.

Charvet 8, place Vendôme, 1er; (tel: 260.30.70; metro: Opéra, Tuileries). The place to get a tailored silk shirt for that Cardin or Dior suit. This is where the young French aristocrats and high flying corporate heads buy their clothes, and the sumptuous selection looks to be fit for a king. Charvet also has tailored three-piece suits and dinner jackets, plus lovely sweaters, scarves, ties and leather jackets.

Christian Dior 30, avenue Montaigne, 8e; (tel: 723.54.44; metro: Roosevelt). Ready-to-wear Dior suits, for business and play, perhaps the best formal wear you can obtain that's not custom tailored. Plus all those posh Dior extras like shirts, shoes, underwear, gloves, ties and belts.

Givenchy 1, avenue George V, 8e; (tel: 723.80.05; metro: George V). Excellent line of suits, shirts and accessories from one of the leaders in French fashion.

Hilditch and Key 252, rue de Rivoli, 1er; (tel: 260.36.09; metro: Tuileries). A bit of Saville Row transplanted to Paris. The finest quality custom-made shirts and suits, plus an unbelievably chic line of extras. Another hangout of top-flight executives and the landed aristocracy. Likely to drain your Swiss bank account.

Lanvin 15, rue du Faubourg St Honoré, 8e; (tel: 265.14.40; metro: Concorde, Madeleine). Custom-made Lanvin suits and accessories, plus a sophisticated line of ready-to-wear sports clothes. Amongst the best quality and classiest designs in Paris.

Renoma 19, avenue Matignon, 8e; (tel: 359.79.31; metro: Roosevelt). Ready-to-wear suits and sportswear for the young executive, plus a fashionable coiffeur upstairs to complete that smart look. Where Richard Gere must buy his clothes, for this is definitely the 'American Gigolo' style. If only they had Venetian blinds.

A. Sulka 2, rue de Castiglione, 1er; (tel: 260.38.08; metro: Tuileries). Where the rich and famous shop. Posh custom-made shirts and accessories at prices to unbalance your bankbook. But if you dare shop at Sulka, need you even ask the price?

Valentino 19, avenue Montaigne, 8e; (tel: 723.64.61; metro: Roosevelt, Alma). Chic Italian sportswear for international jet-setters.

Ermenegildo Zegna 10, rue de la Paix, 2e; (tel: 261.67.61; metro: Opéra). Sophisticated suits and sportswear for the man who wants to stand out from the crowd. Excellent Italian designs and tailoring, but you'll pay for all that chic.

● **Avenue Victor Hugo**

Harrison 130, rue de la Pompe, 16e; (tel: 727.96.62; metro: Pompe). Traditional, but colourful line of Harrison shirts, ties and scarves, as well as the house brand of ready-to-wear suits. For more conservative clothing tastes.

Hemispheres 22, avenue de la Grande Armée, 17e; (tel: 755.61.86; metro: Argentine). Suits, shirts, shoes and other accessories along traditional French lines. Nothing avant-garde here, more for the mature and unobtrusive man. Excellent spread of Roland and Church's English-made shoes.

Lacoste 82, avenue Victor-Hugo, 16e; (tel: 553.39.49; metro: Victor-Hugo). The world famous Lacoste line of sportswear. For those who want to look trendy both on and off the courts or greens. Lots of tennis and running gear, plus Lacoste rackets. Also at 37, boulevard des Capucines, 2e and 44, rue St Placide, 6e.

Ted Lapidus 6, place Victor-Hugo, 16e; (tel: 500.88.11;

metro: Victor-Hugo). Ready-to-wear suits and sportswear from the all-encompassing Mr Ted. Something for just about everyone. Also at 23, rue du Faubourg St Honoré, 8e; 52, rue Bonaparte, 6e; and 37, avenue Pierre 1er de Serbie, 8e.

Georges Rech 23, avenue Victor-Hugo, 16e; (tel: 500.83.19; metro: Victor-Hugo). Not-so-traditional suits and sportswear from one of the cutting edges in Parisian male fashion. Elegant, but comfortable.

Francesco Smalto 5, place Victor-Hugo, 16e; (tel: 500.48.64; metro: Victor-Hugo). One of the lesser known men's custom tailors in Paris, but certainly one of the best. Tailored suits and shirts along with super-posh Italian lines, plus the delightful Smalto selection of ready-to-wear sports clothes and accessories.

● **Les Halles**

Agnes B 3, rue du Jour, 1er; (tel: 233.04.13; metro: Les Halles). Don't be put off by the female name, for Agnes B has an excellent collection of both men's and women's sportswear. A bit trendy, but nothing too far out. Excellent prices.

Hubert Aimetti 41, rue Coquillière, 1er; (tel: 236.29.77; metro: Les Halles, Louvre). Elegant ready-to-wear suits, overcoats and leather jackets for both men and women. Superb Italian styling.

Brummel Estage − 1 at the Forum des Halles, 1er; (tel: 297.44.84; metro: Les Halles). The special men's branch of the great department store Printemps, featuring all of the designers on contract to the parent store including Yves Saint-Laurent, Kenzo, Christian Dior, Guy Laroche, Cerruti and more. The big name line-up changes yearly. A good place to compare the styles and prices of the various fashion houses. Also at 112, rue de Provence, 9e.

Cacharel 5, place des Victoires, 1er; (tel: 233.29.88; metro: Sentier, Palais Royal). Wide range of exciting clothes from one of the top ready-to-wear designers in Paris. The Cacharel collection includes trousers, shirts, overcoats, waistcoats, socks and more. Clothes that look and feel good, at prices you can afford. Also at 34, rue Tronchet, 8e.

Halles Capone 12, rue de Turbigo, 1er; (tel: 233.54.69; metro: Etienne-Marcel). Trendy threads from François and Marithe Girbaud, everything from top-notch designer jeans to leather jackets. Clothes to have fun in, for the young or the young at heart.

Island 3, rue Montmartre, 2e; (tel: 261.77.77; metro: Sentier, Les Halles). Often called the 'English look' by the trendy French, what might translate into 'Sloane' in England or 'preppie' in America. Lots of slightly conservative but very upmarket shirts, sweaters, ties and trousers. Lots of male BCBGs are found sifting through the Island racks. Got to impress the banker's daughter.

Kenzo 3, place des Victoires, 1er; (tel: 236.81.41; metro: Sentier, Palais Royal). For an exercise in fashion contrast, compare the traditional lines of Island with the avant-garde styles of Kenzo just across the square. The Kenzo clothes are for men who aren't square, anyone who is willing to put a bit of dash and flair into his wardrobe. Fun fashions at high prices. Be sure to check out those fabulous Kenzo jackets.

Jeff Sayre 4, place André Malraux, 1er; (metro: Palais Royal). One of the few American names in Paris fashion. Sayre is a former medical student who left a comfortable (and warm) home in California 10 years ago to try and make a name for himself in the world of high fashion. He can now look back at a decade of hard work and steady progress. Sayre is now an unabashed success, the only non-European who has cut his brand name into the higher echelons of French men's fashion. His styles are a self-proclaimed mix of function and comfort, lots of natural fabrics (much of it bought in Ireland and England) and lots of pockets. The knitted sweaters are among the best in town. Look for Sayre to be around the Parisian scene for many years to come.

● Opéra

Boutique Pour Lui 23, boulevard Montmartre, 2e; (metro: Montmartre, Richelieu-Drouot). A great place for overseas visitors to get a quick introduction and education in Paris men's fashion. Lui stocks many of the big names in chic ready-to-wear: Guy Dormeuil, Nino Cerruti, Francesco Smalto, Saint-Laurent, Christian Dior and more. So you can easily compare prices and styles, then decide which look is really for you. Both suits and sportswear, and the selection also includes the fantastic Burberry raincoats and Lacoste sports clothes.

Centmil Chemises 128, rue de Rivoli, 1er; (tel: 233.52.72; metro: Louvre). Amazing selection of high-quality, ready-to-wear shirts for both business and play, plus lots of exciting extras. The prices are more affordable than the famous brand names, but the workmanship at Centmil is often just as good. Great value for price. Also at 126, boulevard Voltaire, 11e and 109, rue du Faubourg St Antoine, 11e.

Lacoste 37, boulevard des Capucines, 2e; (tel: 261.58.20; metro: Opéra). The American college students head straight for this place. For while everyone on campus has an 'Alligator' shirt, who can actually say they bought theirs in Paris instead of the student store? All that world-famous Lacoste sportswear under one roof, but the collection goes far beyond those trendy shirts. Special outfits for tennis, golf and jogging, plus the Lacoste brand tennis and squash rackets. A fraternity boy's heaven. Also at 44, rue St Placide, 62 and 82, avenue Victor-Hugo, 16e.

● Saint Germain

Arny's 14, rue de Sèvres, 7e; (tel: 548.76.99; metro: Sèvres-Babylone). Not one of the big names in men's fashion, but the threads at Arny's are both fun and comfortable. Mostly sports clothes, casual wear and accessories. The designs range from simple and traditional, to outrageous and avant-garde. Take a look at those sexy men's kimonos. Shoes, socks and ties too. And best of all, the prices are much more reasonable than Faubourg St Honoré.

Christian Aujard 15, rue de Tournon, 6e; (tel: 634.26.39; metro: Odéon). Elegant clothes for conservative tastes, and a landmark in Paris fashion for many years. Smart ready-to-wear suits, sweaters, shirts and overcoats, plus other extras. Top-of-the-line are the sumptuous cashmere sweaters and coats.

Burberry's 55, rue de Rennes, 6e; (tel: 548.52.71; metro: St Sulpice). How could you possibly be caught in the spring showers without your Burberry raincoat? High-quality rainwear and overcoats from the house of the Sloane Rangers.

Daniel Hechter 50, avenue des Champs-Elysées, 8e; (tel: 225.06.54; metro: Mabillon). The famous Hechter ready-to-wear sports clothes and jackets, good quality and moderate prices.

Yves Saint-Laurent Rive Gauche 12, place St Sulpice, 6e; (tel: 326.84.40; metro: St Sulpice). Ready-to-wear suits and sportswear from the biggest name in Paris fashion, plus all those famous St Laurent accessories. Ranging from the traditional to the slightly avant-garde (but nothing too wild, of course), so there is something at Rive Gauche to please almost anyone. Many other St Laurent boutiques throughout Paris.

Wylton 30, rue des Sts Pères, 7e; (tel: 222.23.41; metro:

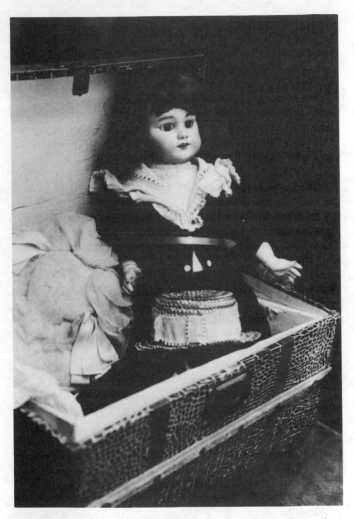

*The Beau Noir/Monsieur Renard in the Saint Germain
district specializes in* poupées anciennes *and has the best
selection of antique dolls in Paris.*

St Germain). Brand new purveyors of the popular 'look Anglais'. Wylton is a joint venture of Jean-Michel Beaumont de St James and Stephane Savary, a boutique meant to water the mouths of that growing band of French Anglophiles. Top-notch suits, shirts, shoes and ties, and even bowler hats.

Yohji Yamamoto 18, rue du Dragon, 6e; (tel: 222.90.49; metro: St Germain). Out-of-this-world menswear from the avant-garde Japanese. Nothing conservative about this lot, and you'll have to be slightly daring even to try these clothes in the shop. Particularly effective are the Yamamoto jackets and scarves.

Men's accessories

Freelance 26, rue Mondetour, 1er; (tel: 233.74.70; metro: Les Halles, Etienne-Marcel). Trendy shoes for under 25s. Something to go with that Kenzo or Yamamoto outfit.

Jocelyn 134, boulevard St Germain, 6e; (metro: Mabillon). Elegant men's footwear from one of the finest houses in Paris.

Charles Jourdan 86, avenue des Champs-Elysées, 8e; (tel: 562.29.28; metro: George V). Perhaps the best range of men's shoes and boots in the city. The leather is the finest, the crafting impeccable, the style up-to-date. Usually something for everyone. Also at 5, boulevard de la Madeleine, 8e; 12, rue du Faubourg St Honoré, 8e; and Estage −3 in the Forum des Halles, 1er.

Kickers 114, avenue des Champs-Elysées, 8e; (tel: 359.57.80; metro: George V). Shoes for any sports, for all ages, at a wide range of prices. Plus lots of athletic extras like sportswear, socks, sweat-bands and head-bands.

Motsch et Fils 42, avenue George V, 8e; (tel: 723.79.22;

metro: George V). Old-fashioned hat store with many elegant styles and prices. Something to fit any head size, although your hat tastes should be more on the traditional side.

Roots 3, rue du Jour, 1er; (tel: 508.09.84; metro: Les Halles). 20, rue St Sulpice, 6e; (tel: 354.78.66; metro: St Sulpice). Direct from Toronto, all your favourite 'earth' shoes, leather boots, Ray Ban sunglasses and other famous Roots accessories.

Children's wear

Alphabet Quilts 69, rue St Honoré, 1er; (metro: Louvre). Superb winter clothes for your little cherubs, including down-filled pyjamas, jumpers and dungarees.

Baby Dior 30, avenue Montaigne, 8e; (tel: 723.54.44; metro: Roosevelt). Chic clothes for future bank managers and debutantes. The special Dior children's boutique has styles to take junior from the crib to prep school, or for little Missy to look her elegant best when the fifth birthday party rolls around. The finest Dior workmanship and prices.

Becotine 111, rue St Denis, 1er; (metro: Les Halles). Smart, colourful and reasonably priced clothes for kids. A good place to pick up a gift for the nephews and nieces back home.

Bonpoint 67, rue de l'Université, 7e and 82, rue de Grenelle, 7e; (tel: 705.09.09; metro: Solferino). Perhaps the best children's boutiques in Paris, a wide range of sizes and styles for almost every mother's taste. You might choose the up-to-date Prince William look, or the more traditional velvet and lace. Clothes for infants up to age 12.

Enfantillage Rive Gauche 260, boulevard St Germain, 7e; (tel: 551.34.28; metro: Bac). More high-quality clothes for infants and children, an exciting collection which includes outfits for both playground and Sunday school.

Junior Pierre Cardin Palais des Congrès, 17e; (tel: 758.23.33; metro: Porte Maillot). Designer clothes from the one and only Uncle Pierre. Modern selection, great quality and lofty prices. For babes with a silver spoon.

Maman Troc 6 bis, rue Fourcroy, 17e; (tel: 766.70.20; metro: Pereire). Good selection of clothes and accessories for infants and children to age 12. Best of all, you get great quality at low prices. Next door is a fascinating old toy and doll shop called Volpone and Company.

Mini-Ted 6, place Victor-Hugo, 16e; (tel: 500.88.11; metro: Victor-Hugo). More high fashion cribwear and play clothes for the discerning infant, this time courtesy of 'Big Daddy' Ted Lapidus. But are the kids really worth all this style and money?

Second-hand, punk and leather

Air Force Surplus 15, rue St Denis, 1er; (metro: Châtelet, Les Halles). Tacky but fun. Take your choice of punk or the army surplus look. The selection includes flack jackets, handcuffs, hand grenades and baseball gear. Appropriately low prices.

Freeway 133, rue St Denis, 1er; (metro: Etienne-Marcel, Les Halles). Leather city. Authentic flight and bombardier jackets for only 850F. Get there early.

Jacqueline Jacquelin 9, rue Pierre Lescot, 1er; (metro: Les Halles). Fifties-style clothes for ex-bobbysoxers.

Japa 3, rue de la Ferronnerie, 1er; (metro: Chatelet, Les Halles). Large selection of leather jackets in many styles and several colours.

Killy Killy Watch 98, rue St Denis, 1er; (metro: Etienne-Marcel, Les Halles). Bizarre assortment of second-hand clothes, T-shirts, punk outfits and general junk at unbelievably low (for Les Halles) prices.

Liberty 20, rue St Denis, 1er; (metro: Châtelet, Les Halles). Assorted punk, leather, army surplus and second hand clothes at reasonable prices. Among the accessories are gas masks, hand grenades and Army spades.

Au Marché des Halles 65, rue Rambuteau, 3e; (metro: Rambuteau). Good selection of second-hand and working clothes, oddball dresses and other funny threads at bargain prices. Opposite the Pompidou Centre.

Marché aux Puces Rue J H Fabré at Rue R J Valles, St Ouen; (metro: Porte de Clignancourt). The great flea market at Clignancourt, the biggest selection of second-hand and cut-rate clothes in Paris. The Malik section of the market at the corner of Fabré and Valles specializes in old clothes. Open from dawn until dusk every Saturday, Sunday and Monday. But get there early for the real bargains and good clothes.

Marché du Temple Rue Eugène-Spuller, 3e; (metro: Temple). Huge flea market under the all-weather protection of a classic Belle Epoque steel and glass canopy. The Marché du Temple has been dispensing second-hand and bargain clothing for over 100 years. Giant selection of cheap jeans, and you can even purchase cut-rate (although somewhat tacky) furs here. Open Tuesday to Sunday from 9 am to noon.

Rag Time 23, rue Roule, 1er; (metro: Châtelet, Louvre). An excellent collection of antique dresses, gowns and accessories from the 1920s and 30s. Fun for a browse.

Rococo 30, rue du Dragon, 6e; (metro: St Germain). More nostalgic styles from the 20s and 30s.

Sigma 3, rue de Tournon, 6e; (metro: Odeon). Leather jackets for pre-teens.

Riding gear

Hermès 24, rue du Faubourg St Honoré, 8e; (tel: 265.21.60; metro: Concorde, Madeleine). Saddles, boots, clothes and tack for those Sunday riders who want to look good on that expensive horse. You might even get some Hermès perfume for your stallion. Hermès makes the finest quality leather goods at prices to match.

J M Weston 97, avenue Victor-Hugo, 16e; (tel: 704.23.75; metro: Victor-Hugo). The finest quality leather riding boots from the famous American manufacturer. Nothing cowboy about this selection, rather très chic.

Cowboy clothes

Cowboy Dream 21, rue de Turbigo, 2e; (tel: 236.30.05; metro: Etienne-Marcel). Everything for the aspiring French cowboy and cowgirl: ten gallon hats, flashy studded shirts, mocassins, turquoise and silver jewellery, leather belts and wallets, playing cards (for you five card stud fanatics) and those marvellous silver tie clasps which Ronald Reagan wears on his days off.

Mexico Lindo 19, rue des Canettes, 6e; (tel: 326.43.55; metro: Mabillon). Authentic Mexican and Wild West gear including fancy cowboy shirts with studded buttons, Tom Mix hats, turquoise and silver jewellery, Indian crafts and pointed boots.

Western House 23, rue des Canettes, 6e; (tel: 354.71.17; metro: Mabillon). Cowboy boots and Western-style shirts, plus authentic American T-shirts, varsity jackets, baseball caps and lettermen sweaters.

Bakeries

Boulangerie Poilane 8, rue du Cherche Midi, 6e; (metro: St Sulpice, Sèvres-Babylone). Forum Les Halles, 1er; (metro: Les Halles). Perhaps the most famous bakery in Paris, known for both its loaves and pastries. Good for snacking at Les Halles or if you're shopping in the St Germain area.

Melot 13, rue Oberkampf, 11e; (metro: Oberkampf). Corinne LaBalme of *Passion* magazine calls Melot's croissants the best in Paris. A little out of the way, but good old fashioned baked goods cooked over a wood-burning fire.

Patisserie Viennese 85 bis, rue de Charenton, 12e; (metro: Ledru-Rollin). At the other end of the spectrum, *Passion* calls this the best-looking bakery in Paris with its exquisite Belle Epoque interior. The croissants and other baked goods aren't bad either.

René Saint Ouen 111, boulevard Haussmann, 8e; (metro: St Augustin). 30, rue de Levis, 17e; (metro: Villiers.) Bring the kids along to René's. The self-styled 'Sculptor of Bread', he specializes in baked goods shaped like elephants, rabbits, dogs, birds, trees and even bicycles. Perfect gifts if home is but a day away. Combination patisserie, tea room and snack bar.

Cheese

Androuet 41, rue d'Amsterdam, 8e; (metro: St Lazare, Liège). The master cheese proprietors of Paris with over 300 varieties and a special cheese restaurant next door. A bit pricey compared to neighbourhood *fromagers* though.

Cremerie Détail 9, rue des Halles, 1er; (metro: Les Halles). Small but excellent selection of cheeses, plus fresh milk, eggs and other dairy products. Convenient to the Forum.

La Maison du Bon Fromage 35, rue du Marché St Honoré, 1er; (metro: Pyramides). You can smell this delightful little cheese shop before you even turn the corner onto the Rue du Marché. Good selection and great prices.

La Maison du Fromager 62, rue de Sèvres, 7e; (metro: Vaneau, Duroc). Huge selection of several hundred varieties of French cheese, a real treat for connoisseurs. Buy just a bite or in bulk.

Au Paradis des Fromages 170, avenue Ledru-Rollin, 11e; (metro: Voltaire). True to its name, a paradise of hundreds of cheese varieties, plus wine, yoghurt, milk and other dairy products. A neighbourhood place with excellent prices.

Fish

Poissonnerie 20, place du Marché St Honoré, 1er; (metro: Pyramides). Fresh fish supermarket (yet another place you can smell long before you get there!) on the southeast corner of the old market square. The place to purchase all those sea and freshwater delicacies they serve in the nearby restaurants.

Gourmet foods

Battendier 8, rue Coquillière, 1er; (metro: Les Halles). A Parisian landmark since 1826, one of the surviving legacies of when Les Halles was the city's giant fresh food market. A mouth-watering shop with an expansive selection of paté, truffles, quiches, escargots, pies, pastries and liqueurs. Battendier also offers delivery service, either to hotel or home.

Boisse Charcuterie 38, rue Coquillière, 1er; (metro: Les Halles, Louvre). Another vestige of old Les Halles, serving up paté, cheese, wines, roast chickens and liqueurs. Among house specialities are escargots (27F for a dozen), roast chicken (45F), half an avocado stuffed with prawns (18F).

La Cave de Gargantua 286, rue St Honoré, 1er; (metro: Pyramides, Tuileries). Over 15,000 gourmet food items in stock including a wide selection of paté, seafood, chocolates, salads, fruit, wine and even crisps (potato chips to you Yanks).

La Cave d'Hediard 17, avenue de Courcelles, 17e; (metro: Courcelles). Perfect for gift or Christmas shopping with its special packages of wine, cheese and sweets. Among the house selection are chocolates, dried and fresh fruits, nuts, cheeses and maple syrup. The round, red syrup containers make great kitchen decorations when they're empty.

Fauchon 28, place de la Madeleine, 8e; (metro: Madeleine). The most famous gourmet food outfit in Paris with literally something for everyone: paté, cheeses, wine, liqueurs, sweets and chocolates, tinned meats and foie gras, caviar, escargots, dried and fresh fruits. The inventory goes on and on. Not as pricey as you would expect.

Flo 42, place du Marché St Honoré, 1er; (metro: Pyramides). Yet another haute cuisine supermarket. Among the best buys are foie gras, smoked salmon.

Foie Gras Import 34, rue Montmartre, 1er; (metro: Les Halles, Etienne Marcel). A wonderful old shop that resembles a general store from the American West. Bite-size or bulk quantities of foie gras, tinned meats, canned fish, spices, sausages and mushrooms.

Foie Gras Luxe 26, rue Montmartre, 1er; (metro: Les Halles, Etienne Marcel). The grande maison of duck livers, plus truffles, cured hams, olives, salmon and goose. Bulk supplies available, but Luxe does a marvellous job of packaging its small gift items. A Paris landmark.

Gourmandises Clos du Parc 16, rue Elzevir, 3e; (metro: St
314

Paul). Good selection of cheese, wine, fruit, vegetables, coffee and sweets. A Marais landmark with its picturesque red facade.

Kaspia 17, place de la Madeleine, 8e; (metro: Madeleine). Where Nicholas and Alexandra might have bought their caviar — a superb shop selling the finest of Russian and Iranian sturgeon eggs from the Caspian Sea. Open 11 am to midnight.

Petrossian 18, boulevard de Latour-Maubourg, 7e; (metro: Latour-Maubourg). The pièce de résistance: the most exquisite and marvellous gourmet shop in Paris. The giant sturgeon and the crates of Moet Chandon in the window give you a clue as to the luxurious style of Petrossian, a shop which packages and markets its own brand of caviar. Among other delicacies are foie gras, Russian vodka, smoked salmon, wines, tinned *soupe de poissons,* canned duck stewed in a wine sauce, and pickled walnuts. You can also purchase silver caviar dispensers. Open Tuesday to Friday 9 am to 1 pm and 1.30 to 7 pm, and Saturday 9.30 am to 7.30 pm. Closed Sunday and Monday.

Herbs and spices

Herboristerie du Palais Royal 11, rue des Petits Champs, 1er; (metro: Bourse, Palais Royal). If Rousseau were still alive he would definitely shop here: a real back to nature place with herbs (several hundred varieties), vitamins, teas, jams, plants, natural shampoos and the other trademarks of the natural lifestyle.

Kosher foods

Chez Raphael 12, rue Grand Marie, 9e; (metro: Rue Montmartre). Kosher delicatessen and restaurant near the Folies Bergère on a street overflowing with Jewish food stores, eating places and hotels.

Jo Goldenberg 4, rue des Rosiers, 4e; (metro: St Paul). Paris's delicatessen supreme, still run by the amiable Mr Goldenberg. In the mouth-watering inventory are pickled herring, caviar, foie gras, matsa and Israeli wines. Restaurant upstairs.

La Mamina 2, rue des Hospitales St Gervais, 4e; (metro: St Paul). Combination kosher delicatessen and food store for Paris's oldest Jewish neighbourhood. Stocks plenty of kosher wine and spirits too.

Outdoor food markets

Abbesses Rue des Abbesses, 18e; (metro: Abbesses). Lots of Montmartre atmosphere. Many famous names have shopped these stalls. Tuesday through Sunday.

Aligre Place and Rue d'Aligre, 12e; (metro; Ledru Rollin). Lots of exotic atmosphere at this sprawling food market because the neighbourhood is heavily populated with North and West Africans. It's not uncommon to see beautiful West African women shopping in their colourful kangas and head scarves. The market features fruit, vegetables, cheese, meat and fish. Daily.

Bastille Centre divider on Avenue Richard Lenoir, 11e; (metro: Bastille). The usual spread of inexpensive fruit, vegetables and other food items. One of Paris's least touristy markets. Daily.

Bretagne Rue de Bretagne at Rue Charlot, 3e; (metro: Filles du Calvaire). Little-known but colourful neighbourhood affair also called the Marché des Enfants Rouges. Where the Red Babies are I can't tell you. Tuesday through Sunday.

Buci Rue de Buci and Rue de Seine, 6e; (metro: Odéon,

Mabillon). Fruit and vegies in the heart of old St Germain, and a great place to pick up seafood delights like shellfish. Tuesday through Sunday.

Edgar-Quinet Centre divider on Boulevard Edgar-Quinet, 14e; (metro: Edgar-Quinet). Food shopping in the shadow of the Tour Montparnasse. Wednesday and Saturday only.

Faubourg St Denis Rue du Faubourg St Denis from Porte St Denis to Rue du Château d'Eau, 10e; (metro: Strasbourg St Denis, Château d'Eau). Heavy North African flavour. Daily.

Menilmontant Centre dividers on Boulevards Menilmontant and Belleville, 11e and 20e; (metro: Père Lachaise). Reputed to be Paris's largest outdoor food market. Tuesday and Friday only, 7 am to 1.30 pm.

Monge Place Monge, 5e; (metro: Place Monge). Food market in the heart of old student Paris with lots of pavement cafés around the square to watch the action. Wednesday, Friday and Sunday only.

Montorgueil Rue Montorgueil and Rue Montmartre, 1er; (metro: Les Halles). A survival from ancient Les Halles days when this was the biggest market district in Paris. The market specializes in meat and poultry items − pork, goose, beef, duck, veal, lamb and chicken − and much of the produce is sold to restaurants. A lot of little speciality shops selling foie gras and tinned meats. It's not unusual to see a butcher cutting up wild boar fresh from the southern woods. Daily.

Mouffetard Rue Mouffetard, 5e; (metro: Place Monge, Censier Daubenton). Sprawling local food market with lots of students. Daily.

St Denis Rue St Denis from Rue de Turbigo to Rue Reaumur, 2e; (metro: Etienne Marcel, Reaumur

Sebastopol). Small market with a definite Basque and South West flavour. Another vestige of old Les Halles days. Daily.

St Germain Rue Clement, 6e; (metro: Mabillon). Tuesday through Sunday.

St Quentin 85, boulevard de Magenta, 10e; (metro: Gare de l'Est). Tuesday through Sunday.

Supermarkets

Codec 11, rue des Deux Boules, 1er; (metro: Châtelet, Pont Neuf).

Codec 81, rue de Seine, 6e; (metro: Odéon, Mabillon).

Franprix 7, rue des Petites Ecuries, 10e; (metro: Château d'Eau).

Shopping Felix Potin 22, rue d'Aligre, 12e; (metro: Ledru Rollin).

A – Z shopping guide

● **Antiques**

Air de Chasse 8, rue des Sts Pères, 7e; (tel: 260.25.98; metro: Bac, St Germain). Paraphernalia of the hunt, including antique walking sticks with carved handles, stag heads, wooden decoy birds, paintings, lithographs and bone carvings.

Alain Lesieutre 9, rue de Beaune, 7e; (tel: 222.79.13/49.31; metro: Bac). A veritable museum of art deco and Belle Epoque antiques with dusty windows and a musty old smell. Statues and figurines, glassware and bottles. Open Tuesday to Friday 3 to 7 pm. Closed Saturday to Monday.

Cremerie Détail 9, rue des Halles, 1 er; (metro: Les Halles). Small but excellent selection of cheeses, plus fresh milk, eggs and other dairy products. Convenient to the Forum.

Brimo de Laroussilhe 7, quai Voltaire, 7e; (tel: 260.74.72; metro: Bac, St Germain). The collection is immense, taking in Egyptian, Greek, Roman, Medieval and Renaissance antiques. Among the items are religious statues, inlaid boxes, carpets, chests, tables, paintings and archaeological finds. Brimo is across the Seine from the Louvre, convenient for purchasing pieces similar to those you have just seen in the museum. Open 10 am to noon and 2.15 to 6.30 pm. Closed Monday.

Brocante Stone 31, rue Jacob, 6e; (tel: 260.24.80; metro: St Germain). For those with a bit of seaspray in the blood. Brocante is a treasure chest of old globes, ships-in-a-bottle, carved whale bone and walrus tusks, nautical instruments, spy glasses, binoculars, compasses, telephones and bottles. Like a nautical museum. Open 10.30 am to 7 pm. Closed Sunday and Monday.

La Cour de Varenne 42, rue de Varenne, 7e; (tel: 544.65.50; metro: Bac). Claude Levy's brilliant showcase of traditional French antiques and art from the 17th to the 19th centuries. Behind the showroom is Serod, a workshop specializing in the restoration of furniture and antiques.

Dehoux 62, rue des Sts Pères, 7e; (tel: 548.28.47; metro: Bac, St Germain). The place to buy your antique fireplace. Various designs from 15th to 18th century.

Jacques Kugel 279, rue St Honoré, 8e; (tel: 260.19.45; metro: Concorde, Madeleine). Antique silver, gold and jewellery, tapestries, carpets and furniture.

Jacques Perrin 3, quai Voltaire, 7e; (tel: 260.27.20; metro: Bac, St Germain). Just get off the train from Versailles at Gare d'Orsay. Then check out this place, a specialist in 18th

century French antiques including relics of Louis XIV and
Louis XV.

Librairie J H Pinault 27 and 36, rue Bonaparte, 6e; (tel:
633.04.24/354.89.99; metro: St Germain). The house forté
at no. 36 is rare books, like medieval manuscripts and
engravings. At no. 27 they specialize in the autographs of
well-known Frenchmen.

Le Louvre des Antiquaires 2, place du Palais Royal, 1er;
(tel: 297.27.00; metro: Palais Royal). The world's largest
antique market, 250 exquisite shops set under one roof, the
old Louvre department store. The collection spreads across
three levels and encompasses almost the entire range of antiques from ancient to modern. Specialities and best buys
include art deco, art nouveau, 18th century French. Asian,
American, African, Middle Eastern and European modes
are represented. A fantastic place for a rainy afternoon.
Open Tuesday to Sunday 11 am to 7 pm.

Lucienne Cella 2, rue des Francs Bourgeois, 3e; (tel:
277.40.53/825.04.01; metro: St Paul). A wide selection of
fine antiques representing Gothic, Renaissance, Louis XIII
and Asia. Collection includes, carpets, tapestries, furniture
and objets d'art.

C Marchal 46, rue de Miromesnil, 8e; (tel: 265.72.79; metro:
Miromesnil). Unique shop dedicated to antique arms (sabres,
swords, knives, etc.), historical souvenirs and mementoes
of the orders of chivalry.

Marway 26, rue de Richelieu, 1er; (tel: 296.88.99; metro:
Palais Royal). Marvellous collection of antique Oriental
fans, many of them made from mother-of-pearl.

Mythes et Legendes 18, place des Vosges, 4e; (tel: 272.63.26;
metro: St Paul, Chemin Vert). New antiquaire with the emphasis on Third World and ancient art: American Indian,
Mexican, Greek, Roman, Chinese, Hindu and Islamic. Open

10 am to 12.30 pm and 2 to 7 pm. Closed Sunday and Monday.

J P Rochefort 14, rue des Sts Pères, 7e; (tel: 296.60.05; metro: Bac, St Germain). Specialist in antique globes, time-pieces and navigational equipment.

Vieille France 364, rue St Honoré, 1er; (tel: 260.01.57; metro: Madeleine, Concorde). Antique sabres and other military equipment, historical documents, tin soldiers and military decorations.

Village Suisse 51, avenue de la Motte-Piquet, 15e; (metro: La Motte Piquet). Similar in design and function to the Louvre antiques market, a collection of 150 small shops and boutiques specializing in a wide variety of wares. The name is misleading because not much of the merchandise is actually Swiss. Open Thursday through Monday 10.30 am to 7 pm.

● Art supplies

Adam 11, boulevard Edgar Quinet, 14e; (tel: 320.68.53; metro: Edgar-Quinet). A department store of art supplies for the beginner or pro: paints, brushes, canvas, scissors, crayons, pens, frames, sketch books, acrylics; something for every medium. Open 9 am to 9 pm. Closed Sunday and Monday. In the heart of the old artists' quarter in Montparnasse.

Rennes 80 80, rue de Rennes, 6e; (tel: 548.54.27; metro: St Sulpice). Large stock at good prices near the gallery district of the Rive Gauche.

● Autographs

Autographes 14, rue de Seine, 6e; (metro: Mabillon). Tiny shops with some mighty signatures, everyone from Napoleon to Picasso. This inventory includes writers, artists, politicians, diplomats and military people. Also stocks historical documents and letters.

J H Pinault 27, rue Bonaparte, 6e; (tel: 354.89.99; metro: St Germain). Specializing in the signatures of famous people, both past and present.

● **Bicycles**

Peugeot 72, avenue de la Grande Armée, 17e; (tel: 574.27.38; metro: Porte Maillot, Argentine). A large selection of France's most famous bikes, plus accessories.

Raleigh 36, avenue de la Grande Armée, 17e; (tel: 380.66.89; metro: Argentine). Supermarket of Raleigh and Brooks bikes and accessories.

● **Books − English**

Brentano's 37, avenue de l'Opéra, 2e; (tel: 261.52.50; metro: Pyramides, 4 Septembre). The world famous purveyor of fine books, operating in Paris since 1895. Good selection but a bit pricey.

Galignani 224, rue de Rivoli, 1er; (tel: 260.76.07; metro: Tuileries). Established in 1856 as the first English language bookshop in Paris. A gargantuan selection of British and American works. Open 9.30 am to 10.30 pm every day but Sunday.

Shakespeare and Company 37, rue de la Bucherie, 5e; (metro: Maubert-Mutualité, St Michel). Not the biggest, not the oldest, but certainly the most famous English bookshop in Paris. Started in the 1930s by a romantic-minded American expatriate as both store and lending library. Among the first card-holders were Gertrude Stein and Ernest Hemingway. After nearly a half century the place is still a bastion of literary Paris (poetry readings at regular intervals) and the epitome of what a book store should be with its cosy corners, comfortable armchairs and friendly, anti-quated atmosphere. Sells both new and used books. Chess on the terrace and message board inside. Open daily noon to midnight.

W H Smith & Son 248, rue de Rivoli, 1er; (tel: 260.37.97; metro: Concorde, Tuileries). The high temple of British literature in Paris, and probably the best all-around English language bookshop in the city. Smith's specializes in best sellers, English classics, tour guides and maps, plus current newspapers and magazines like *The Times* of London and *The Guardian*. You can read your new book at the Tuileries across the street or go upstairs to the first floor restaurant and tea room (see page 166). Open 9 am to 6.30 pm every day but Sunday.

Village Voice 6, rue Princesse, 6e; (tel: 633.36.47; metro: Mabillon, St Germain-des-Près). As the name suggests, something right out of Greenwich Village, a café-bookstore specializing in avant-garde literature. The friendly American owners have followed the guidelines laid down by Shakespeare and Company, creating a warm and comfort-able ambience in which you can browse and read at your pleasure the entire day. If the Americans in Paris do something better than anyone else, it has to be bookstores. Open Tuesday, Friday and Saturday, 11 am to 8 pm, Wednesday and Thursday 11 am to 10 pm. Closed Sunday and Monday.

● **Books – specialized**

Albert Petit Siroux 46, galerie Vivienne, 2e; (metro: Bourse). A *librairie ancienne et moderne* selling new and used books on France and Paris. A museum of old, musty books that looks as if Voltaire and J-J Rousseau could have shopped there.

Atmosphere 1, rue Balzac, 8e; (tel: 256.20.38; metro: George V). 7-9, rue Francis de Pressense, 14e; (tel: 542.29.26; metro:

Pernety). Shops specializing in books and magazines of the cinema, both old and new. Movie posters and publicity photos too. The Balzac store is open Wednesday to Sunday 2.30 to 8.30 pm; the Pressense shop Wednesday to Monday 2.30 to 10.30 pm.

Galerie Documents 53, rue de Seine, 6e; (tel: 354.50.68; metro: Mabillon). Antique and rare books, plus Belle Epoque posters and prints. Open 10 am to 12.30 pm and 2.30 to 7 pm. Closed Sunday and Monday.

Jullien Cornic 29 and 33, avenue Matignon, 8e; (tel: 359.10.90; metro: Roosevelt, Miromesnil). Specialists in books on the fine arts, decorative arts and fashion. Jullien claim they can supply any book old or new from any country on artists and fashions. Large English and French selection.

Librairie Nautique 71, rue Fondary, 15e; (metro: Emile Zola). Seafaring books in all shapes and sizes: how-to, navigational aids, travel and adventure, photograph, biography, sports.

Paralleles 47, rue St Honoré, 1er; (tel: 233.62.70; metro: Les Halles). Paris's most famous house of underground and avant-garde books and periodicals. Lots of Third World and counter-culture titles.

Ulysse 35, rue St Louis en l'Ile, 4e; (tel: 325.17.35; metro: Pont Marie). The well-known travel bookshop in the Ile St Louis. Over 20,000 travel books, maps, historical and cultural accounts in stock dealing with both the practical and romantic sides of travel. Both new and used books. Out of print works can be obtained. Many English titles. Open 2 to 8 pm. Closed Sunday and Monday.

Le Zin Zin d'Hollywood 7, rue des Ursulines, 5e; (tel: 633.48.43; metro: Place Monge). 5, rue de Condé, 6e; (metro: Odéon). Both old and new books dealing with

Hollywood (couldn't you guess by the name?) and the film industry, plus posters and still photographs. Open daily 11 am to 7 pm.

● Camping and backpacking equipment

R Dethy 20, place des Vosges, 4e; (tel: 887.27.01; metro: Bastille, Chemin Vert). Small, but packed with the latest, best and cheapest of camping equipment: tents, cookers, Gaz stoves, backpacks, isotherm coolers, trailers and mini-caravans, crampons, mousquetons and piolets. And what they don't have in the shop they'll quickly order. Open 9 am to 12.30 pm and 2 to 7 pm. Closed Monday.

Randonneurs/Cooperative du Temps Libre 39, rue Trebois, Levallois-Perret; (tel: 758.78.60; metro: Louise Michel, Anatole France). Outdoor boutique in the Levallois suburb stocking backpacks, tents, sleeping bags, hiking and climbing boots, sports shoes, climbing equipment, orientation maps and compasses, canoes, kayaks and even roller skates.

● Candles

C I R 18, rue St Sulpice, 6e; (metro: Mabillon). Making fine candles in France since 1643. They come in every conceivable size, shape and colour; most interesting are the unusual fruit, cheese and wine motifs. Are they real or are they wax? Open 10 am to 7 pm. Closed Monday.

● Candy and sweets

Catalin Estage − 1 Forum les Halles, 1er; (metro: Les Halles). Mouth-watering chocolates, candies, sweets and fruit sculptures. Perfect as gifts.

La Grande Confiserie 1, rue de la Banque, 2e; (metro: Bourse). An old fashioned Parisian sweet shop with the candies displayed in huge glass jars on the pavement and in the window. The shop also sells wine and gourmet tinned meats.

Port Royal 234, rue de Rivoli, 1er; (metro: Tuileries). Paris's premier *chocolatier et confiseur*. Some of the best chocolate candies found anywhere, but look out for the prices.

● **Canes and umbrellas**

Abel 36, passage Jouffroy, 9e; (metro: Montmartre, Richelieu-Drouot). Walking sticks, canes and umbrellas. Many are lovely antiques with carved wooden or ivory handles. Worth a visit just to glance at the Belle Epoque passage Jouffroy. Open 10 am to noon and 1 to 7 pm. Closed Sunday and Monday.

● **Carpets and tapestries**

Braquenie and Company 16, rue Vivienne, 2e; (tel: 261.53.94; metro: Bourse). A fascinating workshop and sales room which could double as a museum. Braquenie has been making and selling fine tapestries, wall hangings and carpets since 1804, in conjunction with the famous Dautzenberger antiques in the same courtyard. They will also upholster furniture. Both ancient and modern designs. Best selection in Paris.

Tapis du Louvre 170, rue de Rivoli at place du Palais Royale, 1er; (metro: Palais Royale). Persian and other Asian weaves.

Robert Four 32, rue Jacob, 6e; (tel: 296.14.19; metro: St Germain). Gorgeous and intriguing modern tapestries. You can even watch them weaving through the corner windows. Open Tuesday to Saturday 10 am to 7 pm, Monday 2 to 7 pm. Closed Sunday.

Tai Ping 30, rue des Sts Pères, 7e; (metro: Bac, St Germain). Vogue's choice as one of the exciting new carpet designers in Paris. Features bold, naturalistic designs in over 300 colours. Open 10.30 am to 12.30 pm and 2.30 to 5.30 pm. Closed Saturday and Sunday.

● Ceramics

Le Cresartisanal 61, rue St Denis, 1er; (metro: Les Halles). Pots, lamps and ceramic articles of every shape and size.

La Soupière Estage – 1 Forum les Halles, 1er; (metro: Les Halles). As the name suggests, a place to buy soup bowls, but they've got about everything else you might need for the dining table including silver place settings and full dinner sets. Ranges from traditional porcelain to modern flatwear designs.

Venini France 95, rue du Bac, 7e; (tel: 548.95.39; metro: Bac). Modern avant-garde glass and ceramics from Venice, including the beautiful *masques au cuir* for a mere 500-700F each. Venini also stocks lamps, mirrors, furniture and various objets d'art. An interesting place to browse even if you can't afford to buy.

● Duty free

Benelux 174, rue de Rivoli, 1er; (metro: Palais Royale). The 'International Shopping Centre' which offers the varied products of Holland, Belgium and Luxembourg, as well as France.

Eiffel Shopping 9, avenue de Suffren, 7e and Les Boutiques du Palais des Congrès, 17e; (metro: Bir Hakeim for Suffren; Porte Maillot for Congrès). Paris's most famous duty free house, with a staff and service to match the top French restaurant. Good range of designer clothes and accessories, plus watches, perfume and jewellery.

Michel Swiss 16, rue de la Paix, 2e (tel: 261.69.44; metro: Opéra). Tax free perfumes, leather, scarves, ties, china and menswear.

Zeina 18-20, rue de la Paix, 2e; (metro: Opéra). Forty per cent discount for export on items such as menswear, leather and perfume. Open 9.30 am to 7 pm daily.

● **Fossils and rocks**

Galerie Michel Cachoux 16-29, rue Guenegaud, 6e; (metro: Odéon). A shop or a geology museum? Possibly the only place in Paris where you can buy a fossil tortoise from South Dakota or a fossil fish embedded in stone. Lots of geodes, just plain rocks and semi-precious stones. A rock hound's paradise.

● **Furniture and household items**

La Bovida Rue Etienne Marcel at Rue Montmartre, 1er; (metro: Les Halles, Etienne Marcel). The latest in pots, pans, knives, utensils, etc.

Dehillerin 18, rue Coquillière, 1er; (tel: 236.53.13; metro: Les Halles). Paris's grand old store for kitchen items since 1820. Stock includes, pots, pans, copperware, electric appliances and an amazing selection of knives. The hardware store supreme. Open 8 am to 12.30 pm and 2 to 6 pm. Closed Sunday.

Habitat Estage 1 Centre Montparnasse, 15e; (tel: 538.69.90; metro: Montparnasse). 35, avenue de Wagram, 17e; (metro: Etoile, Ternes). Everything in furniture and accessories for the contemporary household: pillows, carpets, paint, bookshelves, plants and pots, tables, chairs, glass, pottery, lamps etc. The variety is astounding and the prices quite reasonable. British visitors will know Habitat well from back home; Americans and other colonials will be amazed.

Le Monde Sauvage 101, rue St Denis, 1er; (tel: 261.85.06; metro: Les Halles). Rattan and fibre specialists; a real joy to browse or buy. Sauvage stocks tables, chairs, plant boxes, screens, lamps, hats, baskets, brushes and even hammocks. The 'Wild World' indeed, but such exotic beauty.

Roche-Bobois 213, boulevard St Germain, 7e; (tel: 548.36.76; metro; Bac). Anyone who liked Richard Gere's apartment in *American Gigolo* will love this shop: trendy furnishing to go along with your trendy clothes. Maybe a blue neon telephone, or perhaps a few Japanese-style futons for the sitting room? Avant-garde designs with a touch of fun and a lot of imagination.

Les Quatre Saisons 2-6, rue du Jour, 1er; (tel: 236.80.89; metro: Les Halles, Etienne Marcel). Two shops, one specializing in modern wooden furniture and the other in contemporary accessories to match, including kitchen items and general knick-knacks. Plus a *salon de thé* upstairs.

● **Games**

Le Baguenaudier Estage O Le Centre Gaîté, 68-80 Avenue du Maine, 14e; (tel: 321.60.35; metro: Gaîté, Montparnasse). New shops specializing in chess, checkers, darts, Chinese checkers, cards and adult games.

La Boutique Double 7 Estage − 1 Les Boutiques du Palais des Congrès, 17e; (metro: Porte Maillot). Adult fun shop with Mordillo and Blachon puzzles, playing cards, backgammon, roulette and other gambling games.

La Tortue Electrique 7, rue Frederick Sauton, 5e; (tel: 329.37.08; metro: Maubert Mutualité). Antique games like the famous 'Electric Tortoise'. Open 2 to 7 pm. Closed Sunday and Monday.

● **Gifts and trinkets**

Atelier 12 Objets Insolites 12, rue des Sts Pères, 7e; (tel: 260.81.00; metro; Bac, St Germain). The papier-maché specialists; gorgeous little gift items like boxes, animals, shells and birds. Mother-of-pearl objects too.

Axis 18, rue Guenegaud, 6e; (tel: 329.66.23; metro: Odéon).

A weird assortment of interesting gifts: colourful lamps, rubbish bins, handbags, coffee pots, sponges and cigarette lighters.

Boutique du Palais Royal Passage du Perron at 9 rue de Beaujolais, 1er; (tel: 260.08.22; metro: Palais Royal, Bourse). Curious little shop in a dark passage off the Palais Royal arcade, packed with leather items, kitchen utensils, old dolls and music boxes and other assorted knick-knacks.

Come Bac 23, rue du Bac, 7e; (tel: 261.22.78; metro: Bac). Bizarre and unusual items for the kitchen and home, this shop is an absolute delight just to look around. Alcatraz aprons, Pink Panther T-shirts and glasses, funny shower curtains, masks, stuffed animals and even plastic baguettes. And no pun intended!

Da Capo 14, rue des Ecoles, 5e; (tel: 354.75.47; metro: Maubert-Mutualité). Bizarre but interesting collection of old junk: records, cameras, African tribal statues, gramophones, music books and photo magazines. Rock bottom prices on most items. Open 1 to 7 pm. Closed Sunday.

Délégation de l'Artisanat Morocain 161, rue St Honoré, 1er; (metro: Palais Royal). Straight out of a Casablanca bazaar, gift and art objects from Morocco for those who can't travel to North Africa. Some of the items represent exquisite workmanship by native craftsmen, skills which have often been in the family for generations. Brass, carpets, chests, leather and beautiful Berber dresses.

Dépôt Vente 11, rue Campagne Première, 14e; (tel: 322.17.83; metro: Raspail). Various baubles and bangles as presented by Michèle Maret, including buttons, pins, jewellery, old clothes and assorted junk. Out-of-the-way, but interesting shop.

Didier Ludot 18, galerie Montpensier in the Palais Royal, 1er; (metro: Palais Royale). Things your mother or grandmother might have worn: interesting old clothes, shoes, handbags, hats and costume jewellery from the 1920s, 30s and 40s. A bit like the costume department at MGM or Warner Brothers. Knick-knacks and old bottles too.

Diptyque 34, boulevard St Germain, 5e; (tel: 326.45.27; metro: Maubert-Mutualité). You'll either love or hate this shop the minute you walk through the door: the intense aroma of candles and perfume will knock you dead or remind you of bygone days at grandmama's. A little bit of everything: pens and ink, perfumes and soaps, tweed hats, Oriental carpets, weird jewellery, candles, shaving cream goblets and brushes. Open 10 am to 7 pm. Closed Sunday and Monday.

Esteve 3, rue Jacques-Callot, 6e; (tel: 354.19.10; metro: Odéon). Near to the Cachoux rock shop, Esteve is a bizarre collection of old photos, odd statues, Belle Epoque art objects, jewellery, new and used frames, prints, posters, collages and knick-knacks. Open 10.30 am to 12.30 pm and 1.30 to 6.45 pm. Closed Monday.

Exactement Fauve 5, rue Princesse, 6e; (metro: Mabillon). Weird costume jewellery and lots of odd things for the hair like combs, bracelets, feathers. Mediums include textiles, metal and plastic.

La Marie Galande 65, rue Galande, 5e; (tel: 354.06.47; metro: Maubert-Mutualité, St Michel). For art deco and Belle Epoque fans. Mostly bizarre old clothes, furs, statues, glasses and baubles.

Pain d'Epices 35, passage Jouffroy, 9e; (tel: 770.82.65; metro: Rue Montmartre, Richelieu Drouot). Old signs, imitation flowers, candles, soap, greeting cards and candy. A lot of boxes of various shapes and sizes, plus trendy bathroom accessories. Check out the lovely Belle Epoque passage.

Remember Marilyn 23, rue des Canettes, 6e; (tel: 354.71.17; metro: St Sulpice). Billed as the world's only store devoted to Marilyn Monroe, and they're probably right! Postcards, posters, books, watches, lamps, T-shirts and her famous 1953 nude calendar. A real treat for movie freaks and anyone who reminisces about the good old days of Hollywood. Open 11 am to 1 pm and 2 to 7.15 pm. Closed Monday and holidays.

F Thibault 1, rue de Bourbon-le-Château, 6e; (tel: 326.40.23; metro: Mabillon). A treasure house of Belle Epoque memorabilia including lamps, mirrors, boxes, statues, toys and marionettes.

Victorine 65, rue St Martin, 4e; (tel: 277.95.03; metro: Châtelet). Marvellous marionettes, scarves, costume jewellery, buttons, figurines and other gift items. Near the Pompidou Centre. Open Monday and Tuesday 2 to 7.30 pm; Wednesday to Saturday 11 am to 7.30 pm. Closed Sundays.

● **Jewellery**

Cartier 13, rue de la Paix, 2e; (tel: 261.58.56; metro: Opéra). The original, still a girl's best friend after all these years. And it doesn't cost anything to gaze at the crystalized carbon in the windows. The black and gold marble facade is a work of art too.

Gianmaria Buccellati 4, place Vendôme, 1er; (tel: 260.12.12; metro; Opéra, Tuileries). Traditional jewellery and silver opposite the Ritz.

Mauboussin 20, place Vendôme, 1er; (tel: 260.44.93; metro: Opéra, Tuileries). Fine jewellery and watches. Open 9.30 am to 1 pm and 2.30 to 8.30 pm. Closed Saturday and Monday.

Mellerio 9, rue de la Paix, 1er; (tel: 261.57.53; metro: Opéra). An updated version of Cartier with more modern

Cartier's jewellery boutique in the Rue de la Paix, still a girl's best friend after all these years. It doesn't cost anything to gaze at the crystalized carbon in the windows.

settings and jewellery designs.

Utility Bibi 27, rue du Four, 6e; (tel: 325.53.77; metro: St Germain, Mabillon). Avant-garde, ultra-modern and experimental jewellery, Louis Villevon watches and turquoise. Trendy city.

Van Cleef et Arpels 22, place Vendôme, 1er; (tel: 261.02.36; metro: Opéra, Tuileries). Another famous house of diamonds, right down the street from Cartier.

● **Musical instruments**

Achat et Vente 6, passage de la Mule, 3e; (tel: 287.20.15; metro: Chemin Vert, Breguet Sabin, Bastille). A veritable museum of antique music makers: harps, guitars, drums, trumpets, violins, clarinets, mandolins, bugles, music boxes and gramophones. Open 2 to 7 pm. Closed Sunday and holidays.

Quincampoix 38, rue Quincampoix, 4e; (tel: 277.48.02; metro: Rambuteau, Les Halles). Purveyors of fine stringed instruments since 1815 (right after the Battle of Waterloo). Selection includes steel and wood guitars, mandolins, dulcimers, bouzoukis and Hungarian epinettes.

● **Newspapers and magazines**

Carnavalette 2, rue des Francs Bourgeois, 3e; (metro: St Paul, Chemin Vert). Wonderful shop selling old newspapers and magazines dating back to the 1850s, engravings, books, prints and postcards. Proof that good shops come in small packages. Just off the Place des Vosges.

Le Journal Anniversaire Estage – 1 Forum les Halles, 1er; (metro: Les Halles). Old magazine and newspaper covers from around the world. Both 19th and 20th century. Huge selection.

Whaam 29, rue Aubry le Boucher, 4e; (metro; Les Halles, Rambuteau). French comic books and movie posters.

● Paper and stationery

L'Escritoire 61, rue St Martin, 4e; (metro: Chatelet). Everything for the aspiring writer: fountain pens, ink pots, diaries and fancy paper, plus art supplies, old postcards and posters.

Papeterie de la Poste 66, rue J-J Rousseau, 1er; (metro: Les Halles). Pens, paper and postcards, plus lighters, watches, leather goods, briefcases, toys and games.

Papeterie Moderne 12, rue de la Ferronnerie, 1er; (metro: Les Halles). Tiny shop with a huge collection of signs of every colour, size and description. Parisian street signs (with either the real name of the street or your name), restaurant and café signs, made-to-order door and office signs, calling cards. Balls of string too.

Papier + 9, rue du Pont Louis Philippe, 4e; (metro; Pont Marie, St Paul). For real paper freaks. Laurent Tisne's exquisite collection of paper in almost every colour of the rainbow, plus coloured pencils, pens, inks, notebooks, drawing pads and other art supplies. You can buy almost everything in bulk. Open noon to 7.30 pm. Closed Monday.

Sterns Graveur 47, passage des Panoramas, 2e; (metro: Rue Montmartre). The premier Parisian engravers, an elegant premises and a stylish reputation. Sterns produces almost anything you can engrave on: calling cards, Christmas cards, menus, invitations, letterhead, monograms and even bronze plaques.

● Perfume

Note: when searching for perfume in Paris, keep in mind that many of the major clothes designers also market their own brands of scent. The list of fashion-inspired fragrance is endless, including such big names as Chanel, Dior, Givenchy, Laroche, Saint Laurent, Rabanne and Ricci. When searching for these perfumes, it's often best to head directly to the haute couture outlet. For addresses, look under the appropriate designer heading in the Womenswear and Menswear sections.

L'Artisan Parfumeur 5, rue des Capucines, 1er; (tel: 296.35.13; metro: Madeleine) or 84 bis, rue de Grenelle, 7e; (metro: Bac). Jean Laporte collection of fine perfumes, plus assorted soaps and scents for bath and bedroom. Fascinating window displays.

Beauté 97, rue du Bac, 7e; (tel: 548.30.30; metro: Bac) and 34, place du Marché St Honoré, 1er; (metro: Pyramides).

Capucines 122, rue Faubourg St Honoré, 8e; (tel: 562.36.50; metro: St Philippe-du-Boule) and 18, rue des Capucines, 2e; (metro: Opéra, Madeleine).

Concordances 4, place André Malraux, 1er; (tel: 296.07.45; metro: Palais Royal).

Gray 27, rue Danielle-Casanova, 1er; (tel: 261.73.11; metro: Opéra) and 2, place du Palais Royal, 1er; (metro: Palais Royal). Good selection of Gucci, Revlon, Hermès and Armaus perfumes.

Guerlain 2, place Vendôme, 1er; (tel: 260.68.61; metro: Opéra, Tuileries). Exclusive home of Guerlain perfumes. Other boutiques at 29 Rue de Sèvres, 6e, 68 avenue des Champs-Elysées, 8e and 93 Rue de Passy, 16e.

● **Pets**

La Niche Royale 113, rue de la Faisanderie, 16e; (tel: 504.32.74; metro: Rue de la Pompe). *Toilette pour Chiens*, a chic boutique for the canine in your family. Anything you could ever want for a dog: toys, beds, food, collars, clothes, bowls, leads, books, artwork (paintings of dogs) and doggie transporters. Open 9 am to noon and 2 to 6.30 pm. Closed Sunday.

Quai de la Megisserie Between Pont Neuf and Place du Châtelet, 1er; (metro: Pont Neuf, Châtelet). Paris's famous pet market along the Seine where you can purchase just about anything in the way of pets and accessories: dogs, cats, mice, rabbits, chickens, birds, chipmunks and fish. Among the larger shops are Au Paradis des Oiseaux (no. 22), Cheuil Oisellerie (no. 18) and Oisellerie Pont Neuf (no. 8). Many of these folks set up at the Flower Market on Sundays for the one-day Pet Market.

● **Photo equipment**

FNAC Etage — 1 Forum les Halles, 1er; (tel: 261.81.18; metro: Les Halles). Biggest photo supermarket this side of Japan, part of the FNAC department store in the Forum. Everything you need: film, new and used cameras and lenses, tripods, flash units, camera bags, processing chemicals and papers, how-to and art books, cinema and video equipment. For both professionals and amateurs. Special photo exhibits in the FNAC gallery. And a special camera repair desk for the shutter-stuck tourist.

Kodak 38, avenue George V, 8e; (tel: 723.57.40; metro: George V, Alma Marceau). Everything you ever wanted to know about Kodak cameras and films. But this place is both an information centre and a sales room, so you can buy too. Small, but fantastic photo library stocking current and back issues of photo magazines from America, France, Germany, England, Italy and other places. Special exhibits of photo art and photo journalism.

Photo Verdeau 16, passage Verdeau, 9e; (tel: 770.51.91; metro: Le Peletier, Rue Montmartre). Antique cameras, accessories and opticals. Among the gems are ancient Kodak cameras and exquisite opera glasses.

Shop Photo 33, rue du Com. Mouchotte and 26, rue Vercingetorix, 14e; (tel: 320.15.35; metro: Gaîté, Montparnasse). The Montparnasse answer to FNAC, 1,200 square metres of photo, cinema and video equipment. Almost every major camera maker has a display stand, and there is a vast array of accessories like flashes, tripods and filters. On the spot cibachromes and quick film processing. Radio, television and stereo equipment too. You can spend hours here just looking around.

● **Pipes and tobacco**

A La Civette 157, rue St Honoré, 1er; (tel: 261.61.07; metro: Palais Royal). Superb smokeshop on the Place Colette opposite the Comédie Française. Features Cuban and Dutch cigars, numerous brands of international cigarettes, Cartier and Dunhill lighters (at only 1,850F), Waterman and Sheaffer ink pens, and pipes.

Alfred Dunhill 15, rue de la Paix, 2e; (tel: 261.57.58; metro: Opéra). The one and only, right down the block from Cartier. The famous Dunhill pipes, lighters, snuff and cigar boxes, silver ashtrays and gold-plated letter openers, watches and fountain pens. The prices match the quality. Open 9.30 am to 1 pm and 2 to 6.30 pm. Closed Sunday.

A L'Oriental 19, galerie de Chartres, 1er; (metro: Palais Royal). Interesting collection of antique and new pipes in a small shop in the Palais Royal arcade. One of the oldest establishments in Paris for smoking gear.

● **Postcards and posters**

La Banque de l'Image 51, rue Mouffetard, 5e; (metro: Place Monge). Large selection of posters and postcards in the heart of student Paris.

Beaubourg Boulevard de Sebastopol at Rue Aubry le Boucher, 4e; (metro: Les Halles, Rambuteau). Largest postcard collection in Paris, a stupendous collection of scenic, humorous, art, soft porn and other cards. The place where everyone stops enroute from the Pompidou Centre to Les Halles.

Beaubourg Diffusion Rue Aubry le Boucher at Rue St Martin, 4e; (metro: Rambuteau). The second largest postcard collection in the neighbourhood, but they also have a great selection of art and photo books, posters, calendars and even film. Open until 11 pm for post-dinner browsing.

Cartes d'Art 9, rue du Dragon, 6e; (metro: St Germain). Insiders say this is the best postcard shop in Paris. Large selection, and like a library everything is catalogued according to artist's name or subject.

Galerie Hit Melody 62, rue des Ecoles, 5e; (metro: Maubert Mutualité). Postcards and posters.

Poster Shop 7, quai St Michel, 5e; (metro: St Michel). Tiny shop specializing in high quality posters and frames. Selection includes both ancient and modern art, photos, scenic, advertising, cinema, music, theatrical. An art gallery in its own right.

Soho 4, rue Aubry le Boucher, 4e; (metro: Les Halles, Rambuteau). Imported English postcards, posters and gift items. Take your pick: American car number plates, Pink Panther paraphernalia, pop art lamps, etc. Some call it trendy, some call it kitsch.

● **Records**

Cécile Musique 84, rue Mouffetard, 5e; (metro: Place Monge). French and international rock, soul, jazz and disco at student prices.

FNAC 1, rue Pierre Lescot, 1er; (metro: Les Halles, Etienne Marcel). Billed as the largest selection of records and tapes in Paris, covering everything from Bob Marley to Mozart, Elvis to the Eurythmics.

Juke Box Estage 1 Le Centre Gaîté at 68-80 Avenue du Maine, 14e; (metro: Gaîté, Montparnasse). New disc spinners with the emphasis on rock and pop.

Paralleles 47, rue St Honoré, 1er; (metro: Les Halles, Louvre). Rock, pop, jazz, reggae and Third World music, as well as avant-garde and left wing literature. Counter-culture hangout.

● **Religious**

Maison Bleue 6 bis, rue des Petits Pères, 2e; (tel: 260.94.80; metro: Bourse). The Roman Catholic supermarket in what is a very Catholic city. Statues, books, records, candles, plaques, holy cards, crucifixes and colour posters of Pope John Paul II. Not bad for Christmas decorations either, if you're into manger scenes and guardian angels.

● **Sports equipment**

Athletic Attic 118 rue de Rivoli at Rue des Déchargeurs, 1er; (tel: 233.69.55; metro: Les Halles, Châtelet). Part of the new wave of American-style athletic boutiques now hitting Paris. Shoes, bags, shirts, shorts, socks and various balls. Open 10 am to 7 pm. Closed Sunday.

La Boule Obut 39, rue Coquillière, 1er; (metro: Les Halles, Louvre). Shoes, balls, weights, shirts, socks, shorts, and tennis rackets at reasonable prices. Open Monday 1 to 6.45 pm, Tuesday to Friday 9.30 am to 2.30 pm and 3 to 6.45 pm. Closed Saturday and Sunday.

LaCoste 37, boulevard des Capucines, 2e; (tel: 261.58.20; metro: Opéra). 44, rue St Placide, 6e; (metro; St Placide).

82, avenue Victor Hugo, 16e; (tel: 553.39.49; metro: Etoile, Kleber). The alligator people. Trendy sportswear straight off American college campuses and the beach at Antibes. LaCoste tennis outfits and rackets. Pricey but cool.

Emeraude Marine 5, rue Petits Champs, 1er; (tel: 296.33.85; metro: Bourse, Palais Royal). Paris's ocean sports centre. Catamarans, life jackets, sailing supplies and clothes.

Randonneurs/Cooperative du Temps Libre 39, rue Trebois, Levallois-Perret; (tel: 758.78.60; metro: Louise Michel, Anatole France). Specialized outdoor sports equipment like kayaks, canoes, cycles and climbing equipment. They also rent bikes.

● **Stamps, coins and medals**

A Bacqueville 7, galerie de Montpensier, 1er; (tel: 296.26.90; metro; Palais Royal). Fabulous collection of ancient French military campaign medals: Ivory Coast, Senegal, Gabon, Madagascar, Algeria, Morocco and Indo-China. American Volunteers with the French Army (1914-17) medals for 150F.

Daniele Dutertie Galerie Chartres, 1er; (tel: 296.09.29; metro: Palais Royal). Another of the gorgeous shops in the Palais Royal arcade, this one specializing in old stamps and medals.

Empire Philatélique 49, galerie de Montpensier, 1er; (tel: 297.45.28; metro: Palais Royal). Storehouse of French and foreign stamps.

Marché aux Timbres Avenue Champs-Elysées at Avenue de Marigny, 8e; (metro: Clemenceau). Paris's weekend stamp and coin market off Place Clemenceau. Saturday and Sunday only.

Philatélie G Behr 26, avenue de l'Opéra, 1er; (tel: 297.42.62; metro: Pyramides). The prestigious stamp dealers featuring rare and expensive items. Bring your chequebook and safety deposit box.

● Telescopes and optics

Cerf 20, quai de la Megisserie, 1er; (tel: 233.54.42; metro: Pont Neuf, Châtelet). Supermarket of optical equipment for recreation, business and laboratory. Selection includes binoculars, monoculars, telescopes, opera glasses, tripods, clamps, microscopes, thermometers, and magnifying glasses. Specialist in Zeiss, Optolyth, CBS Beck and Perl.

● Toys

Au Nain Bleu 408, rue St Honoré, 8e; (tel: 260.39.01; metro: Madeleine). Toys for little rich kids. You will either be amazed by the imagination (and prices) or disgusted that so much cash could be spent on a little brat. The 'Blue Dwarf' has giant Snoopy dolls, toy soldiers, videos for kids, space ships, puppets, model airplanes and go-carts with petrol engines. A Paris landmark since 1836.

Aux Soldats d'Anton 12, rue de l'Université, 7e; (tel: 260.89.56; metro: Bac). For kids aged six to sixty, a marvellous collection of antique tin soldiers, swords, war medals and miniature canons.

Beau Noir/Monsieur Renard 6, rue de l'Echaude, 6e; (tel: 325.70.72; metro: Mabillon). Specializing in *poupées anciennes,* this is the best selection of antique dolls in Paris. A wonderful shop for children or adults. Also has dolls' houses and furniture, old masks and assorted toys. Good for a lunchtime browse.

La Boîte à Joujoux 41, passage Jouffroy, 9e; (tel: 824.58.37; metro: Rue Montmartre, Richelieu Drouot). Toys, games, masks, unusual chess sets, tarot cards and playing cards in a lovely Belle Epoque galerie. Open 10 am to 7 pm. Closed Sunday.

Canard Roulettes 60, rue Mazarine, 6e; (tel: 354.79.08; metro: Odéon). Excellent collection of antique toys, puppets, marionettes, dolls, dolls' houses and furniture. Open 10 am to 7 pm. Closed Sunday and Monday.

Drapeaux France 34, galerie de Montpensier, 1er; (metro: Palais Royal). Watch the master of the tin soldier at work. This is Jacques Bittard's workshop and salesroom of superb, hand-made toy soldiers. And what more perfect location for the 'French Flag' than the Palais Royal arcade?

B H Maquettes 3, rue Franklin, 16e; (metro: Passy). Huge display of model automobiles, submarines, battle ships, racing cars, aeroplanes and sailing ships. They crowd into the windows and display shelves, hang from the ceiling.

La Ruche du Montparnasse 54, boulevard Edgar Quinet, 14e; (metro: Edgar-Quinet). Modern toys, furniture and eating equipment for youngsters at budget prices. Good selection of tin boxes and wooden stools.

Si Tu Veux Galerie Vivienne, 2e; (metro: Bourse). Unusual, avant-garde toys, games and puzzles for kids, plus children's furniture. Open 11 am to 7 pm Monday to Friday, and 2 to 6 pm Saturday.

Au Tambourin Passage Grand Cerf, 2e; (tel: 236.65.87; metro: Etienne Marcel). A dusty old shop full of games, toys, gadgets, party gags and grotesque masks. Looks like it's been there since the French Revolution, a spooky place on a dark passage. Open Tuesday to Saturday 10 am to 7 pm and Monday 2 to 7 pm. Closed Sunday.

Vieille France 364, rue St Honoré, 1er; (tel: 260.01.57; metro: Madeleine, Concorde). Toy soldiers, medals, medallions, decorations, antique sabres and historical documents. More for the adult than children.

● Trains

Baby Train 9-11, rue St Jacques, 5e; (tel: 633.90.79; metro: St Michel). Department store of model trains and accessories. Includes Marklin, Fleischmann, Roco, Rivarossi, Jouef, Faller, Lima, Minitrix and Pola brands. Open 9 am to 11 pm daily.

Modelisme Ferroviaire Clarel 25, rue de la Roquette, 11e; (tel: 700.98.94; metro: Bastille, Bréguet Sabin). Marklin, Lima and Roco brands, including the new orange TGV models. Open 9.30 am to 7 pm. Closed Sunday and Monday.

● Trophies

Jim Rue Perrée at Rue Paul Dubois, 3e; (metro: Temple). Awards and trophies for any sport or occasion, in bronze, silver, chrome or gold. Get yourself a bronze tennis racket or copper bicycle.

● Typewriters

Olivetti 91, rue du Faubourg St Honoré, 8e; (tel: 266.91.44; metro: St Philippe, Miromesnil). The latest in electronic typewriters, word processors and home computers in the chicest hardware store in town. A model in how to market electronic products in the same neighbourhood as Gucci and Yves St Laurent.

● Watches and clocks

Mappin & Webb Rue de la Paix at Rue des Capucines, 2e; (tel: 261.50.13; metro: Opéra). Paris's Rolex representative and a specialist in fine watches in silver, diamond or gold settings.

J P Rochefort 14, rue des Sts Pères, 7e; (tel: 296.60.05; metro: Bac, St Germain). Beautiful antique clocks, navigational instruments and globes.

CHAPTER ELEVEN

Sports and recreation

Your opinion on getting a little fun and exercise in the French capital will be formed largely on the basis of where you come from. Americans will find Paris and suburbs sadly lacking in basic sports facilities, especially the tennis courts and golf courses which seem to permeate most Yank cities. The British, however, might find Paris a downright athletic paradise compared to tennis-court-starved central London.

Like most European cities, Paris grew large and crowded long before sport was a vital human activity. Thus, most of the athletic facilities which have been added in the past century are situated far from the centre of town, most of them on the periphery of the City of Paris or in the suburbs. But the guiding fathers of Paris were thoughtful enough to finance a marvellous network of public swimming pools which can be found in nearly every district, including right across the street from the Pompidou Centre.

Until the 1970s these pools were about the only recreation facilities you found in the city centre. Then sports became big business in France, and entrepreneurs began to modify their theory that you could only make money by setting up facilities on cheap land in the suburbs. The growing demand for centrally-situated recreation led to a blossoming of tennis and squash clubs, aerobic and dance classes close to the heart of Paris, which is a boon for both residents and tourists. Tennis, in particular, has skyrocketed in popularity amongst the French; squash is on the verge of a major boom; and nearly every Parisian woman knows the name Jane Fonda (and not from the movies either).

Paris has not been immune to other recreational fads. The French very early picked up a love for ice skating, thus there are dozens of ice skating rinks (*patinoires*) in the Paris region (compared to only three in London). They acquired an itch for American ten-pin bowling in the 1950s — no doubt influenced by the American movies of the period — and up came dozens of American-style bowling alleys. The 'kung-fu' movie genre had its effect in the 1970s, thus Paris saw a rapid expansion of martial arts clubs.

The city is also strong on horse sports — racing, riding and even polo — but this has always been the case, for that is the sport of kings and Paris has always been a royal city.

Those with an interest in spectator sports might find Paris a notch down from, say, London or New York. The French have never been as avid on team play as the British or Americans. But you can find first division soccer at the aged Colombes Stadium and the Parc des Princes Stadium. Paris St Germain is the best local club, and the French national squad holds its own among the best in Europe. Rugby fans will know Parc des Princes well, for this is where the big rugby matches between France (usually the best side in Europe) and the British Isles are set. Paris has not been grand on indoor spectator sports, due mostly to the lack of a proper indoor facility for big audiences. But that will be remedied by the brand new Omni-Sports Complex, which opened in January 1984 in the 12th district.

Aerobics and dance

American Centre 261, boulevard Raspail, 14e; (tel: 321.42.20; metro: Raspail). Courses in ballet, modern jazz and Latin dance.

Centre de Danse du Marais 41, rue du Temple, 4e; (tel:

277.58.19; metro: Hotel-de-Ville). Classes in aerobics, ballet, gymnastics, jazz, modern and classical dance, for adults and children. Open all year.

Club California 41, rue du Temple, 4e; (tel: 277.58.19; metro: Hotel-de-Ville). 119, avenue General Leclerc, 14e; (tel: 541.02.82; metro: Porte d'Orléans). Paris's trendy new aerobics salon, run in conjunction with the Centre de Danse du Marais and the Centre Culturel Chorégraphique. The classes are taught by three 'authentic California professors' who promise both exciting California music and the original California method. While this may all sound like the marshmallow approach to exercise, insiders say this is the best and toughest aerobics in town. Fees: 50F per class, 450F for 10 classes, 730F for one month of unlimited classes.

Gymnase Club Maillot 17, rue du Debarcadère, 17e; (tel: 574.14.04; metro: Porte Maillot). *Culture physique* from TV aerobics stars Veronique and Davida.

Gymnase Club Monceau 24, rue de Chazelles, 17e; (tel: 380.66.14; metro: Monceau). Aerobics, energy-dancing and body-building, plus a sauna to relax in afterwards and ultra-violet lamps.

Studio Magenia 16, rue St Marc, 2e; (tel: 261.99.14; metro: Bourse). Aerobics, acrobatics, dance and jazz dance, plus mime and pantomime classes for adults and children.

Studios Pleyel 252, rue du Faubourg St Honoré, 8e; (tel: 561.06.30; metro: Ternes). Wide variety of courses in aerobics, gymnastics, body building, yoga, modern, classic, Hindu, Spanish, tap and jazz dance. At least 24 resident instructors. The Centre 'Body Ligne' has a sauna, solarium and ultra-violet lamps.

Body building

Club 52 52, rue de Levis, 17e; (tel: 755.80.32; metro: Malesherbes). 12, rue de Madrid, 8e; (tel: 522.23.17; metro: Europe). Weightlifting, sauna and kinesitherapy. Open daily 8 am to 9 pm.

Garden Gym 65, avenue des Champs-Elysées, 8e; (tel: 225.87.20; metro: George V). 123, avenue De Gaulle, Neuilly; (tel: 747.62.62; metro: Sablons). A club for 'getting in shape' with weights, aerobics, gymnastics and solarium.

Praxitele 50, rue du Faubourg St Denis, 10e; (tel: 523.10.58; metro: Château d'Eau). Scenes from Muscle Beach: a traditional athletic gym.

Rivoli Centre 140, rue de Rivoli, 1er; (tel: 236.85.25; metro: Louvre). Modern body building techniques from weights to aerobics, plus sauna, ultra-violet lamps and burnishing.

Samourai 26, rue de Berri, 8e; (tel: 562.57.94; metro: George V). Aerobics and body building. Open Monday to Friday 8 am to 9 pm, Saturday 9 am to 5 pm.

Bowling

Bowling de l'Académie 66, avenue d'Ivry, 13e; (tel: 586.55.52; metro: Tolbiac). 16 lanes. Part of the Académie de Billard with its 10 French billiard tables and 4 American pool tables. Bar. Open 2 pm to 2 am daily.

Bowling de Montparnasse 27, rue du Comm. Mouchotte, 14e; (tel: 321.61.32; metro: Gaîté, Montparnasse). 16 lanes. Under the Sheraton Hotel in the new Gaîté Shopping Complex. Next door is an ice skating and curling rink. Bar. Open 10 am to 2 am daily.

Bowling de Paris Avenue de Madrid, Neuilly; (tel: 747.77.55; metro: Sablons). 24 lanes. The largest bowling alley in Paris. Always crowded on weekends. Bar and restaurant. Open until 2 am every night.

Bowling Mouffetard 73, rue Mouffetard, 5e; (tel: 331.09.35; metro: Monge). More like the seedy American bowling alleys, if you know them. Lots of students, electronic games, a bar and 8 lanes. Open 10 am to 2 am daily.

Cycling

French drivers are not the kindest to cyclists and like most big cities Paris isn't a biker's paradise. But there are ways to escape the crush of traffic and the hectic inner-city streets. There is a pleasant and lengthy bicycle path through the Bois de Boulogne known as the Piste Cyclable. It runs a rambling course from the Place de la Porte Maillot (it starts next to the Pavillon de l'Orée du Bois) to the Porte de Boulogne, passing the Jardin d'Acclimatation, the Bagatelle and the Grand Cascade. You can also use the paved roads of the Bois, but you must compete with cars for space on these routes.

The Bois de Vincennes also offers untold miles of good paved biking roads, although there is not a specific bike path yet. And Vincennes is the home of Paris's municipal velodrome, down on the southwest side near the Avenue de Gravelle.

For those who want some real riding, you'll have to hop on a train and leave the city with your bike. The SNCF can tell you which trains will take bicycles as baggage, and they have a special scheme in which you can combine rail tickets with cycle rental at over 140 stations in France. Likewise, the RATP rents bikes at five RER stations: St Germain-en-Laye, Courcelle-sur-Yvette. Noisiel and Vincennes in the suburbs and Châtelet-Les Halles in the middle of Paris.

Following is a list of bicycle rental agencies and touring organizations.

One means of escaping the hectic traffic of inner Paris is hiring a bi-cycle for a ride through the Bois de Vincennes, the Bois de Boulogne or one of the city's other large parks.

Bicy-Club de France 8, place de la Porte-de-Champerret, 17e; (tel: 766.55.92; metro: Champerret). National cycle touring club which stages weekend and holiday outings for up to 15 people from March to November. Two-day trips cost approximately 300F including food and accommodation, but day trips can be organized for as little as 35F per person a day. A great way to explore the French countryside.

La Fédération Française de Cyclotourisme 8, rue Jean-Marie-Jego, 13e; (tel: 580.30.21; metro: Corvisart). Governing body which organizes bicycle tours and competitions, plus regular training sessions for both sprint and long distance riders. Monthly cycling magazine and comprehensive club list.

Paris Velo 2, rue du Fer-à-Moulin, 5e; (tel: 337.59.22; metro: Censier-Daubenton). Bois de Vincennes, Avenue de Nogent at Carrefour de la Porte Jaune. Bike rental by the day, week or month. Cost is 25F per day, 175F per week or 300F per month, plus deposit.

RER Velo Esplanade du Château opp. the Château de Vincennes, 20e; (metro: Château de Vincennes). Great place to hire a bike for a ride in the park. Cycles are dispensed from a bus owned by the Bicy-Club de France and cost 10F for one hour, 20F for two hours, 30F for three or four hours and 40F for five hours, with a 20F deposit. Open 9 am to 8 pm on weekends and holidays. There is also service available at Châtelet/Les Halles, St Germain-en-Laye, Courcelle-sur-Yvette and Noisiel RER stations. For information telephone 346.14.14.

Velocipederie de la Grande Gerbe 92 St Cloud in the Parc de St Cloud; metro: Porte de St Cloud). Large selection of bikes for hire in the midst of a 1,100 acre park on the edge of metropolitan Paris.

Fencing

Ligue Française d'Escrime 13, rue de Londres, 9e; (tel: 874.49.92; metro: Trinité). Ruling body of French sabres and epées. They can give you information on classes, competitions and a list of the 50 plus fencing clubs in Paris.

Golf

There are dozens of golf courses in the Paris metropolitan region and the Ile de France, and many of these clubs are more than happy to accept visiting players from overseas, especially from Britain and America. You can play on your home club cards, and both rental and green fees are similar to back home. The only problem is transportation, for most of Paris's courses are situated far from the city centre. Unless you have your own car, or a French friend with transport, then forget trying to haul your own clubs to the course. Those without clubs can take public transport and then hire the desired equipment. The following are three golf clubs which accept visiting players and which are eager to build up overseas contacts.

Racing Club de France La Boulie — Pont Colbert, Versailles; (tel: 950.59.41). Two excellent 18-hole courses in the lovely setting of the Bois des Gonards south of Versailles. Both are par 72. Open daily except Tuesday, but green fees over twice as high on weekends. The problem is getting there if you don't have a car. Take RER Line C5 from the Gare d'Orsay to Versailles station (16.80F return trip) or the SNCF commuter line from the Gare Montparnasse to Versailles-Chantiers station. The taxi drivers outside either station will know the way to the course.

Saint-Cloud — Buzenval Parc de Buzenval, St Cloud; (tel: 970.22.83). Two 18-hole courses, one par 68 the other par 72. This is the closest golfing to the centre of Paris, but it has the highest green fees in the region. Open daily except

Monday. Take the SNCF commuter line from the Gare St Lazare to Garches station (one past St Cloud). Then grab a taxi to the Parc de Buzenval.

Saint-Nom-la-Breteche Fôret de Marly, St Nom-la-Breteche; (tel: 460.90.80). Again, two 18-hole courses. Both are par 73 and one is of championship calibre. Open daily except Thursday. Green fees doubled on weekends. Take the SNCF commuter line from the Gare St Lazare to St Nom-la-Breteche station, then it's a short walk or taxi ride into the Marly Forest.

Horse racing

There are eight tracks in the Paris metro area and you can usually find some sort of racing any day of the year. Entrance usually runs about 10F and the card normally includes seven races. For those who can't make it to the track, bets can be placed in any café or tabac displaying a PMU sign in the window. Wagers are accepted from 8.30 am until the racing starts, usually just after noon.

The highlight of the Parisian racing season is the Prix de la République at Longchamp the first Sunday in October, the local equivalent to the Derby or the Kentucky Derby. It's one of the world's top stakes races and the winner nets over a half million pounds in prize money. The other big one is the Grande Semaine or Great Week, which kicks off the last Sunday in June. This includes nine racing events at three tracks — Longchamp, Auteuil and St Cloud — and is a not-to-be-missed event for any serious racing fans.

Auteuil Route d'Auteuil in the Bois de Boulogne, 16e; (tel: 723.54.12; metro: Porte d'Auteuil). France's premier steeplechase track, with an obstacle course of jumps and ponds that would make a Marine cringe. The season runs from mid-February to mid-December with breaks in May, August and September. The biggest events of the year are the Prix du Président de la Republique (Sunday before

Easter), the Grand Prix d'Automne (beginning of November) and the Grand Steeplechase de Paris (third and fourth Sunday of June).

Chantilly Autoroute A1 north to Chantilly; (tel: 266.92.02). Flat racing in June, July and September. Highlights of the season are the Prix du Jockey-Club and the Prix de Diane de Revlon.

Enghien N14 north to Enghien; (tel: 723.54.12). Steeplechase and harness racing from February to December.

Evry Autoroute A6 south to Evry; (tel: 227.47.36). Flat racing from March to July and September to November.

Longchamp Carrefour des Tribunes in the Bois de Boulogne, 16e; (tel: 266.92.02). The most famous track in France, a bastion of flat racing and Parisian high society since it was opened by Napoleon III in 1857. The season runs from April to June and September to October, but undoubtedly the climax of the season is the Prix de l'Arc de Triomphe the last Sunday in October, the most important single horse race in France. Other big races are the Grand Prix de Paris (last Sunday in June) and the Prix Berteux (last Tuesday in June). For seating, take your choice of two luxurious restaurants, the huge grandstands, or the exclusive (and private) tribune boxes.

Maisons-Laffitte N308 north to Courbevoie; (tel: 359.20.70). Flat racing from March to July and September to December.

Vincennes Route de la Ferme in the Bois de Vincennes, 12e; (tel: 742.07.70). Harness racing in the afternoons and evenings, August to September.

Ice skating

L'Igloo Place du Maréchal-Leclerc (Nogent-sur-Marne); (tel:

877.32.66; RER: Nogent-sur-Marne; buses: 113, 114, 120 and 313F). Open Monday, Tuesday and Thursday 6 to 11 pm, Wednesday 2 to 11 pm, Friday 6 pm to midnight, Saturday 2 pm to midnight and Sunday 10 am to 12.30 pm and 3 to 7 pm. Fee 14F Tuesday to Friday, 22F Saturday and Sunday.

La Main Jaune Place de la Porte-de-Champerret, 17e; (tel: 763.26.47; metro: Champerret). Open every day but Monday 3 to 10.30 pm. Fee: 35-70F.

Patinoire de Charenton le Pont Avenue Jean-Jaurès at Avenue Anatole-France, Charenton; (tel: 368.59.18; metro: Charenton Ecoles). Near the Bois de Vincennes. Day sessions: Wednesday, Saturday and Sunday 2.30 to 6 pm, Tuesday and Thursday 2.30 to 6.30 pm. Night sessions: 9 to 11 pm except Sunday and Monday. Morning session: Sunday 10 am to 12.30 pm. Fee: 15-17.50F. Cafeteria.

Patinoire de la Gaîté Montparnasse 16, rue Vercingetorix, 14e; (tel: 321.60.60; metro: Gaîté). Paris's newest ice skating rink, part of the giant Gaîté shopping complex. Also includes curling facilities, and there's a bowling alley next door. Open Monday to Friday 10 am to noon, and 8.30 to 11 pm; open Saturday 10 am to 12.30 pm, 2 to 6.30 pm and 8.30 to 11.30 pm; open Sunday 9.30 am to 12.30 pm, and 2.30 to 6.30. Fee: 19.50F, under 16s 17.50F, from noon to 2 pm 15F.

Kart racing

Parc du Bois Guyon N12 in the Zone Industrielle Nord (Dreux). Karting for adults and children in a 10 hectares park and forest.

Racing Kart Buffo N19 (Les Etards); (tel: 407.61.66). Large karting centre 35 kms southeast of Paris in Les Etards. Also includes a bar.

Martial arts

Dojo de la Main d'Or 4, passage de la Main-d'Or, 11e; (tel: 805.78.82; metro: Ledru Rollin). Courses in aikido, tai-chi and yoga for adults.

Dojo Number One 73-75, rue Brillat-Savarin, 13e; (tel: 589.36.37; metro: Corvisart). Classes in aikido, karate and judo, as well as a pool to cool down and sauna to relax those tired muscles.

Fed. Française de Tai-Chi et de Kung-Fu American school, 65 quai d'Orsay, 7e; (tel: 577.44.71; metro: Invalides). As the name says, tai-chi and kung-fu as taught by the folks at the national federation. For adults and children.

Georges Zsiga American school, 65 quai d'Orsay, 7e; (tel: 877.60.15; metro: Invalides). Karate for men and women from ex-French champion Georges Zsiga.

Mountain climbing

Club Alpin Français 7, rue la Boetie, 8e; (tel: 742.36.77; metro: Miromesnil). The Paris office of France's greatest climbing club. They can give you information on mountaineering anywhere in France. CAF organize trips which leave every Sunday for climbs in the Paris region. The office is open noon to 6 pm daily except Monday.

Polo

Polo de Paris Route des Moulins in the Bois de Boulogne, 16e; (tel: 506.11.92). The ponies come out to play on this lovely field by the Seine from spring to autumn. Paris's exclusive club.

Martial arts students practice their sublime rites amongst the greenery of the Bois de Vincennes; just like everywhere else in the world, Asian sports have caught fire in the French capital.

Riding

As with running and cycling, the Bois de Boulogne and Bois de Vincennes offer the best riding opportunities for those who don't want to stray far from the heart of Paris. Both have resident riding clubs which offer courses and trail rides in the park. The Bois de Boulogne, for instance, has miles of *allées cavalières* or bridle paths which take you to nearly every major attraction in the park.

In order to ride in France you must purchase a Carte Nationale de Cavalier for 70F from either the Fédération Equestre Française (164, rue du Faubourg St Honoré 8e; tel: 225.11.22; metro: St Philippe du Boule) or an authorized riding club like those in the parks. In addition, you must supply your own helmet, boots and crop.

Bayard Ucpa Avenue du Polygone in the Bois de Vincennes, 12e; (tel: 365.46.87; metro: Vincennes). Trail rides and lessons at about the most reasonable rates in the city.

Cercle de l'Etrier Route de Madrid aux Lacs in the Bois de Boulogne, 16e; (tel: 624.28.02; metro: Porte Maillot, Porte Dauphine). Where Paris high society rides. It's hard at times to tell whose nose is further in the air: the horses' or their riders'. A two-year waiting list for membership, but you must have two recommendations by members before you even reach the list!

Manège Howine — Neuilly 19, rue d'Orléans, Neuilly; (tel: 624.06.41; metro: Sablons). Riding lessons in the house ring, plus trail rides in the nearby Bois de Boulogne. Among the best prices in town at 65F per hour for trail rides.

Société d'Equitation de Paris Route de la Muette à Neuilly in the Bois de Boulogne, 16e; (tel: 722.87.06; metro: Sablons). Another exclusive riding school, this one on the grounds of the Jardin d'Acclimatation at the north end of the park. Prices are higher than Manège Howine but lower than l'Etrier.

Running

Exhaust fumes, obnoxious motorists and ferocious dogs (not to mention what the canines leave behind on the pavement) plague runners in Paris as in any other big city in the world. But these multiple problems don't seem to discourage people from running for both health and fun in every district of the city.

Far and away the best places to run in Paris are our old favourites, the Bois de Vincennes and the Bois de Boulogne. Just take the metro to a park entrance (Porte Maillot, Porte Dauphine and Porte d'Auteuil for Boulogne; Château Vincennes, Porte Dorée, Porte de Charenton or Liberté for Vincennes) and streak away into the wild, green yonder. There are miles of both paved and unpaved trails in both parks, plus benches to rest along the way. But you may have to contend with the ubiquitous park obstacles: horses and bicycles, plus the extra added hazard of hookers in the Bois de Boulogne.

Those who want their running closer to the city centre might opt for a number of smaller, but useful parks: the Jardin des Plantes (5e; metro: Austerlitz), the Jardin du Luxembourg (6e; metro: Luxembourg), the Parc du Mars (7e; metro: Ecole Militaire), the Parc de Monceau (8e; metro: Monceau), the Jardin des Tuileries (1er; metro: Tuileries, Concorde, Palais Royal) or the Parc des Buttes Chaumont (19e; metro: Buttes Chaumont or Botzaris). The trail distances aren't as great as the big parks so you may have to take several circuits over the same territory. And go in the early morning so as to avoid the school children and tourists.

Real masochists might want to try a route up and over the Montmartre hill. Take the metro to Anvers and proceed up the Rue de Steinkerque to the Place Suz Valaden. Towering before you is the Rue Foyetier, the giant staircase which leads up to Sacré Coeur. You can run up and down this as many times as you like, a jog to the right at the top and proceed via Rue Lamarck, Rue du Mont Cenis and Rue St Eleuthère in a circular route around the great church.

Exhaust fumes, obnoxious motorists and ferocious dogs not withstanding, there are pleasant places to run in Paris, like the gravel footpaths of the Champ du Mars near the Eiffel Tower.

But I still think the best running in Paris is along the Seine in the heart of the old city. I've devised what I call the 'Seven Bridges' run from the Ile de la Cité to the Eiffel Tower along the quays. The run includes crossings of the Pont Neuf, Pont du Carrousel, Pont Royal, Pont de la Concorde, Pont Alexandre, Pont de l'Alma and Pont d'Iena. Then you take the metro back from Trocadero. But you can devise your own quay-side run over as many bridges as you like. It's best to run the Seine in the early morning hours before the traffic and the tourists take over.

Paris is not without its competitive running either. The big race each year is the Paris Marathon in May, a major international event which attracts famous names and tens of thousands of runners. There's the 20 Kilometres of Paris each October, a circular romp around many of the city's famous monuments; the Cross du Figaro in December, two days of racing in the Bois de Boulogne now in its 23rd year; and the Paris to Versailles run in October, a 16-km jaunt from the Eiffel Tower to Louis XIV's palace in the suburbs.

Sports grounds

These are general and all-purpose sports areas open to the public which are suitable for impromptu games or team sports like soccer, hockey, rugby, baseball or even cricket.

Bois de Boulogne The park has a large sports ground and training fields between the Route de Sèvres at Neuilly and the Allée du Bord de l'Eau in the west, next to the Seine.

Bois de Vincennes Headquarters of the Institut National Sportif et d'Education Physique, this park has Paris's largest selection of sports fields. There are three major grounds along the Route de Pyramide in the middle of the park.

Squash and rackets

Club de France 24, rue Richard Lenoir, 11e; (tel: 367.13.98; metro: Voltaire). Opened in October 1983 as the first racket-ball club in France, but the facility also includes three squash courts, sauna, solarium, gym, bar and boutique, plus yoga and dance classes. Open daily 9 am to 10 pm.

Squash-Club Stadium 66, avenue d'Ivry, 13e; (tel: 586.55.40; metro: Porte d'Ivry, Tolbiac). Open every day from 9 am to 5 pm. Annual and weekly membership available.

Squash Front de Seine 21, rue Gaston de Caillavet, 15e; (tel: 575.35.37; metro: Javel, Charles Michels). Opened five years ago, a modern facility with nine courts near the Seine. Squash 24 hours a day for the real die-hards.

Squash Montmartre 14, rue Achille-Martinet, 18e; (tel: 255.38.30; metro: Lamarck). Squash and tennis club in the shadow of Sacré Coeur, with sauna, gym, solarium and bar. Open daily 10 am to 11 pm.

Squash Montparnasse 37, avenue du Maine, 15e; (tel: 538.66.20; metro: Montparnasse). Paris's best known squash club, located right under the Tour Montparnasse with an entrance in the Place Raoul Dautry. There are six courts, a gym, solarium and restaurant. Open Monday to Friday 7 am to midnight, Saturday and Sunday 8 am to 8 pm. Best to avoid weekdays at lunch because of the rush for courts from local businessmen.

Steambaths and saunas

Bains Vapeur des Rosiers 4, rue des Rosiers, 4e; (tel: 272.71.82; metro: St. Paul). Steambaths and sauna in the heart of Paris's old Jewish neighbourhood. Men: Thursday 10 am to 8 pm and Saturday 9 am to 8 pm. Women: Wednesday and Friday 10 am to 8 pm. Entry: 60F.

Gym Drouot 2, rue Drouot, 9e; (tel: 246.60.14; metro: Richelieu Drouot). Sauna, jacuzi and sunlamps are just part of this all-round physical fitness centre.

Hammam de la Mosquée 39, rue Geoffroy St Hilare, 5e; (tel: 331.18.14; metro: Monge). Authentic Turkish baths where you can steam away the day for only 35F, and get a massage on the side for only 20F more. Towel included in the price. Women: Monday, Thursday and Saturday 11 am to 5 pm. Men: Wednesday, Friday and Sunday 11 am to 5 pm.

Vitatop 58, boulevard Gouvion St Cyr, 17e; (tel: 758.12.34; metro: Porte Maillot). 118-122, rue de Vaugirard, 6e; (tel: 544.38.01; metro: Rennes). Jacuzi, sauna, swimming pool, gym, solarium, restaurant and bar in one of Paris's most relaxed and refreshing atmospheres.

Swimming

Paris has 26 municipal swimming pools spread across 13 different arrondissements. The standard entrance fee for each one is 7.80F for adults, 3.90F for children under 16, people over 65, disabled or members of certified sports clubs under the age of 21. For those who swim frequently, you can purchase a 'Carte Piscine' for 113F which entitles you to three months unlimited swimming at all public pools. These pools are open to the general public Monday 2 to 7.30 pm, Tuesday to Saturday 7 am to 7.30 pm and Sunday 8 am to 6 pm. But check with each pool to see what times each week are given over to students and swim classes. Also, there are at least two pools in the city open until 8 pm each night.

In addition, there are six municipal pools not managed by the Mairie de Paris and four private pools which are all open to members of the general public. The entrance fees and swim times vary from pool to pool.

A brochure listing both public and private pools is

available upon request at the Mairie de Paris, Direction de la Jeunesse et des Sports (17, boulevard Morland, 75004 Paris; tel: 276.54.54); from the Offices of Municipal Sport at the Mairie annexes in each arrondissement; and from the swimming pools themselves.

Below are listed several of the more interesting and convenient pools for visitors to Paris.

Armand-Massard Pool 66, boulevard du Montparnasse, 15e; (tel: 538.65.19; metro: Montparnasse). One of Paris's newest and most impressive swimming facilities, three pools located deep underground beneath the Maine-Montparnasse Centre. More water than anywhere else in Paris.

Deligny 25, quai Anatole-France, 7e; (tel: 551.72.15; metro: Chambre des Deputés). The oldest pool in Paris, an outdoor facility on the Seine with a huge sun deck always crowded with beautiful bodies. Packed to the rafters on hot summer days, so get there early to find a patch for your towel. Private, so the fees are higher.

Etoile 32, rue de Tilsitt, 17e; (tel: 380.50.99; metro: Etoile). Private indoor pool with a bar, sauna and solarium, once a haunt of Parisian high society. Convenient for the hotels in the 8th arrondissement.

Jean Taris 16, rue de Thouin, 5e; (tel: 325.54.03; metro: Cardinal Lemoine). Two indoor pools just off the Place de la Contrescarpe, very close to the hotels of St Michel and St Germain. In the heart of student Paris near the University, so the place is heavily used by students.

Molitor 2-8, avenue de la Porte Molitor, 16e; (tel: 651.10.61; metro: Molitor, Porte d'Auteuil). An indoor pool for winter swimming and a very popular outdoor pool for the hot months, just outside the Bois de Boulogne.

Pontoise 19, rue de Pontoise, 5e; (tel: 354.82.45; metro: Maubert-Mutualité). A Left Bank fixture for many years, the closest aquatics facility to the heart of old St Michel. Lots of students and young people, and very convenient for visitors staying in Left Bank hotels or the nearby islands.

Saint Merri 18, rue de Renard, 4e; (tel: 272.29.45; metro: Rambuteau, Hotel-de-Ville). The pool across the street from the Pompidou Centre, the only place where you can go for a dip in the Marais or Beaubourg. This is an ultra-modern facility which also includes public showers and baths.

Tennis

The tennis court situation in Paris is appalling, especially to those who've just come from the wide-open spaces of America or Australia where there are about as many courts as past Wimbledon champions. It's because tennis — while it may now be the fastest growing and most popular sport in France — is a relative latecomer to the Parisian sports scene. Thus, all the good, cheap land was taken up years ago.

But this dire situation is correcting itself rather quickly, especially in the suburbs, where there seems to be a new tennis club or complex under construction at any given time. You have two choices in playing tennis in Paris: pay less money, wait longer and dodge the rocks on the somewhat shoddy municipal courts; or bring your home club card, pay more money, wait less and play at the super-posh private clubs in the 16th arrondissement. The alternatives to this 'caste' madness are the new, more democratic clubs in the suburbs, often with superb courts at moderate prices.

Information on municipal courts can be obtained from 'Allo Sports by dialling 276.54.54. Reservations are accepted up to 48 hours in advance. Fees are 18F for outdoor courts in the daytime, 27F for outdoor courts at night, and 42F for indoor courts. With private clubs it's also best to call ahead and try to reserve a court. Best to avoid weekends, lunch hours and the early evening hours in the summer, for this is when the French are batting their balls around. The clubs may be a bit on the snobbish side, but they are also friendly and eager to build up contacts with tennis clubs in America, Britain and Australia.

ABC Protennis 21, boulevard Poniatowski, 12e; (tel: 345.92.91). Six new tennis centres: La Defense, Bourg-la-Reine, Porte d'Aubervilliers, Porte de la Chapelle, Porte d'Ivry, Porte de Montreuil and Porte d'Orleans. Classes for beginners.

Action Tennis 145, rue de Vaugirard, 15e; (tel: 734.36.36). Paris's biggest tennis conglomerate with eight tennis centres: Porte d'Orléans, Porte de Neuilly, Porte de la Chapelle, Porte d'Ivry, La Defense, Meudon, Paris 16e and Fontenay-sous-Bois. Features instruction for both adults and children.

Eurotennis (tel: 451.76.92). Training courses under the direction of Paul Waroquiers at four tennis centres (La Defense, Bourg-la-Reine, St Ouen and Mairie de Montreuil) using videotape techniques.

Forest Hill 40, avenue du Maréchal de Lattre-de-Tassigny, Meudon-la-Foret; (tel: 630.22.55; RER: Meudon-Val Fleury). Another big tennis group, offering 45 indoor and 8 outdoor courts at four modern locations: Meudon, La Defense, Fontenay and Montrouge. Forest Hill Meudon is the home facility, with 9 indoor courts, 3 all-weather outdoor surfaces, a heated pool, club house, bar and restaurant.; La Defense is the largest, with 12 indoor clay courts, 2 squash courts, indoor pool, gym, sauna, clubhouse, bar and restaurant. Fontenay has 10 indoor Greenset courts, while Montrouge has 14 indoor Greenset courts and 5 all-weather outdoor courts. Hourly rates, annual and summer membership, lessons.

Mondial Tennis 58, avenue du President Wilson, La Plaine-St Denis; (tel: 607.62.69; metro: Porte de la Chapelle). Tennis courts, saunas and a restaurant just outside the north boundary of Paris.

Paris Central Tennis 9, rue des Petites Ecuries. 10e; (tel: 770.74.45; metro: Château d'Eau). Small and modern tennis club with several indoor courts, a solarium, bar and grill. One of the few places to play close to central Paris and the business and hotel districts.

Roland Garros 2, Avenue Gordon Bennett, 16e; (tel: 743.96.87). Home of the French Open Tennis Championships in late May and early June each year, one of the four top tournaments in the world with Wimbledon, Forest Hills and the Australian Open.

Stade Français Porte de St Cloud, 16e; (tel: 602.03.19; metro: Porte St Cloud). Large private facility with 23 outdoor courts which will gladly accept visiting players from overseas.

Stage-System-Tennis 30, rue Ste Felicité, 15e; (tel: 638.92.41; metro: Volontaires). Offers long-term, weekend or single training courses for players of any age or level.

Tennis Club de la Croix Blanche Sainte Geneviève-des-Bois, 91; (tel: 016.93.25; RER: St Geneviève-des-Bois). Three indoor courts in a lovely, rural setting. Monthly, weekly or weekend courses offered. Take RER line C4 or C6 south from Gare Austerlitz.

Tennis Club de la Defense 45, boulevard des Bouvets, Nanterre; (tel: 773.04.40; RER Nanterre-Ville). New squash and tennis club in suburban Nanterre with 8 indoor courts, tennis school, gym, sauna and restaurant. Take RER line A1 from Châtelet-Les Halles.

Tennis Club St James 23, boulevard General Koenig, Neuilly; (tel: 624.11.15; metro: Pont de Neuilly). Private club with 8 courts near the Seine and the Bois de Boulogne.

Tennis Club de Paris 15, avenue Felix d'Herelle (Boulogne); (tel: 647.55.54; metro: Porte St Cloud). Posh and private, where Paris high society plays its tennis. The club has a dozen excellent courts, but there's little chance of rank amateurs getting to play here. Best opportunities for visitors who belong to a famous tennis club back home, or for those with famous names (ie movie stars and politicians).

Yachting

Yacht Moteur Club de France Allée du Bord de l'Eau in the Bois de Boulogne, 16e; (tel: 605.32.23). The folks who guide those little motorboats and big cabin cruisers up and down the Seine. Welcomes visitors with overseas yachting club ties.

Yoga

Centre Sivananda de Yoga 123, boulevard de Sebastopol, 2e; (tel: 261.77.49; metro: Reaumur). Yoga for beginners or advanced. First lesson free.